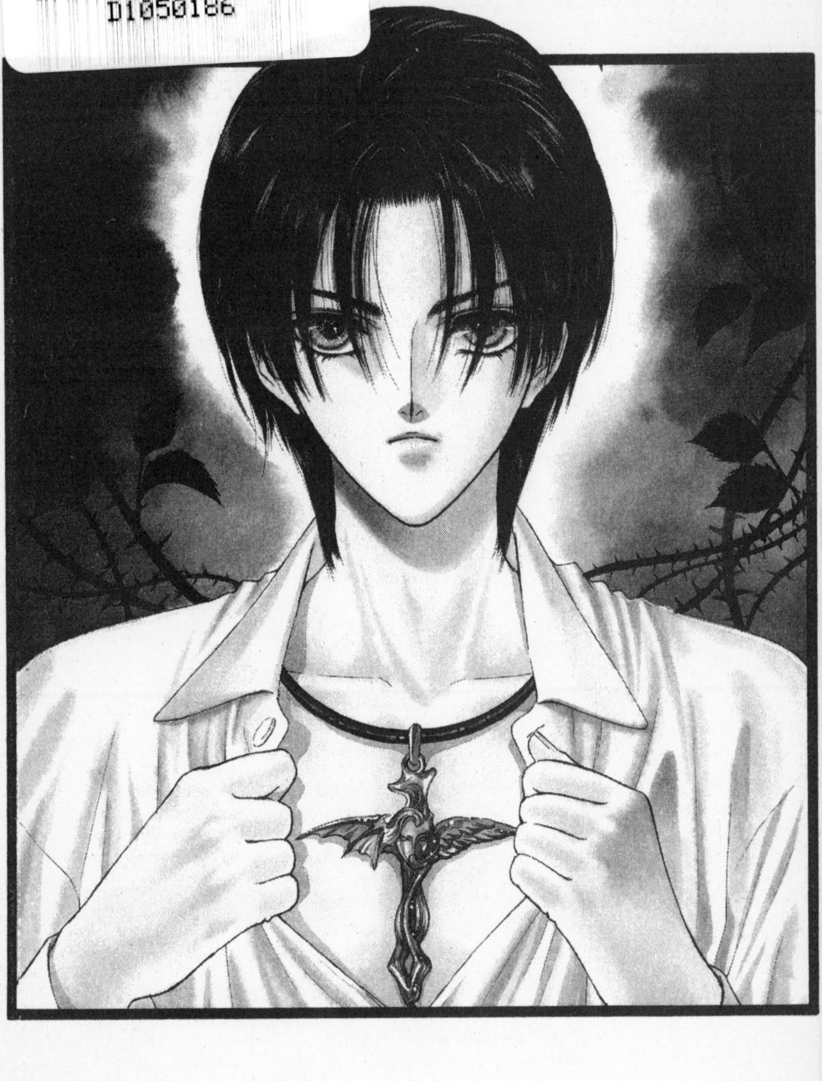

Cross Vol. 3
Created by Sumiko Amakawa

Translation - Yuko Fukami
English Adaptation - Len Wein
Copy Editor - Suzanne Waldman
Retouch and Lettering - Pete Sattler
Production Artist - Vicente Rivera, Jr.
Cover Design - Matt Alford

Editor - Bryce P. Coleman
Digital Imaging Manager - Chris Buford
Pre-Press Manager - Antonio DePietro
Production Managers - Jennifer Miller and Mutsumi Miyazaki
Art Director - Matt Alford
Managing Editor - Jill Freshney
VP of Production - Ron Klamert
Editor-in-Chief - Mike Kiley
President and C.O.O. - John Parker
Publisher and C.E.O. - Stuart Levy

A  Manga

TOKYOPOP Inc.
5900 Wilshire Blvd. Suite 2000
Los Angeles, CA 90036

E-mail: info@TOKYOPOP.com
Come visit us online at www.TOKYOPOP.com

ISBN: 1-59532-229-9

First TOKYOPOP printing: May 2005
10 9 8 7 6 5 4 3 2 1
Printed in the USA

Cross

Volume 3

created by
Sumiko Amakawa

HAMBURG // LONDON // LOS ANGELES // TOKYO

Summary

Takara Amakusa, son of an expert exorcist father and a mother whose family that has been exorcists through the ages, is already a top-notch exorcist attending high school. One day he rescues Shizuha, who had escaped from becoming the ritual sacrifice of a heretic organization. He soon finds that the symbols that appear on Shizuha's body are the "Scripturas." Shizuha and her family are sent away to the Vatican to keep them safe from the heretical organization, but fed up with the restrictions placed on her, Shizuha leaves and becomes a teacher at Takara's school.

Summary and Character Introduction

The heir of the house of Amakusa, the keepers and the owners of Stella Cross Church. An exorcist with the code name "Cross." He possesses a cross with an enormous power hidden within his forehead.

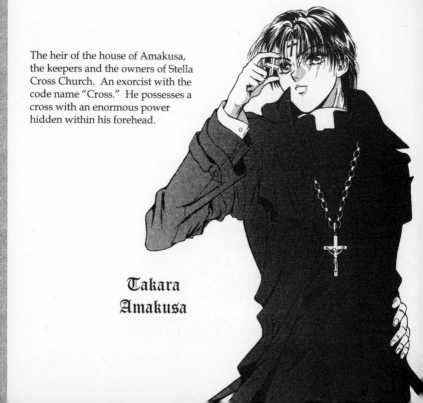

Takara Amakusa

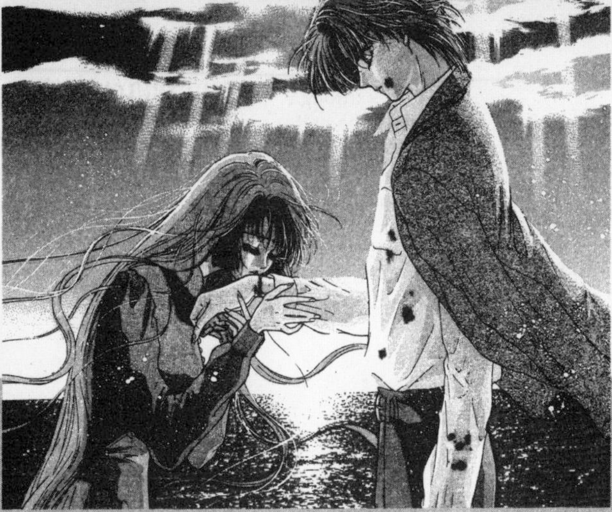

At about that time, mysterious killings began taking place in the old city of Kamakura, the eyes of the victims brutally removed. Behind the murders, one could sense the presence of the Devil… Takara defeated the Devil with his "Holy Cross," and rescued Shizuha from the Prince of Darkness.

And so the battle against evil continues…

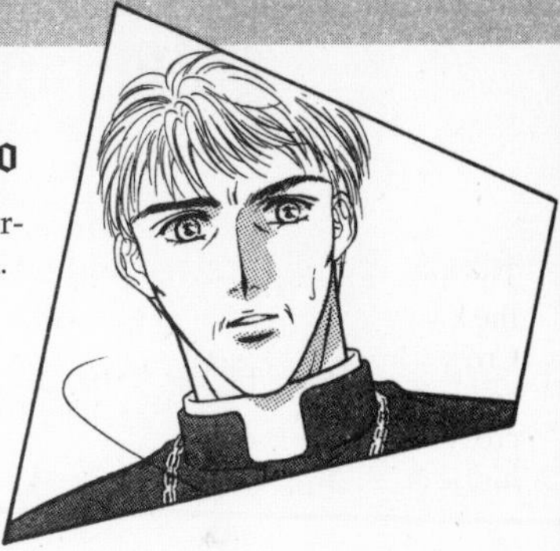

Gerardo Bernardo Serlio

Takara's father and also a first-class exorcist and a priest of Stella Cross Church.

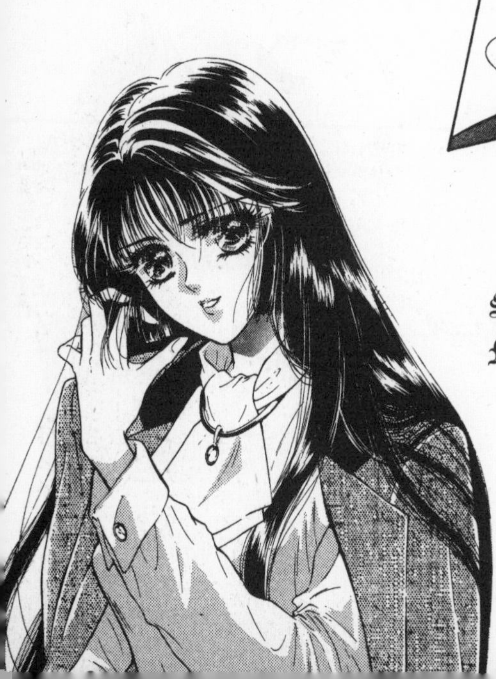

Shizuha Matsuri

Manipulated by the heretical organization, her own parents tried to sacrifice her. She escaped and was saved by Takara. Later, she became a teacher at Takara's high school.

Cross

Table of Contents

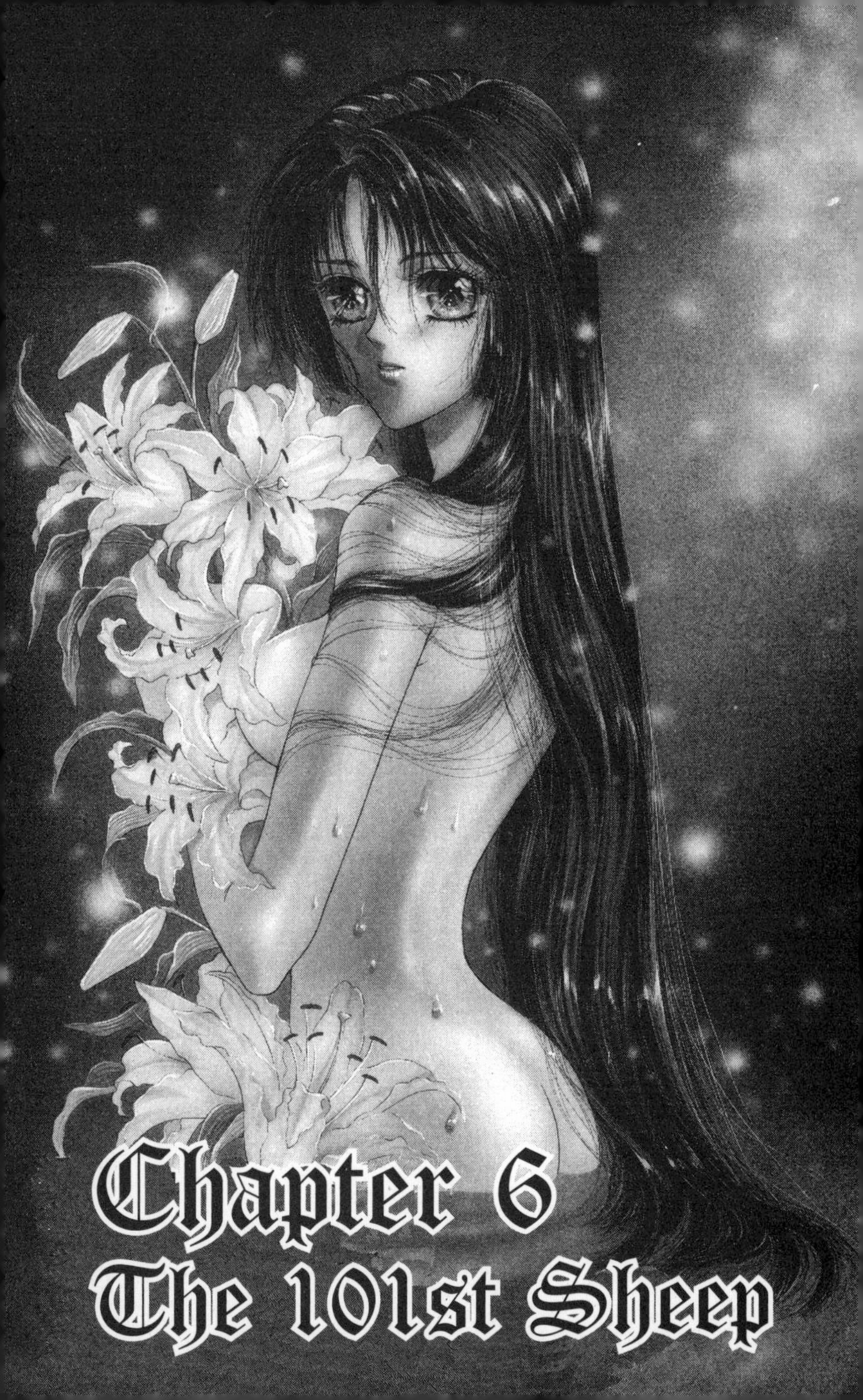

Chapter 6
The 101st Sheep

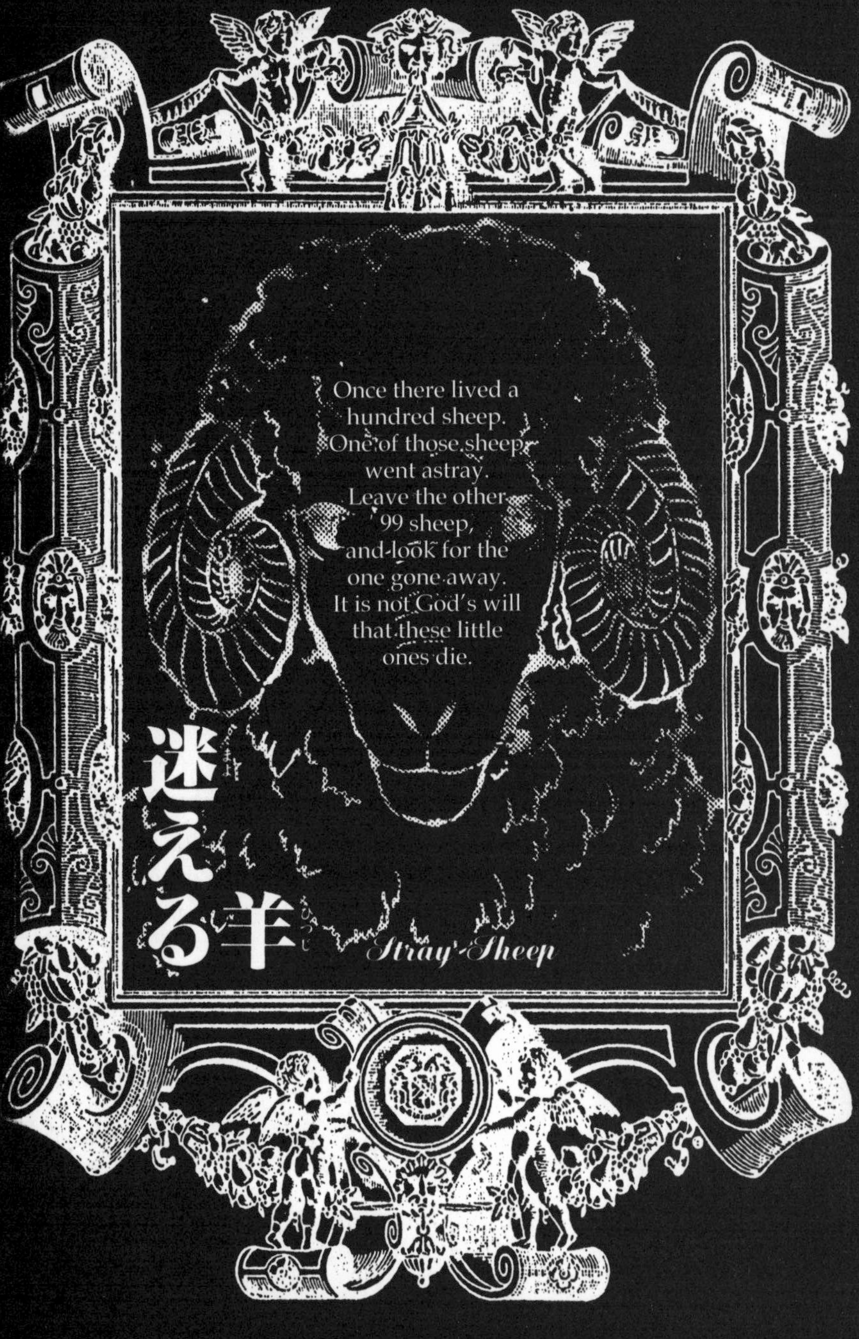
Once there lived a hundred sheep. One of those sheep went astray. Leave the other 99 sheep, and look for the one gone away. It is not God's will that these little ones die.
迷える羊
Stray Sheep

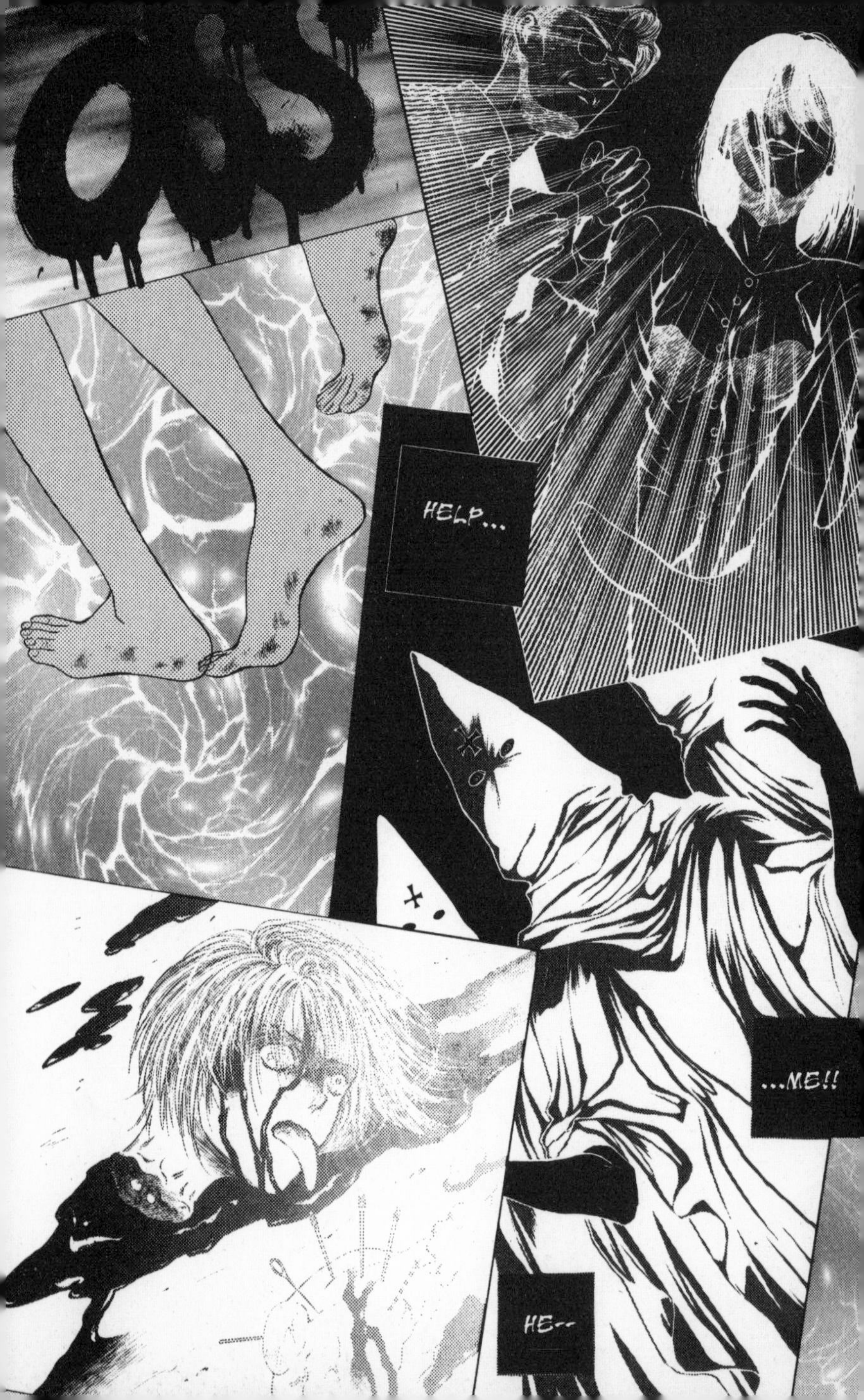
HELP...
...ME!!
HE--

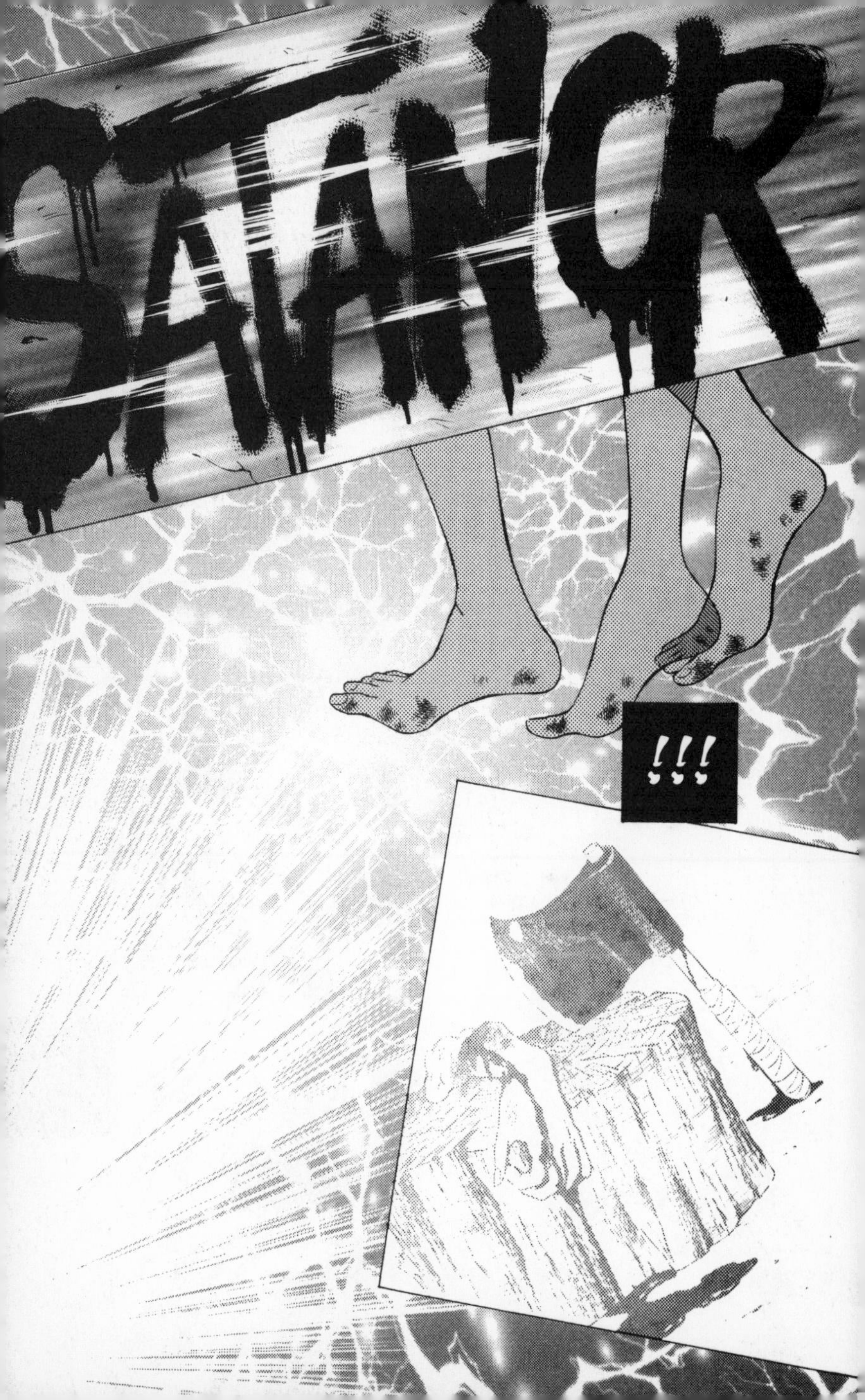
!!!

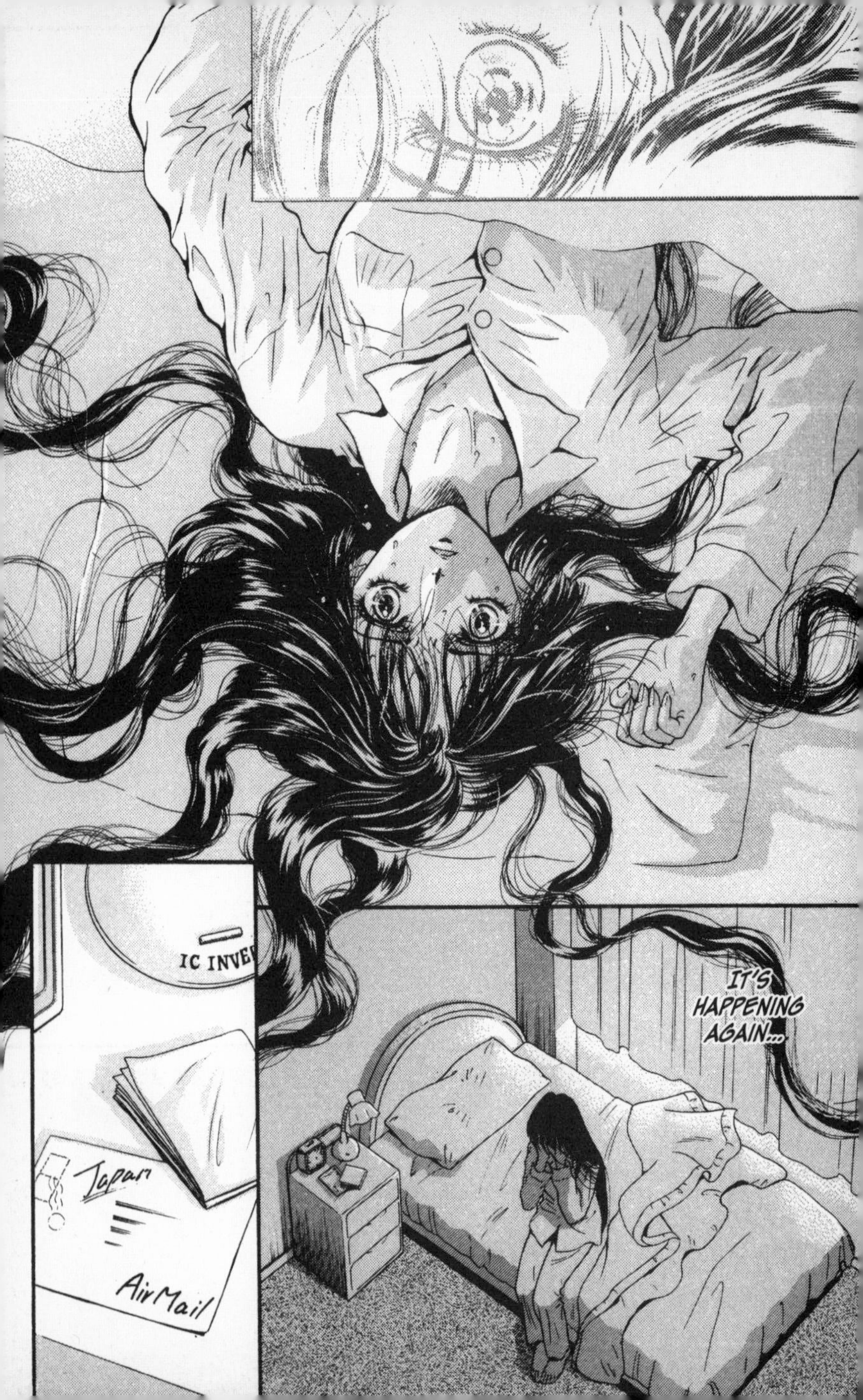
IT'S HAPPENING AGAIN...
IC INVE
Japan
Air Mail

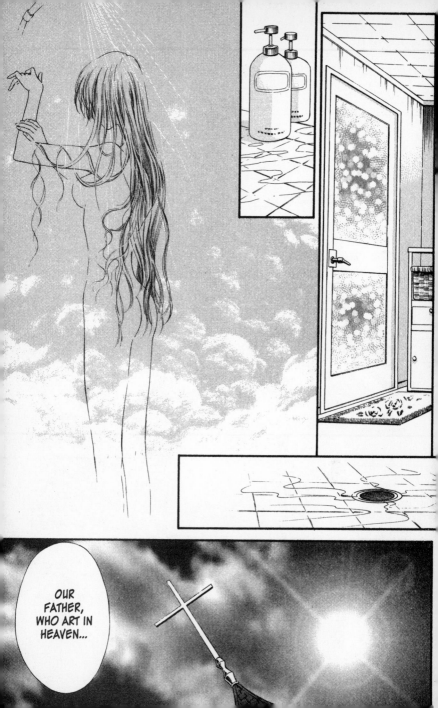

OUR FATHER, WHO ART IN HEAVEN...

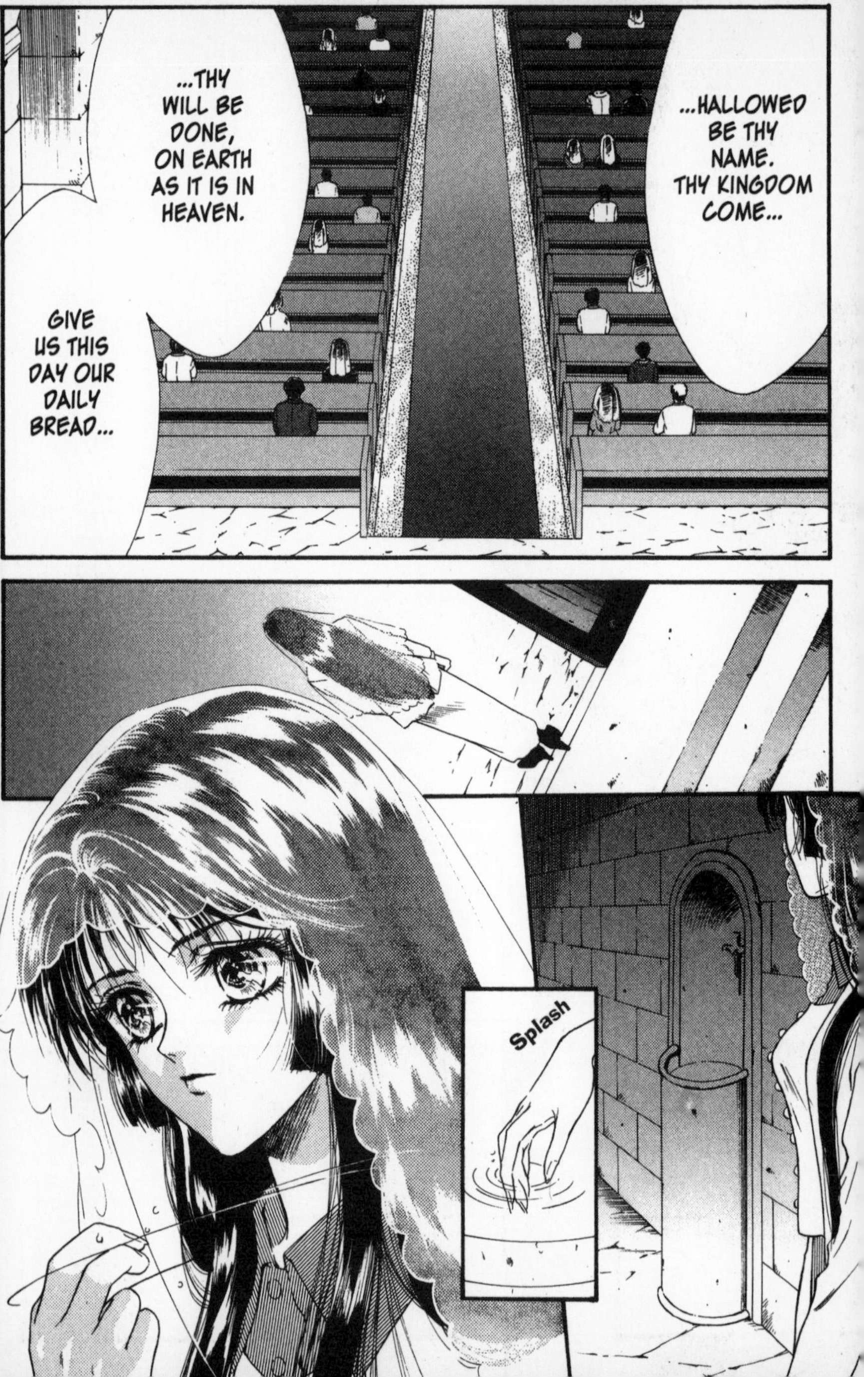
...HALLOWED BE THY NAME. THY KINGDOM COME...
...THY WILL BE DONE, ON EARTH AS IT IS IN HEAVEN.
GIVE US THIS DAY OUR DAILY BREAD...
Splash

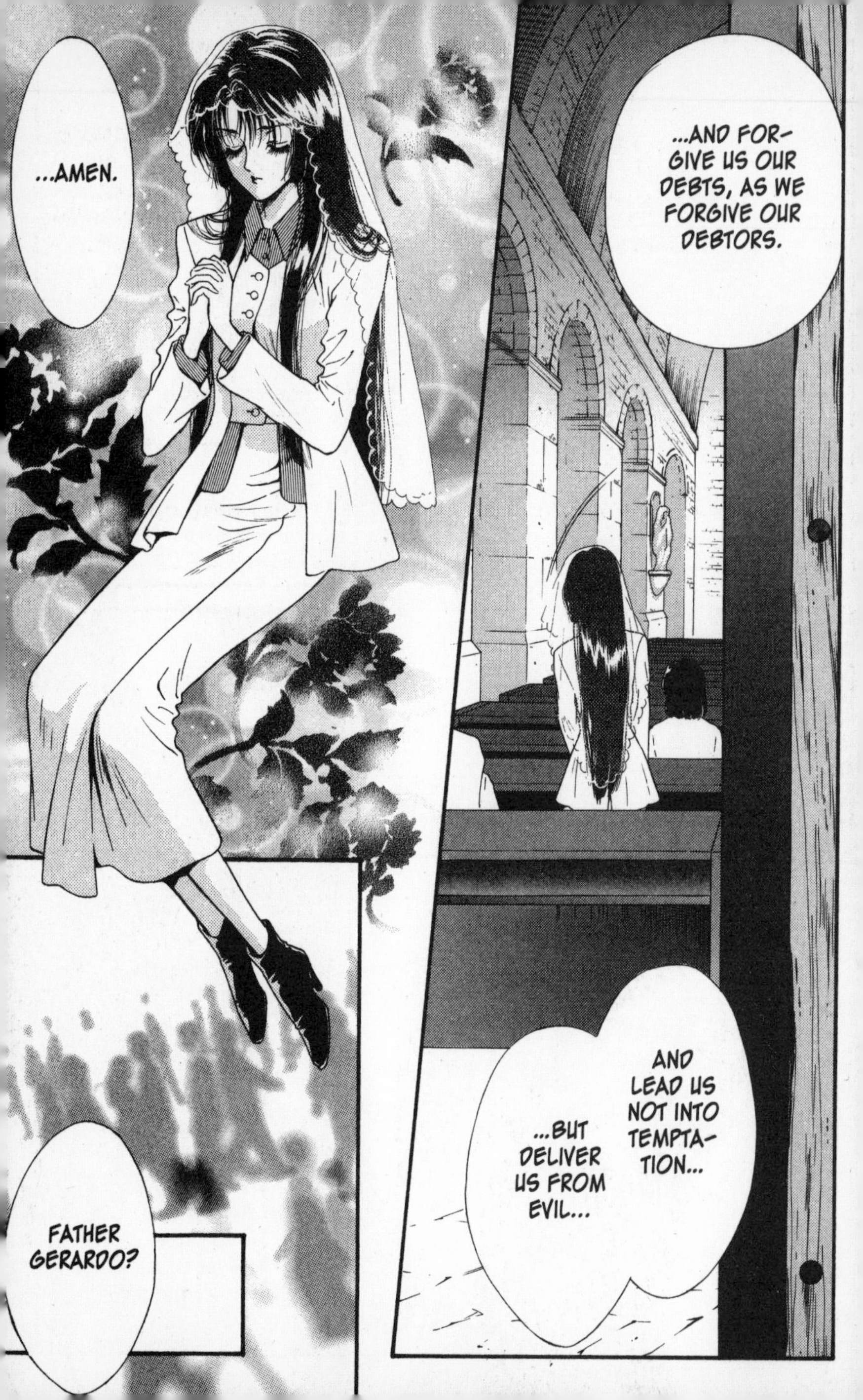
...AND FOR-GIVE US OUR DEBTS, AS WE FORGIVE OUR DEBTORS.
AND LEAD US NOT INTO TEMPTA-TION...
...BUT DELIVER US FROM EVIL...
...AMEN.
FATHER GERARDO?

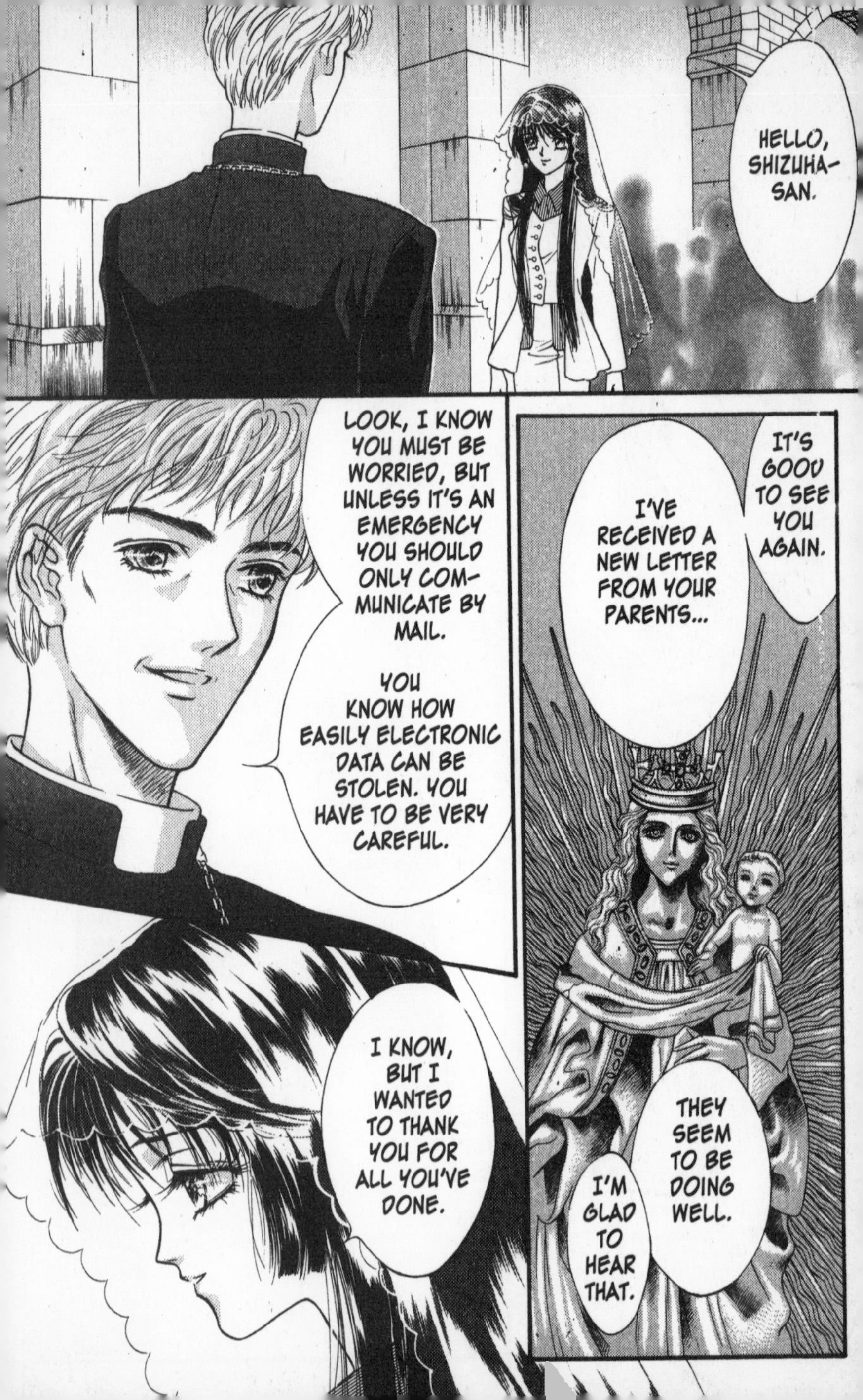
HELLO, SHIZUHA-SAN.
IT'S GOOD TO SEE YOU AGAIN.
I'VE RECEIVED A NEW LETTER FROM YOUR PARENTS...
THEY SEEM TO BE DOING WELL.
I'M GLAD TO HEAR THAT.
LOOK, I KNOW YOU MUST BE WORRIED, BUT UNLESS IT'S AN EMERGENCY YOU SHOULD ONLY COM-MUNICATE BY MAIL.
YOU KNOW HOW EASILY ELECTRONIC DATA CAN BE STOLEN. YOU HAVE TO BE VERY CAREFUL.
I KNOW, BUT I WANTED TO THANK YOU FOR ALL YOU'VE DONE.

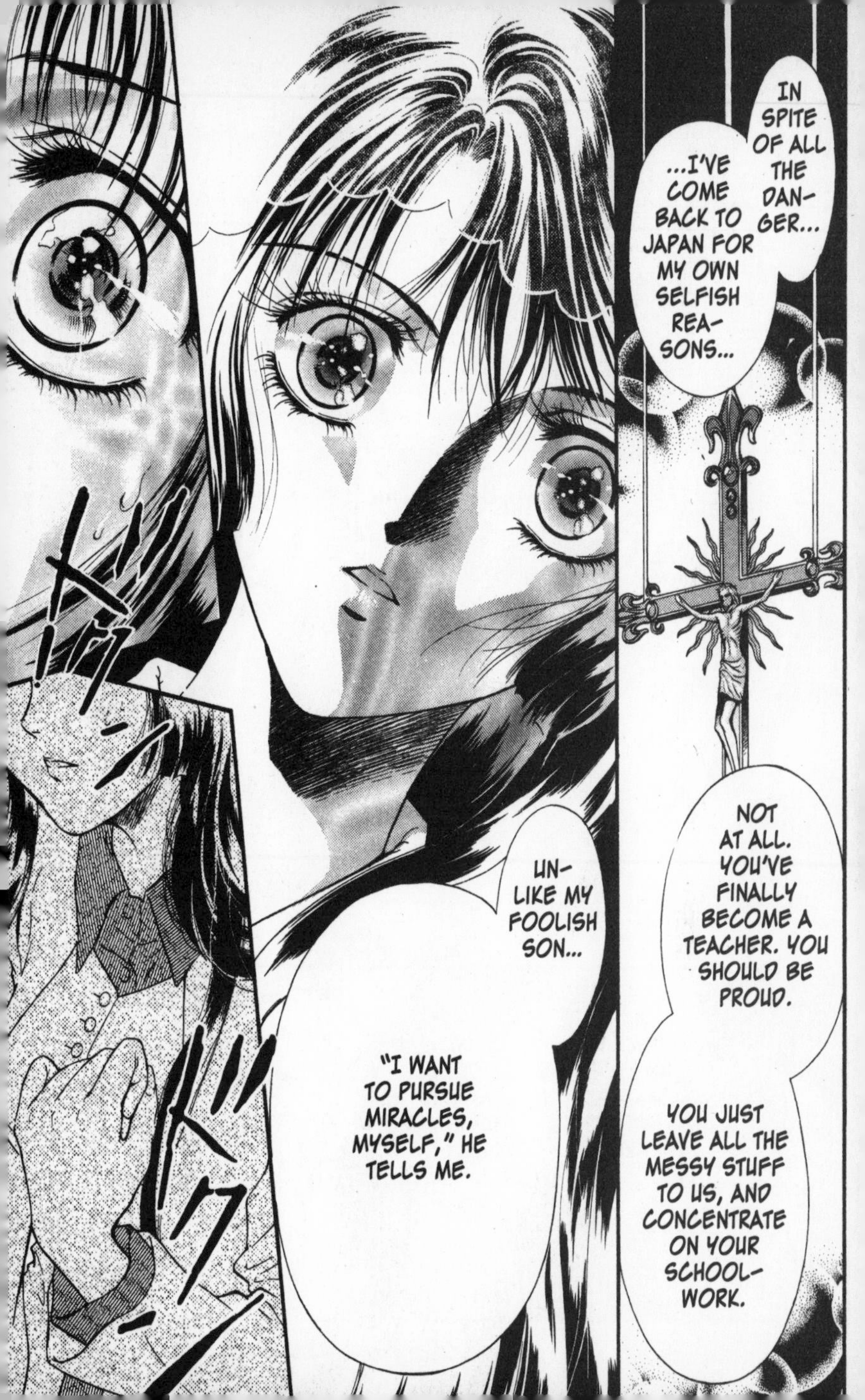
IN SPITE OF ALL THE DANGER...
...I'VE COME BACK TO JAPAN FOR MY OWN SELFISH REASONS...
NOT AT ALL. YOU'VE FINALLY BECOME A TEACHER. YOU SHOULD BE PROUD.
YOU JUST LEAVE ALL THE MESSY STUFF TO US, AND CONCENTRATE ON YOUR SCHOOLWORK.
UNLIKE MY FOOLISH SON...
"I WANT TO PURSUE MIRACLES, MYSELF," HE TELLS ME.

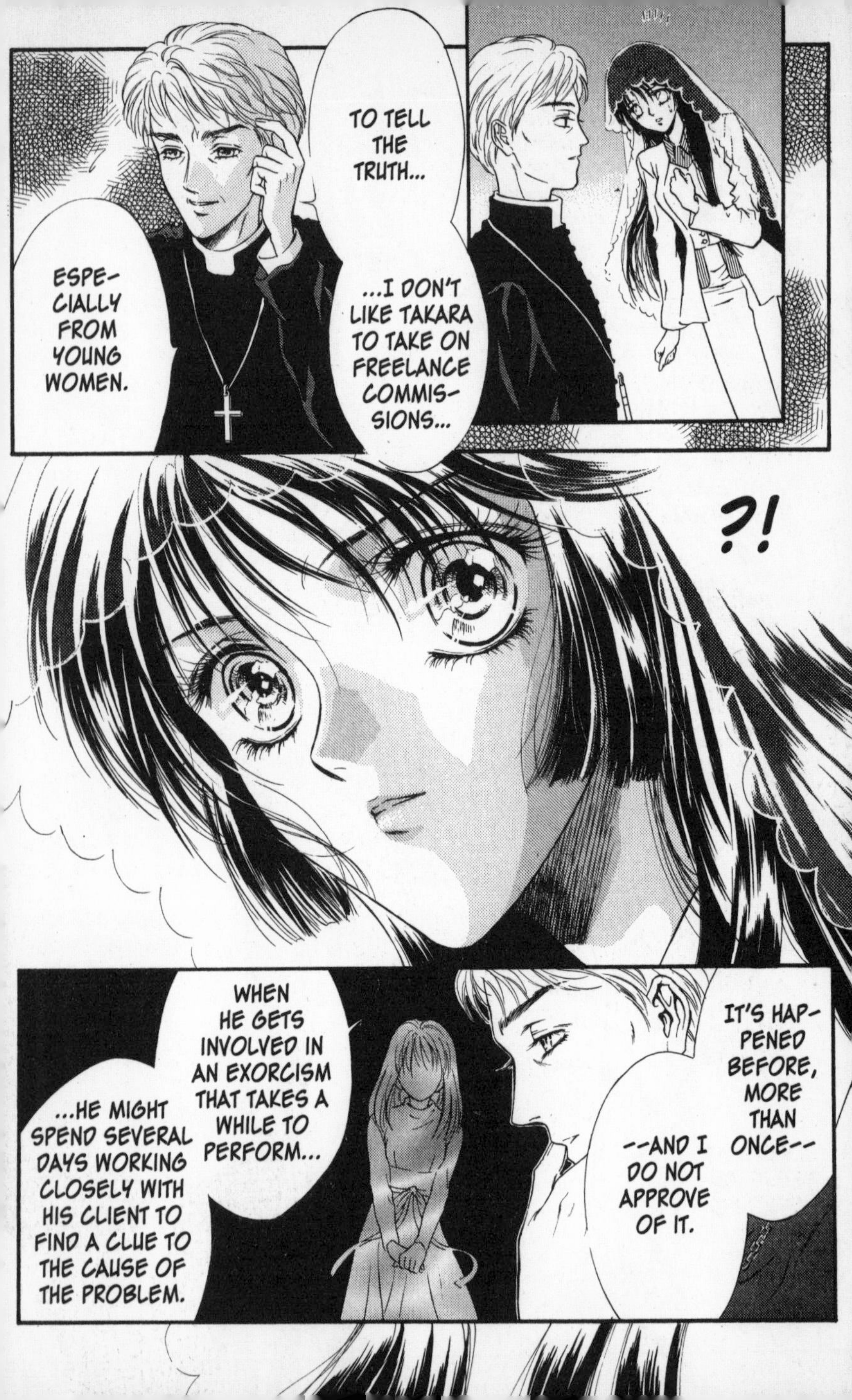
TO TELL THE TRUTH...
...I DON'T LIKE TAKARA TO TAKE ON FREELANCE COMMIS-SIONS...
ESPE-CIALLY FROM YOUNG WOMEN.
?!
IT'S HAP-PENED BEFORE, MORE THAN ONCE--
--AND I DO NOT APPROVE OF IT.
WHEN HE GETS INVOLVED IN AN EXORCISM THAT TAKES A WHILE TO PERFORM...
...HE MIGHT SPEND SEVERAL DAYS WORKING CLOSELY WITH HIS CLIENT TO FIND A CLUE TO THE CAUSE OF THE PROBLEM.

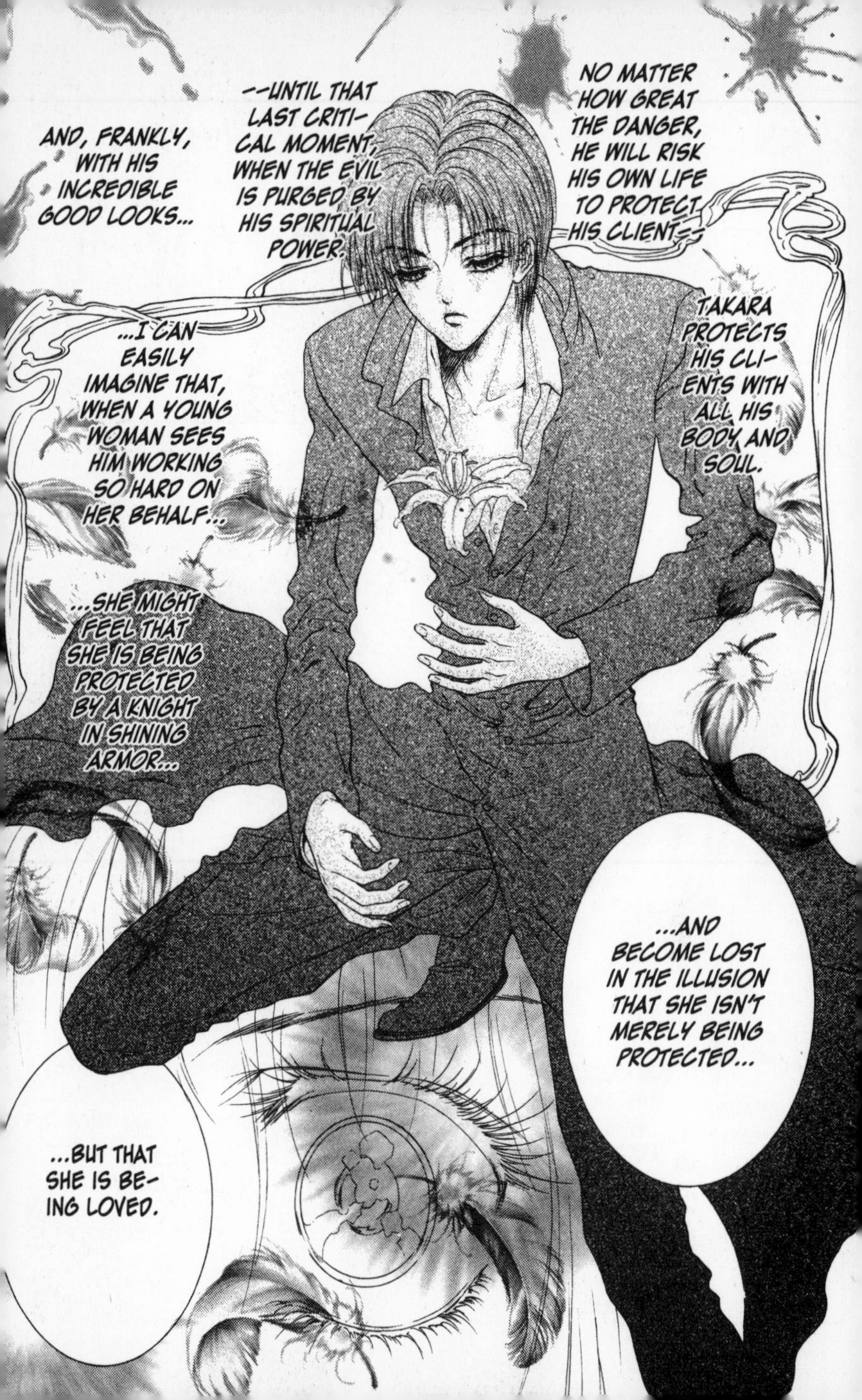
NO MATTER HOW GREAT THE DANGER, HE WILL RISK HIS OWN LIFE TO PROTECT HIS CLIENT--
--UNTIL THAT LAST CRITICAL MOMENT, WHEN THE EVIL IS PURGED BY HIS SPIRITUAL POWER.
AND, FRANKLY, WITH HIS INCREDIBLE GOOD LOOKS...
TAKARA PROTECTS HIS CLIENTS WITH ALL HIS BODY AND SOUL.
...I CAN EASILY IMAGINE THAT, WHEN A YOUNG WOMAN SEES HIM WORKING SO HARD ON HER BEHALF...
...SHE MIGHT FEEL THAT SHE IS BEING PROTECTED BY A KNIGHT IN SHINING ARMOR...
...AND BECOME LOST IN THE ILLUSION THAT SHE ISN'T MERELY BEING PROTECTED...
...BUT THAT SHE IS BEING LOVED.

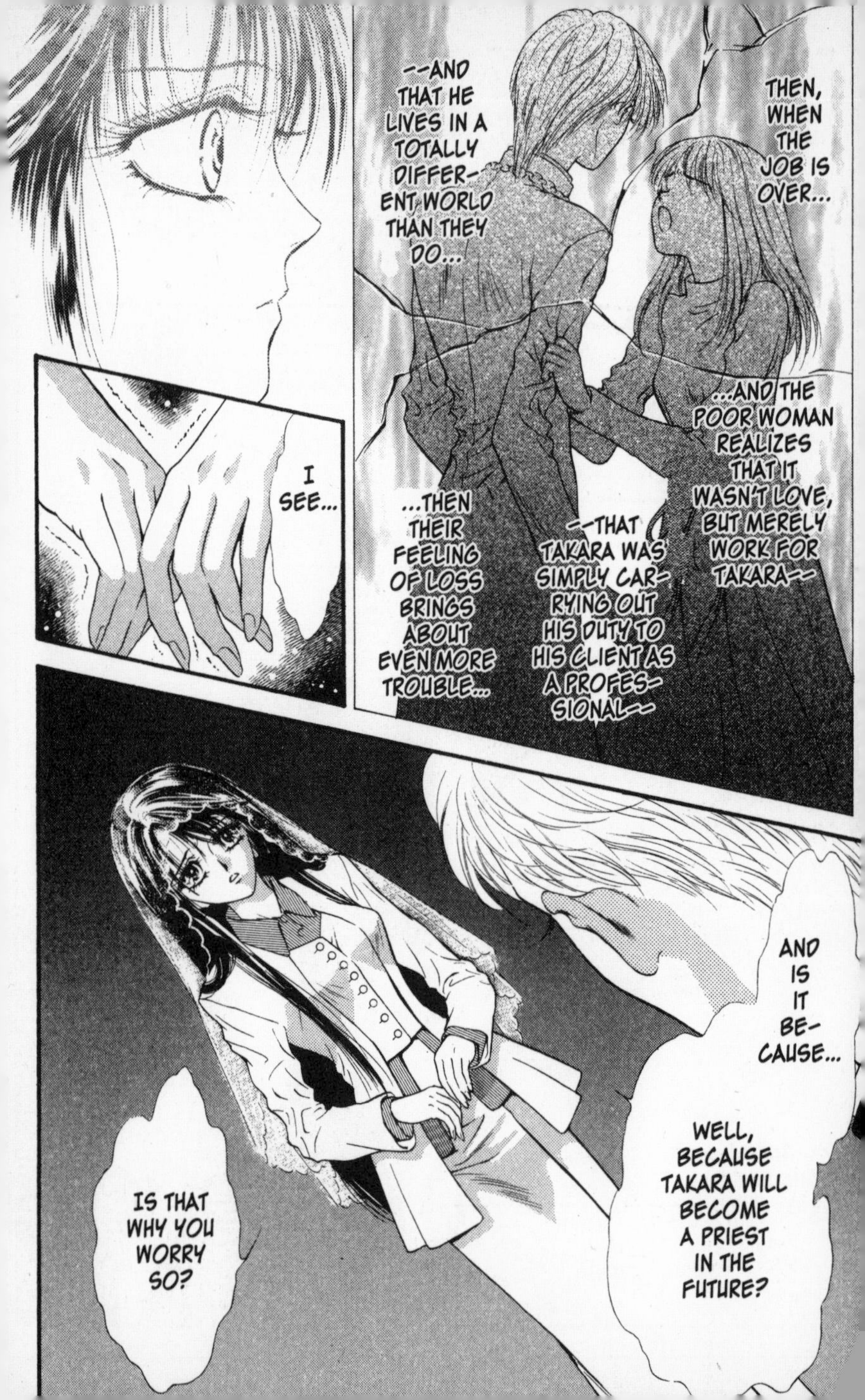
THEN, WHEN THE JOB IS OVER...
...AND THE POOR WOMAN REALIZES THAT IT WASN'T LOVE, BUT MERELY WORK FOR TAKARA--
--THAT TAKARA WAS SIMPLY CARRYING OUT HIS DUTY TO HIS CLIENT AS A PROFESSIONAL--
--AND THAT HE LIVES IN A TOTALLY DIFFERENT WORLD THAN THEY DO...
...THEN THEIR FEELING OF LOSS BRINGS ABOUT EVEN MORE TROUBLE...
I SEE...
AND IS IT BECAUSE...
WELL, BECAUSE TAKARA WILL BECOME A PRIEST IN THE FUTURE?
IS THAT WHY YOU WORRY SO?

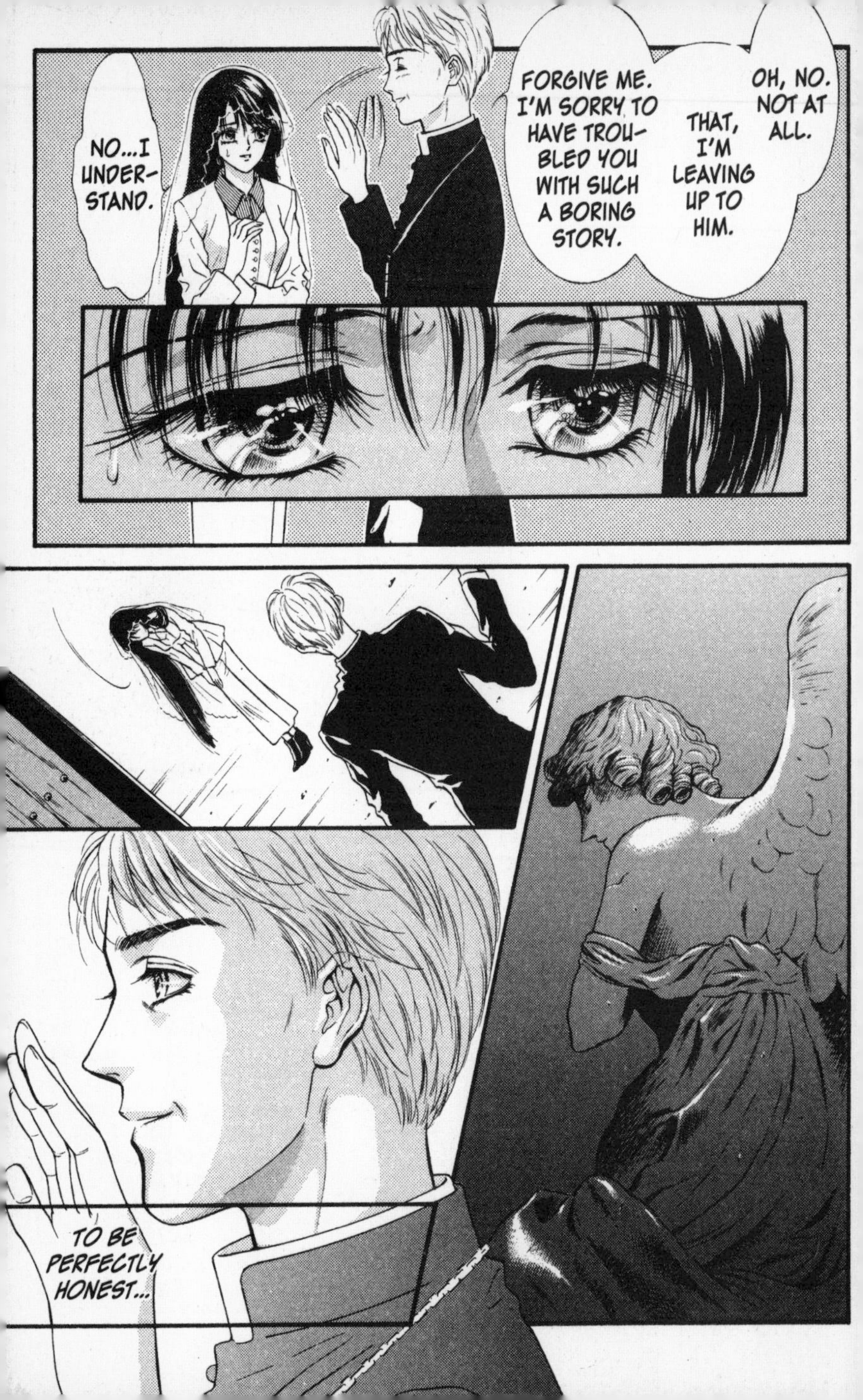
OH, NO. NOT AT ALL.
THAT, I'M LEAVING UP TO HIM.
FORGIVE ME. I'M SORRY TO HAVE TROUBLED YOU WITH SUCH A BORING STORY.
NO...I UNDERSTAND.
TO BE PERFECTLY HONEST...

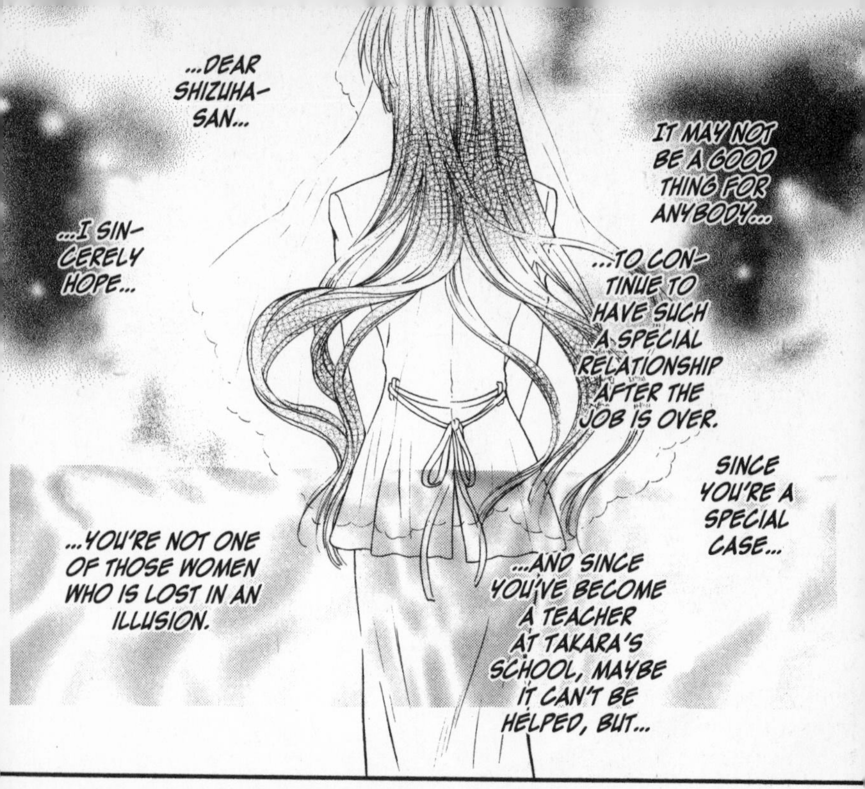
IT MAY NOT BE A GOOD THING FOR ANYBODY...
...TO CONTINUE TO HAVE SUCH A SPECIAL RELATIONSHIP AFTER THE JOB IS OVER.
SINCE YOU'RE A SPECIAL CASE...
...AND SINCE YOU'VE BECOME A TEACHER AT TAKARA'S SCHOOL, MAYBE IT CAN'T BE HELPED, BUT...
...DEAR SHIZUHA-SAN...
...I SINCERELY HOPE...
...YOU'RE NOT ONE OF THOSE WOMEN WHO IS LOST IN AN ILLUSION.

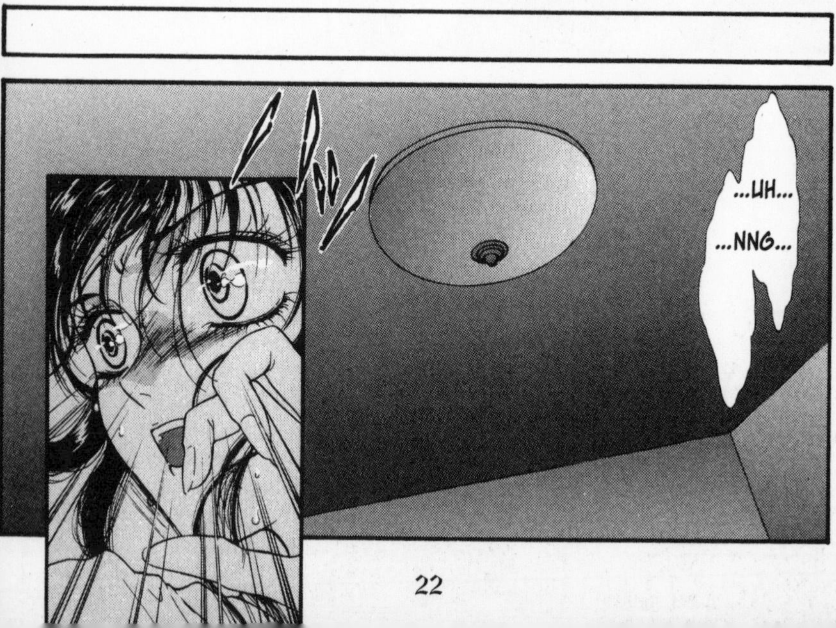
...UH...
...NNG...

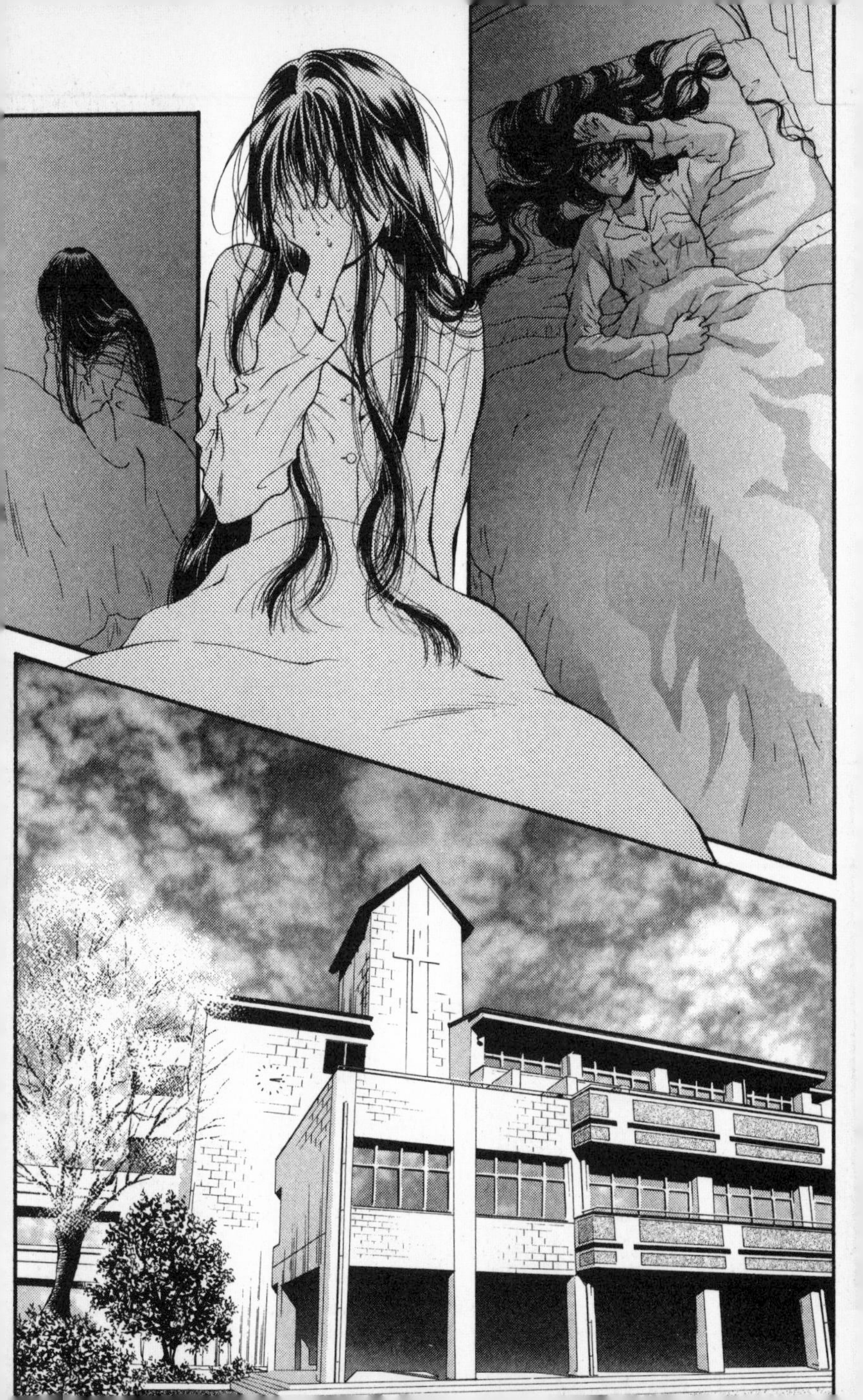

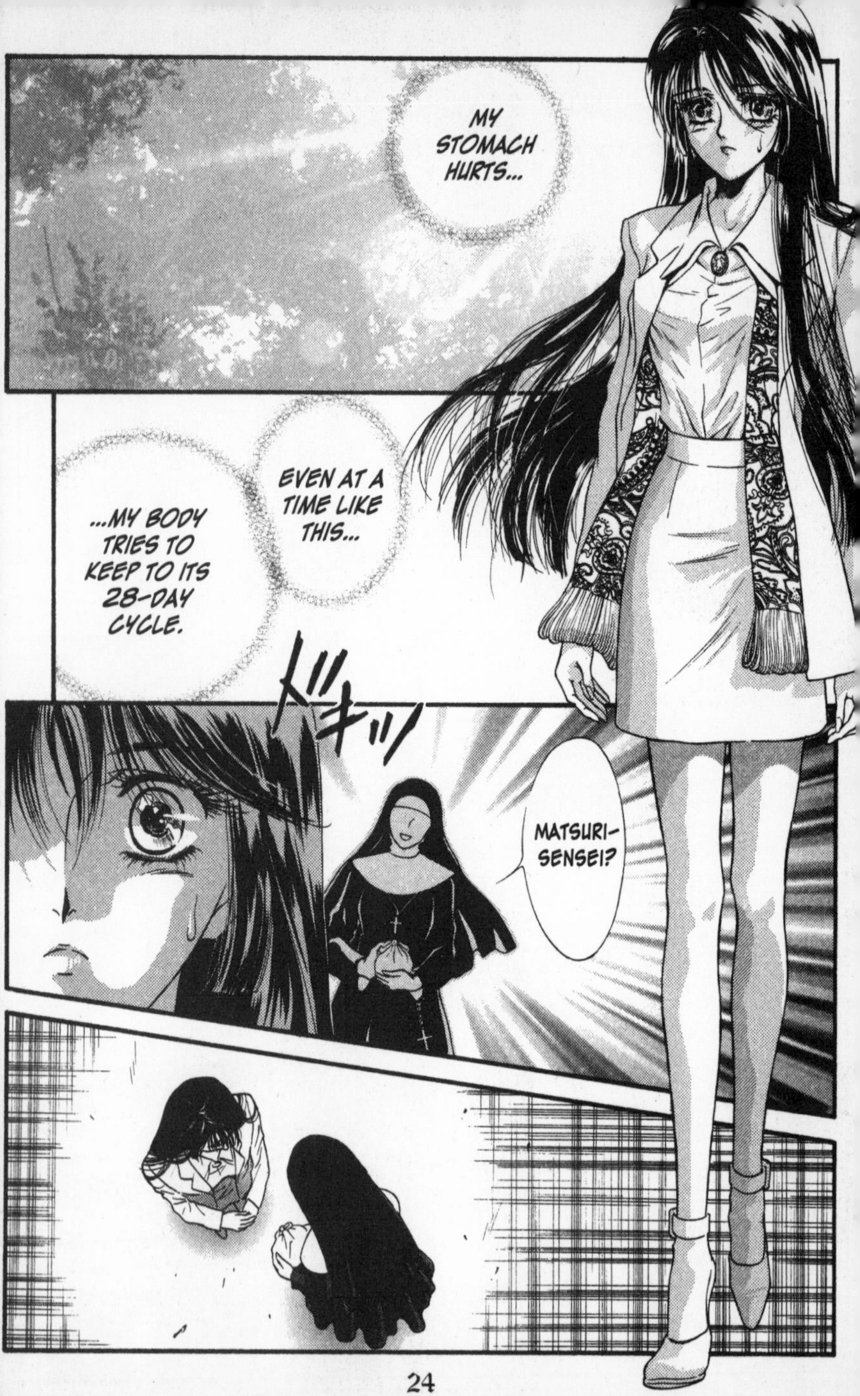
MY STOMACH HURTS...
EVEN AT A TIME LIKE THIS...
...MY BODY TRIES TO KEEP TO ITS 28-DAY CYCLE.
ドキッ
MATSURI-SENSEI?

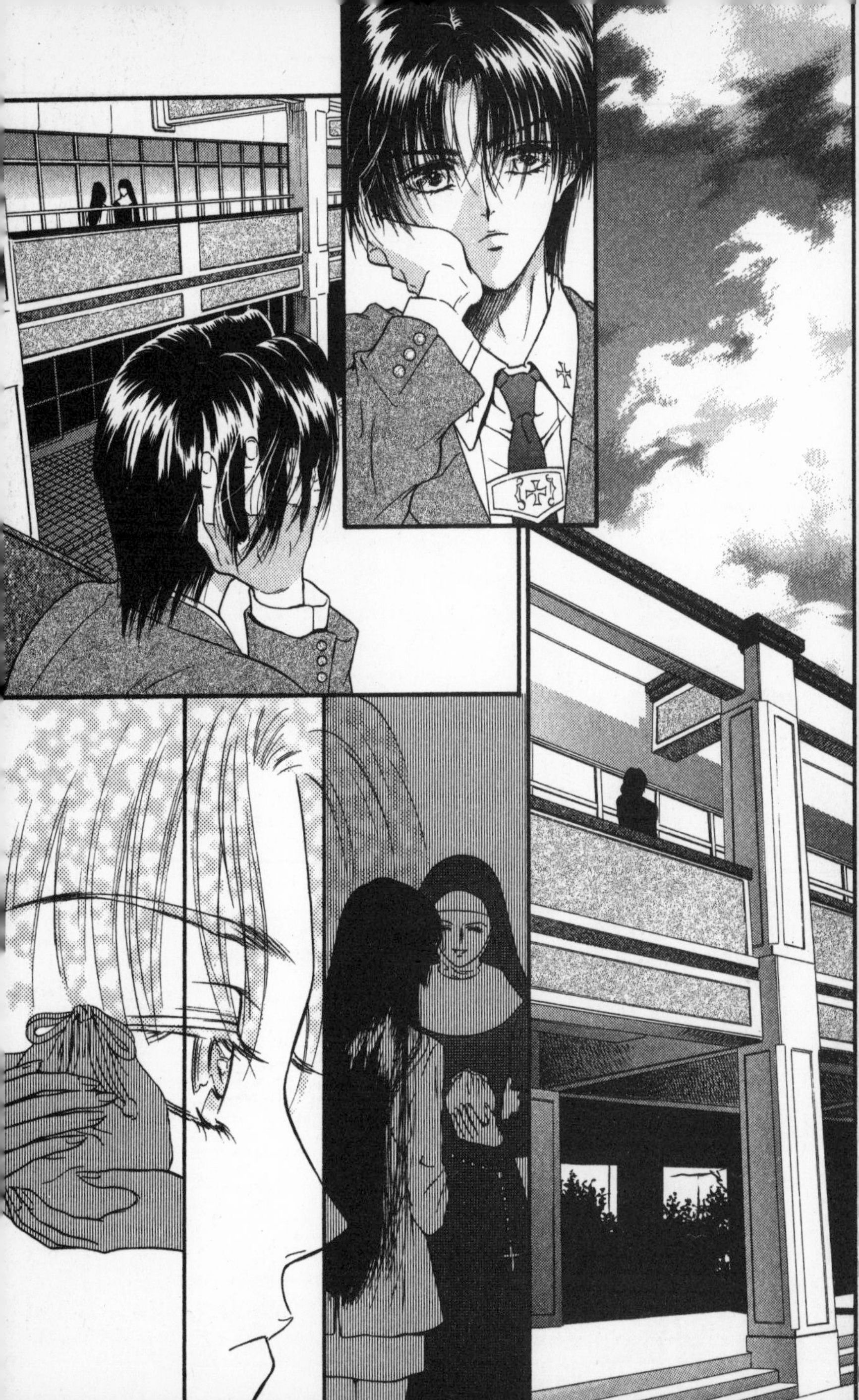

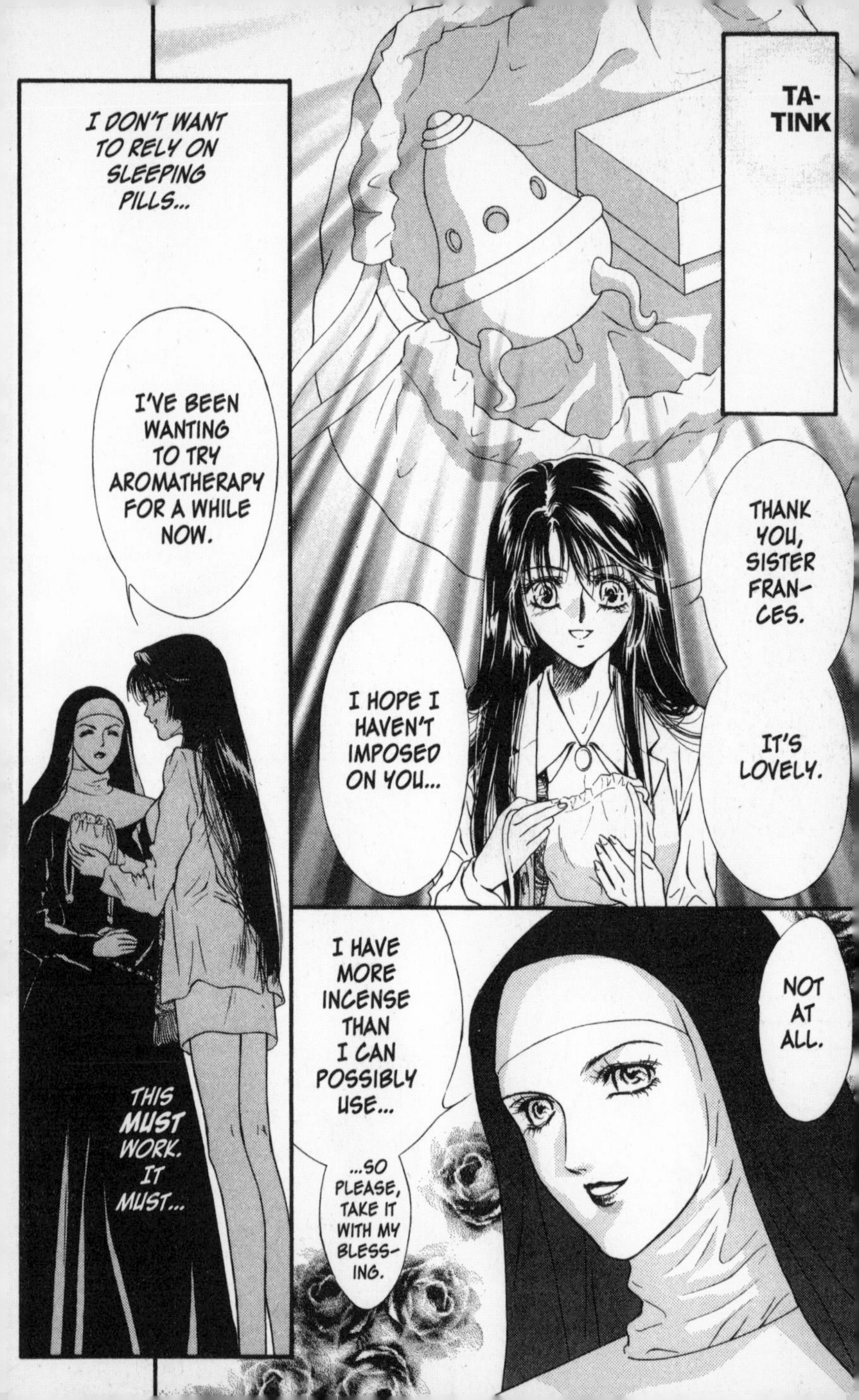

TA-TINK
THANK YOU, SISTER FRANCES.
IT'S LOVELY.
I HOPE I HAVEN'T IMPOSED ON YOU...
NOT AT ALL.
I HAVE MORE INCENSE THAN I CAN POSSIBLY USE...
...SO PLEASE, TAKE IT WITH MY BLESSING.
I DON'T WANT TO RELY ON SLEEPING PILLS...
I'VE BEEN WANTING TO TRY AROMATHERAPY FOR A WHILE NOW.
THIS MUST WORK. IT MUST...

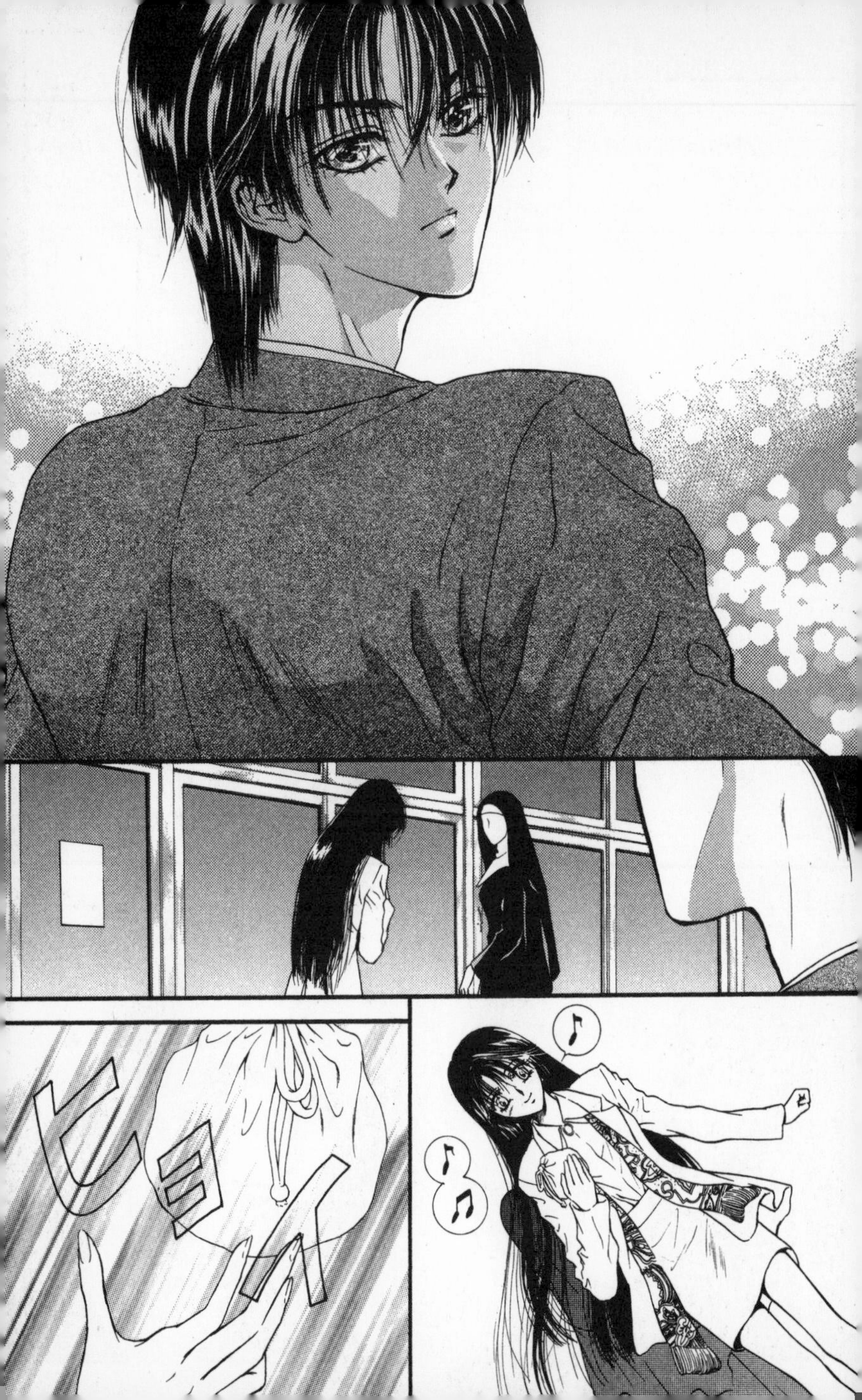
♪
♪
♫
ヒョイ

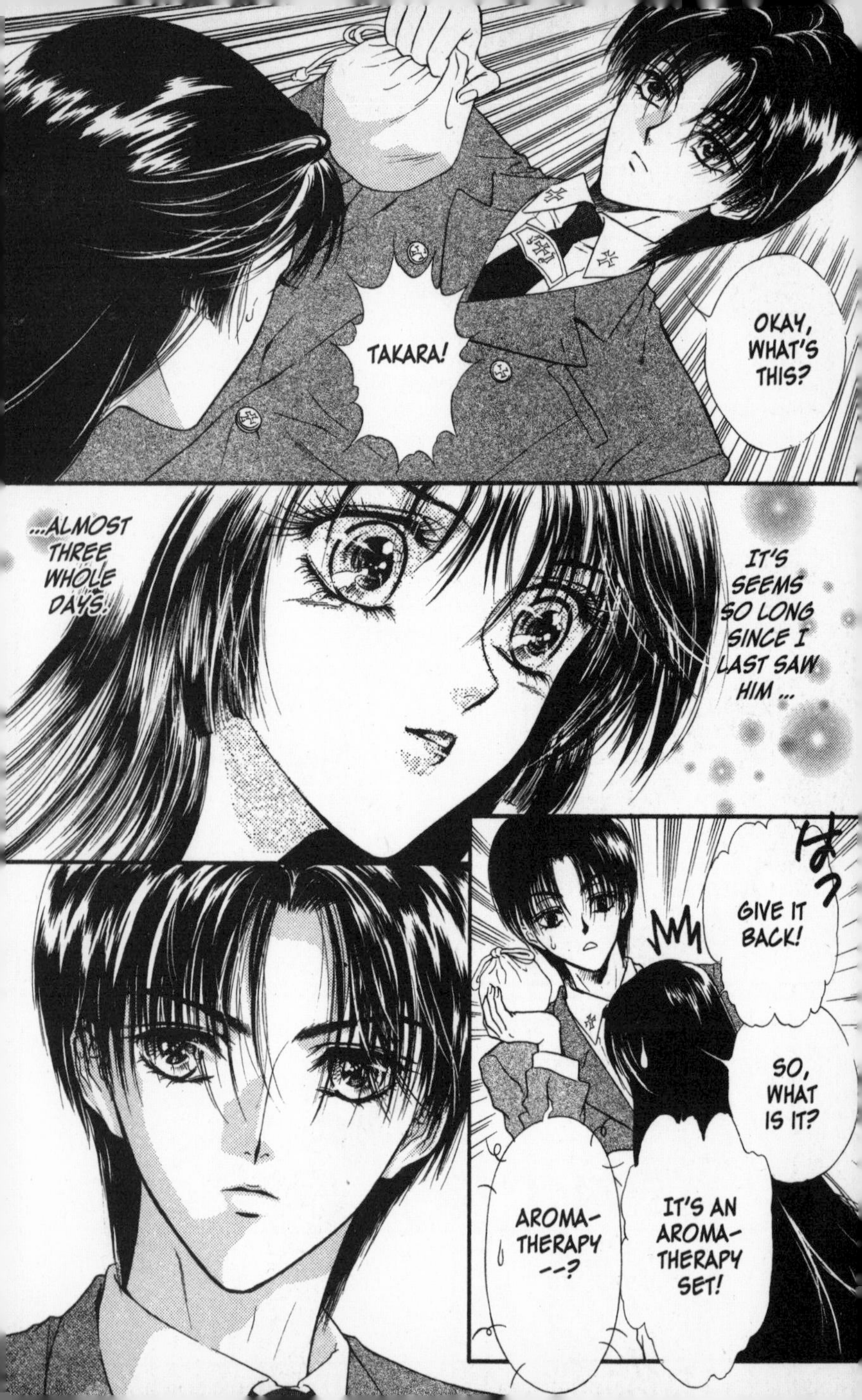
OKAY, WHAT'S THIS?
TAKARA!
IT'S SEEMS SO LONG SINCE I LAST SAW HIM ...
...ALMOST THREE WHOLE DAYS!
はっ
GIVE IT BACK!
SO, WHAT IS IT?
IT'S AN AROMA-THERAPY SET!
AROMA-THERAPY --?

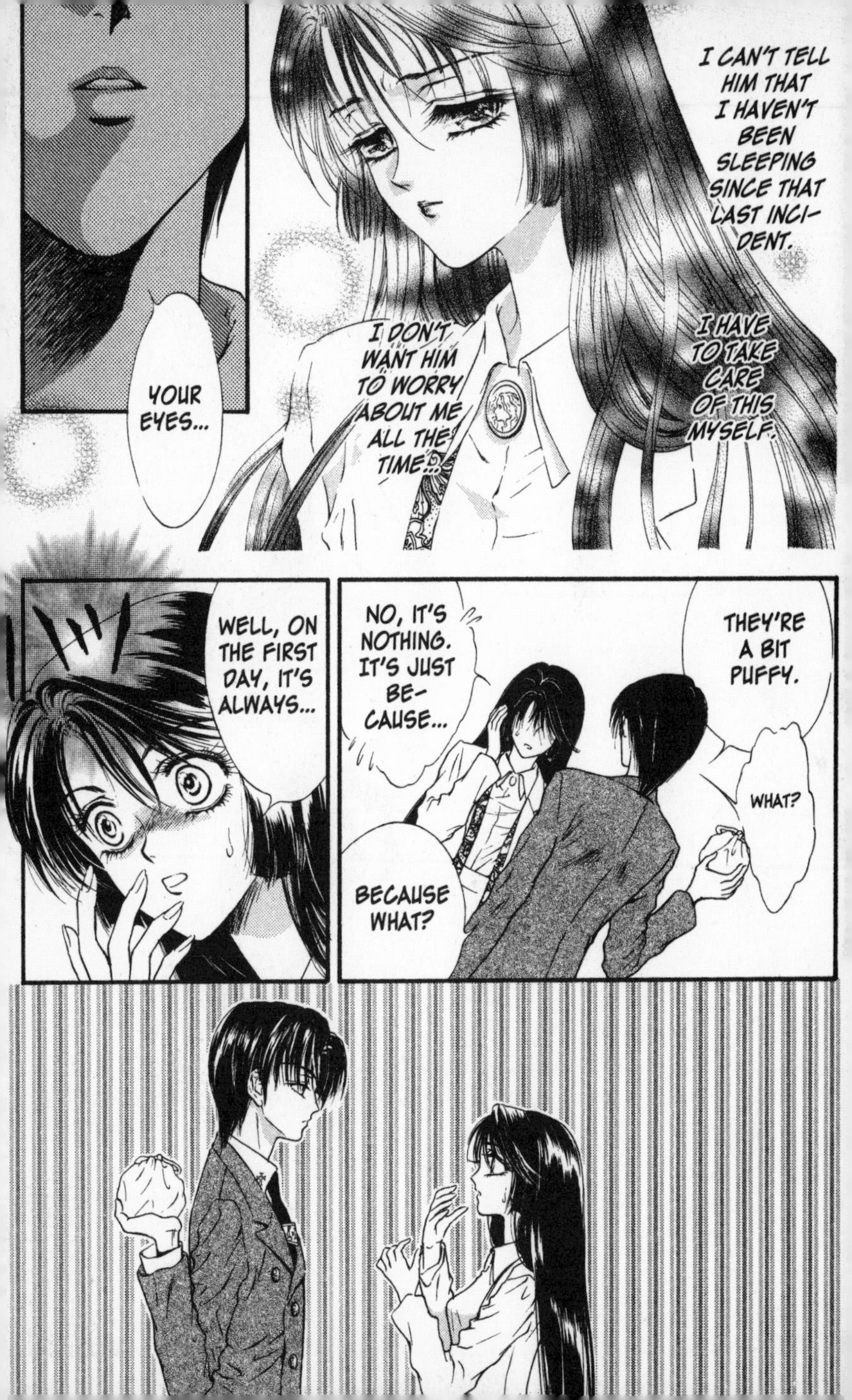
I CAN'T TELL HIM THAT I HAVEN'T BEEN SLEEPING SINCE THAT LAST INCI-DENT.
I HAVE TO TAKE CARE OF THIS MYSELF.
I DON'T WANT HIM TO WORRY ABOUT ME ALL THE TIME...
YOUR EYES...
THEY'RE A BIT PUFFY.
NO, IT'S NOTHING. IT'S JUST BE-CAUSE...
WHAT?
BECAUSE WHAT?
WELL, ON THE FIRST DAY, IT'S ALWAYS...

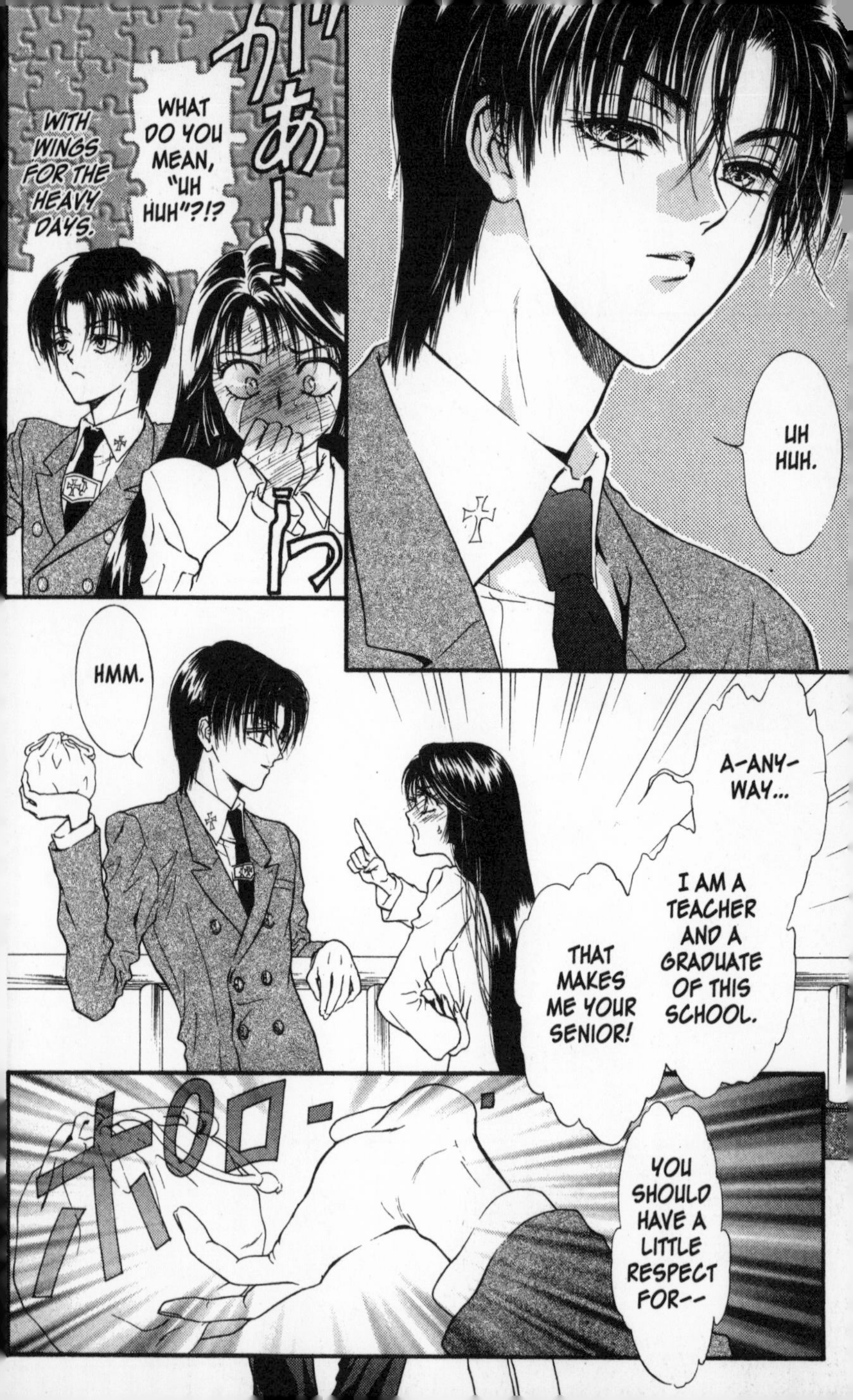

UH HUH.
WHAT DO YOU MEAN, "UH HUH"?!?
WITH WINGS FOR THE HEAVY DAYS.
A-ANY-WAY...
I AM A TEACHER AND A GRADUATE OF THIS SCHOOL.
THAT MAKES ME YOUR SENIOR!
HMM.
YOU SHOULD HAVE A LITTLE RESPECT FOR--

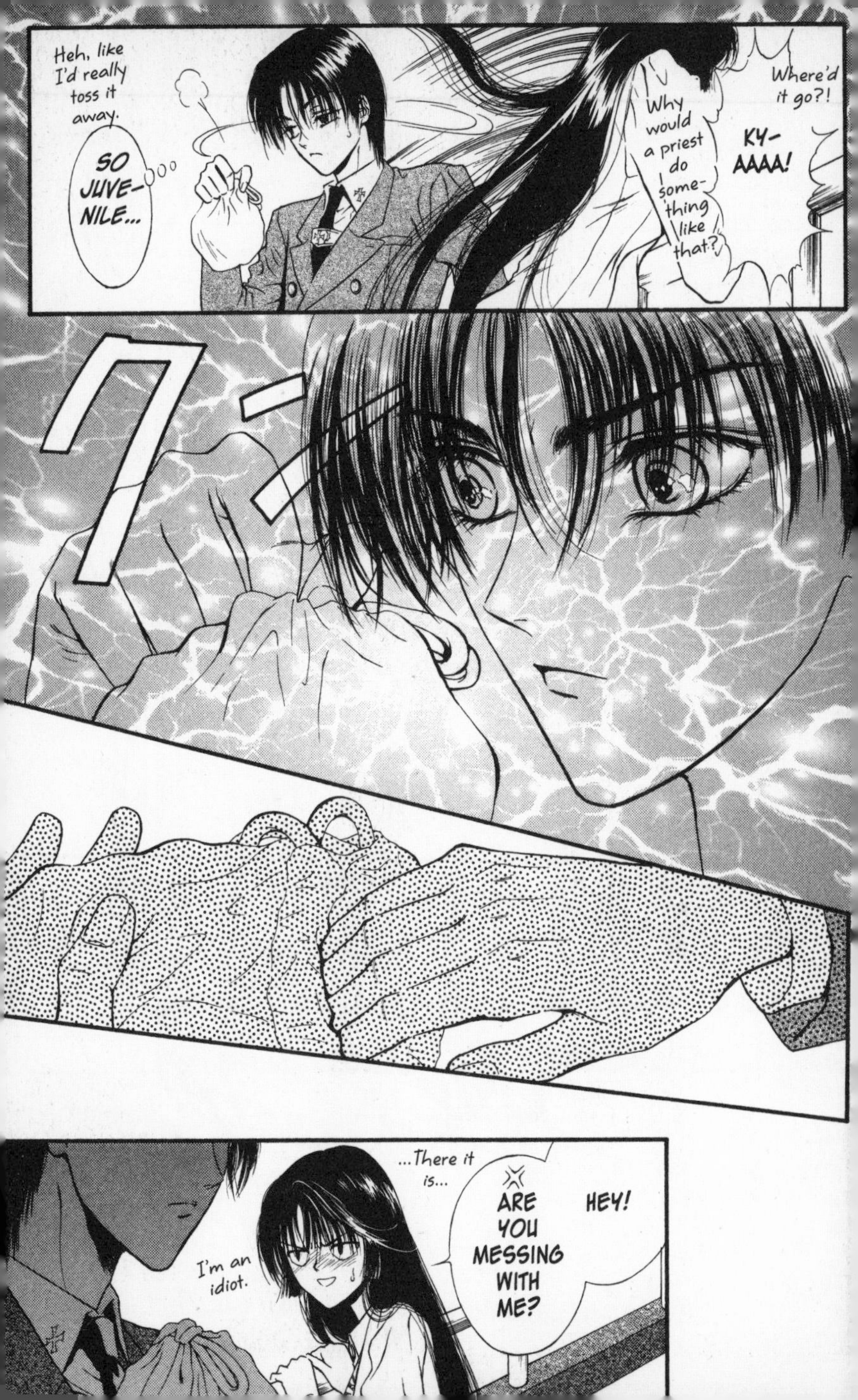
Where'd it go?!
KY-AAAA!
Why would a priest do something like that?
Heh, like I'd really toss it away.
SO JUVENILE...
HEY!
ARE YOU MESSING WITH ME?
...There it is...
I'm an idiot.

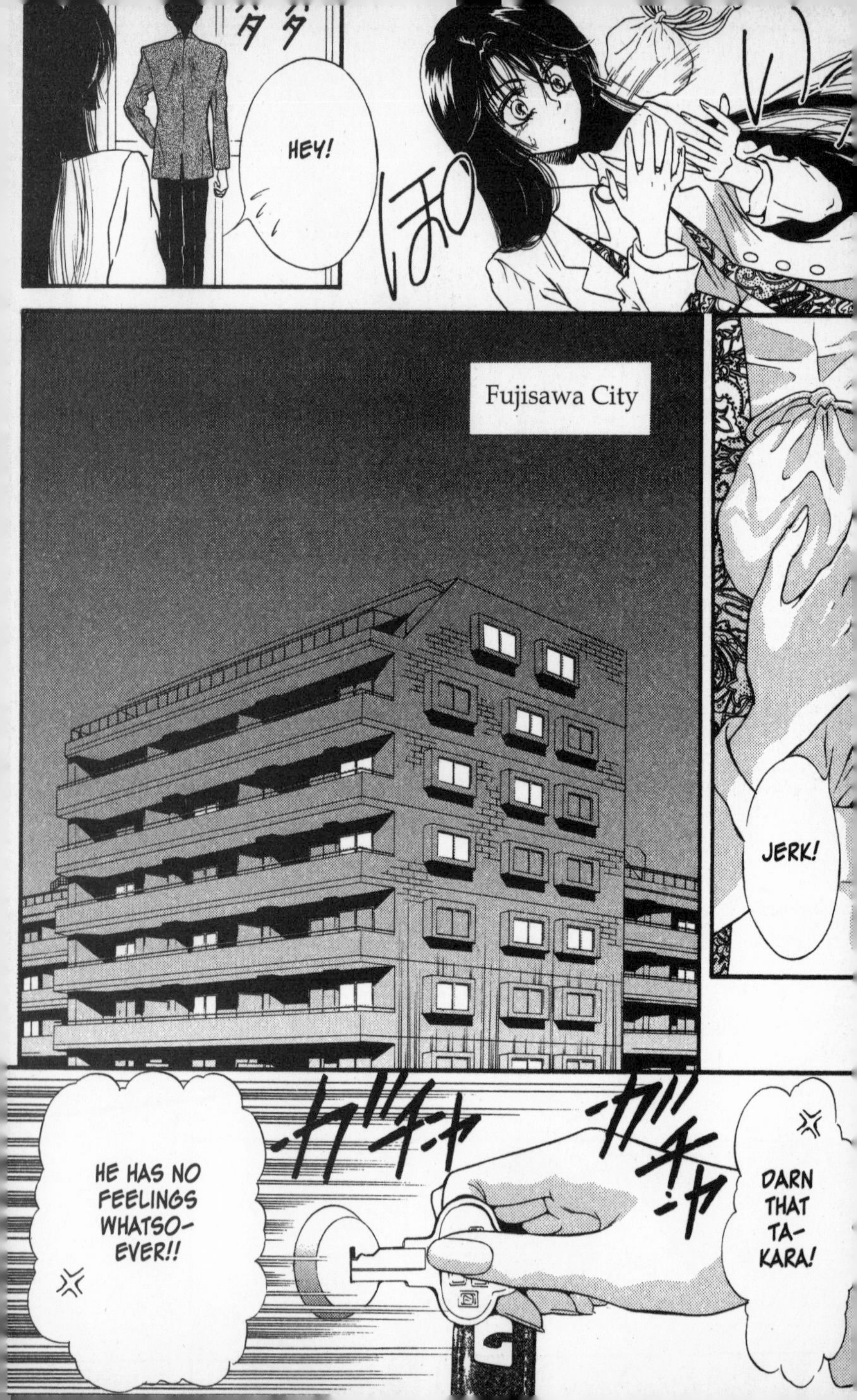
ほっ
タタ
HEY!
JERK!
Fujisawa City
DARN THAT TA-KARA!
ガチャ
ガチャ
HE HAS NO FEELINGS WHATSO-EVER!!

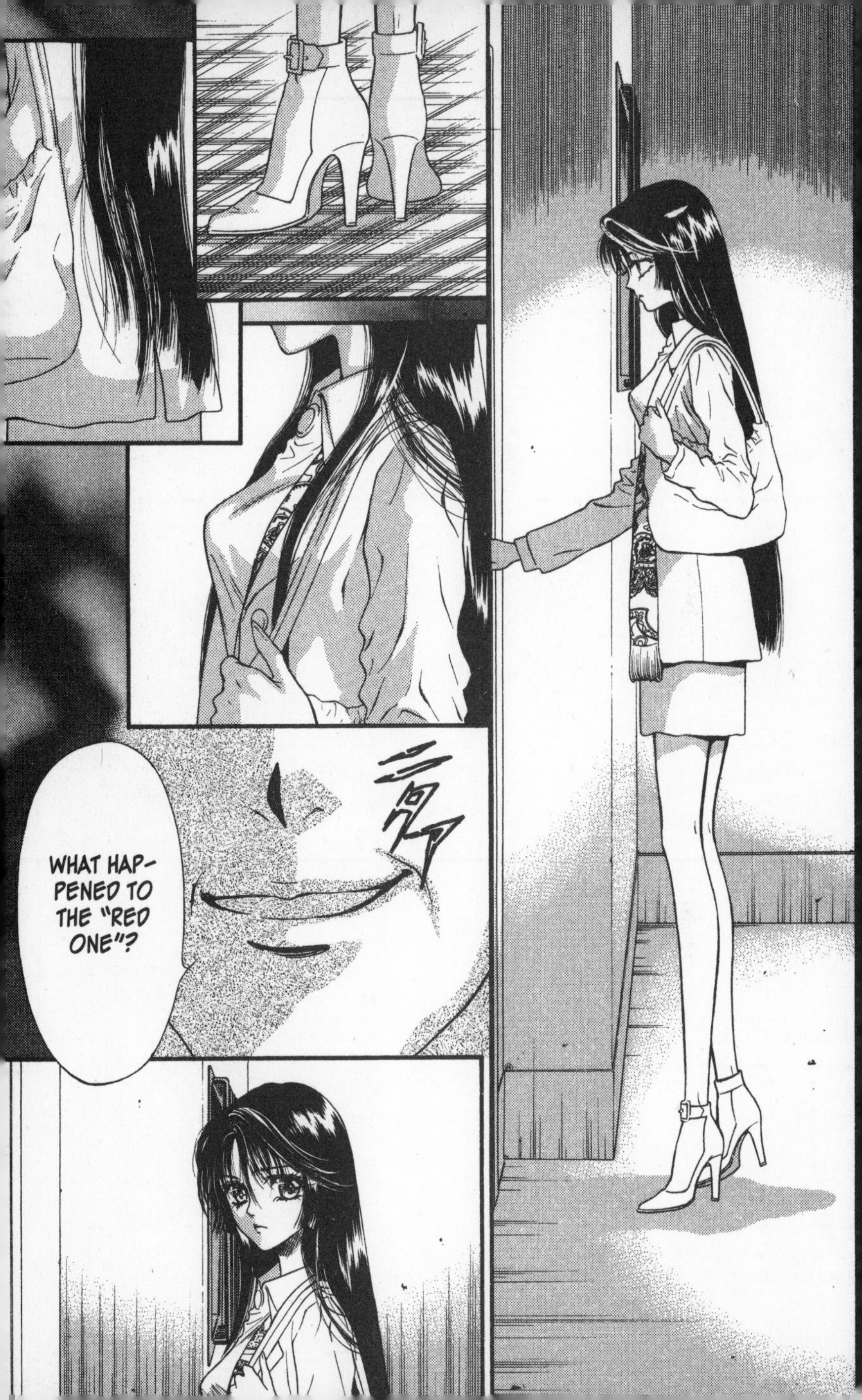
WHAT HAP-PENED TO THE "RED ONE"?

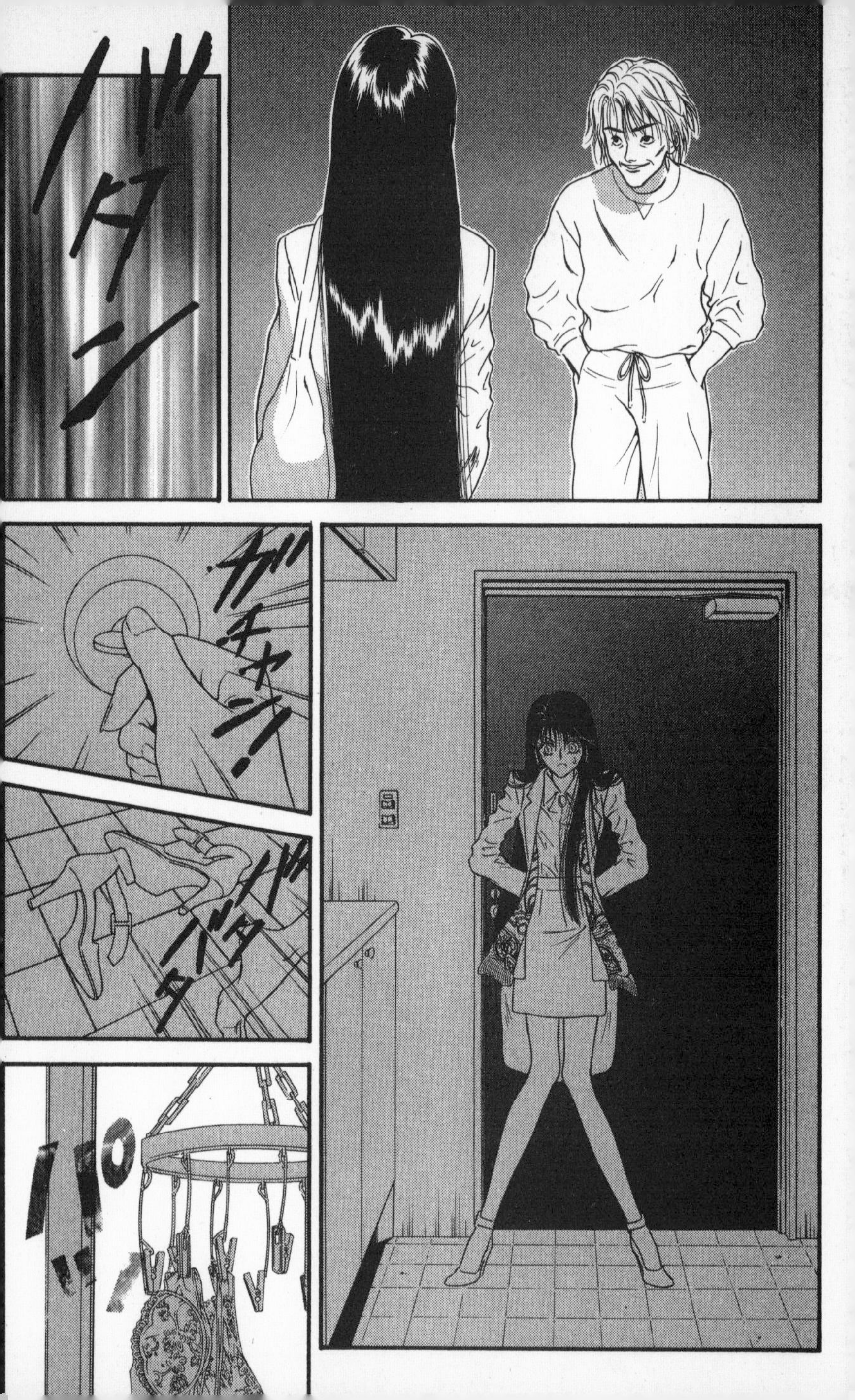
バタン
ガチャン!
バタバタ

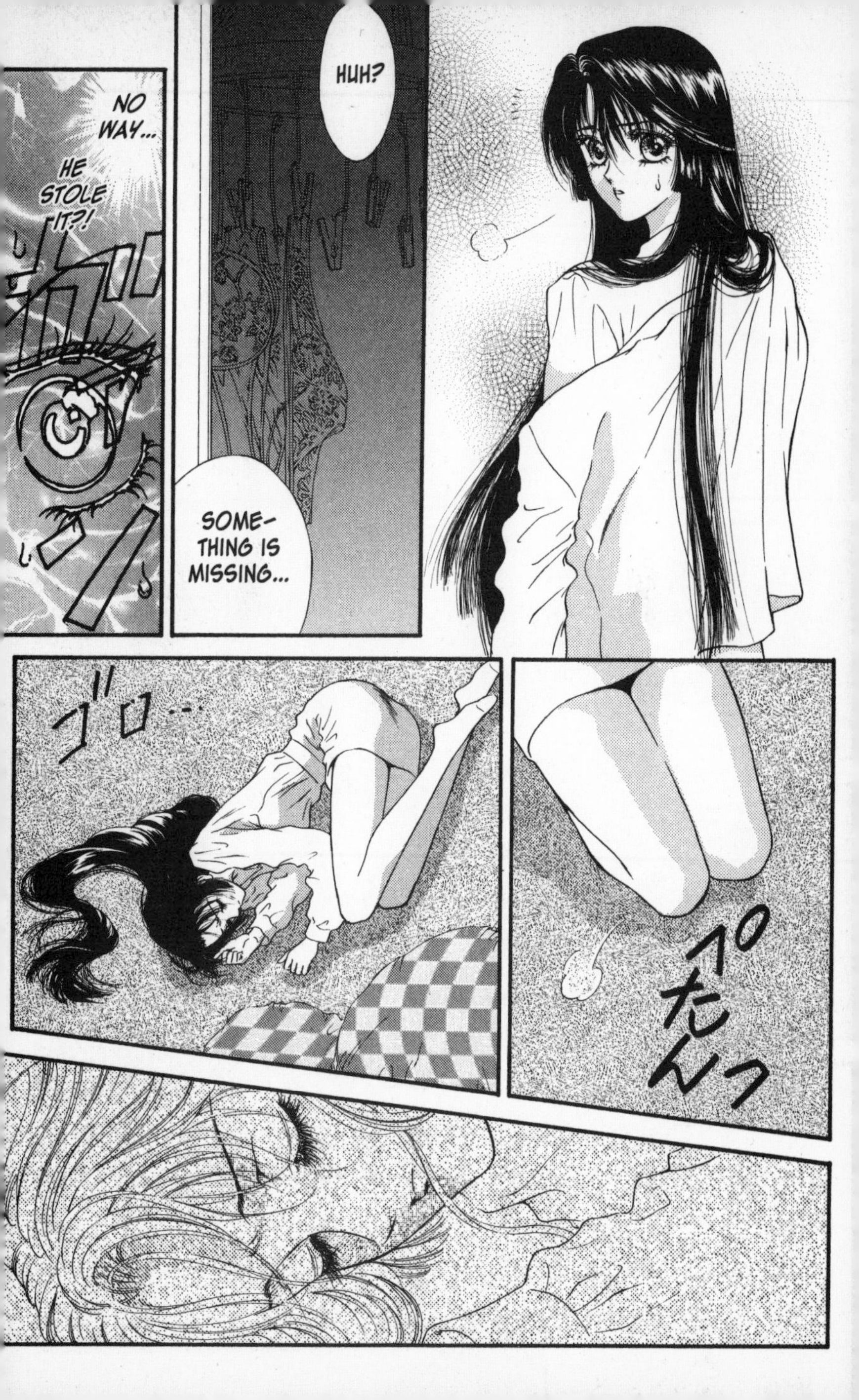
HUH?
SOME-THING IS MISSING...
NO WAY... HE STOLE IT?!
ぺたんっ
ゴロ…

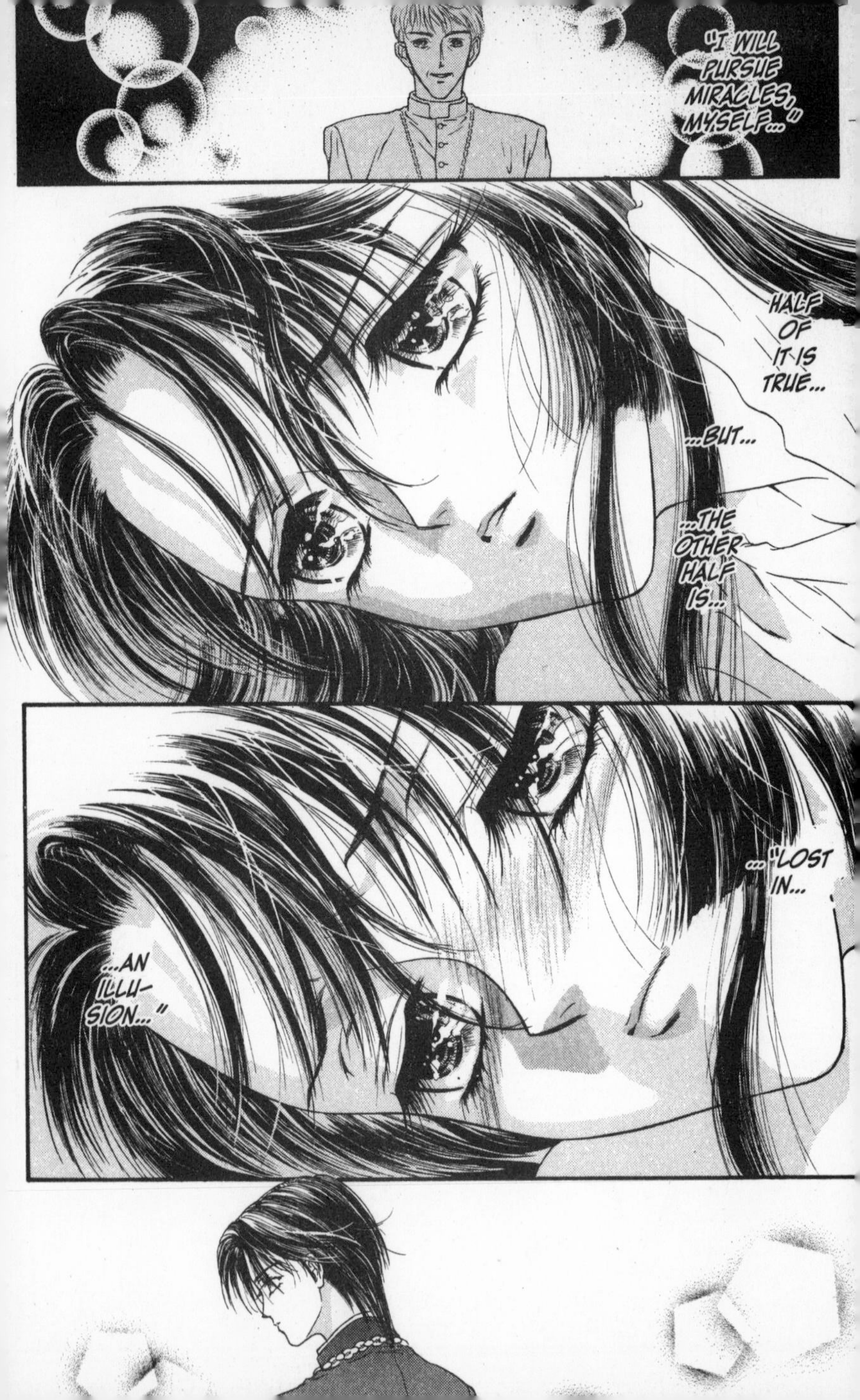
"I WILL PURSUE MIRACLES, MYSELF..."
HALF OF IT IS TRUE...
...BUT...
...THE OTHER HALF IS...
..."LOST IN...
...AN ILLU-SION..."

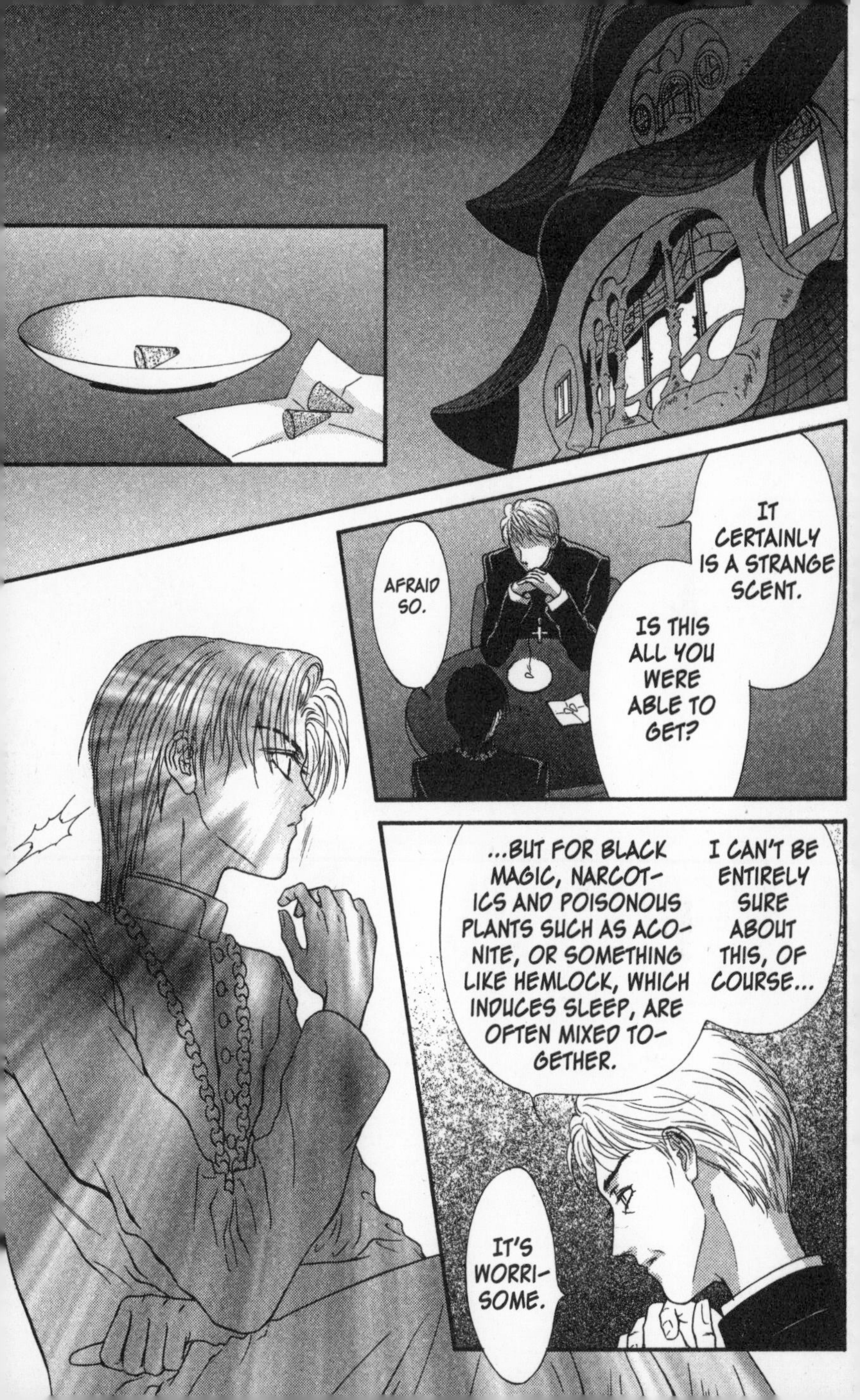
IT CERTAINLY IS A STRANGE SCENT.
IS THIS ALL YOU WERE ABLE TO GET?
AFRAID SO.
I CAN'T BE ENTIRELY SURE ABOUT THIS, OF COURSE...
...BUT FOR BLACK MAGIC, NARCOTICS AND POISONOUS PLANTS SUCH AS ACONITE, OR SOMETHING LIKE HEMLOCK, WHICH INDUCES SLEEP, ARE OFTEN MIXED TOGETHER.
IT'S WORRISOME.

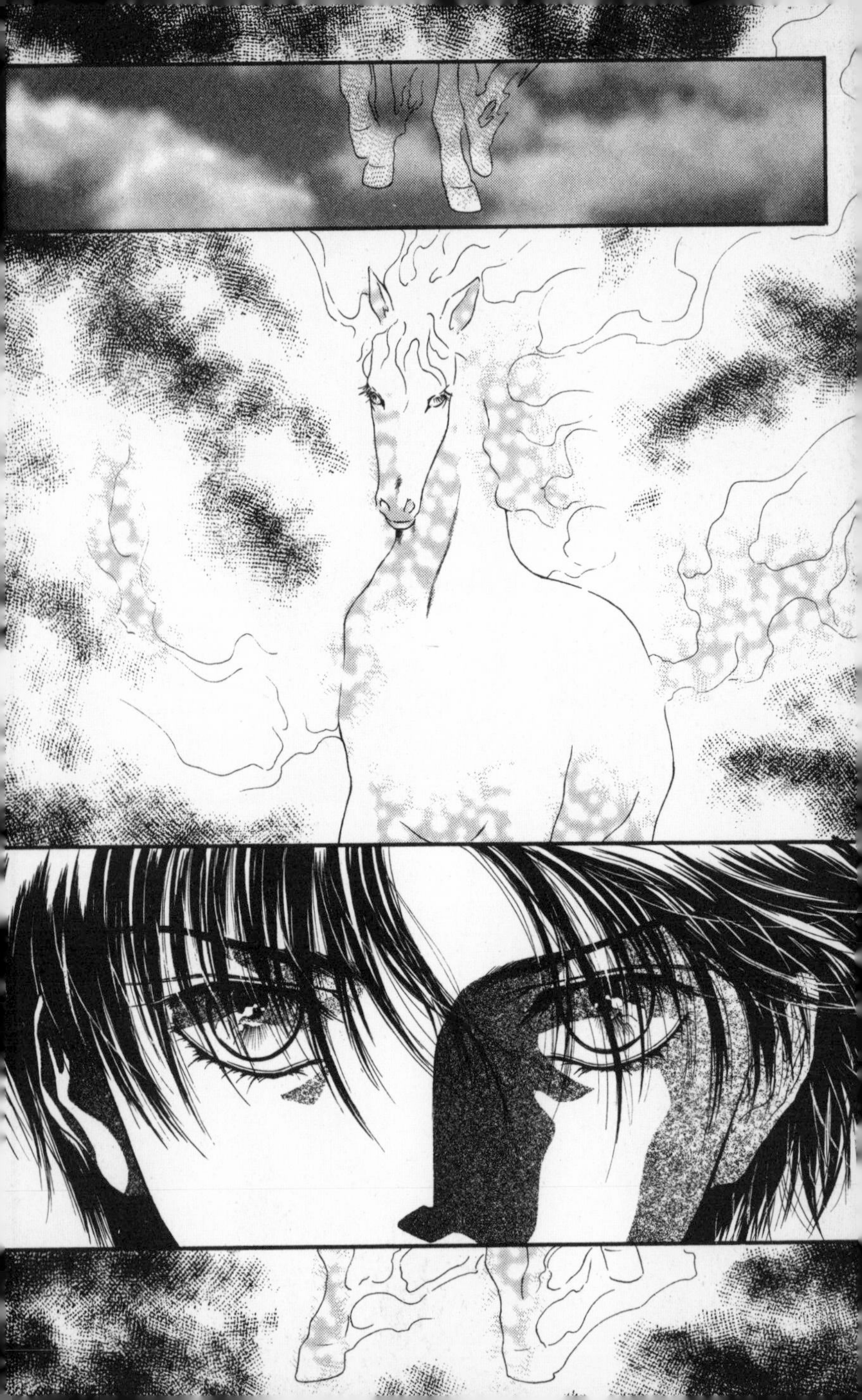

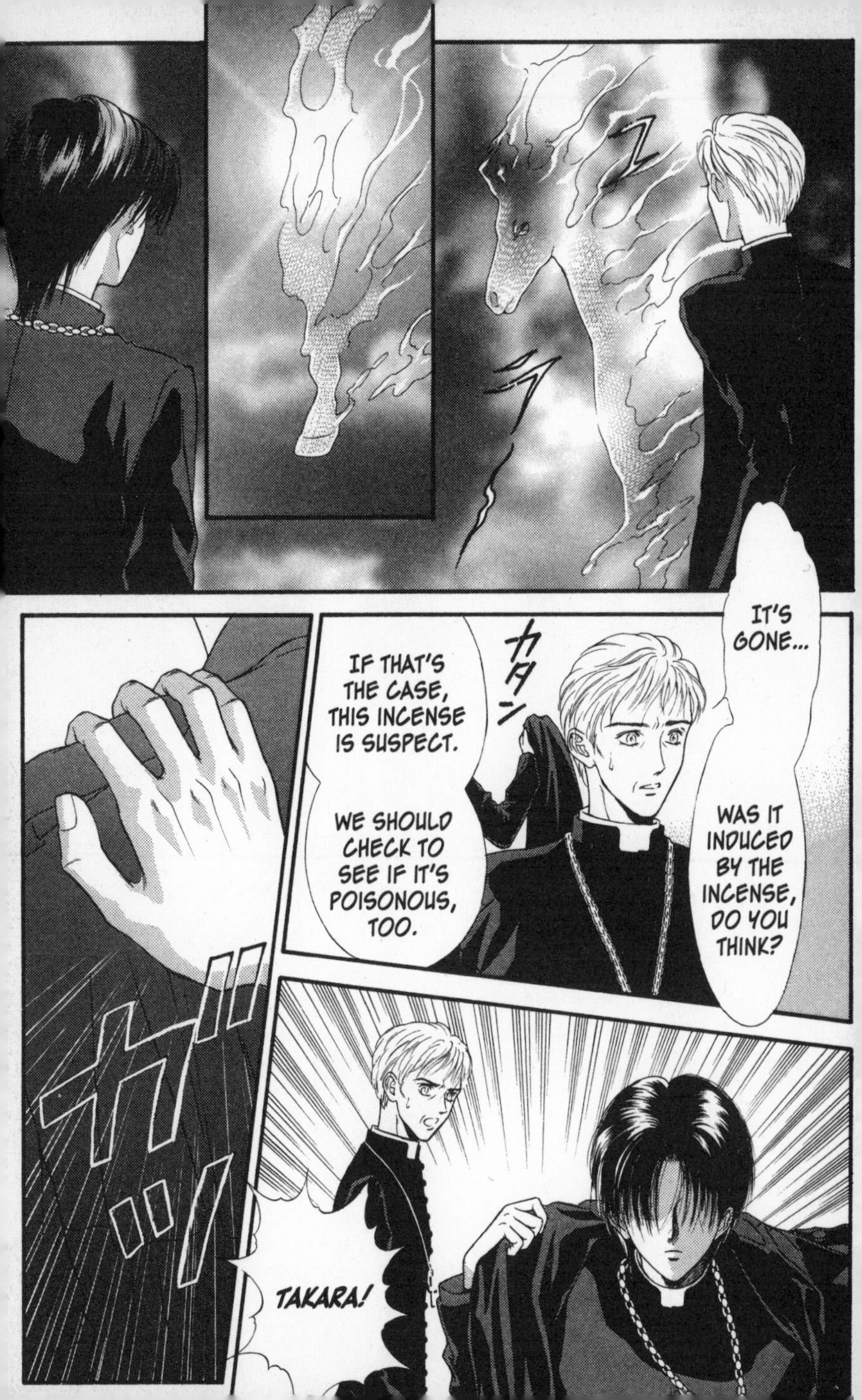
IT'S GONE...
WAS IT INDUCED BY THE INCENSE, DO YOU THINK?
カタン
IF THAT'S THE CASE, THIS INCENSE IS SUSPECT.
WE SHOULD CHECK TO SEE IF IT'S POISONOUS, TOO.
TAKARA!

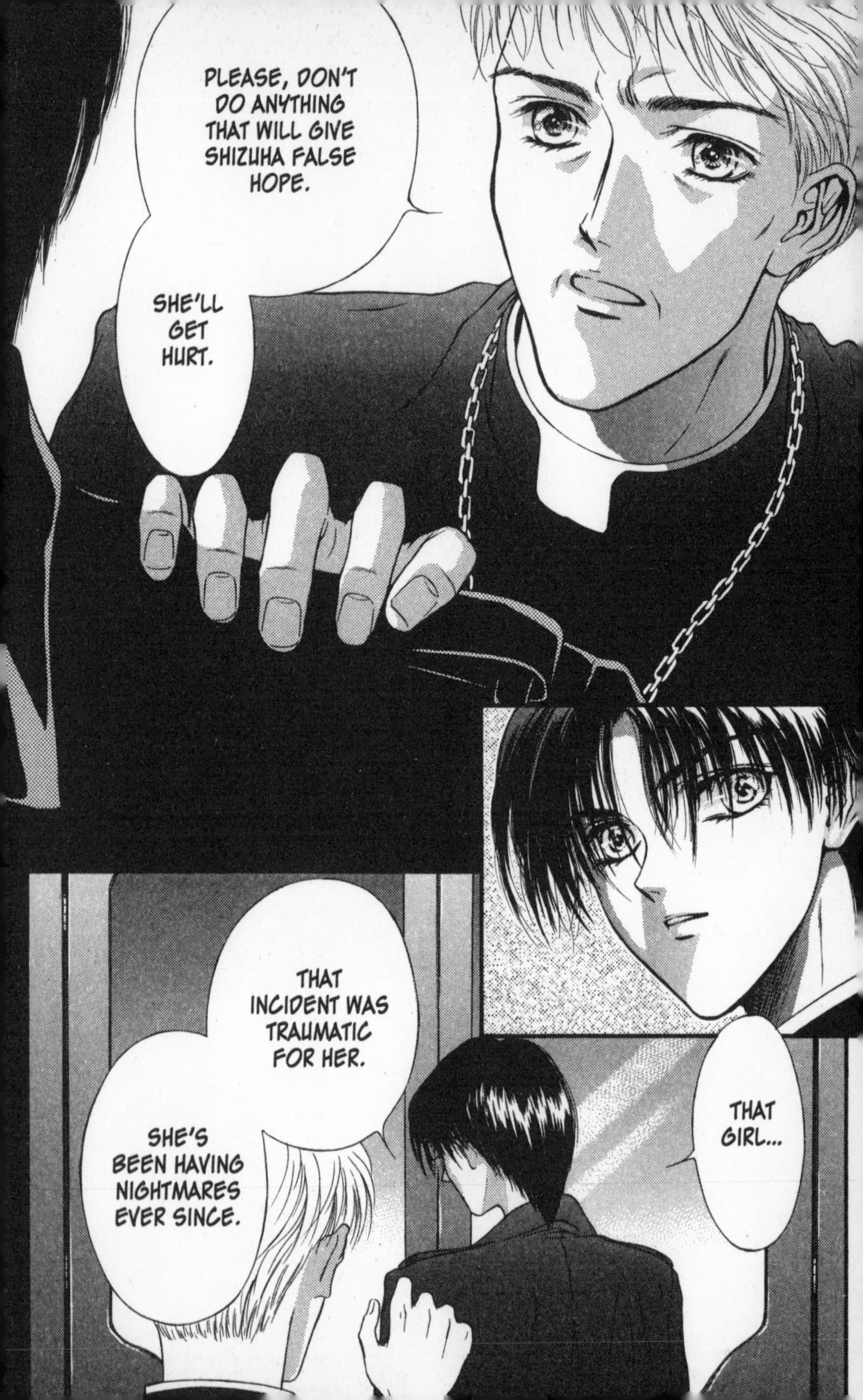

PLEASE, DON'T DO ANYTHING THAT WILL GIVE SHIZUHA FALSE HOPE.
SHE'LL GET HURT.
THAT GIRL...
THAT INCIDENT WAS TRAUMATIC FOR HER.
SHE'S BEEN HAVING NIGHTMARES EVER SINCE.

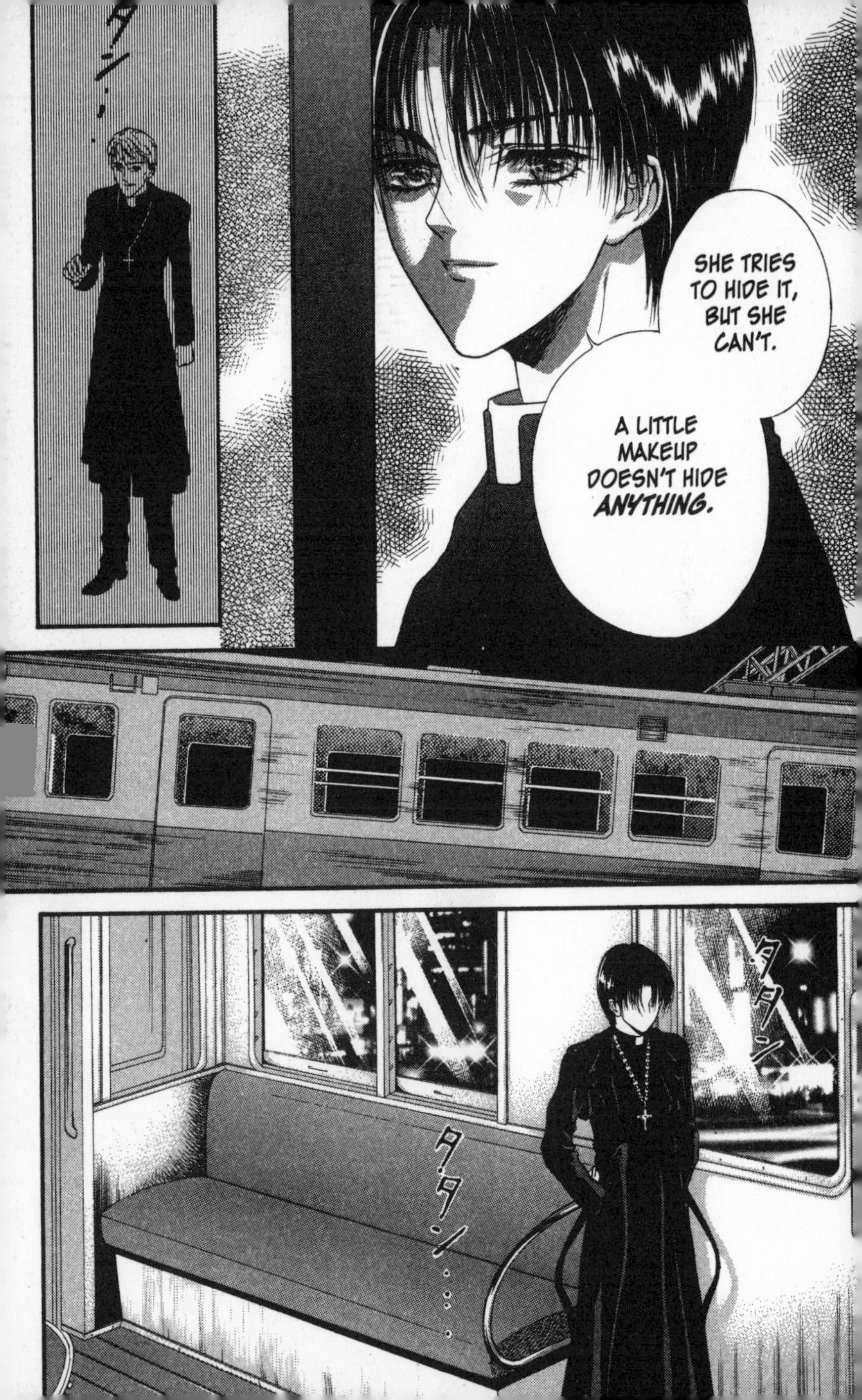
SHE TRIES TO HIDE IT, BUT SHE CAN'T.
A LITTLE MAKEUP DOESN'T HIDE **ANYTHING.**

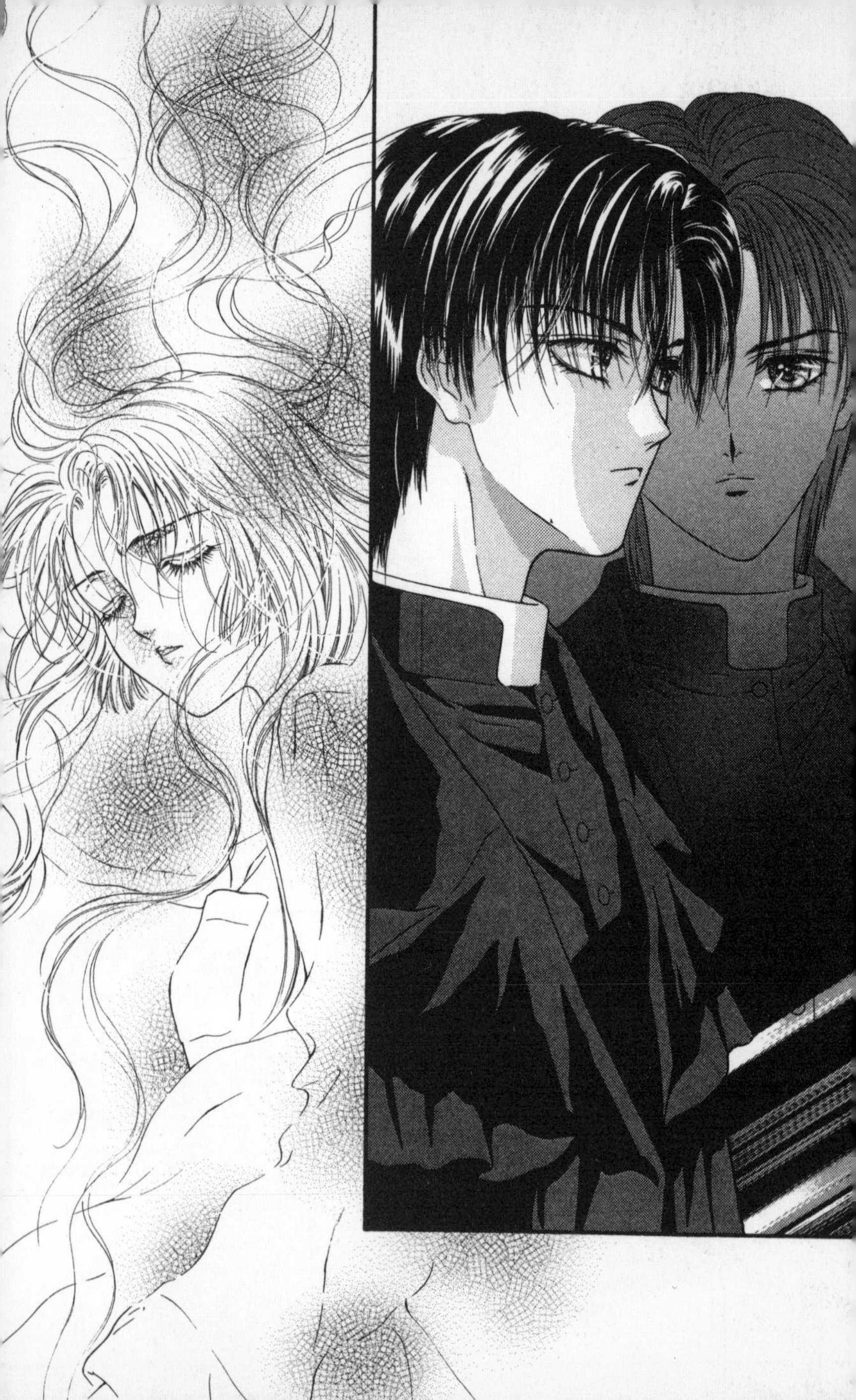

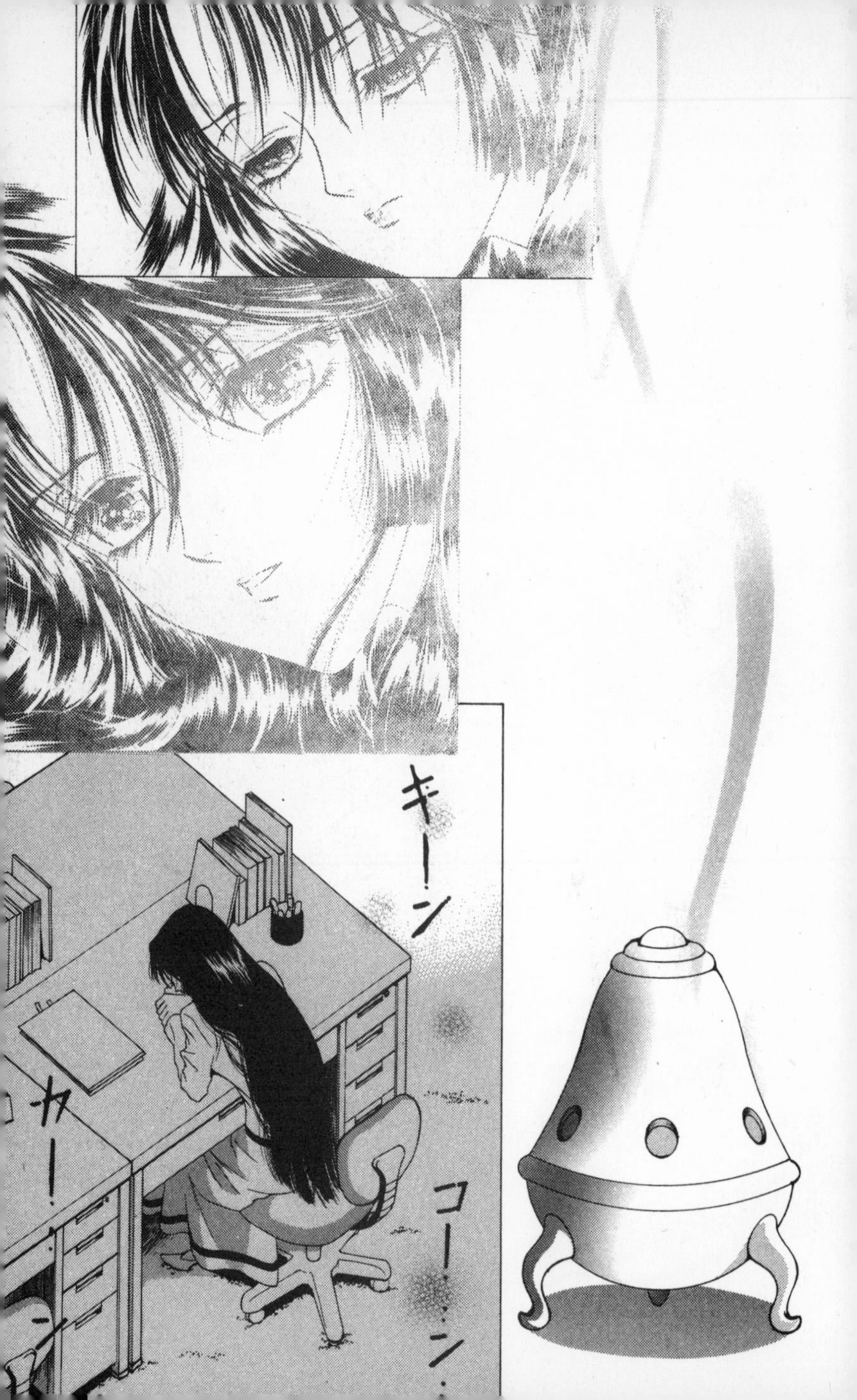
キーン
コーン・
カー！

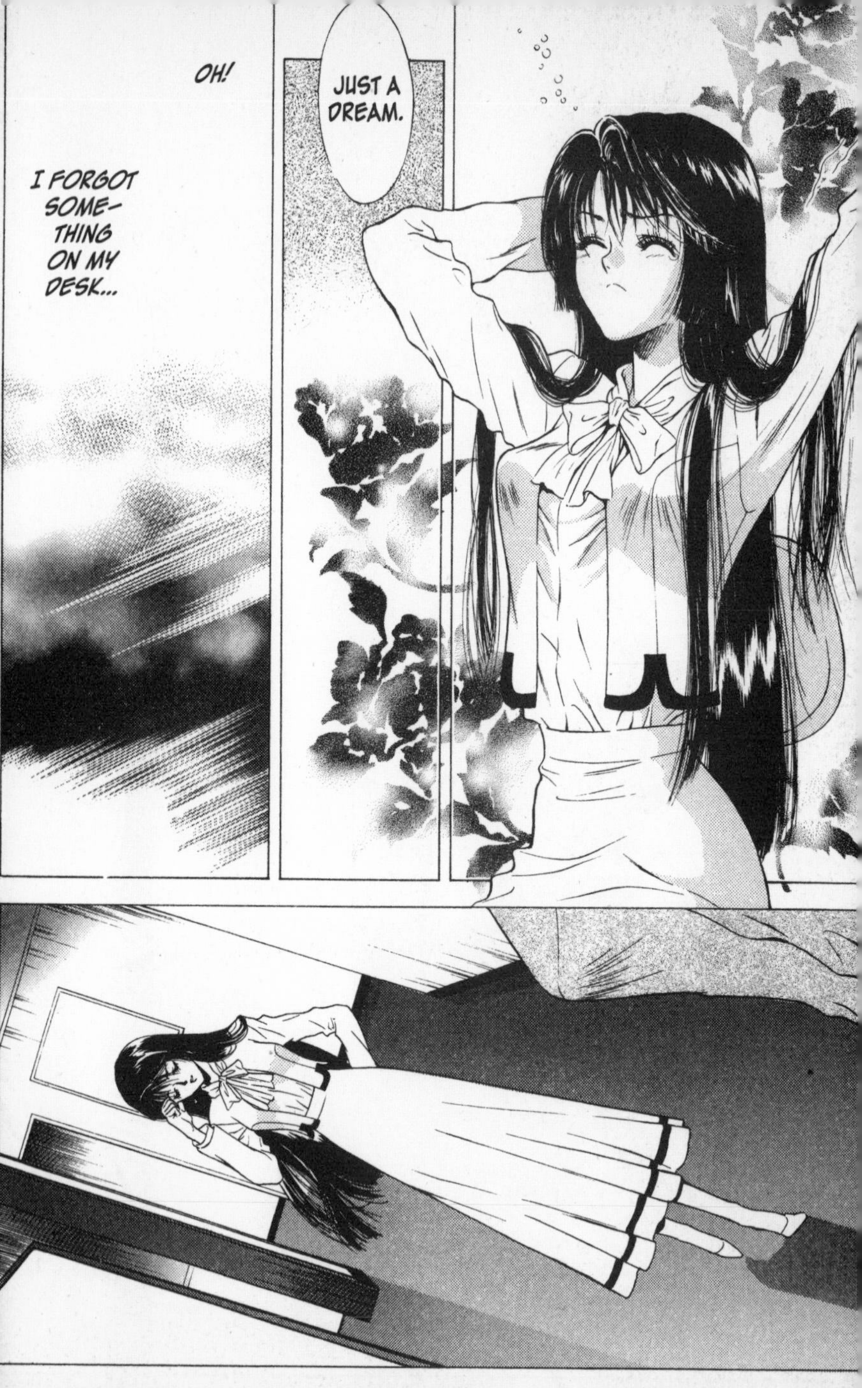
JUST A DREAM.
OH!
I FORGOT SOME-THING ON MY DESK...

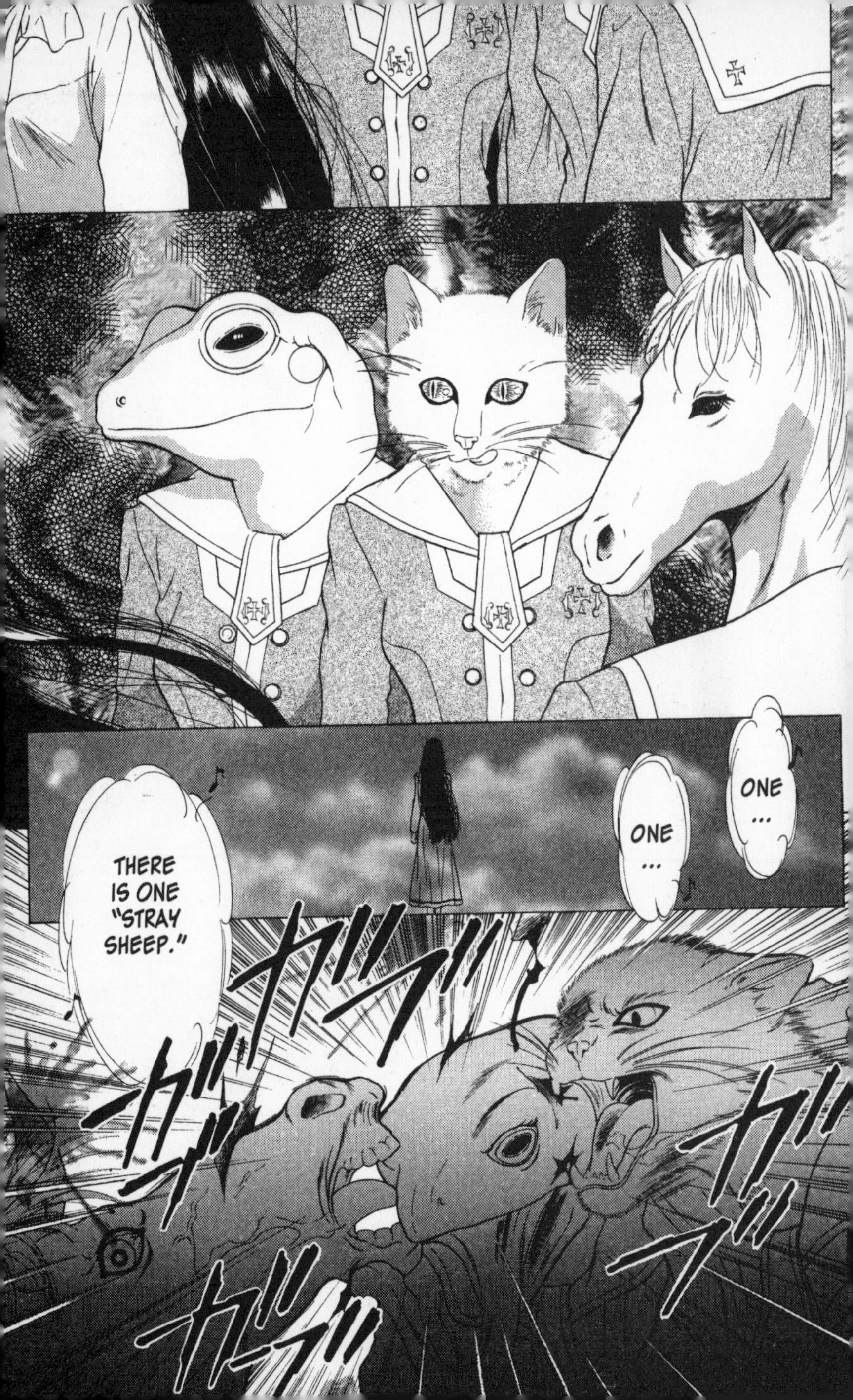
ONE ...
ONE ...
THERE IS ONE "STRAY SHEEP."

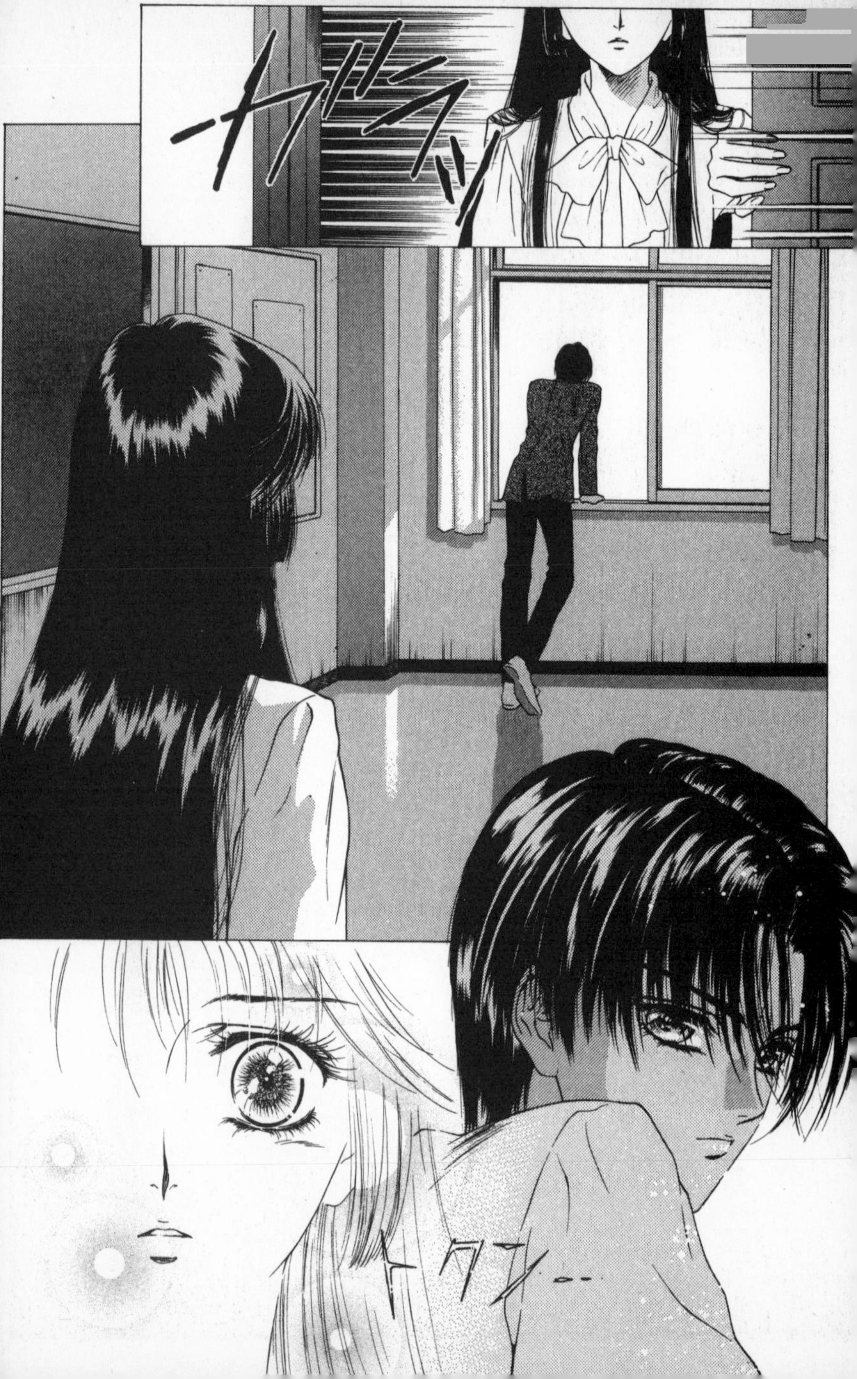
ガラッ
トクン――

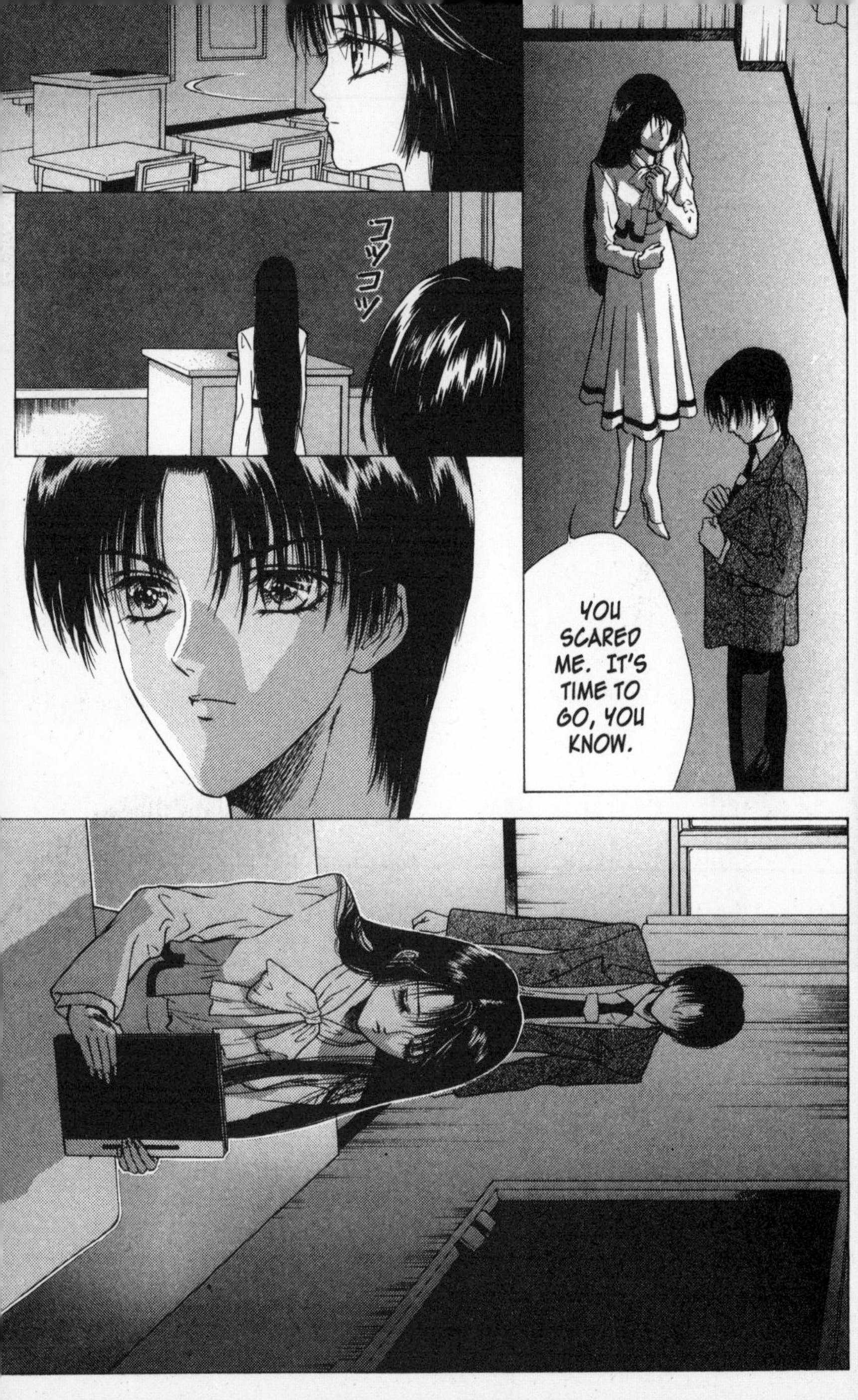
コツコツ
YOU SCARED ME. IT'S TIME TO GO, YOU KNOW.

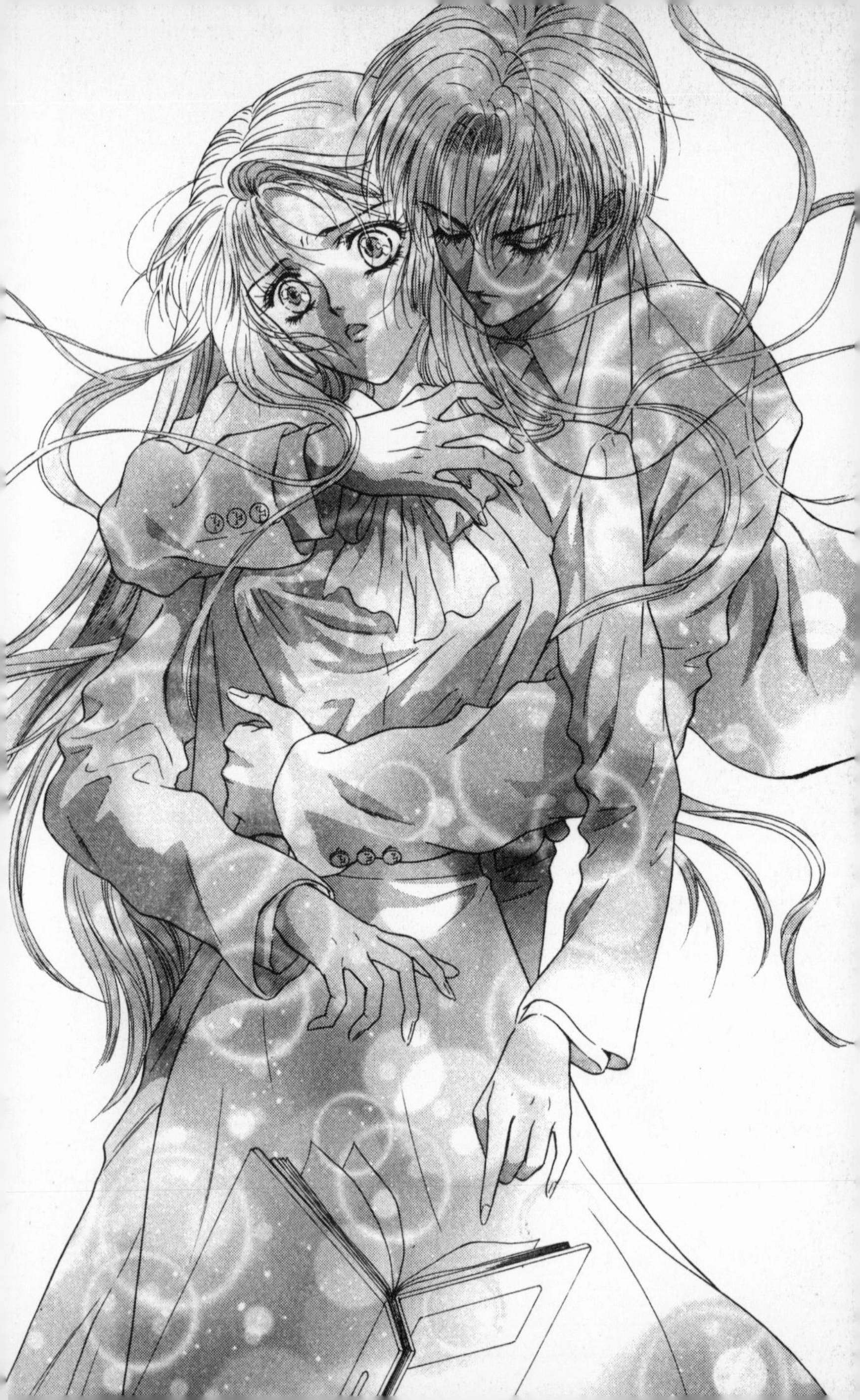

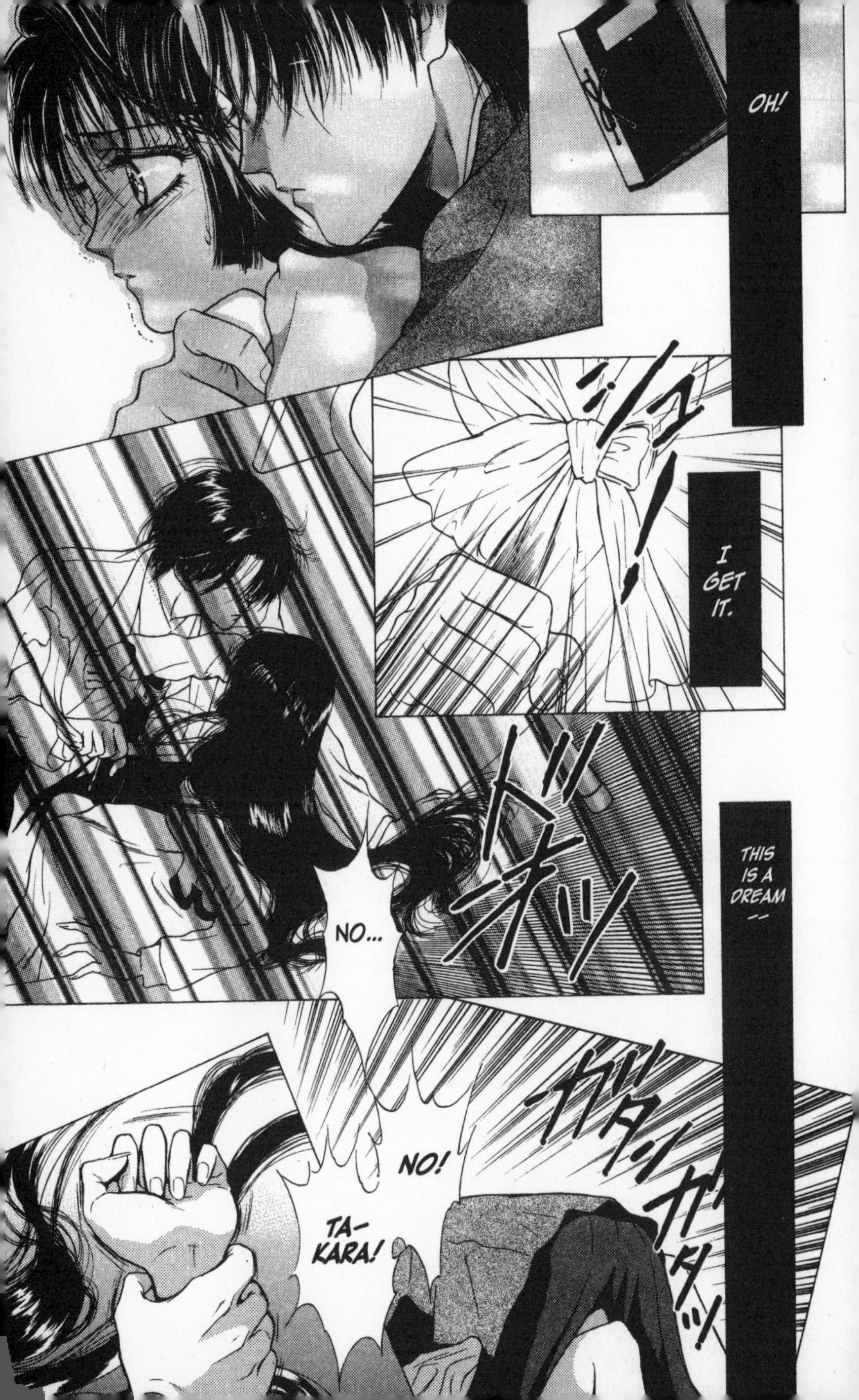
OH!
シュ！
I GET IT.
ドオッ
THIS IS A DREAM --
NO...
ガタッ ガタッ
NO!
TA-KARA!

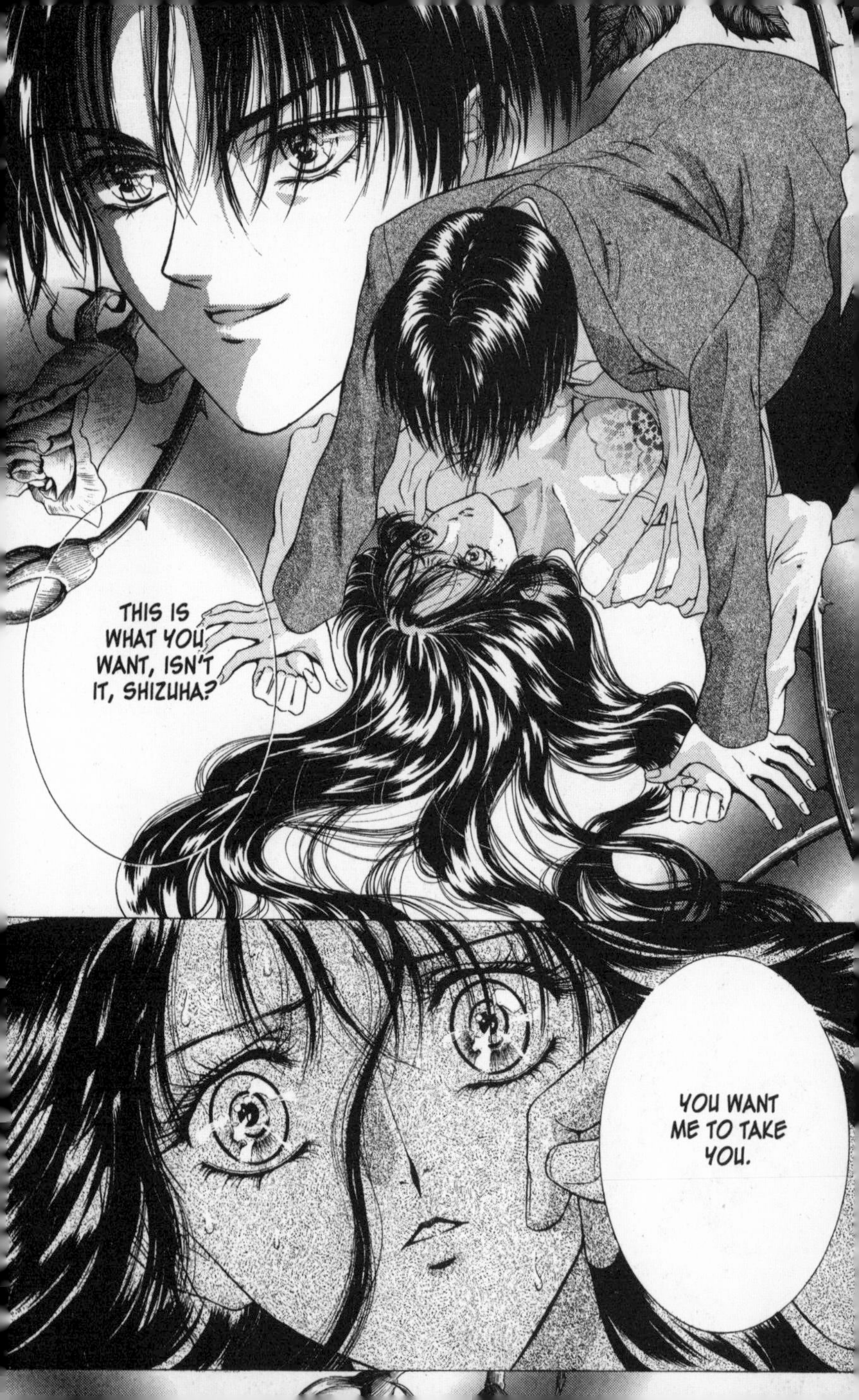
THIS IS WHAT YOU WANT, ISN'T IT, SHIZUHA?
YOU WANT ME TO TAKE YOU.

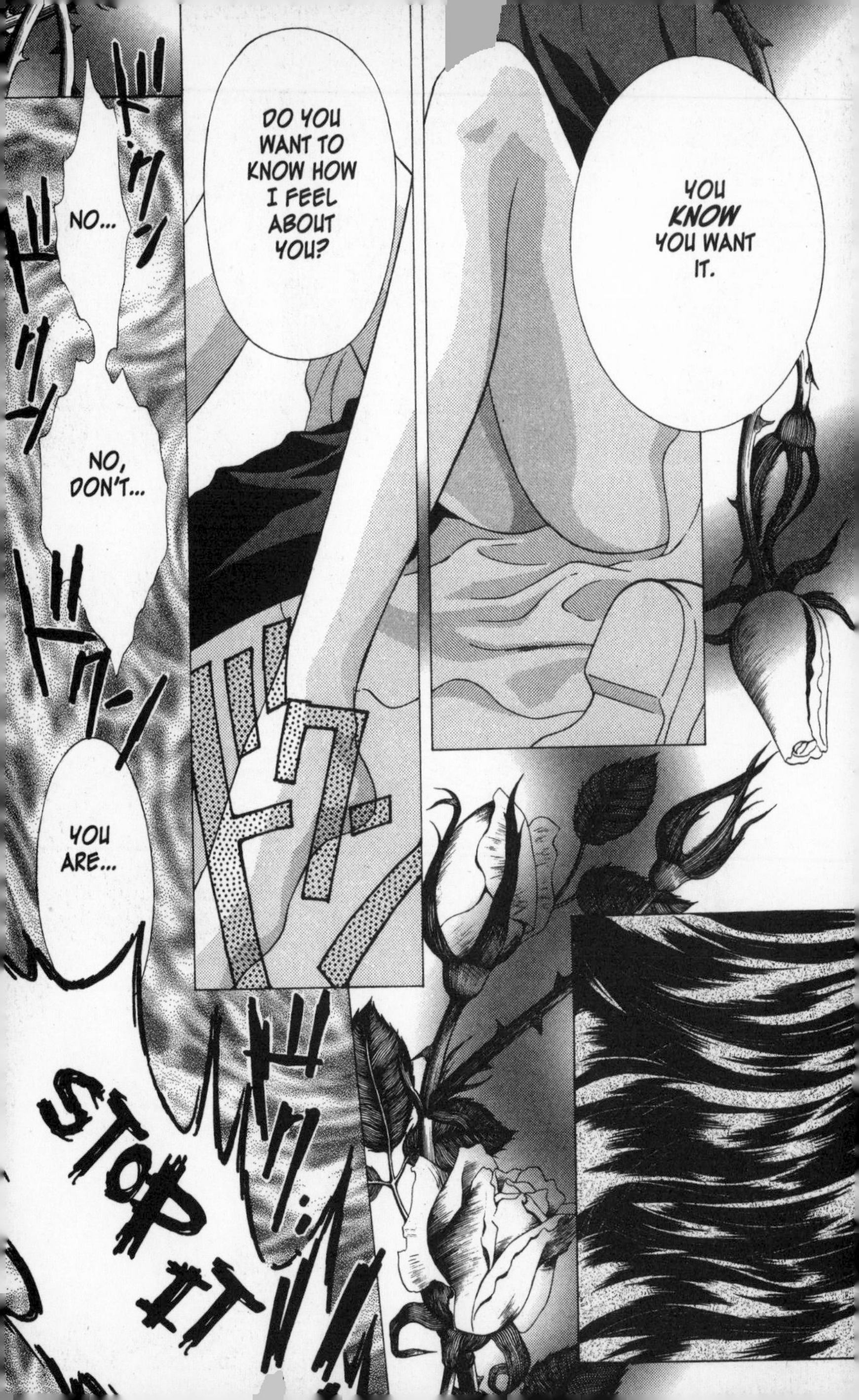
YOU KNOW YOU WANT IT.
DO YOU WANT TO KNOW HOW I FEEL ABOUT YOU?
NO...
NO, DON'T...
YOU ARE...
STOP IT

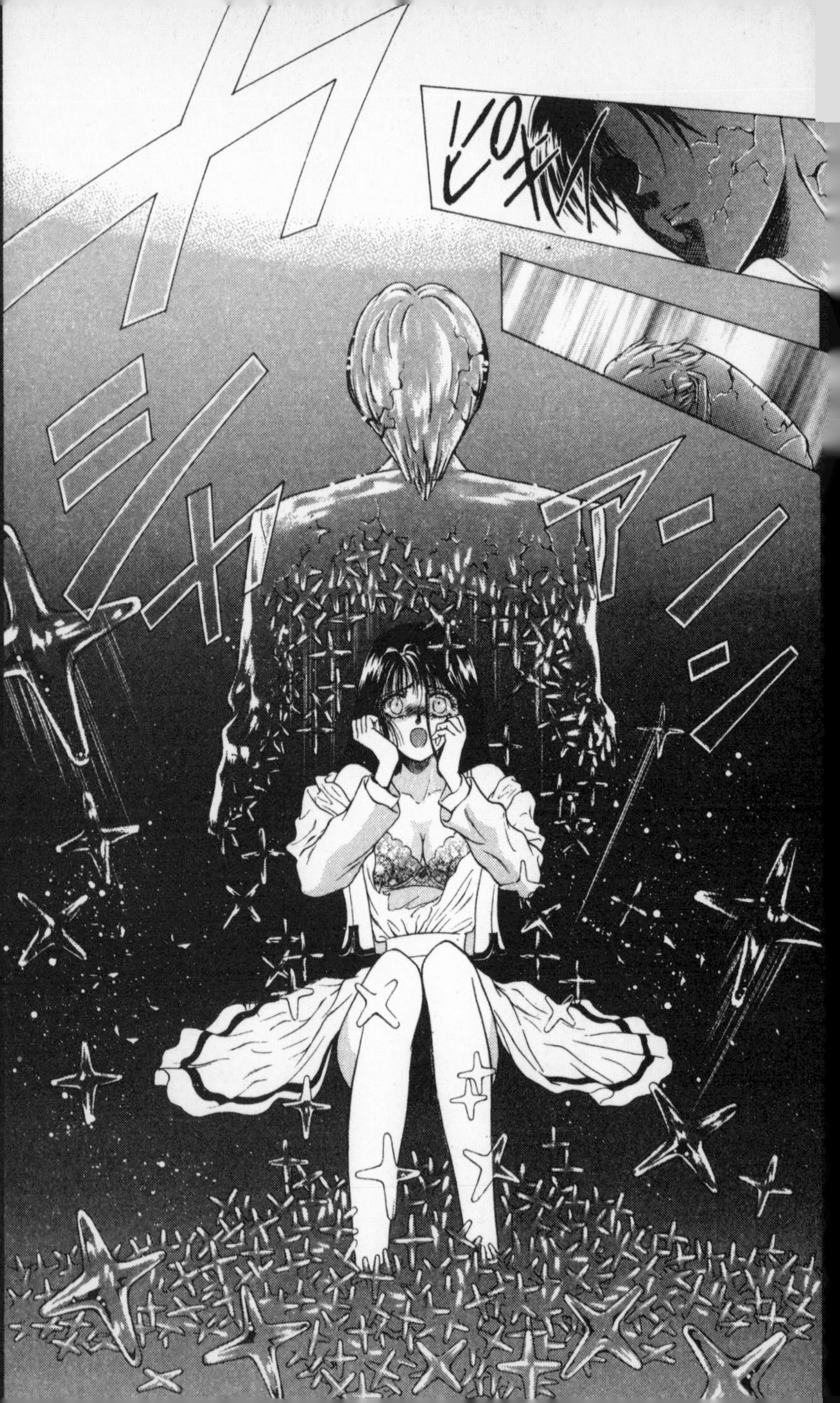
ピキ
ミシィ
アーン

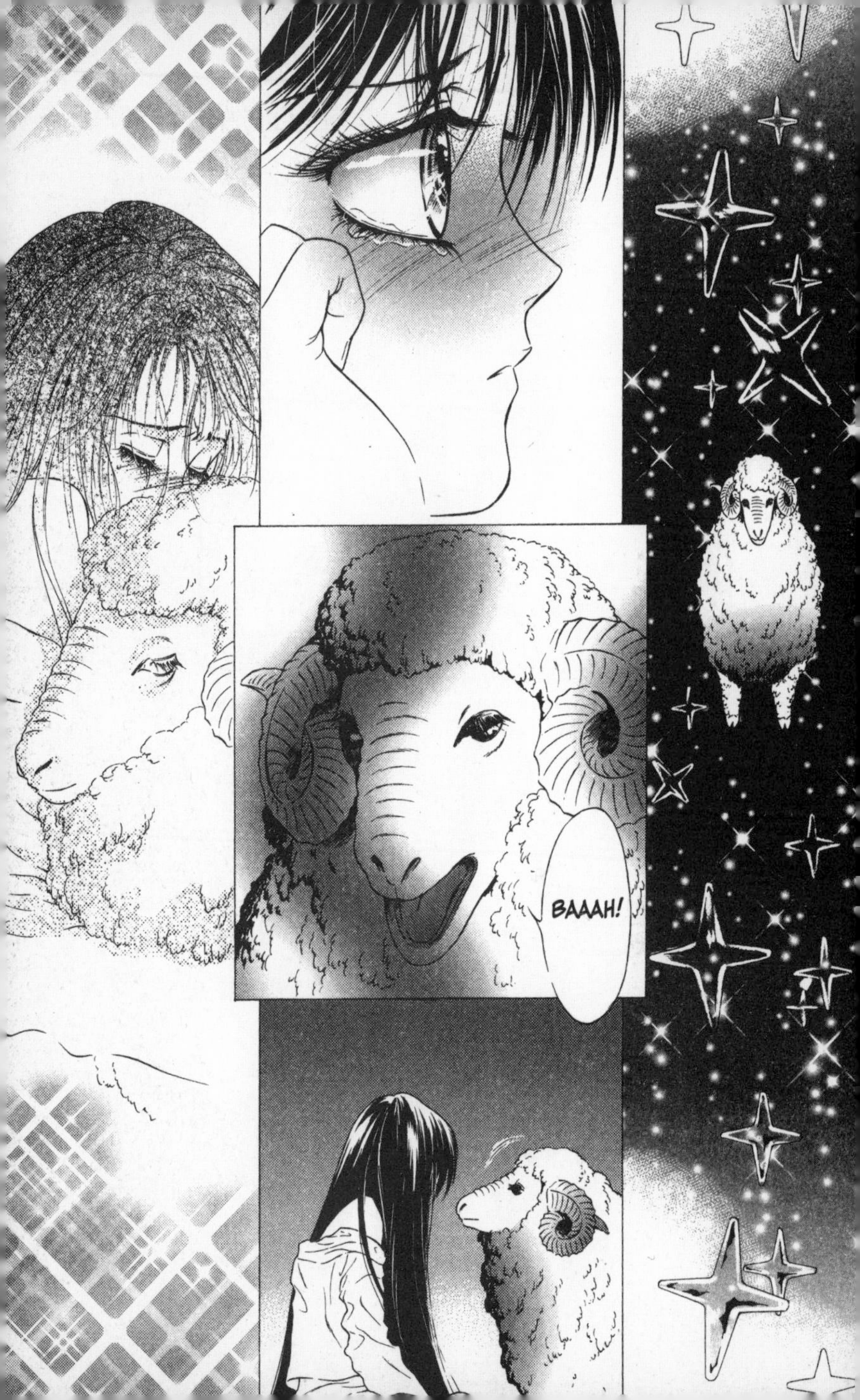
BAAAH!

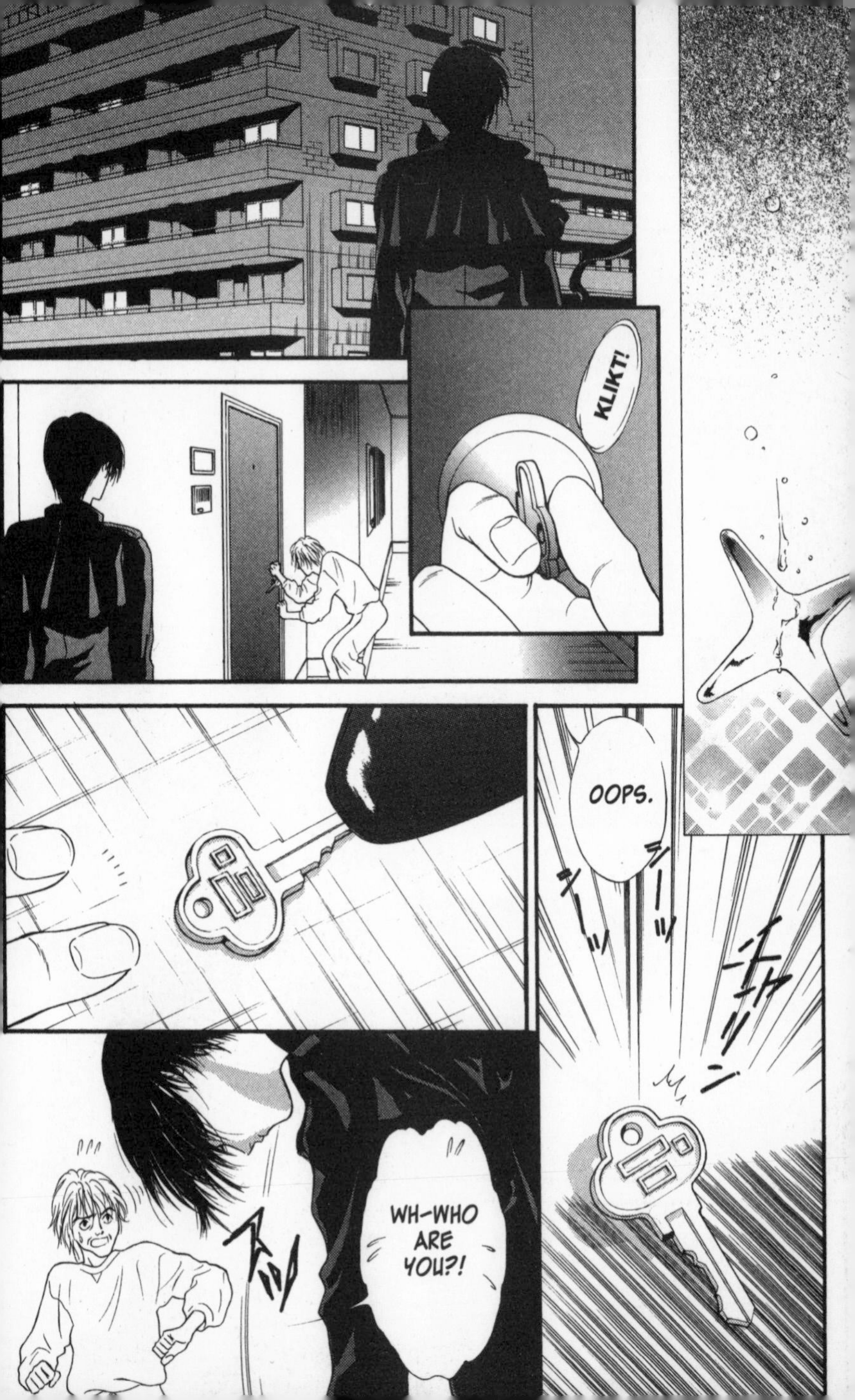
KLIKT!
OOPS.
WH-WHO ARE YOU?!

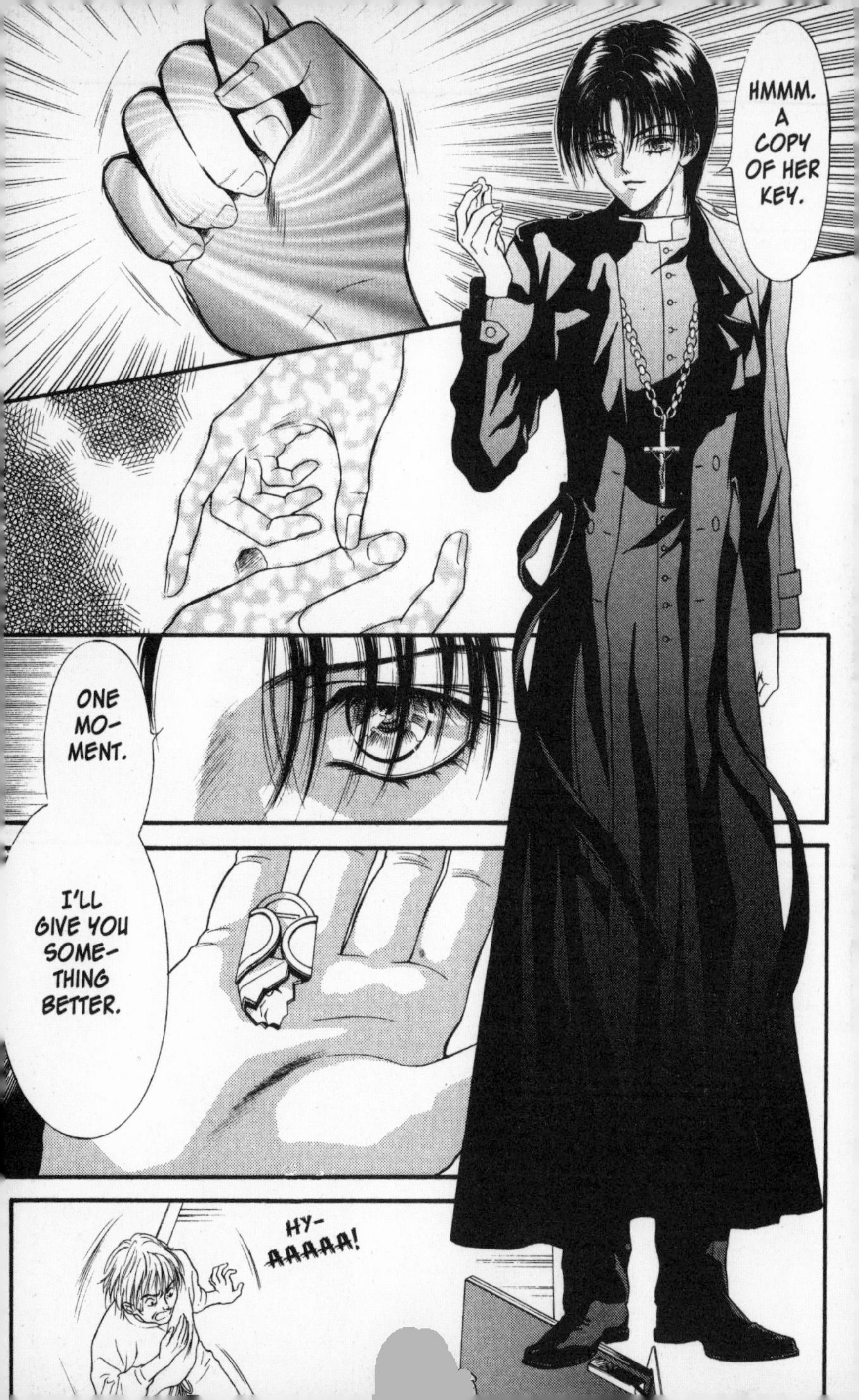
HMMM. A COPY OF HER KEY.
ONE MOMENT.
I'LL GIVE YOU SOMETHING BETTER.
HY-AAAAA!

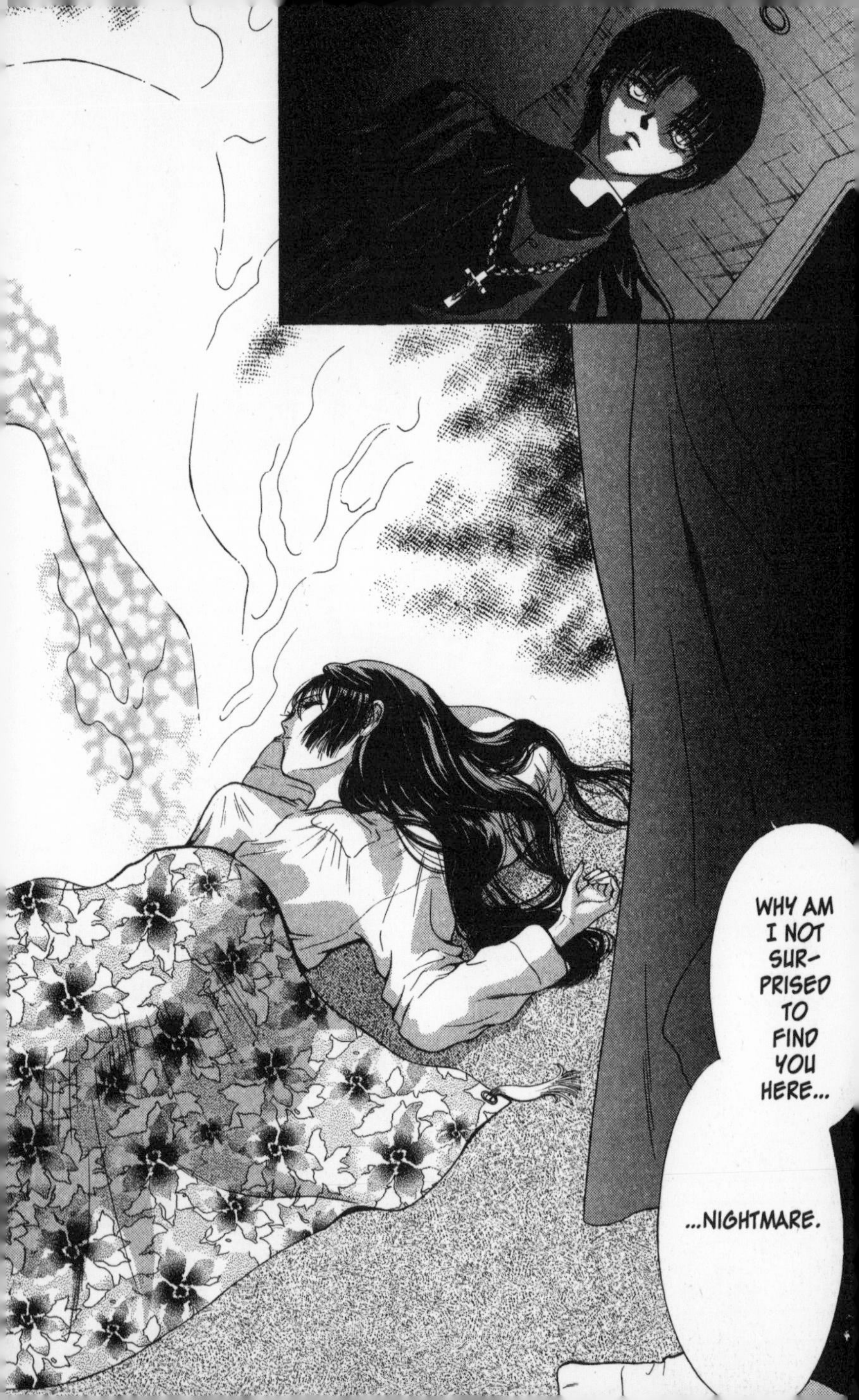
WHY AM I NOT SUR-PRISED TO FIND YOU HERE...
...NIGHTMARE.

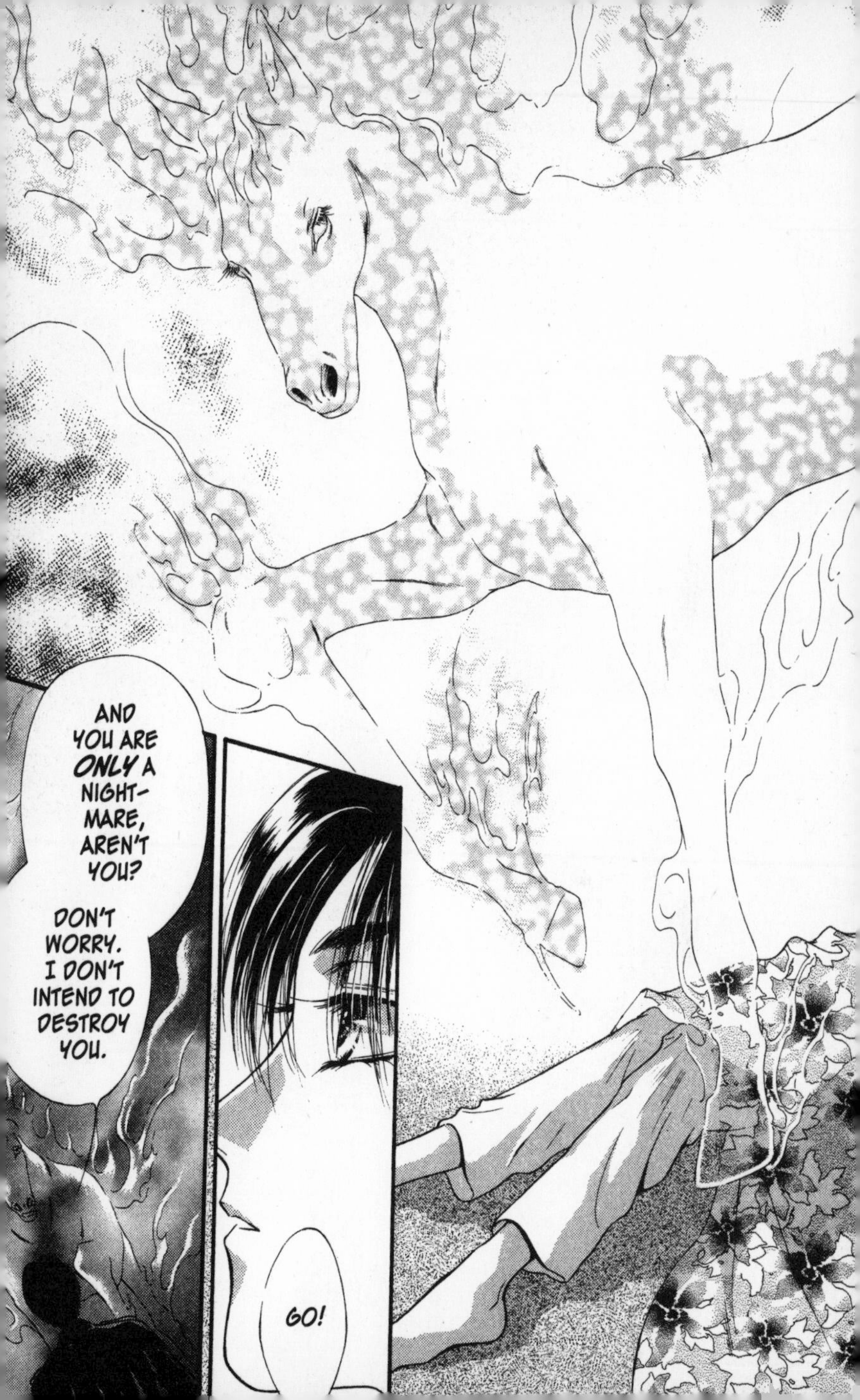
AND YOU ARE ONLY A NIGHT-MARE, AREN'T YOU?
DON'T WORRY. I DON'T INTEND TO DESTROY YOU.
GO!

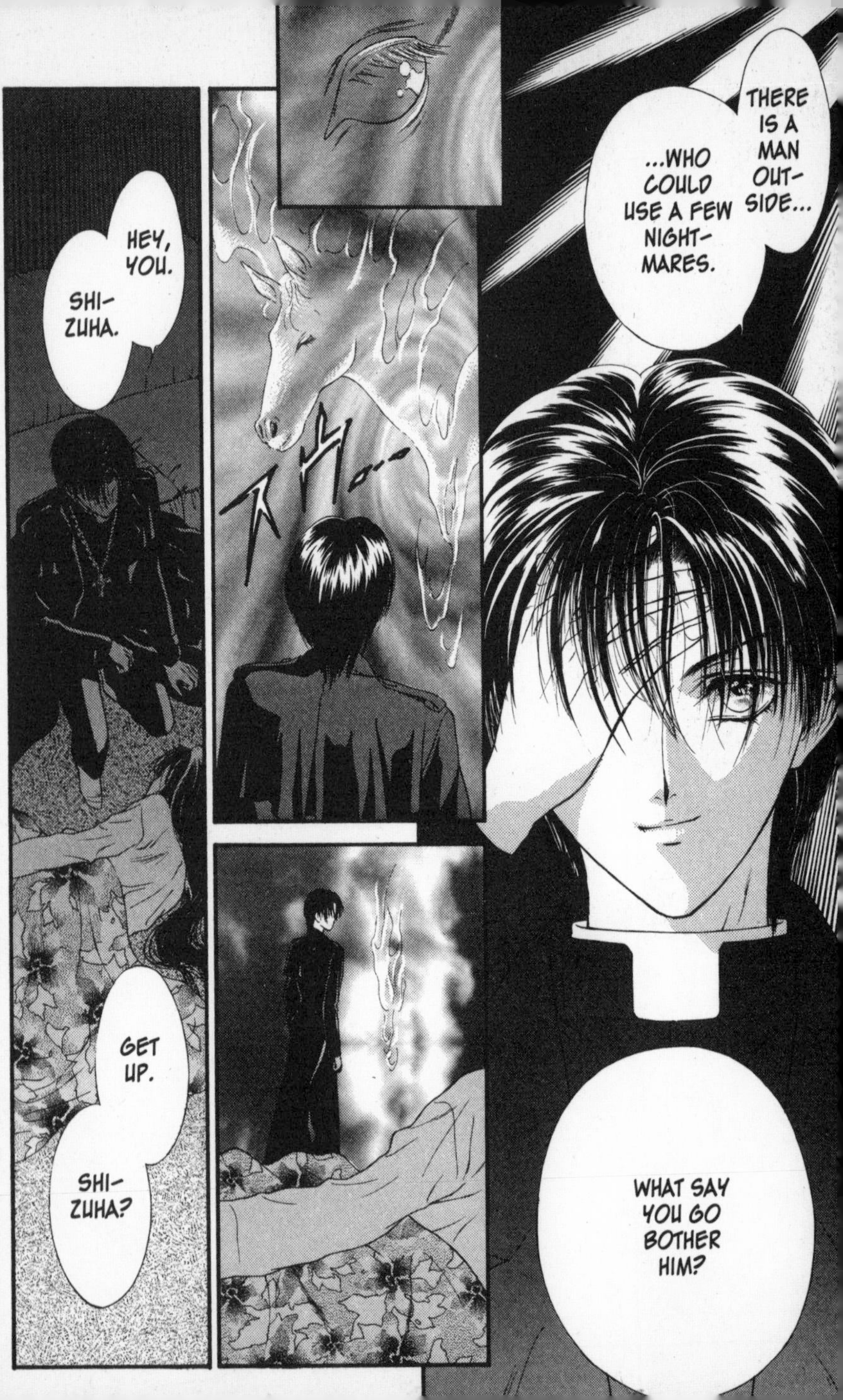
THERE IS A MAN OUTSIDE...
...WHO COULD USE A FEW NIGHTMARES.
WHAT SAY YOU GO BOTHER HIM?
HEY, YOU.
SHIZUHA.
GET UP.
SHIZUHA?

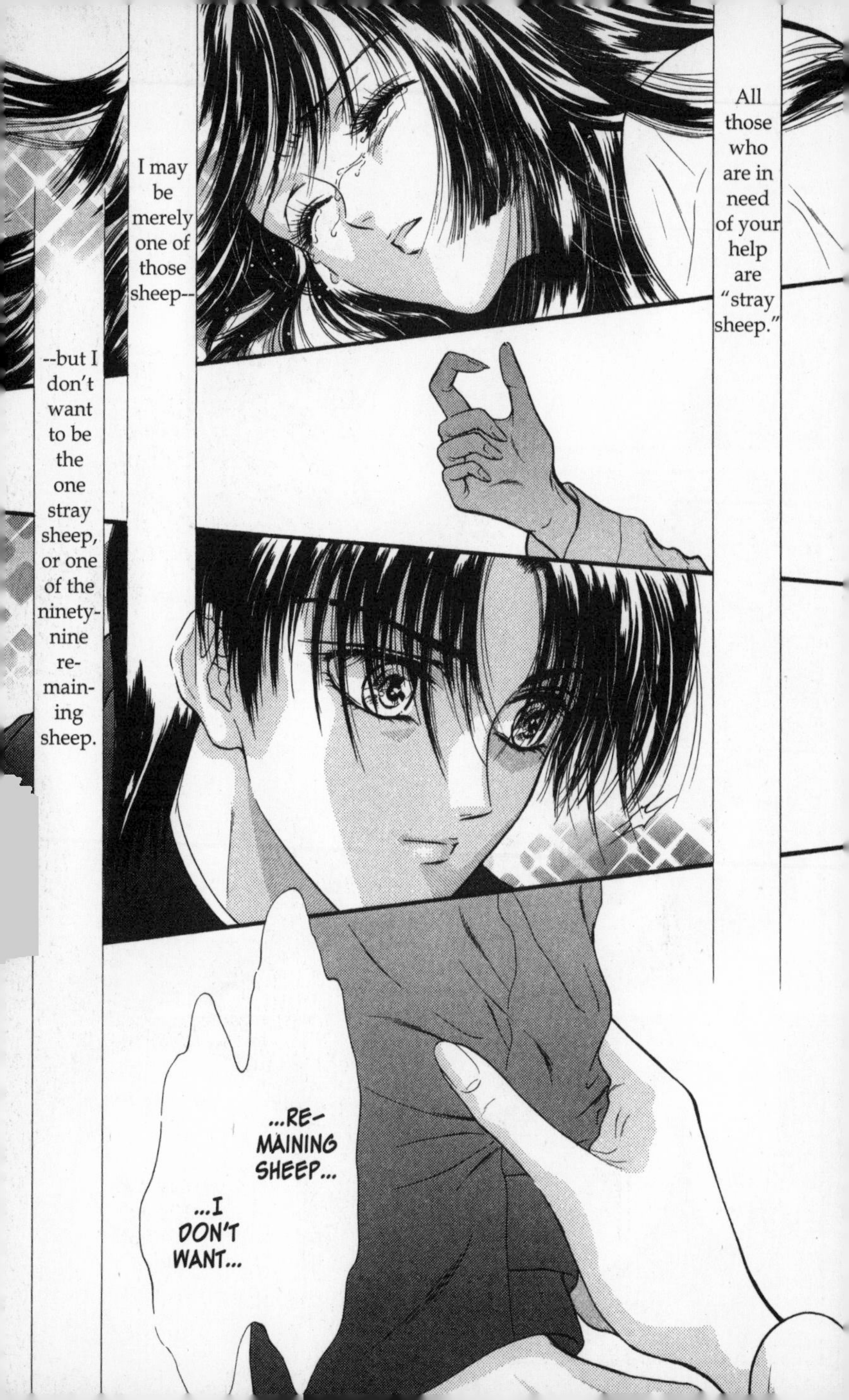
All those who are in need of your help are "stray sheep."
I may be merely one of those sheep--
--but I don't want to be the one stray sheep, or one of the ninety-nine re-maining sheep.
...RE-MAINING SHEEP...
...I DON'T WANT...

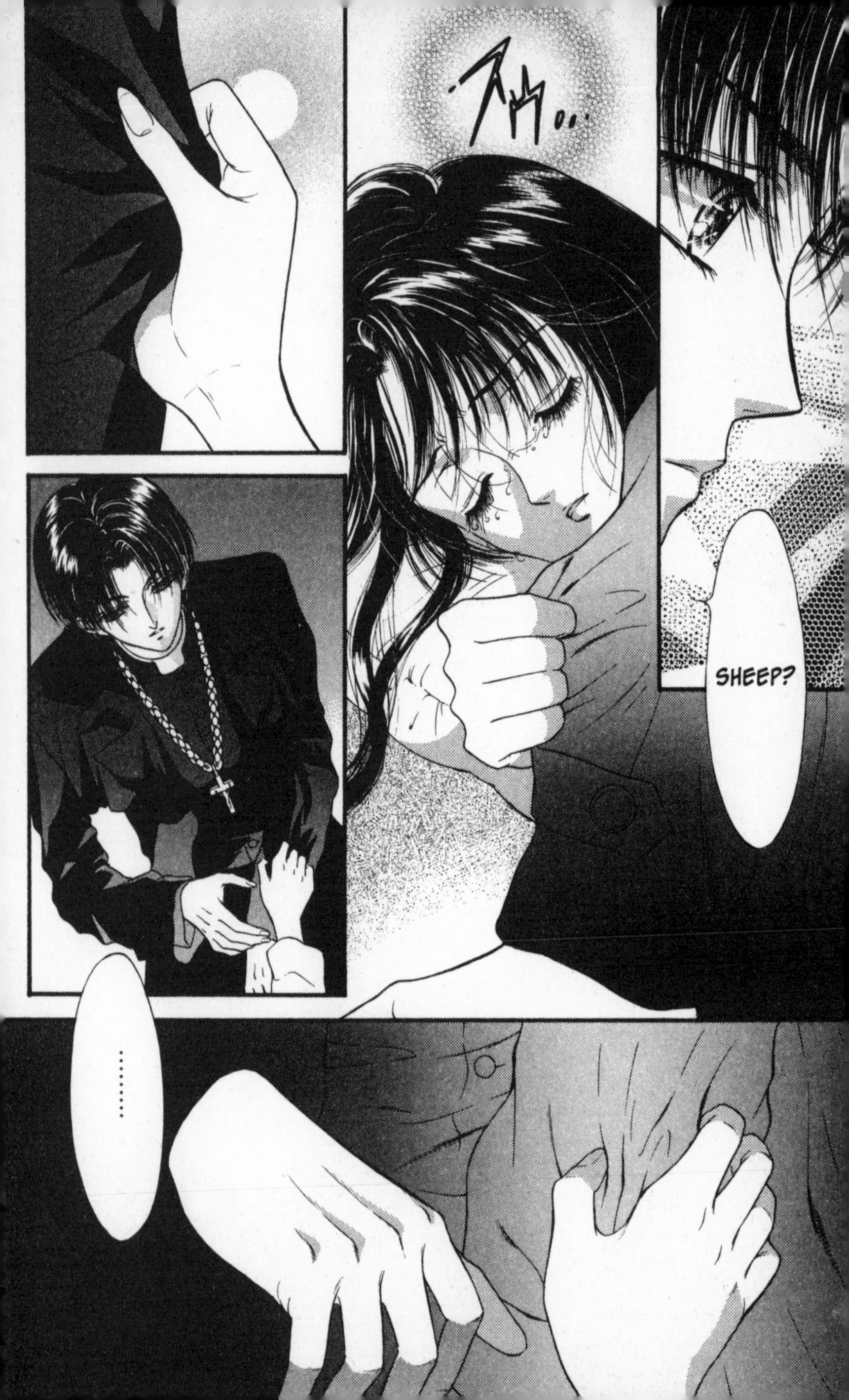
SHEEP?
......

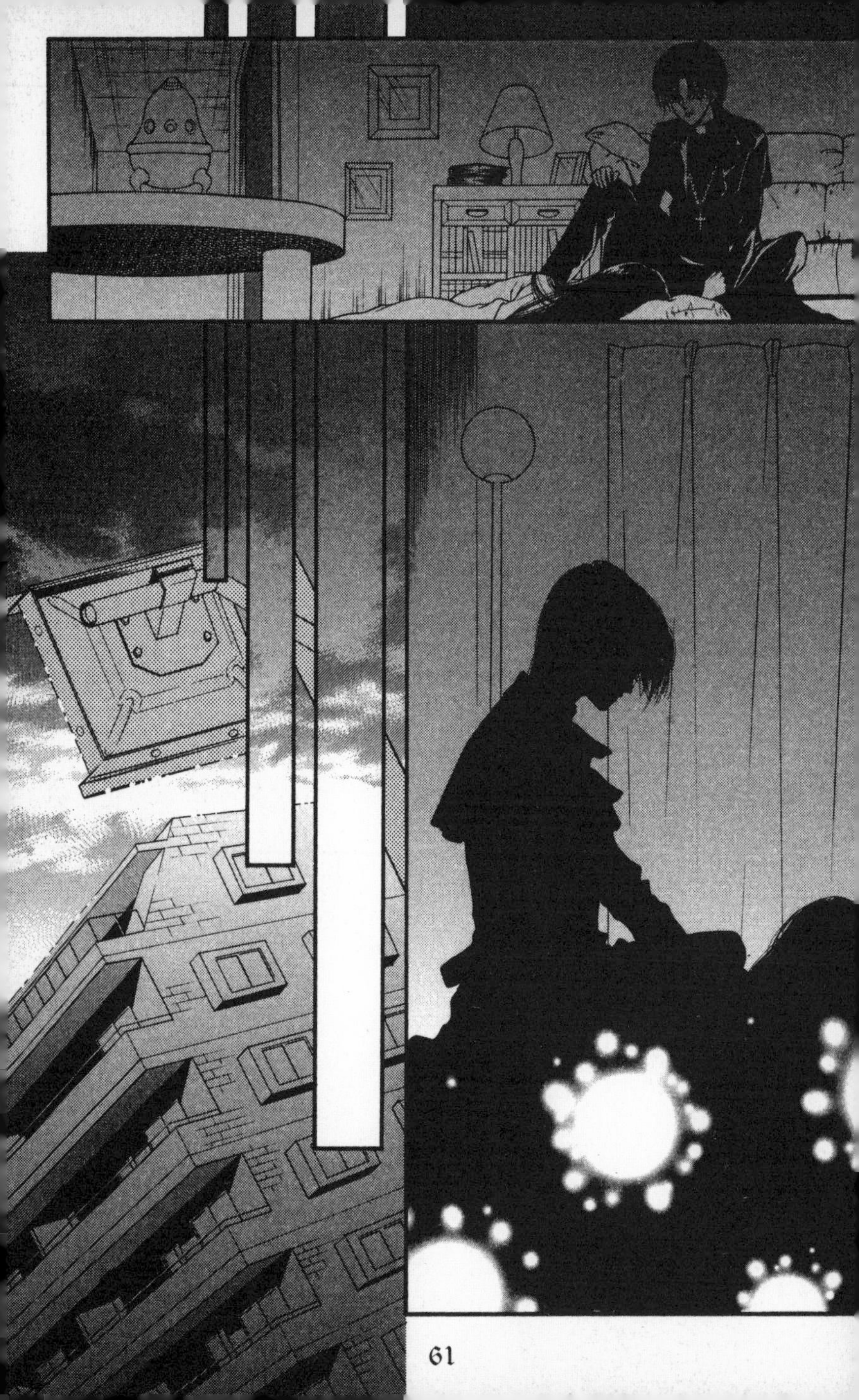

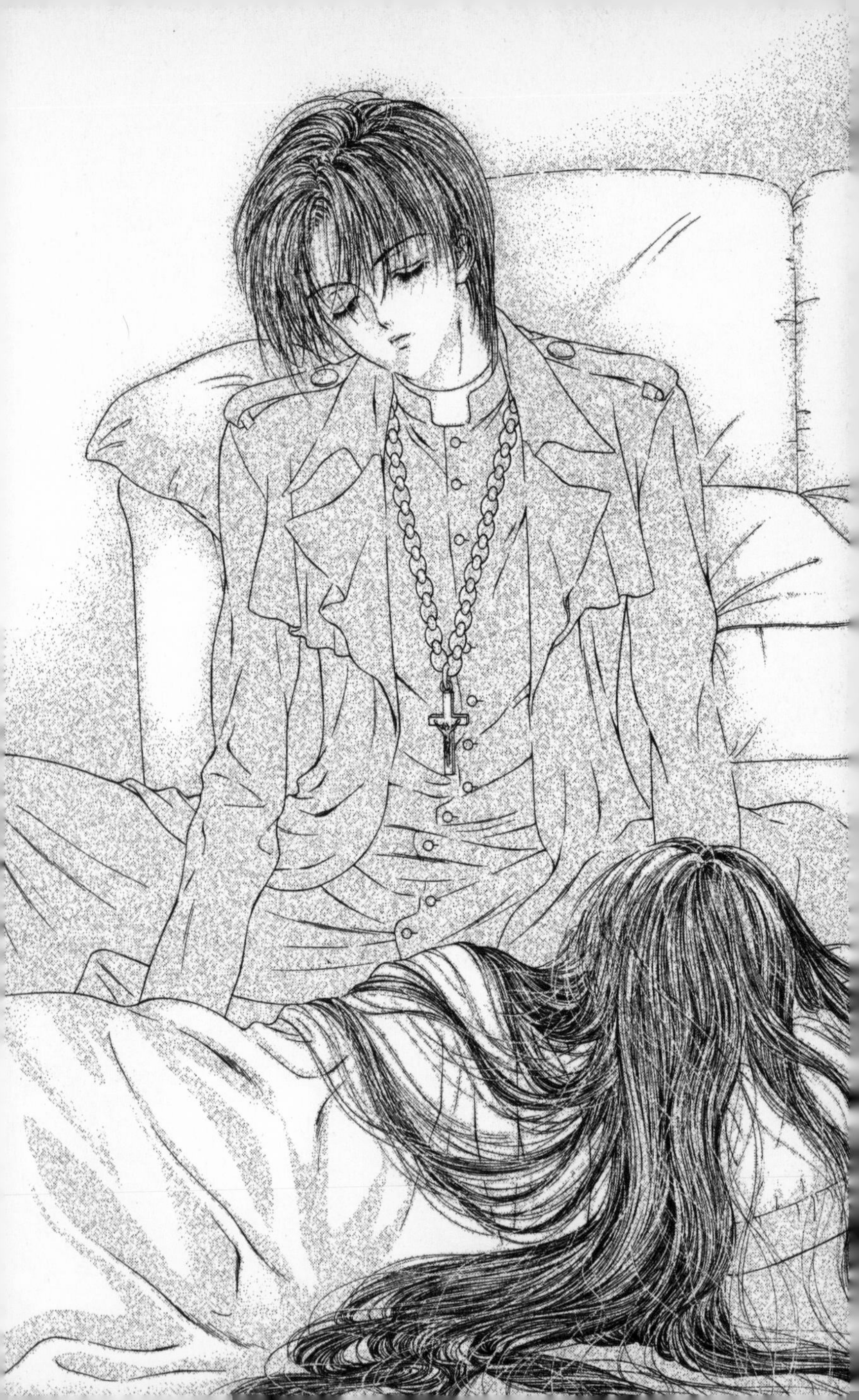

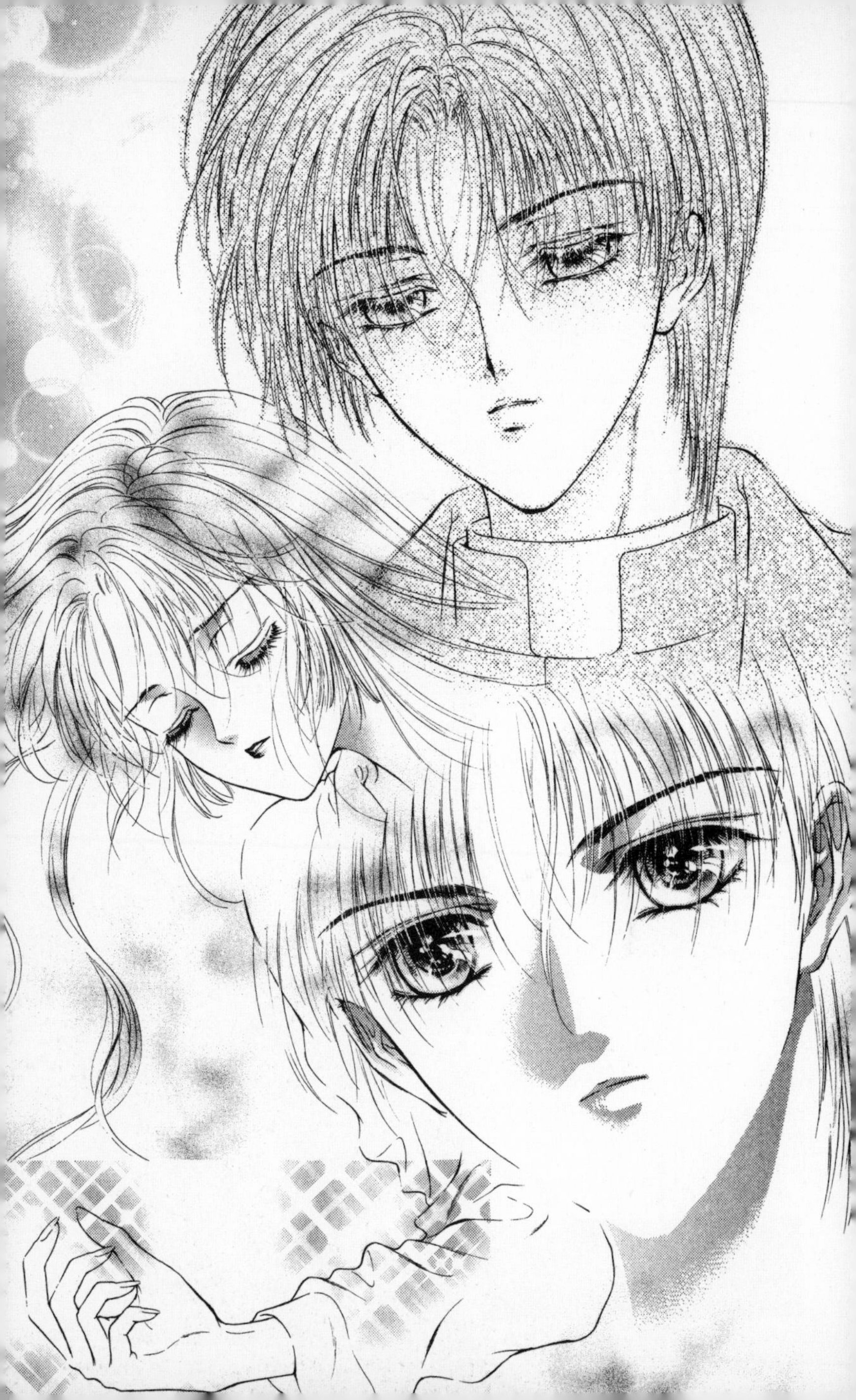

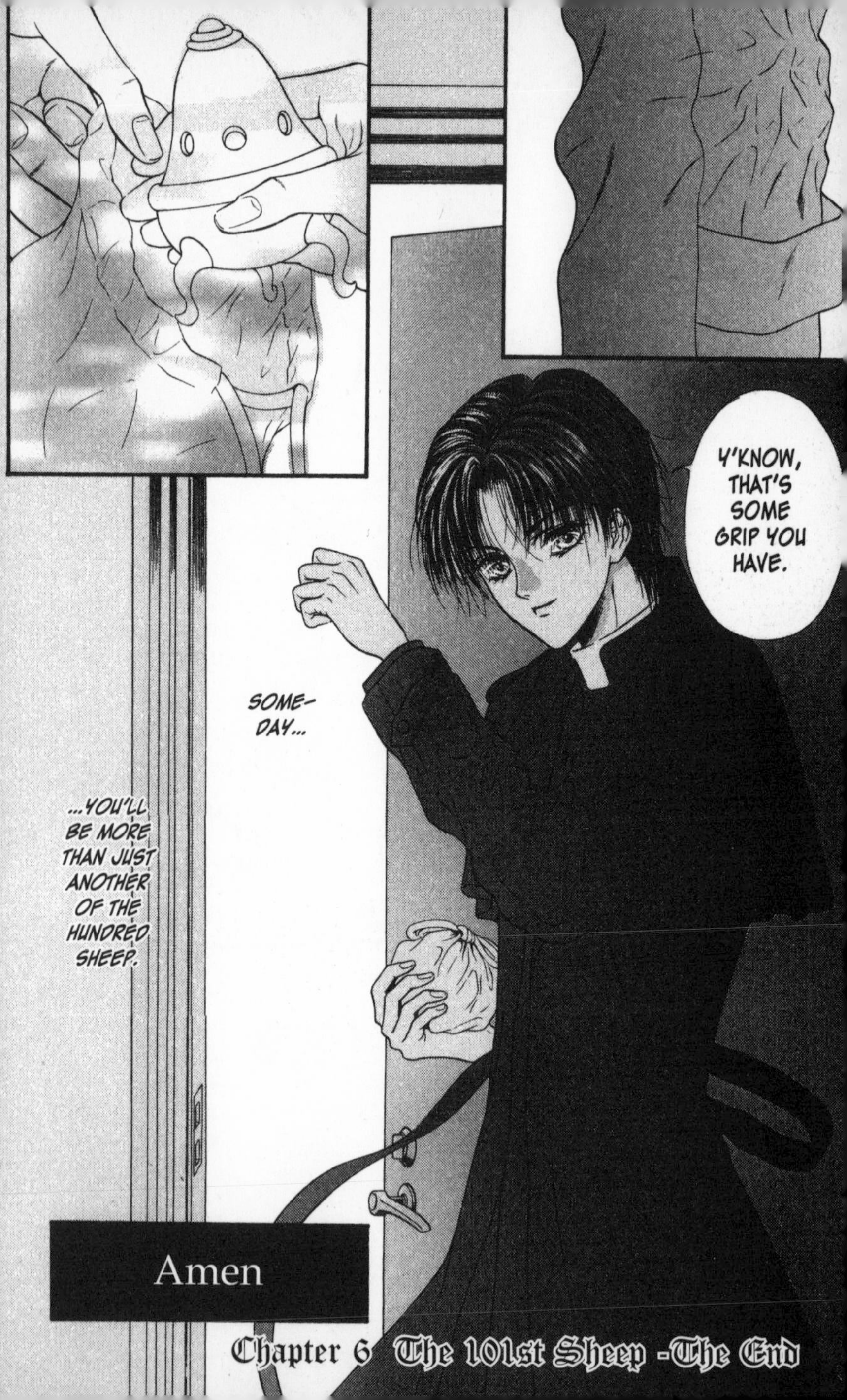
Y'KNOW, THAT'S SOME GRIP YOU HAVE.
SOME-DAY...
...YOU'LL BE MORE THAN JUST ANOTHER OF THE HUNDRED SHEEP.
Amen
Chapter 6 The 101st Sheep -The End

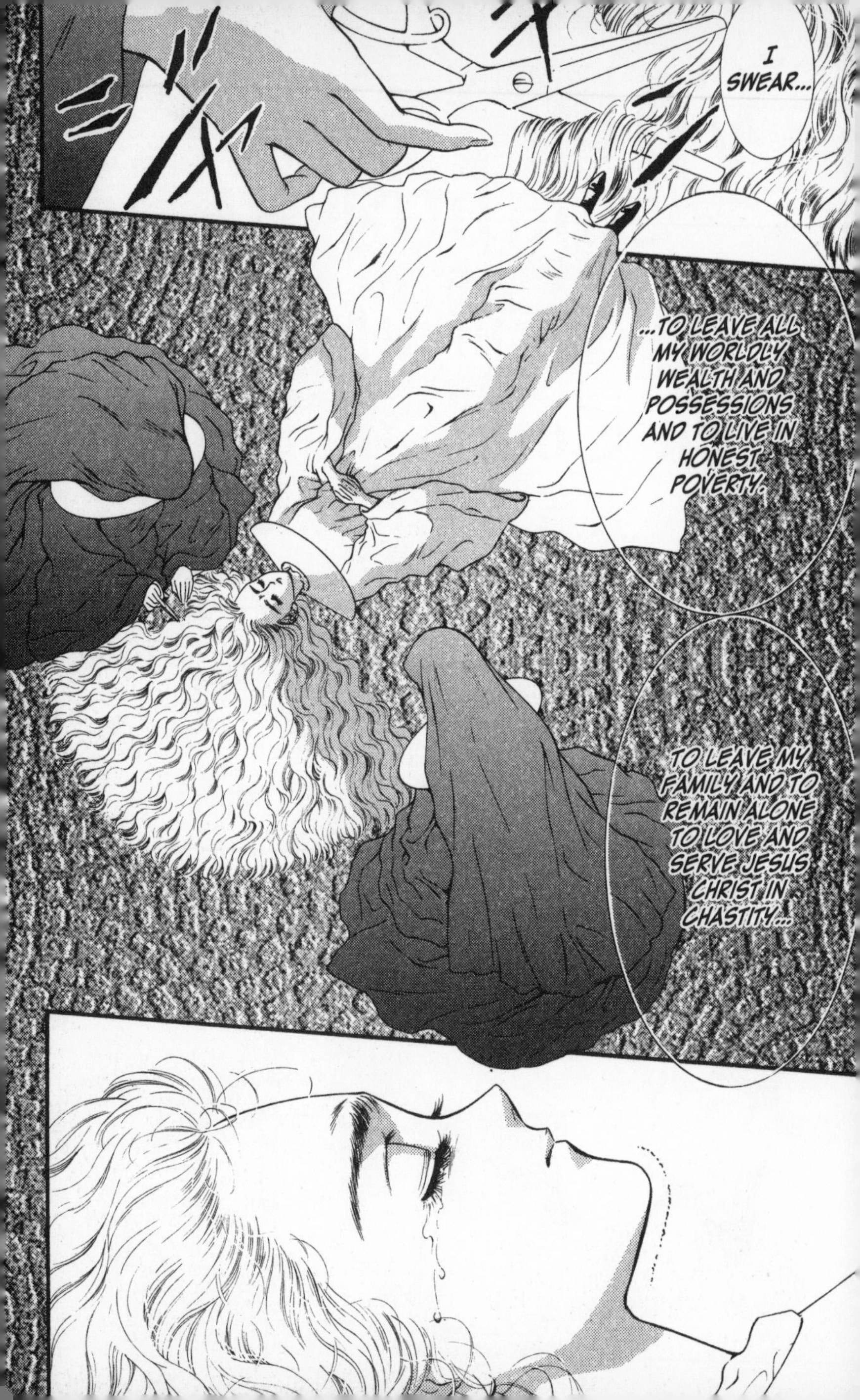
I SWEAR...
...TO LEAVE ALL MY WORLDLY WEALTH AND POSSESSIONS AND TO LIVE IN HONEST POVERTY.
TO LEAVE MY FAMILY AND TO REMAIN ALONE TO LOVE AND SERVE JESUS CHRIST IN CHASTITY...

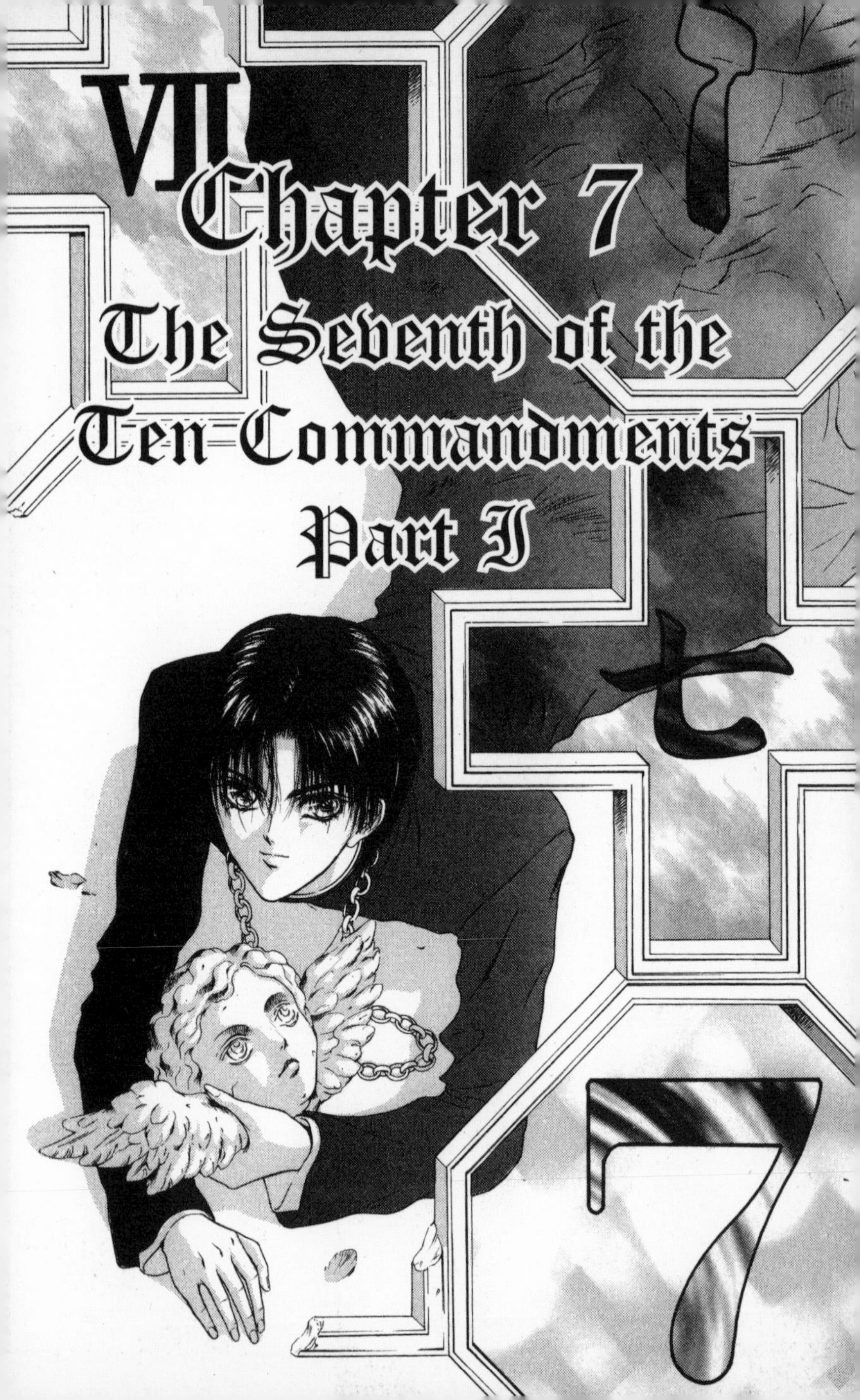
VII
Chapter 7
The Seventh of the Ten Commandments Part I
七
7

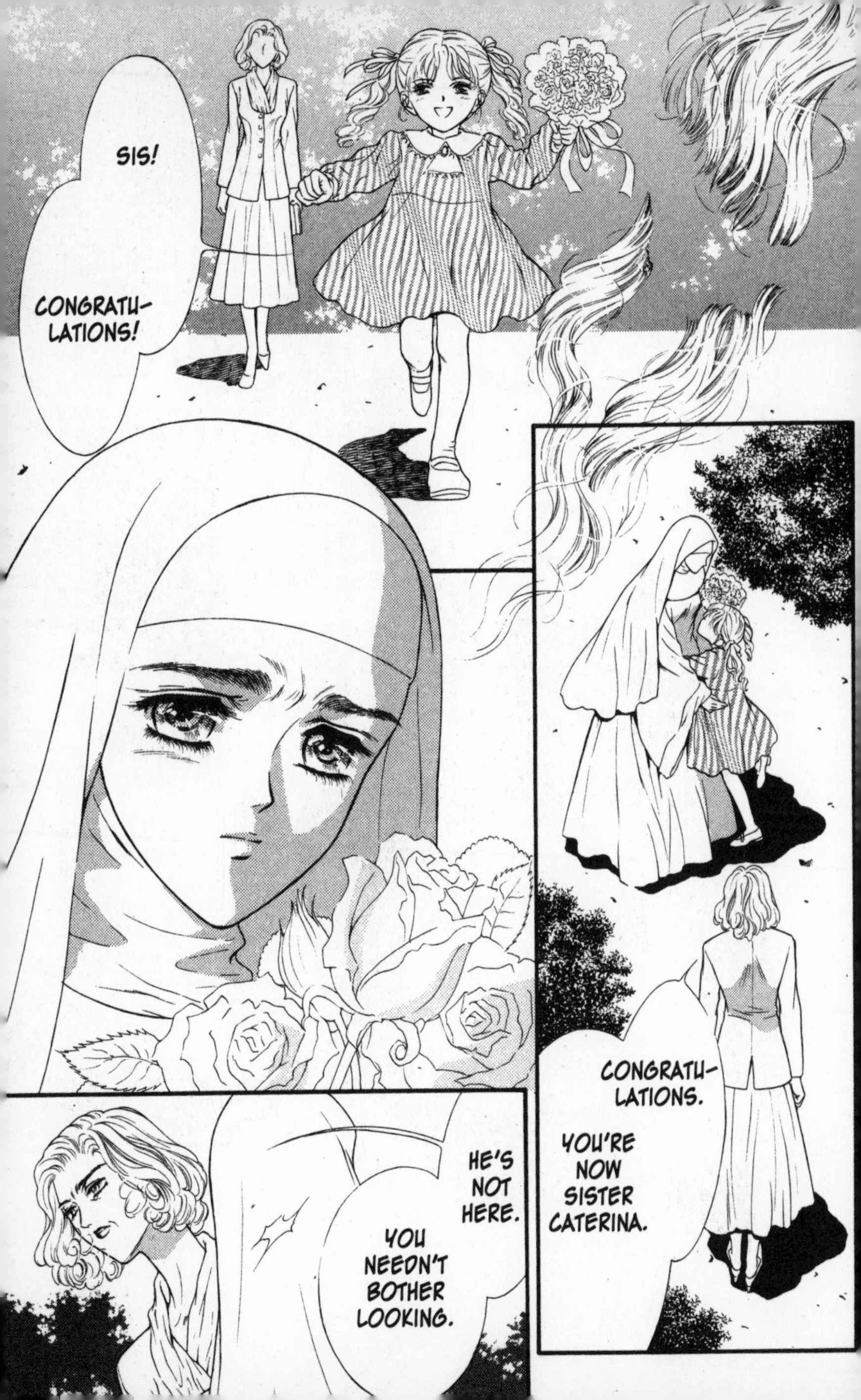
SIS!
CONGRATU-LATIONS!
CONGRATU-LATIONS.
YOU'RE NOW SISTER CATERINA.
HE'S NOT HERE.
YOU NEEDN'T BOTHER LOOKING.

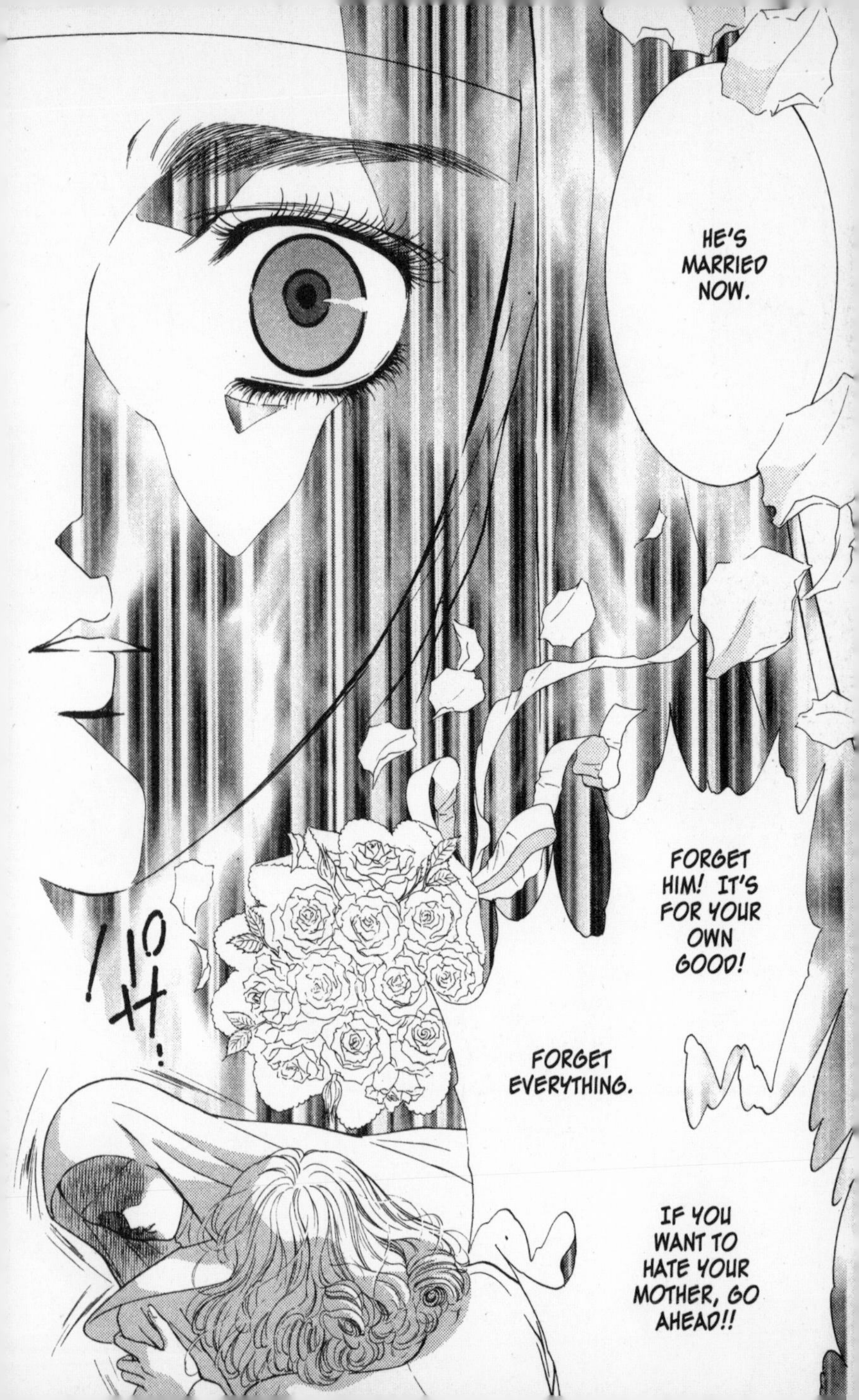
HE'S MARRIED NOW.
FORGET HIM! IT'S FOR YOUR OWN GOOD!
FORGET EVERYTHING.
IF YOU WANT TO HATE YOUR MOTHER, GO AHEAD!!

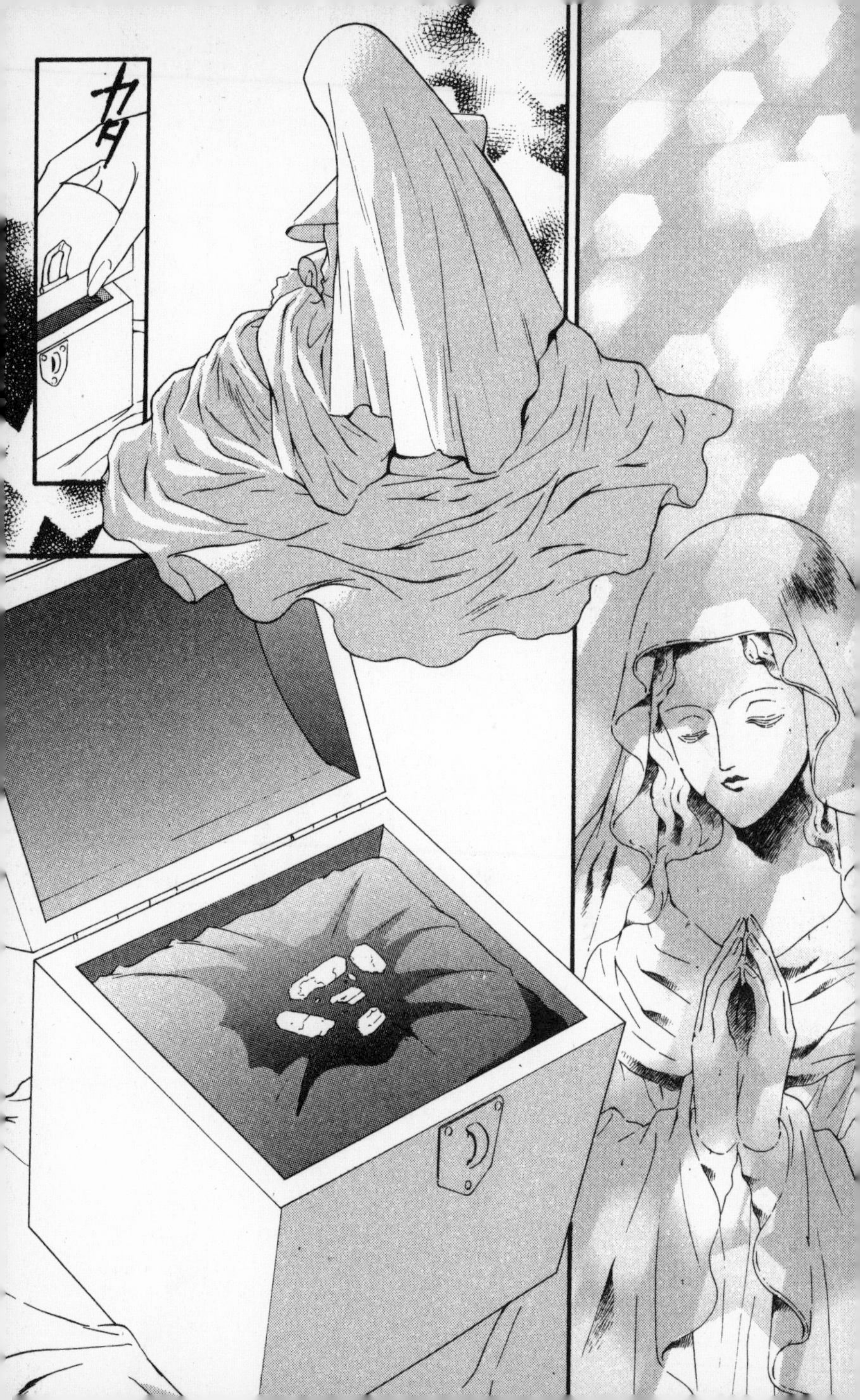
カタ

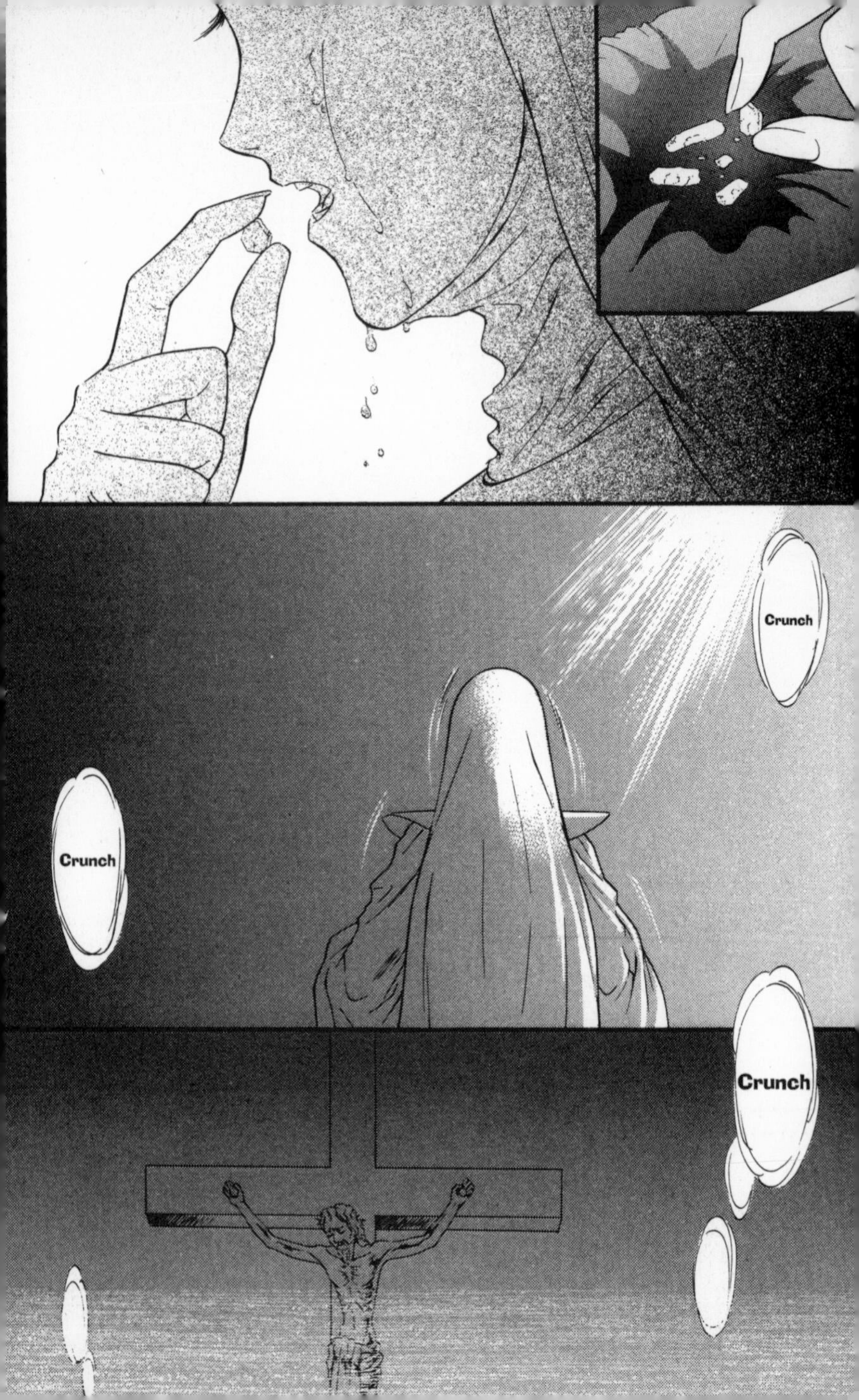
Crunch
Crunch
Crunch

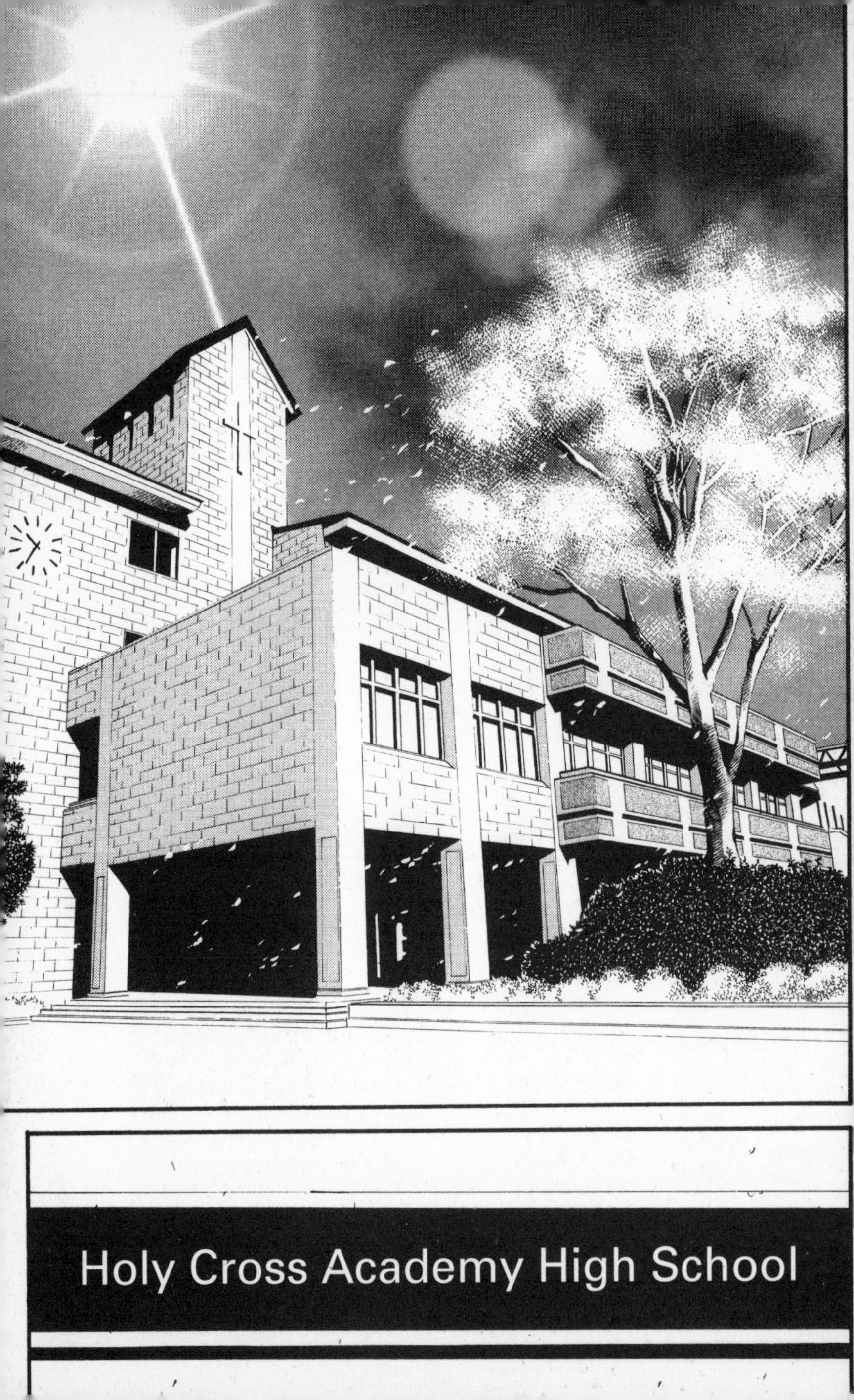
Holy Cross Academy High School

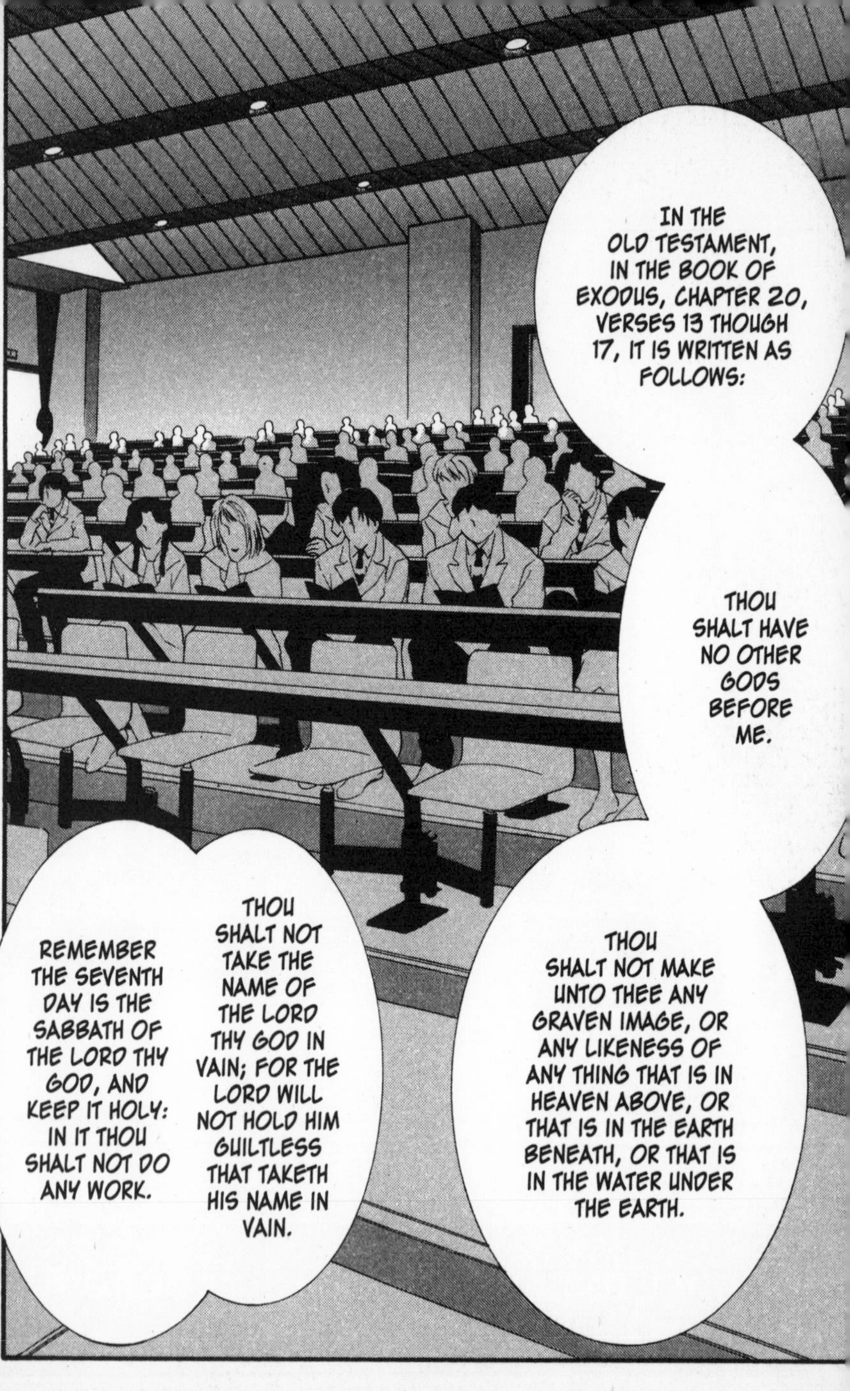
IN THE OLD TESTAMENT, IN THE BOOK OF EXODUS, CHAPTER 20, VERSES 13 THOUGH 17, IT IS WRITTEN AS FOLLOWS:
THOU SHALT HAVE NO OTHER GODS BEFORE ME.
THOU SHALT NOT MAKE UNTO THEE ANY GRAVEN IMAGE, OR ANY LIKENESS OF ANY THING THAT IS IN HEAVEN ABOVE, OR THAT IS IN THE EARTH BENEATH, OR THAT IS IN THE WATER UNDER THE EARTH.
THOU SHALT NOT TAKE THE NAME OF THE LORD THY GOD IN VAIN; FOR THE LORD WILL NOT HOLD HIM GUILTLESS THAT TAKETH HIS NAME IN VAIN.
REMEMBER THE SEVENTH DAY IS THE SABBATH OF THE LORD THY GOD, AND KEEP IT HOLY: IN IT THOU SHALT NOT DO ANY WORK.

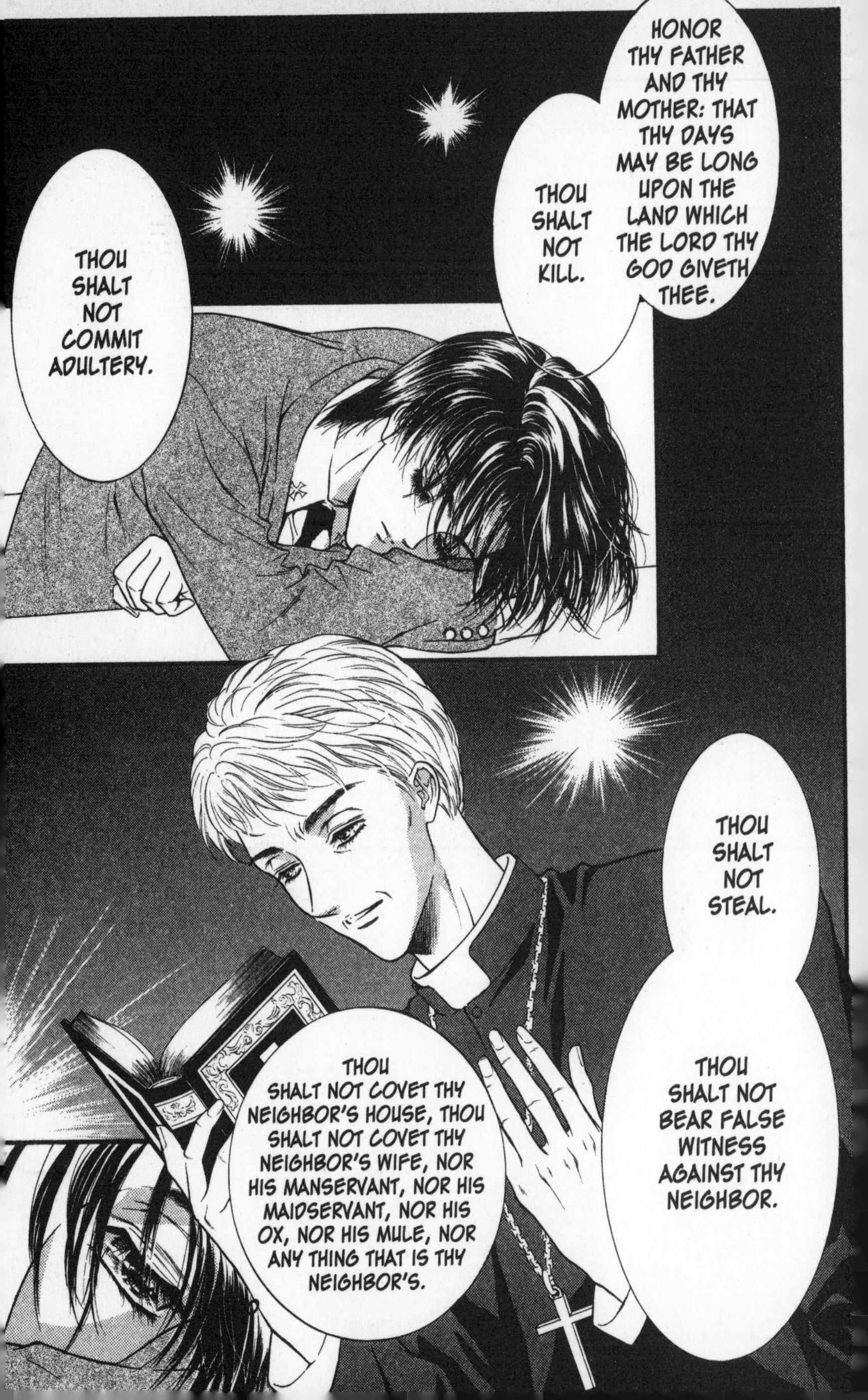
HONOR THY FATHER AND THY MOTHER: THAT THY DAYS MAY BE LONG UPON THE LAND WHICH THE LORD THY GOD GIVETH THEE.
THOU SHALT NOT KILL.
THOU SHALT NOT COMMIT ADULTERY.
THOU SHALT NOT STEAL.
THOU SHALT NOT BEAR FALSE WITNESS AGAINST THY NEIGHBOR.
THOU SHALT NOT COVET THY NEIGHBOR'S HOUSE, THOU SHALT NOT COVET THY NEIGHBOR'S WIFE, NOR HIS MANSERVANT, NOR HIS MAIDSERVANT, NOR HIS OX, NOR HIS MULE, NOR ANY THING THAT IS THY NEIGHBOR'S.

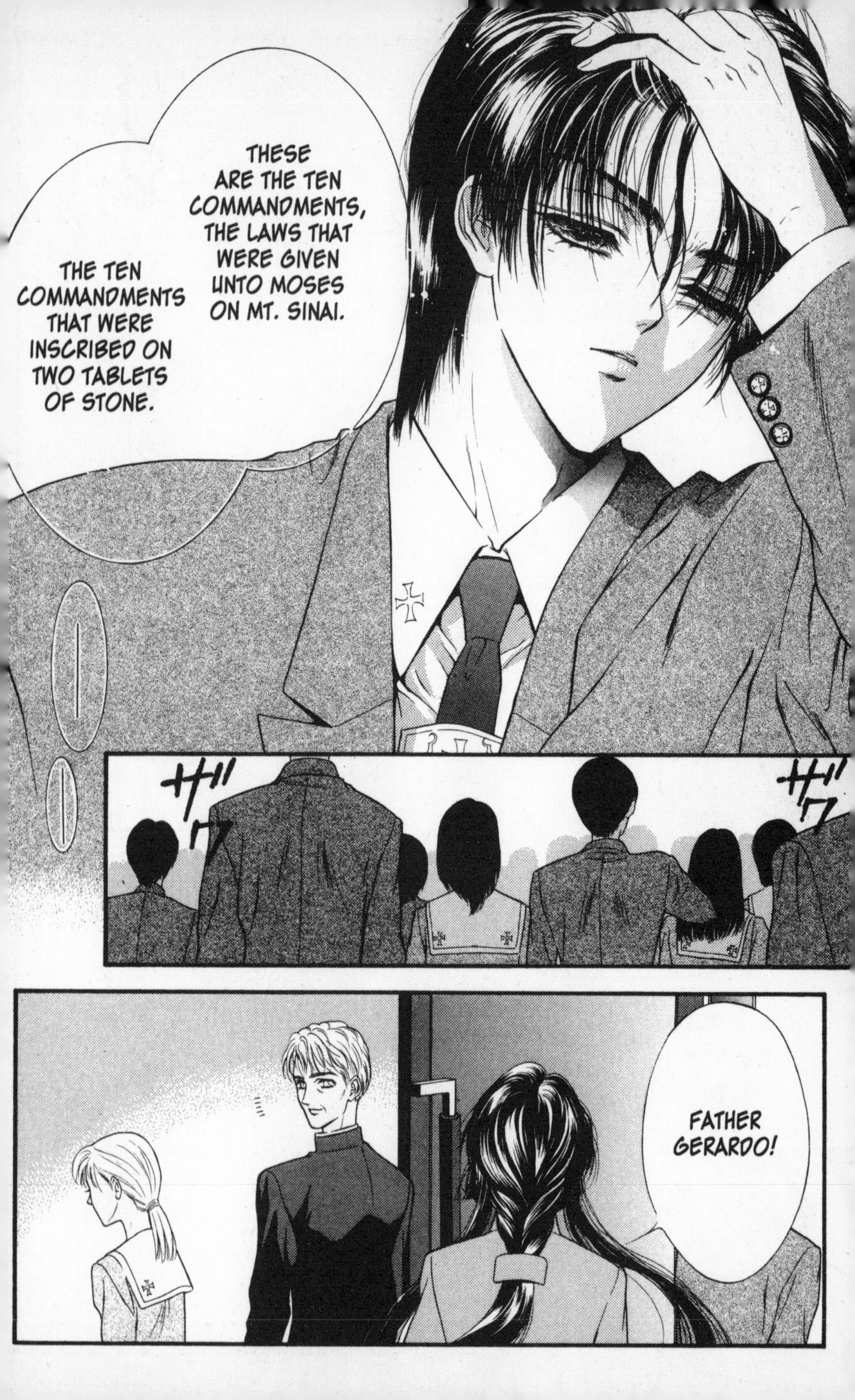
THESE ARE THE TEN COMMANDMENTS, THE LAWS THAT WERE GIVEN UNTO MOSES ON MT. SINAI.
THE TEN COMMANDMENTS THAT WERE INSCRIBED ON TWO TABLETS OF STONE.
ザワ
ザワ
FATHER GERARDO!

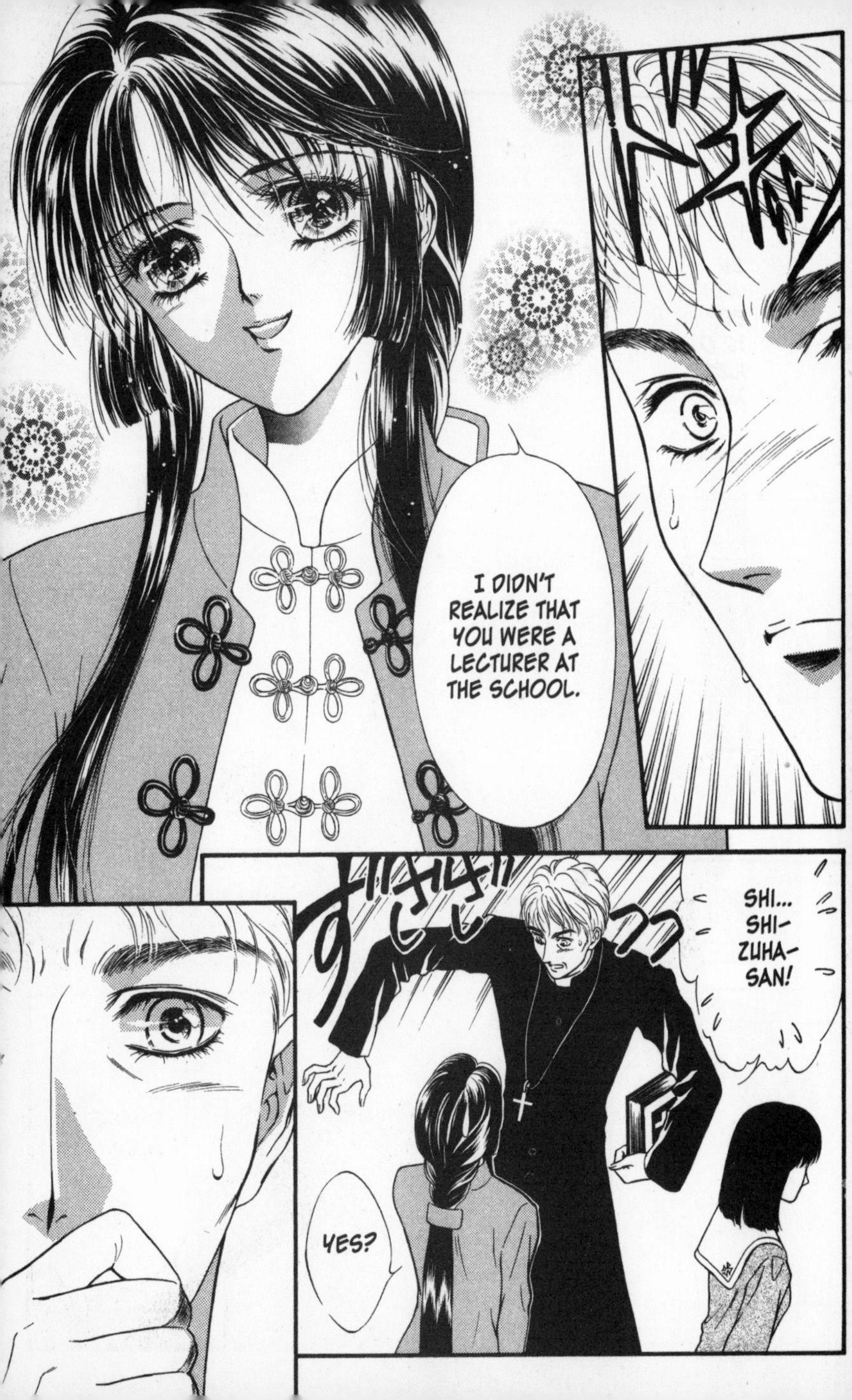
I DIDN'T REALIZE THAT YOU WERE A LECTURER AT THE SCHOOL.
SHI... SHI-ZUHA-SAN!
YES?

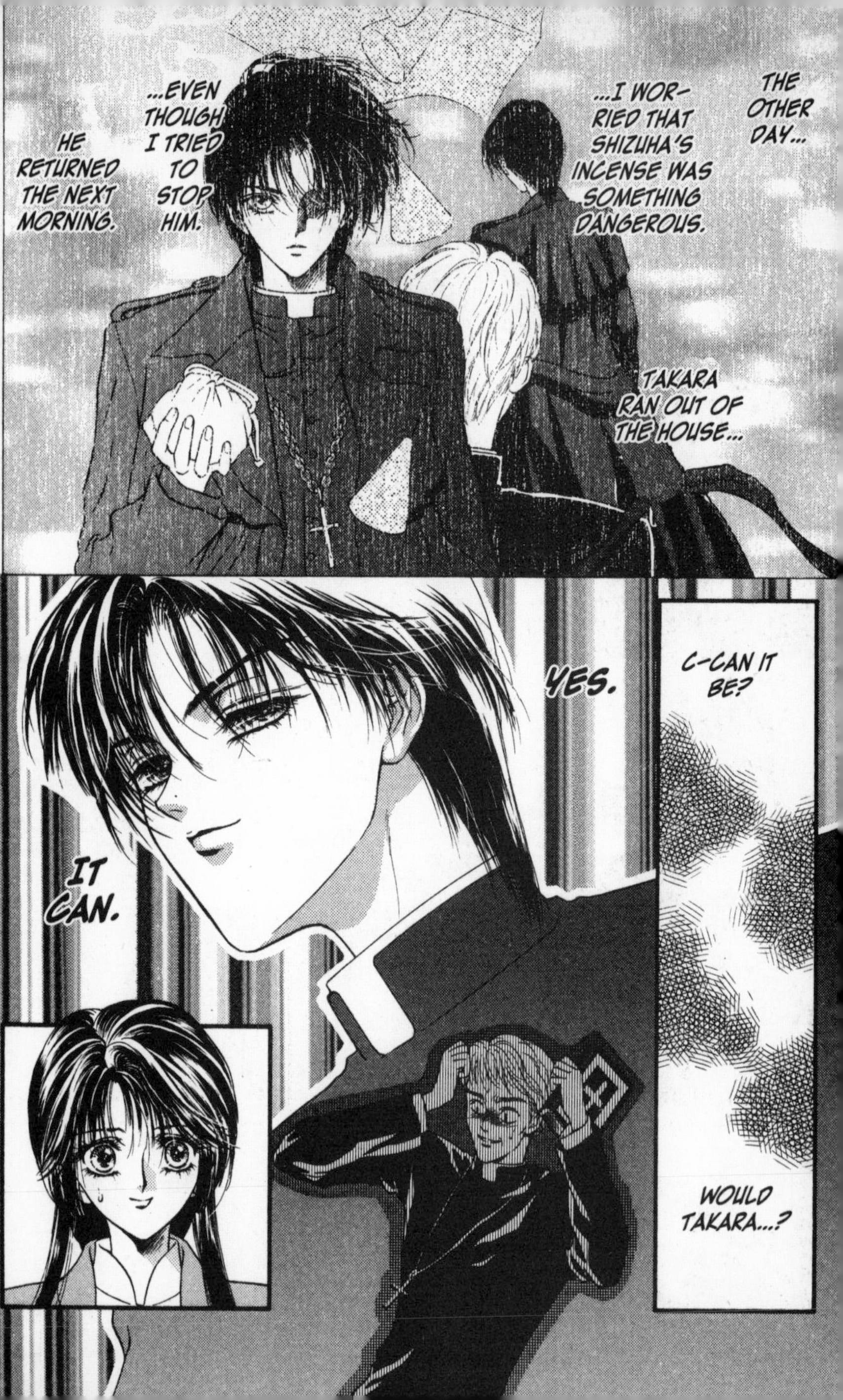
THE OTHER DAY...
...I WORRIED THAT SHIZUHA'S INCENSE WAS SOMETHING DANGEROUS.
TAKARA RAN OUT OF THE HOUSE...
...EVEN THOUGH I TRIED TO STOP HIM.
HE RETURNED THE NEXT MORNING.
C-CAN IT BE?
WOULD TAKARA...?
YES.
IT CAN.

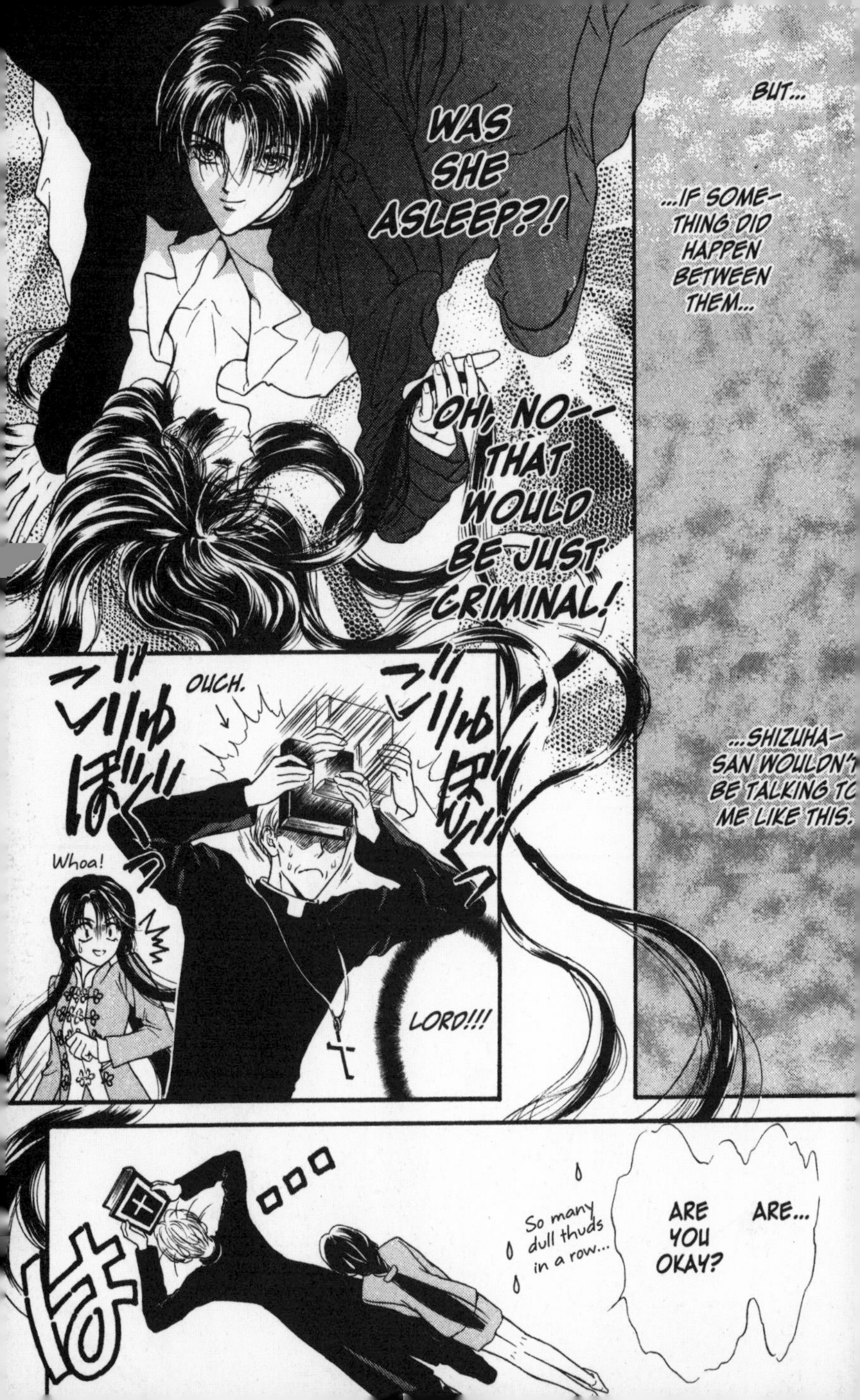
BUT...
...IF SOME-THING DID HAPPEN BETWEEN THEM...
...SHIZUHA-SAN WOULDN'T BE TALKING TO ME LIKE THIS.
WAS SHE ASLEEP?!
OH, NO-- THAT WOULD BE JUST CRIMINAL!
OUCH.
Whoa!
LORD!!!
ARE... ARE YOU OKAY?
So many dull thuds in a row...

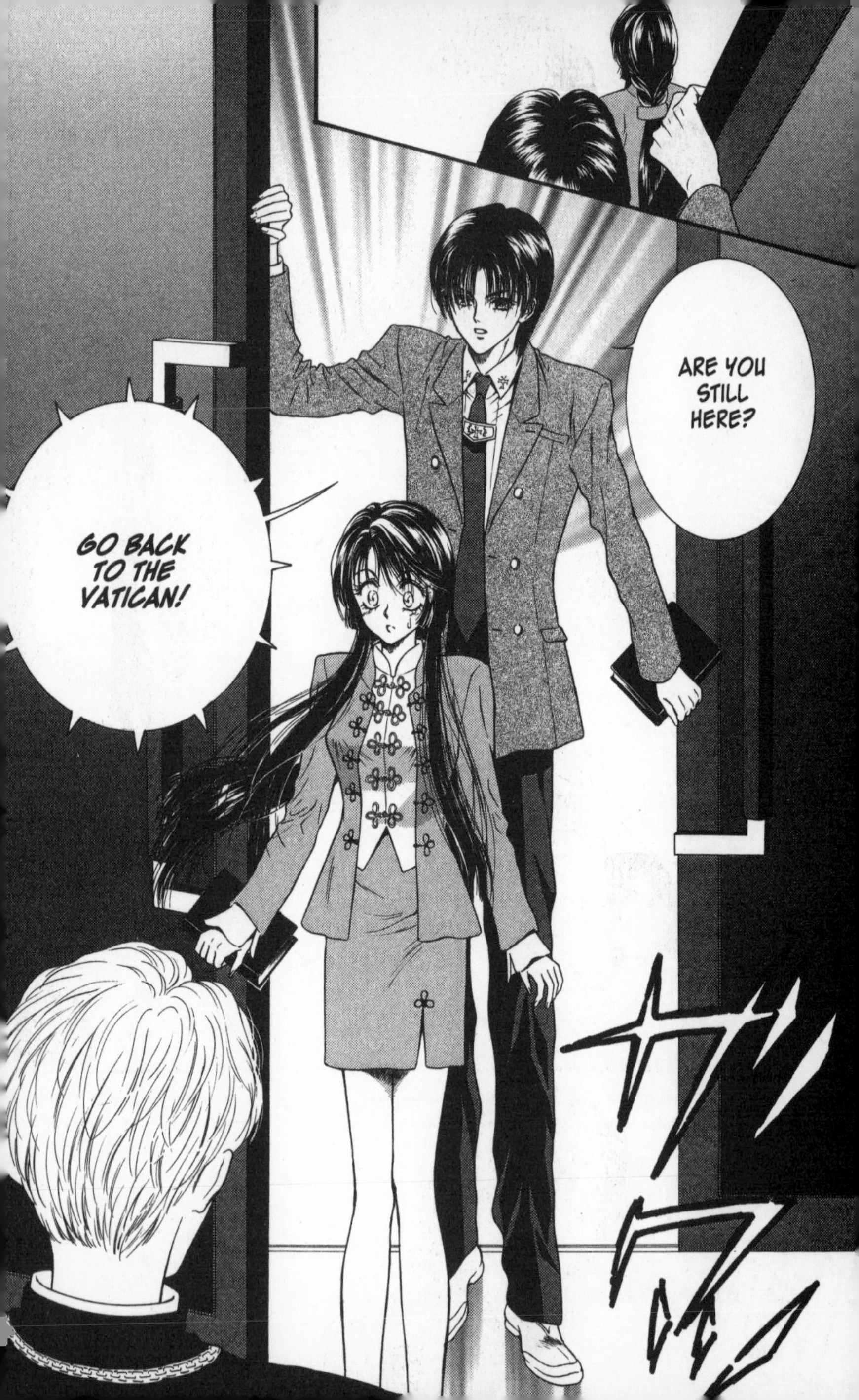
ARE YOU STILL HERE?
GO BACK TO THE VATICAN!

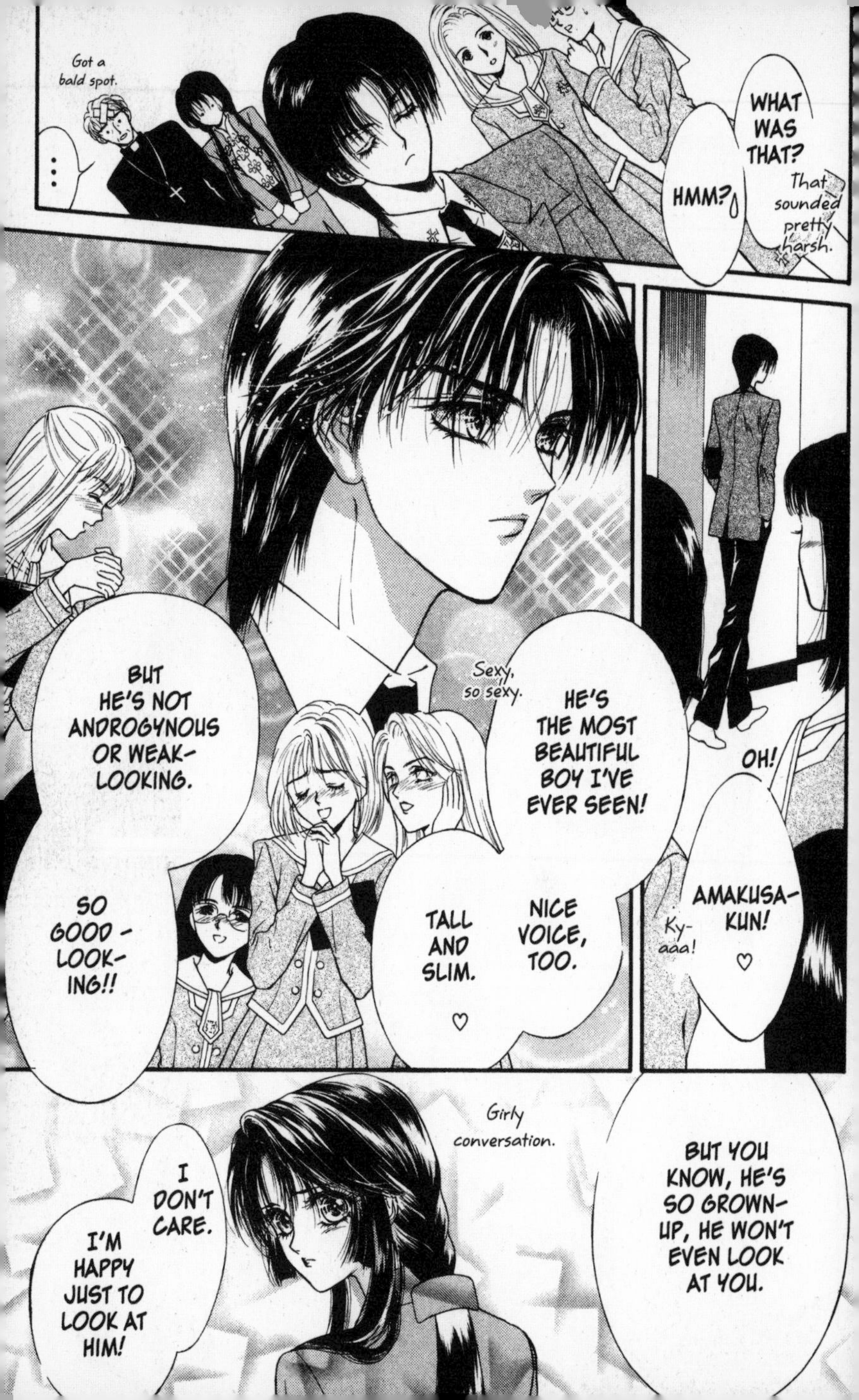
WHAT WAS THAT?
That sounded pretty harsh.
HMM?
Got a bald spot.
...
OH!
AMAKUSA-KUN! ♡
Ky-aaa!
HE'S THE MOST BEAUTIFUL BOY I'VE EVER SEEN!
Sexy, so sexy.
NICE VOICE, TOO.
TALL AND SLIM. ♡
BUT HE'S NOT ANDROGYNOUS OR WEAK-LOOKING.
SO GOOD-LOOKING!!
BUT YOU KNOW, HE'S SO GROWN-UP, HE WON'T EVEN LOOK AT YOU.
Girly conversation.
I DON'T CARE.
I'M HAPPY JUST TO LOOK AT HIM!

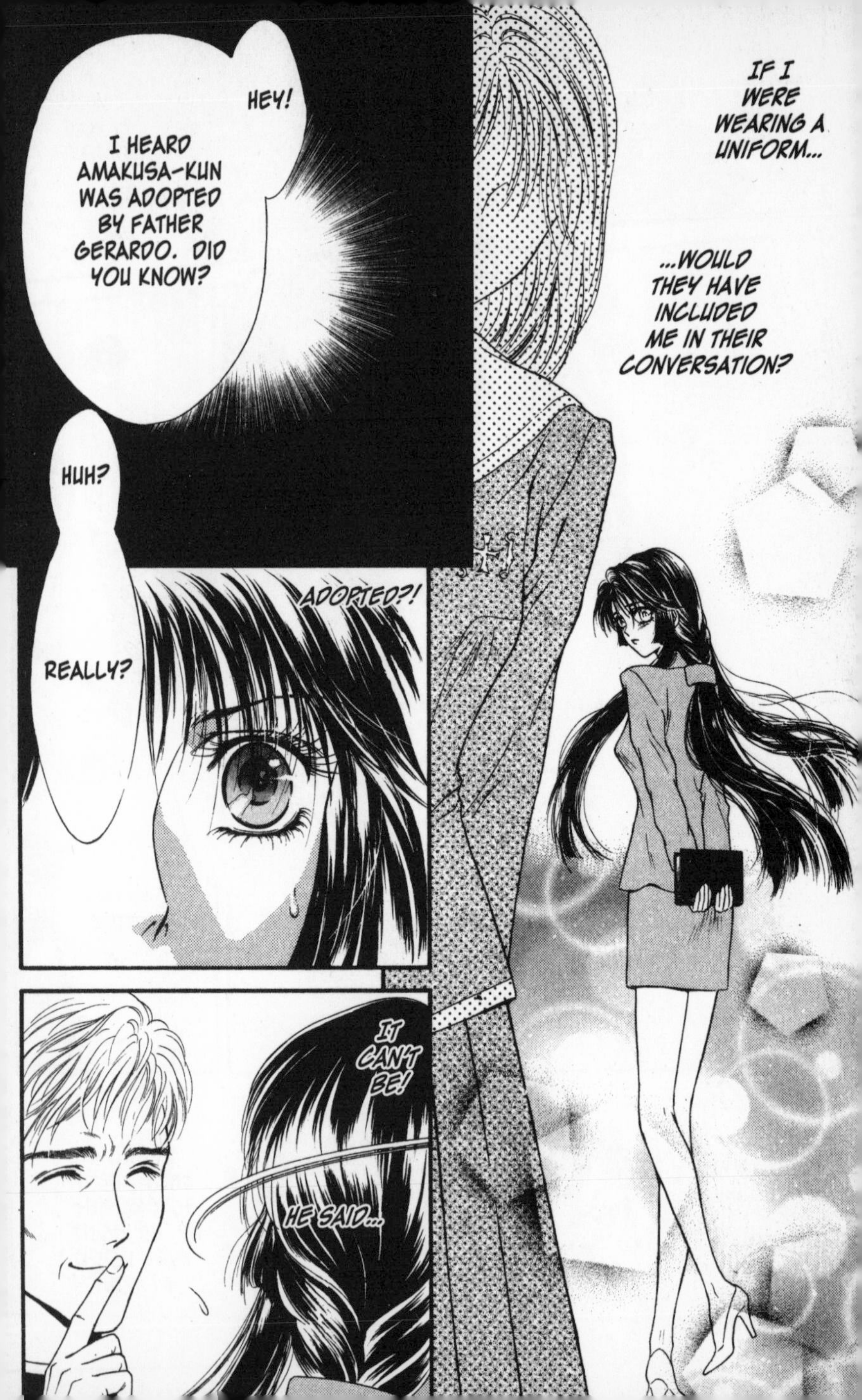
IF I WERE WEARING A UNIFORM...
...WOULD THEY HAVE INCLUDED ME IN THEIR CONVERSATION?
HEY!
I HEARD AMAKUSA-KUN WAS ADOPTED BY FATHER GERARDO. DID YOU KNOW?
HUH?
REALLY?
ADOPTED?!
IT CAN'T BE!
HE SAID...

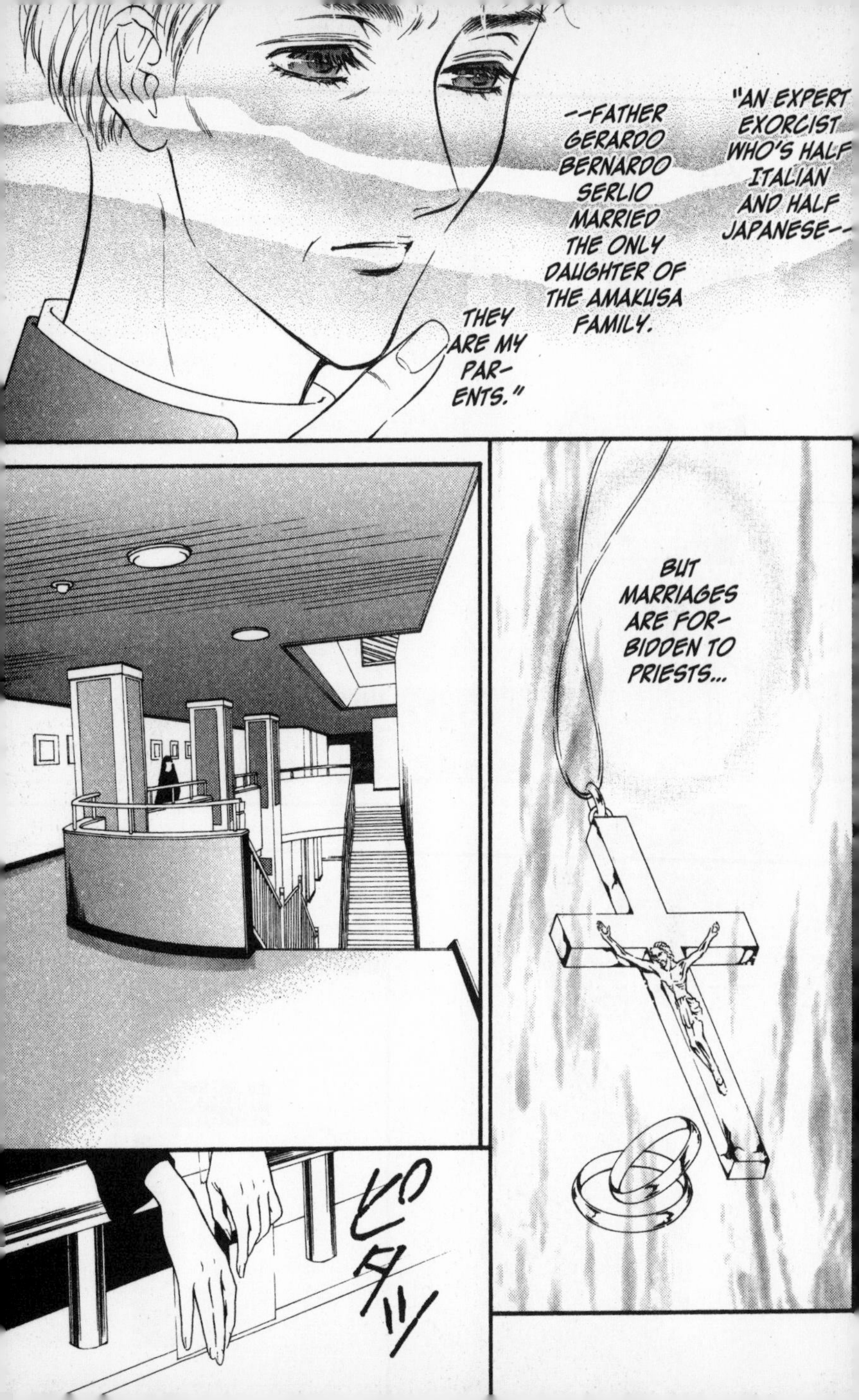
"AN EXPERT EXORCIST WHO'S HALF ITALIAN AND HALF JAPANESE--
--FATHER GERARDO BERNARDO SERLIO MARRIED THE ONLY DAUGHTER OF THE AMAKUSA FAMILY.
THEY ARE MY PAR-ENTS."
BUT MARRIAGES ARE FOR-BIDDEN TO PRIESTS...
ピタッ

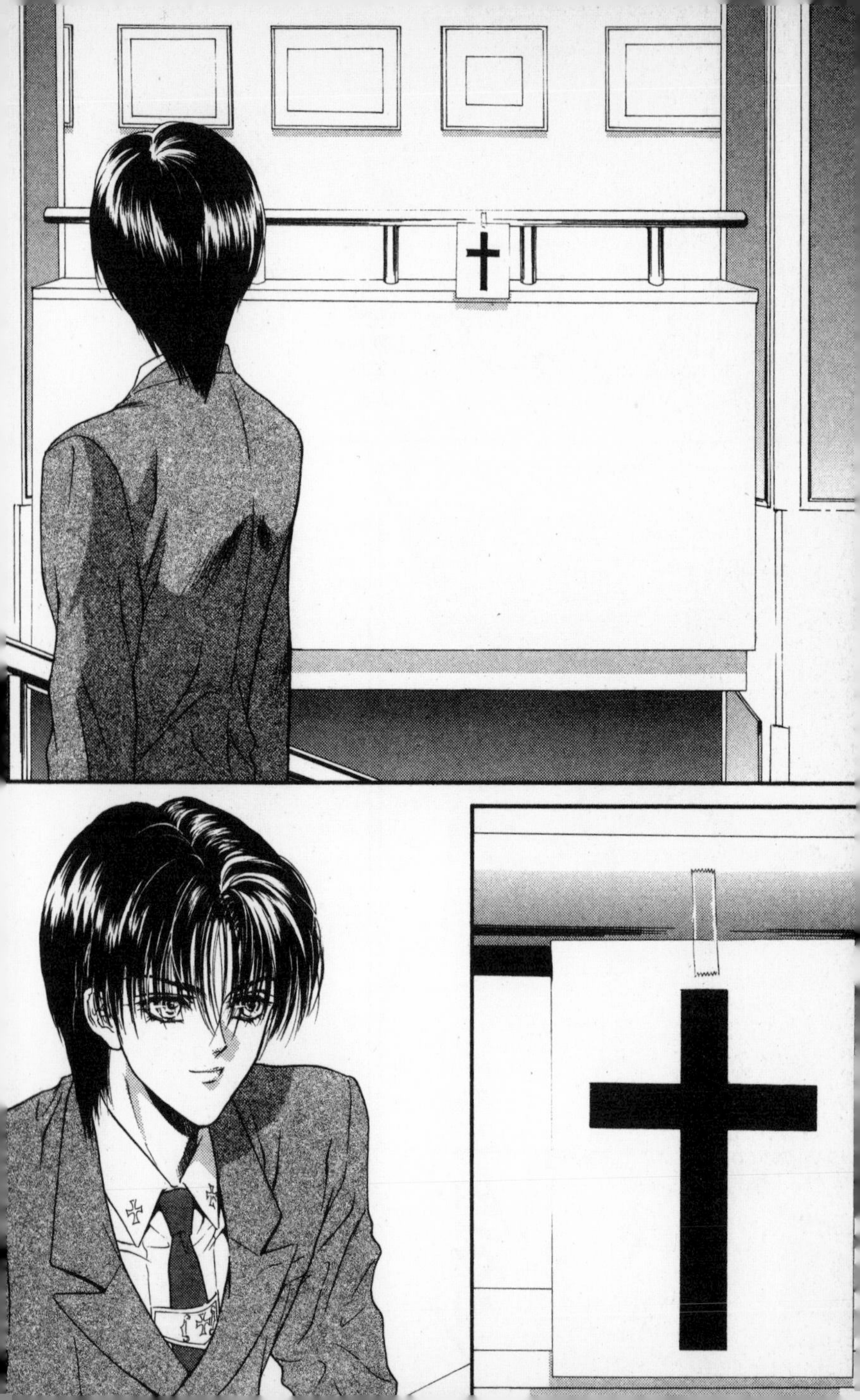

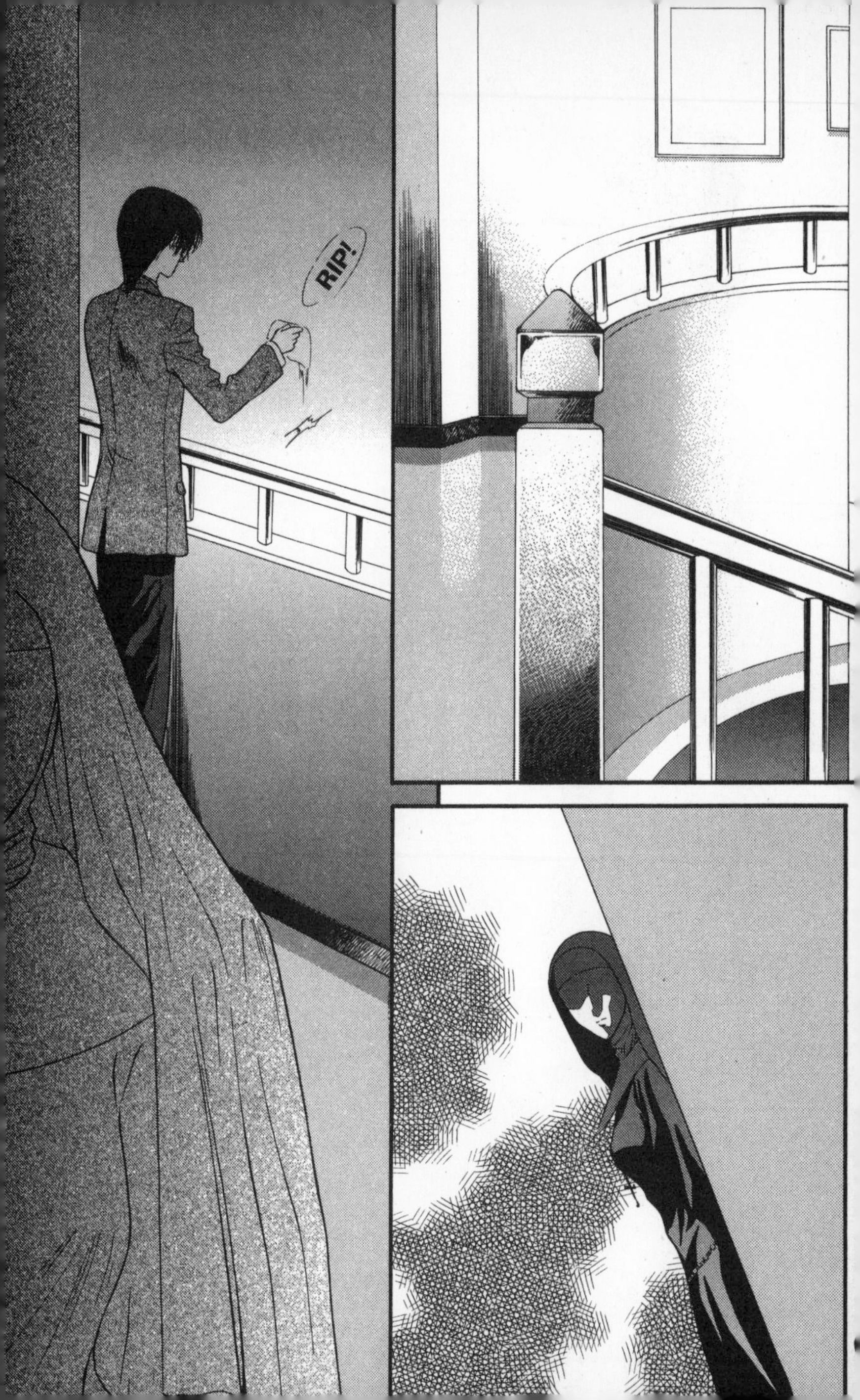
RIP!

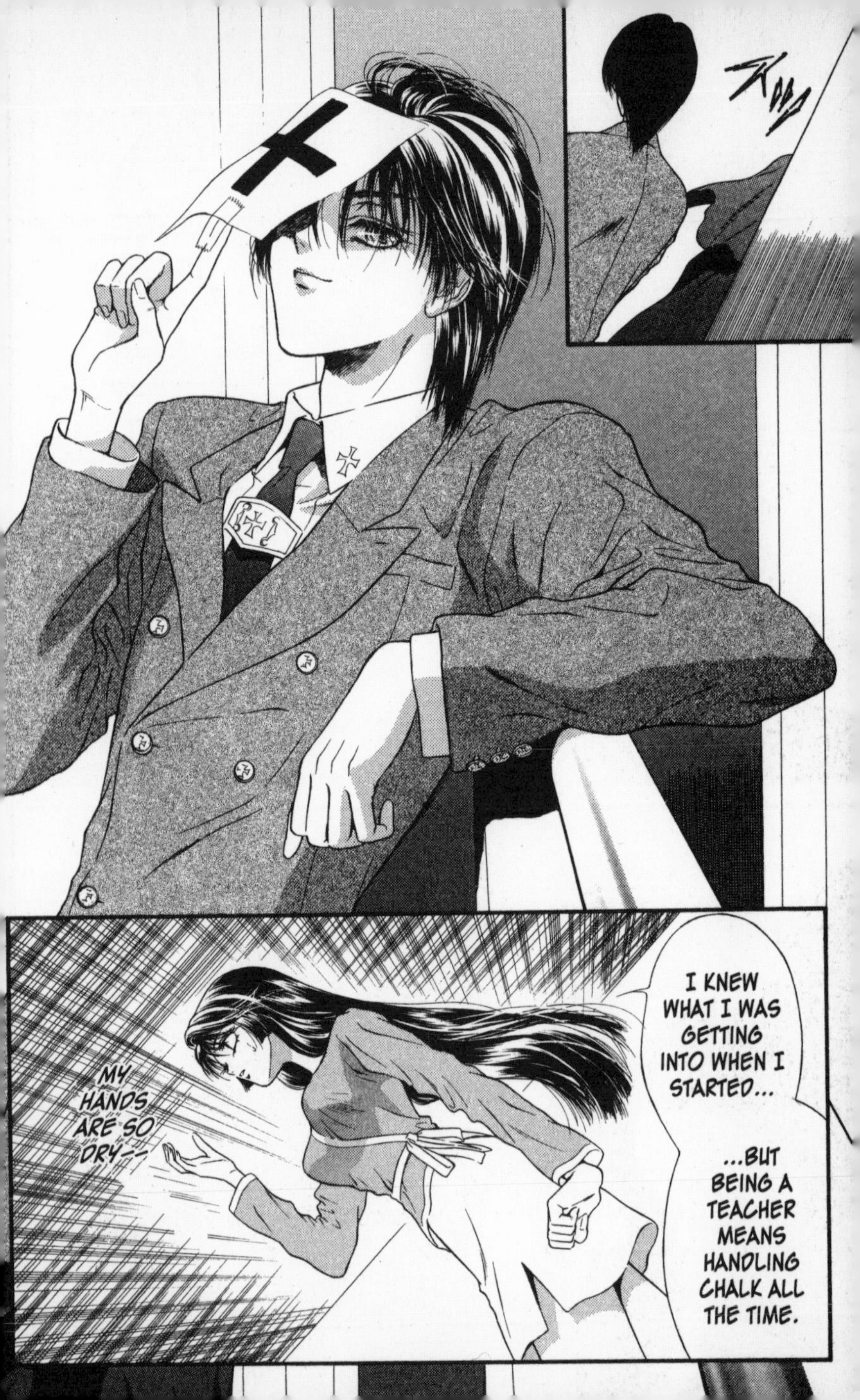
I KNEW WHAT I WAS GETTING INTO WHEN I STARTED...
...BUT BEING A TEACHER MEANS HANDLING CHALK ALL THE TIME.
MY HANDS ARE SO DRY--

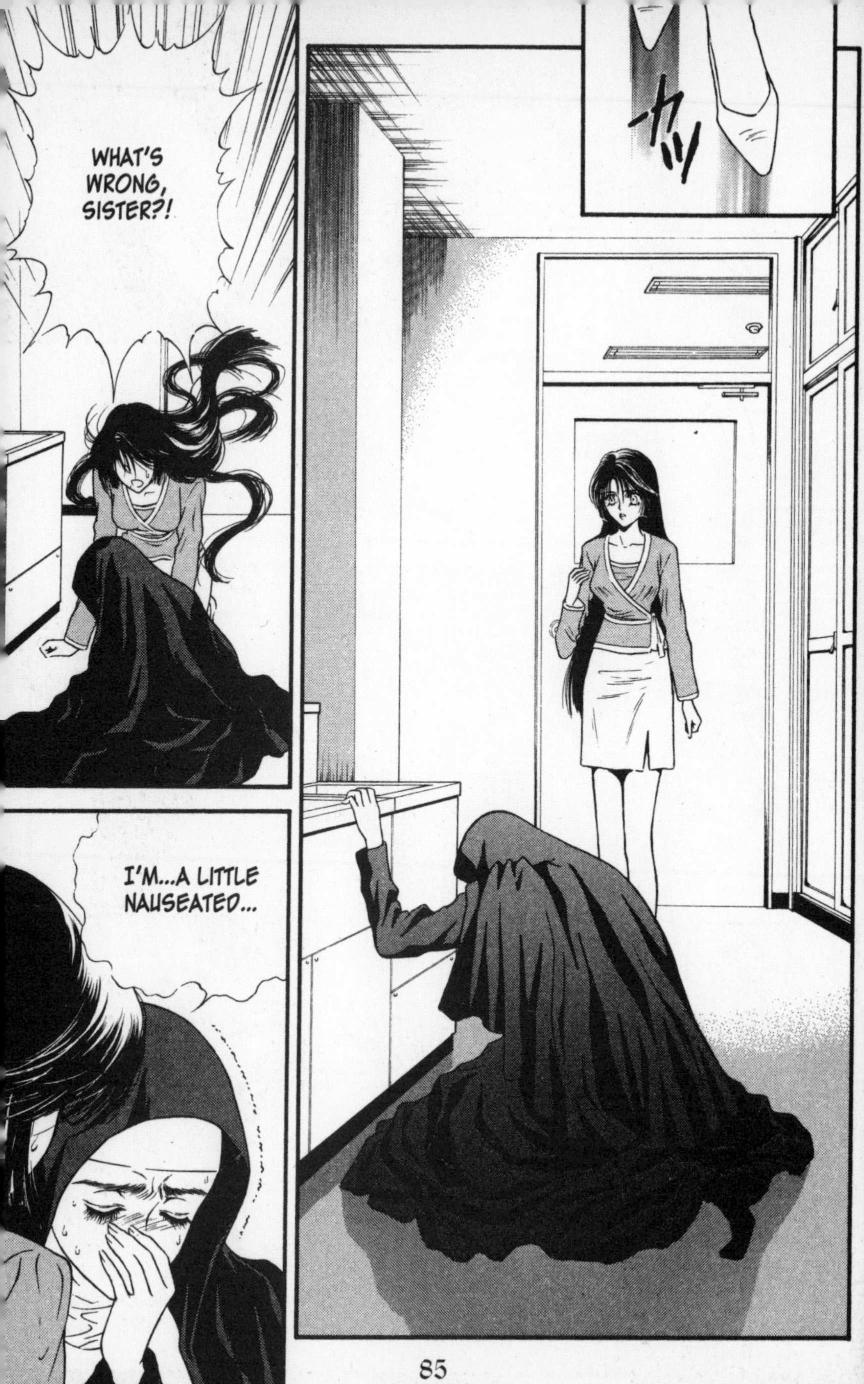
カッ
WHAT'S WRONG, SISTER?!
I'M...A LITTLE NAUSEATED...

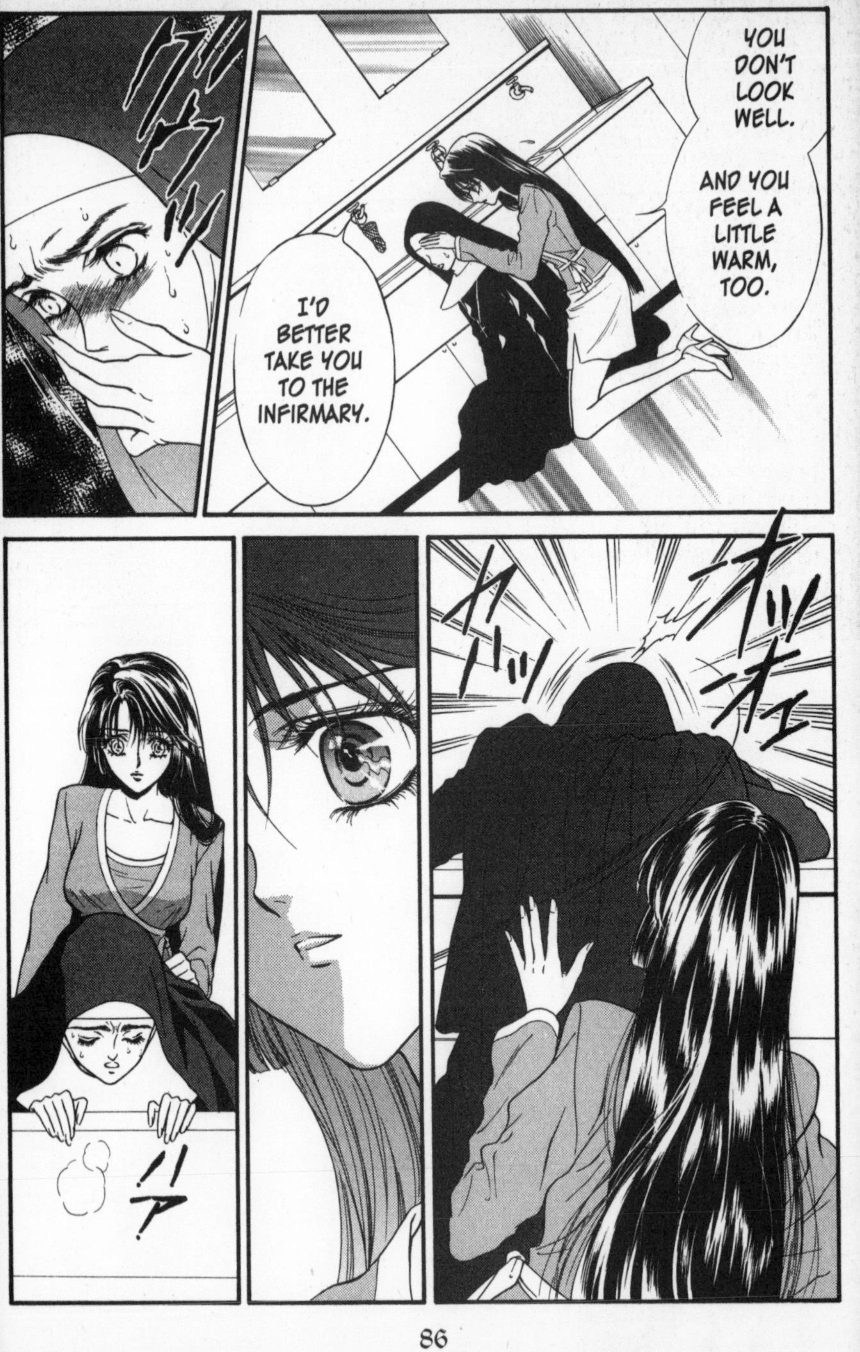
YOU DON'T LOOK WELL.
AND YOU FEEL A LITTLE WARM, TOO.
I'D BETTER TAKE YOU TO THE INFIRMARY.

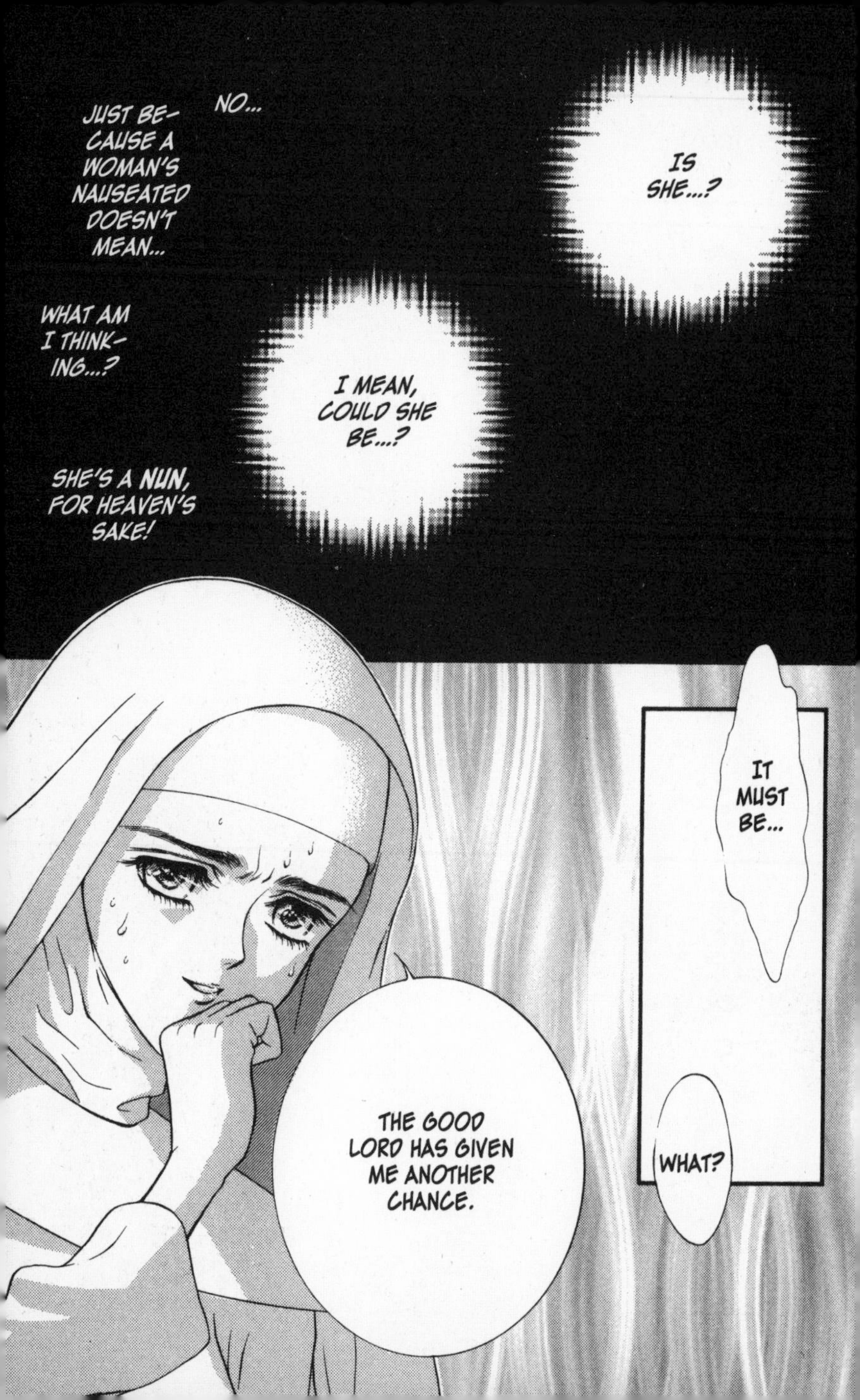
IS SHE...?
NO...
JUST BE-CAUSE A WOMAN'S NAUSEATED DOESN'T MEAN...
I MEAN, COULD SHE BE...?
WHAT AM I THINK-ING...?
SHE'S A **NUN**, FOR HEAVEN'S SAKE!
IT MUST BE...
WHAT?
THE GOOD LORD HAS GIVEN ME ANOTHER CHANCE.

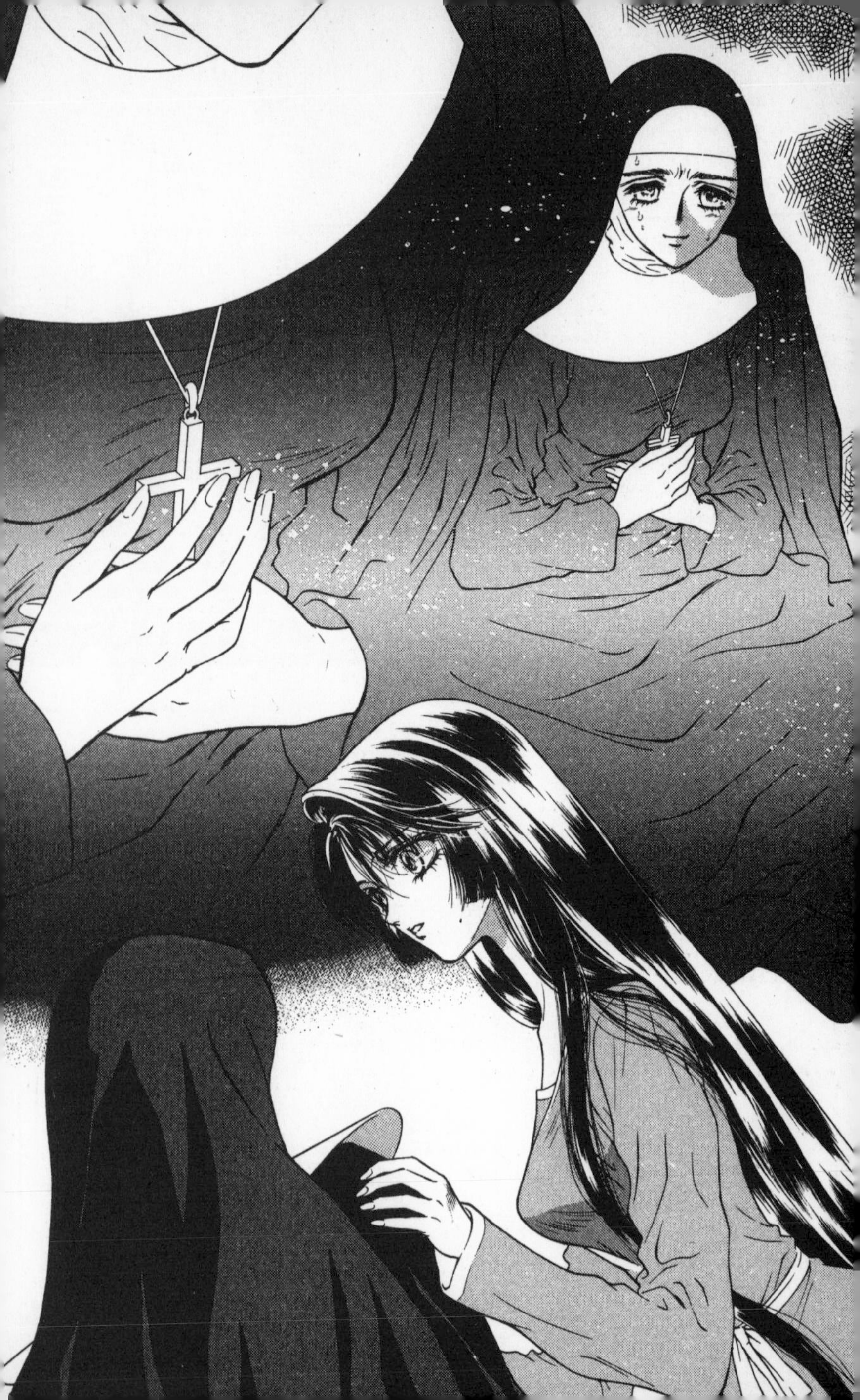

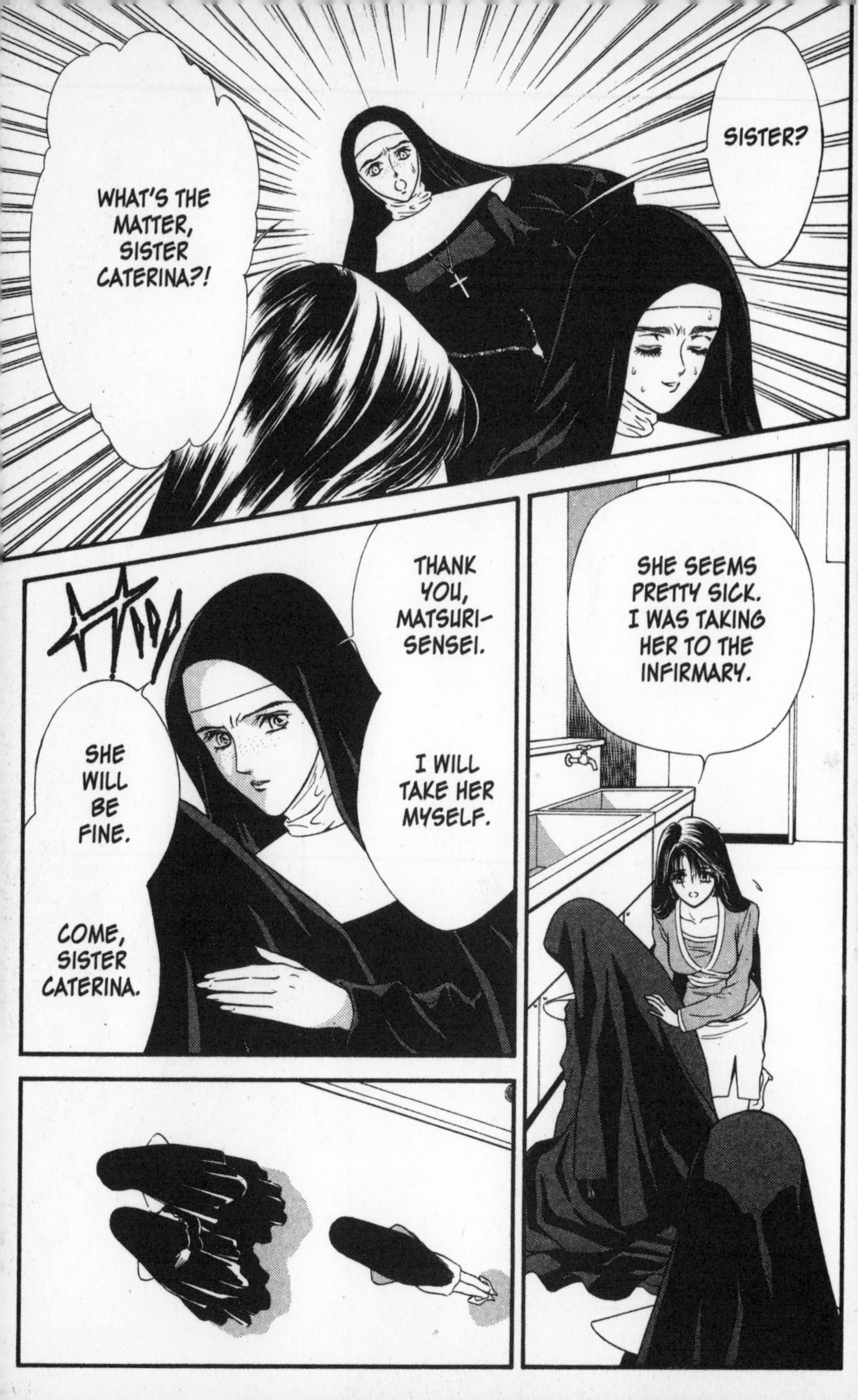
SISTER?
WHAT'S THE MATTER, SISTER CATERINA?!
SHE SEEMS PRETTY SICK. I WAS TAKING HER TO THE INFIRMARY.
THANK YOU, MATSURI-SENSEI.
I WILL TAKE HER MYSELF.
SHE WILL BE FINE.
COME, SISTER CATERINA.

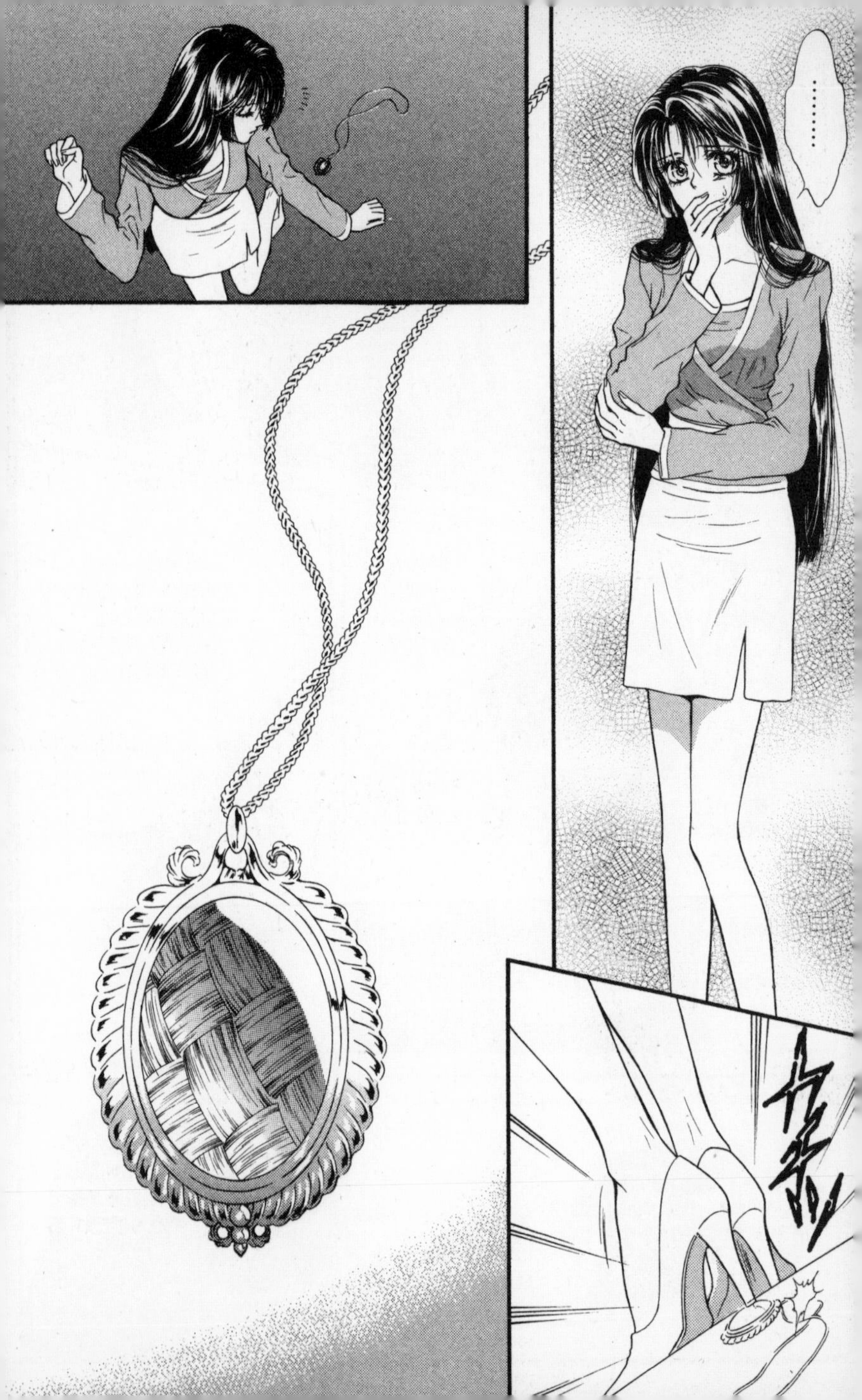
……
ガシャッ

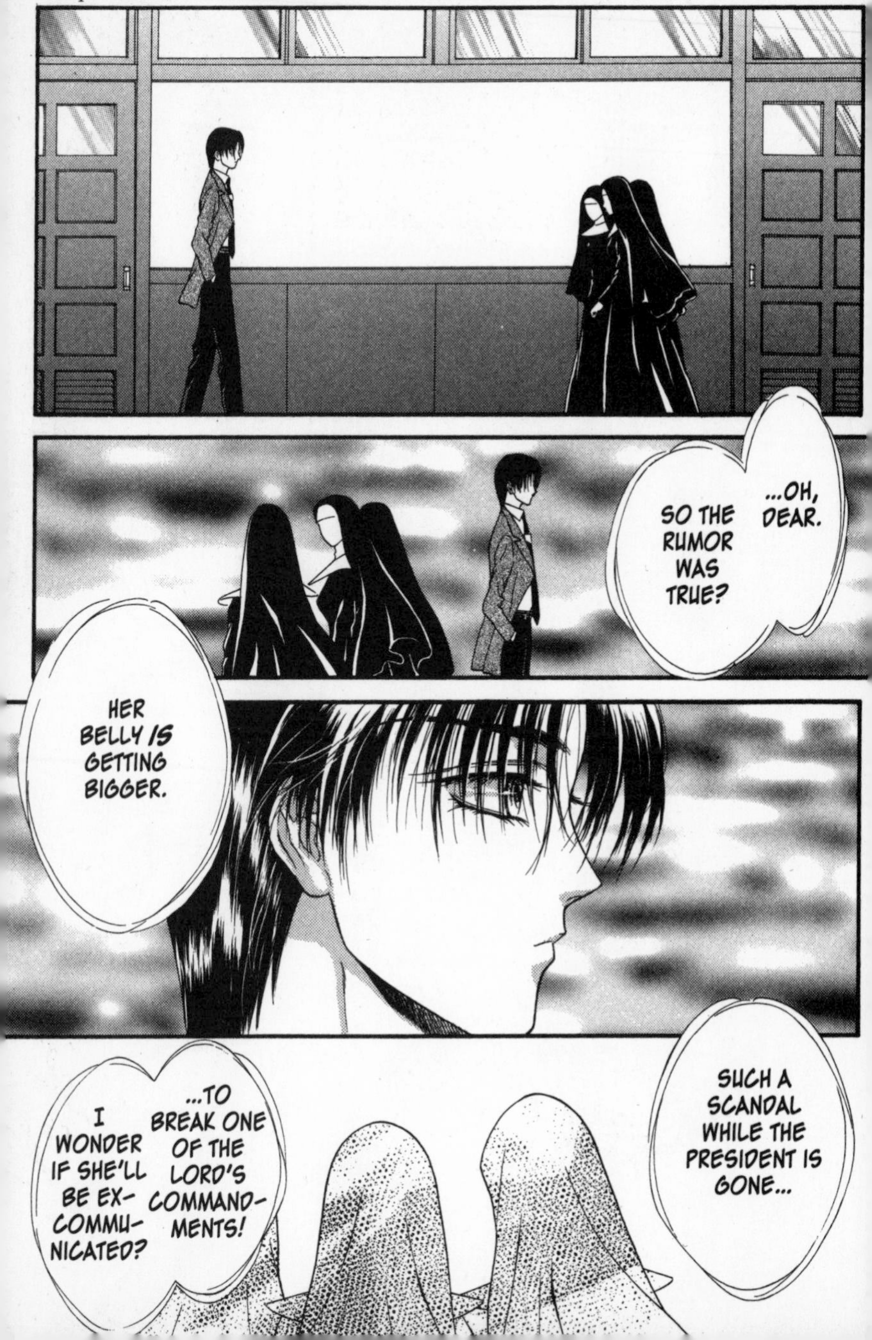
...OH, DEAR.
SO THE RUMOR WAS TRUE?
HER BELLY IS GETTING BIGGER.
SUCH A SCANDAL WHILE THE PRESIDENT IS GONE...
...TO BREAK ONE OF THE LORD'S COMMAND-MENTS!
I WONDER IF SHE'LL BE EX-COMMU-NICATED?

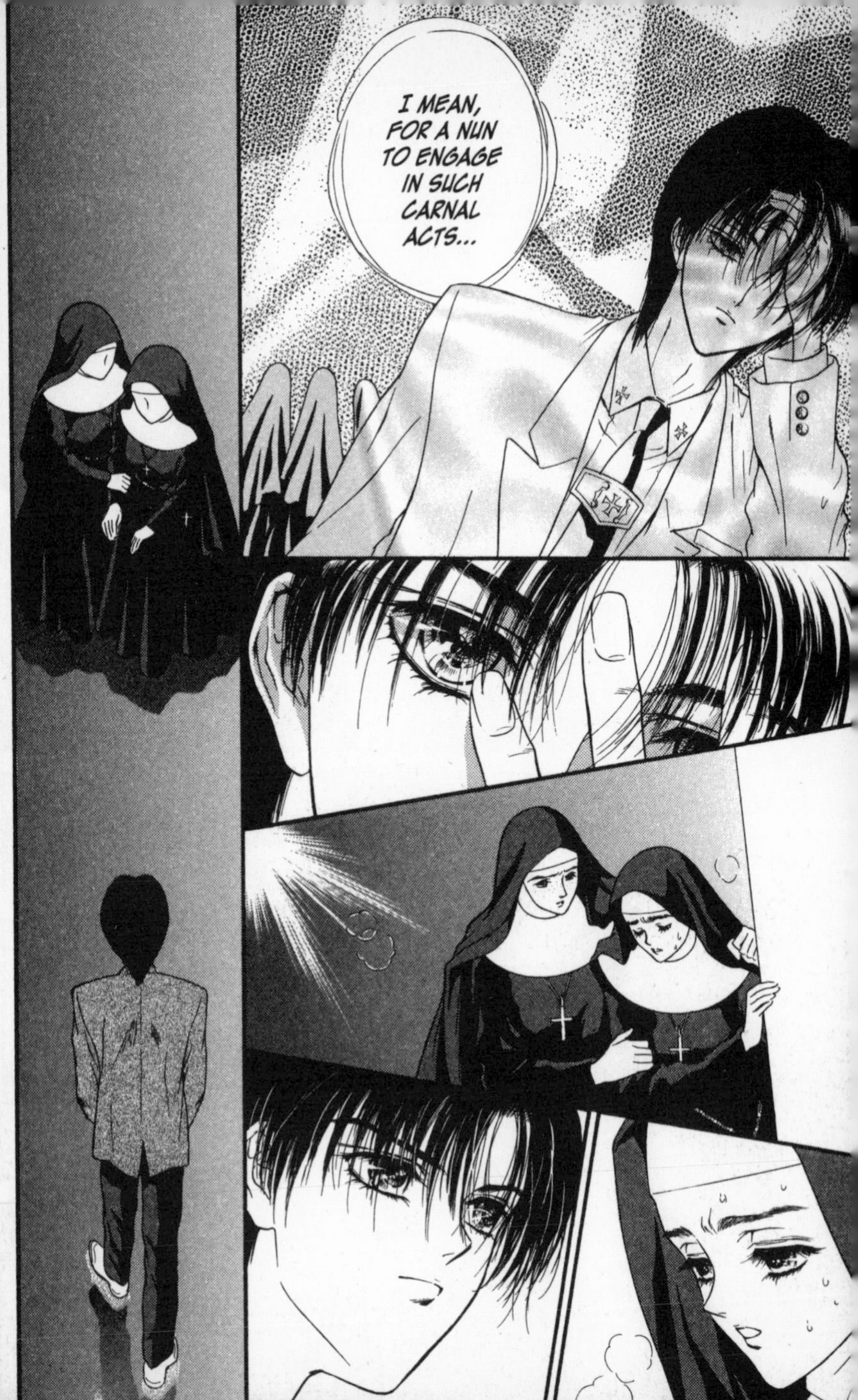
I MEAN, FOR A NUN TO ENGAGE IN SUCH CARNAL ACTS...

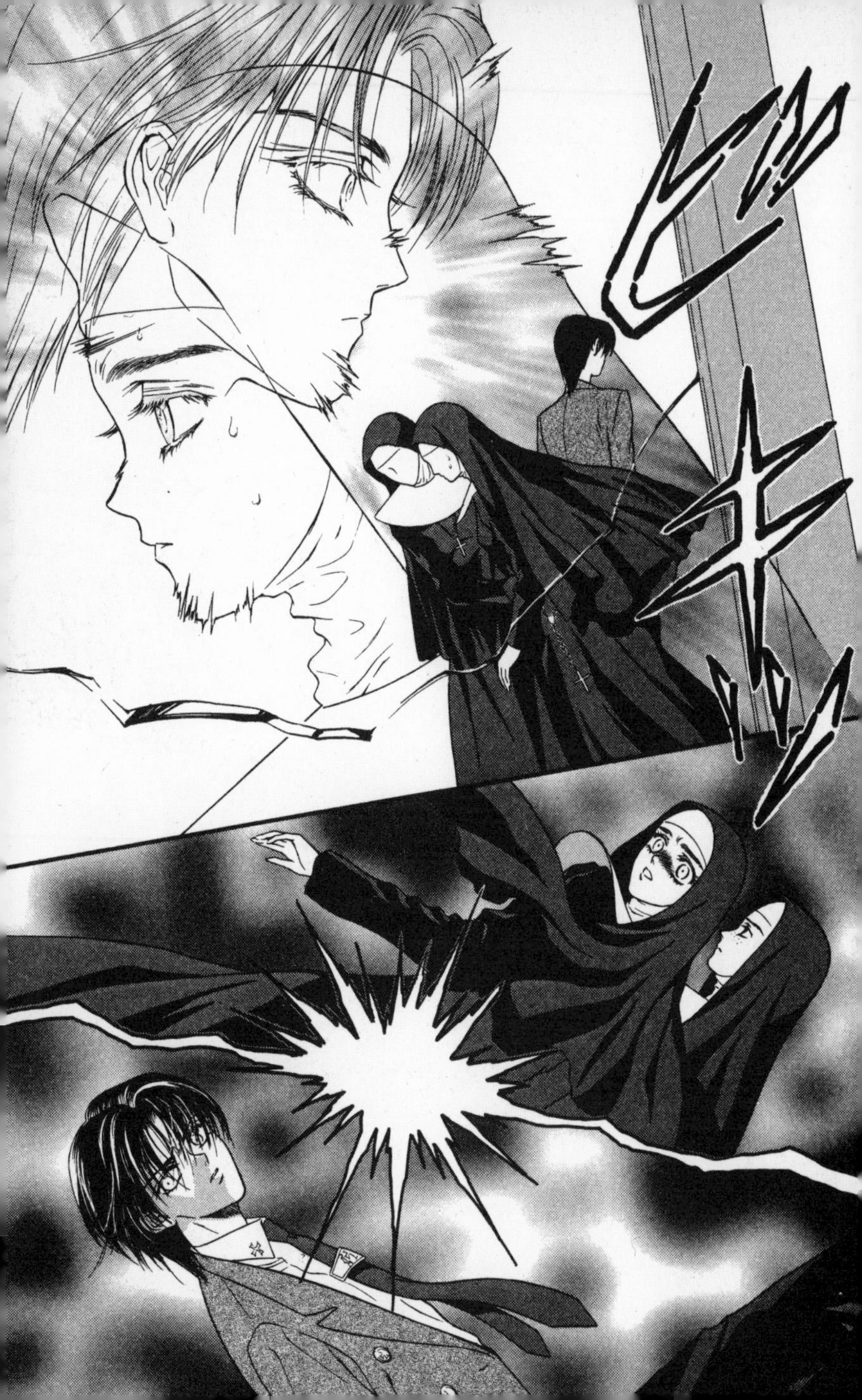
ビキィン

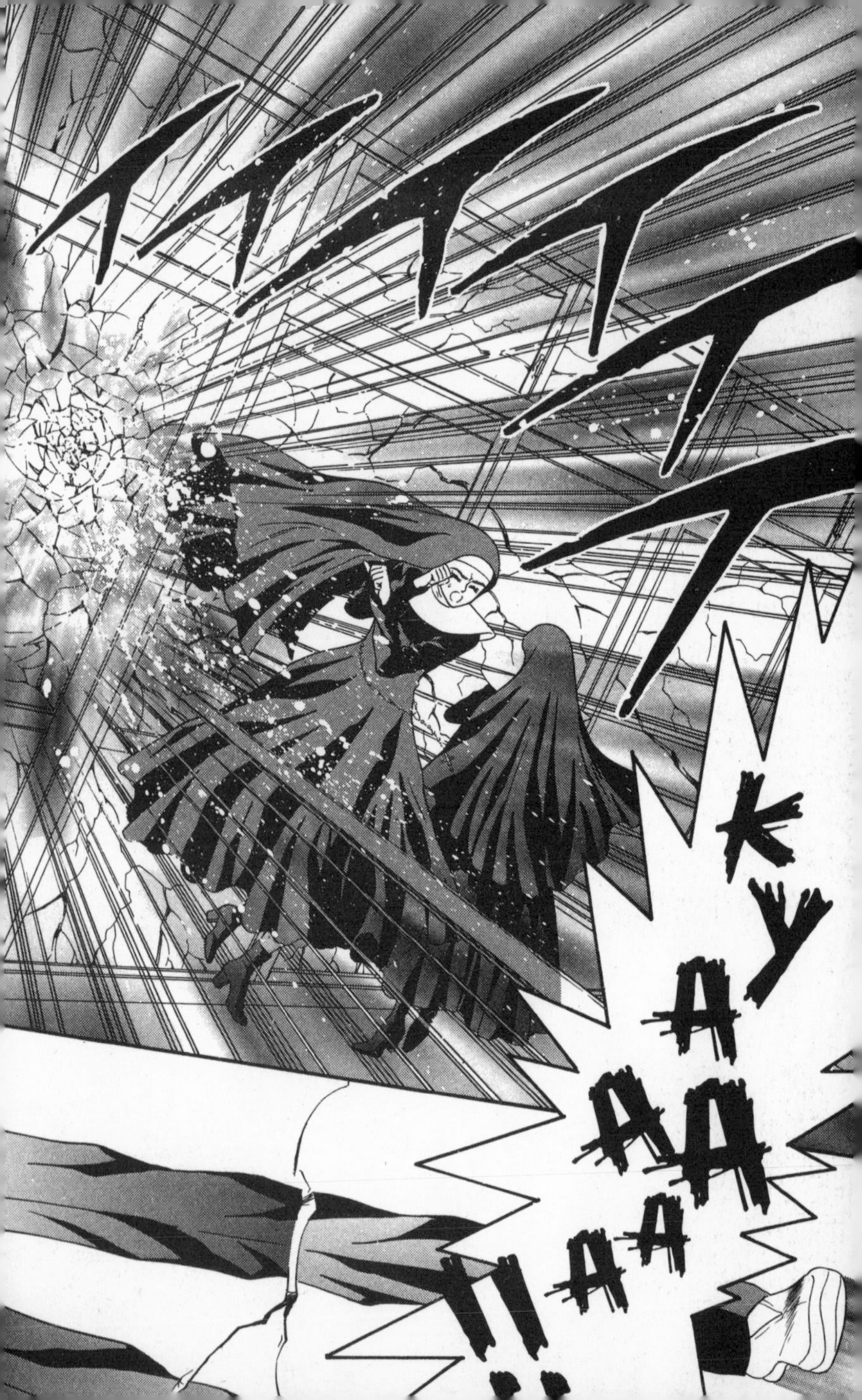
KYAAAAA!!

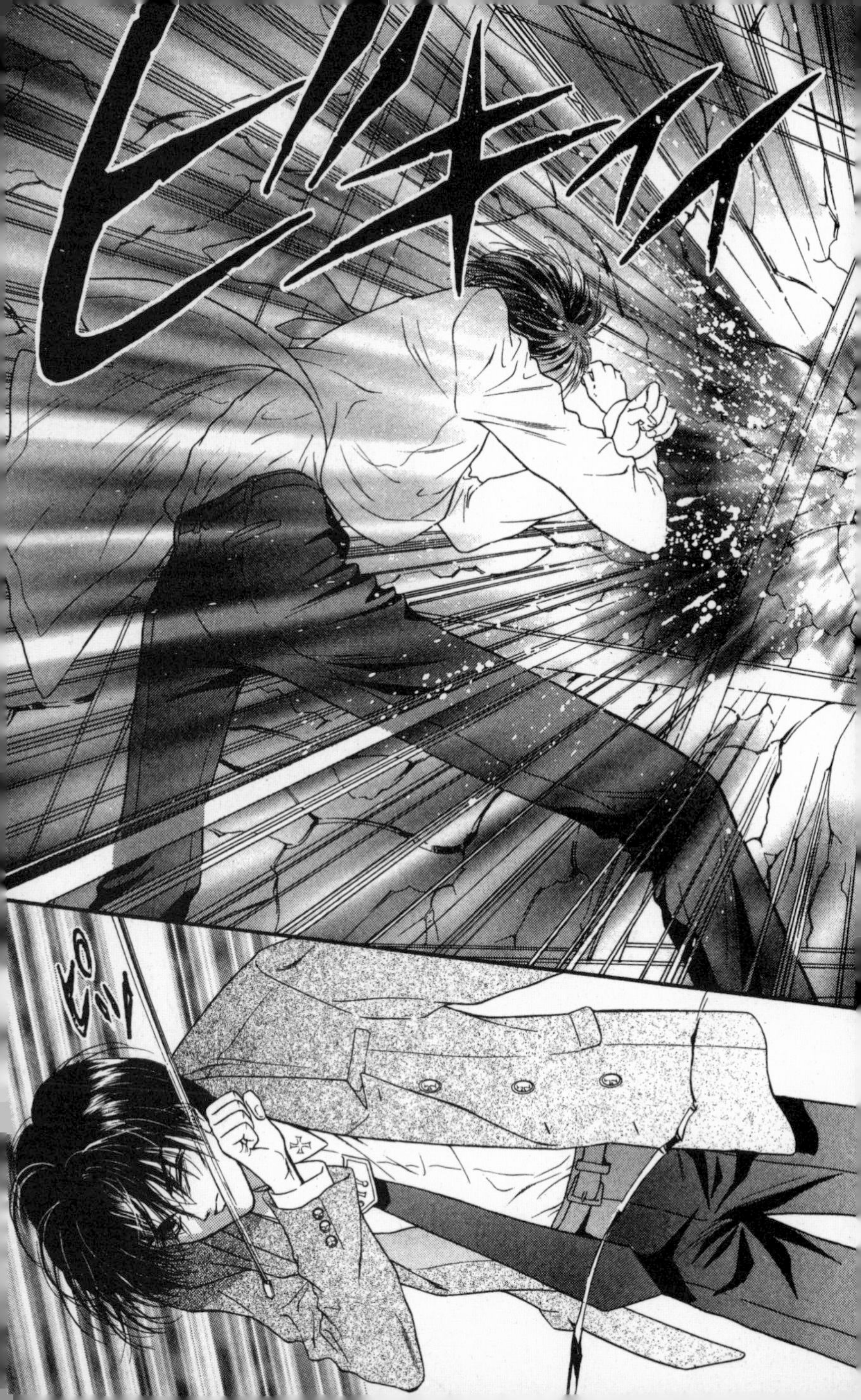

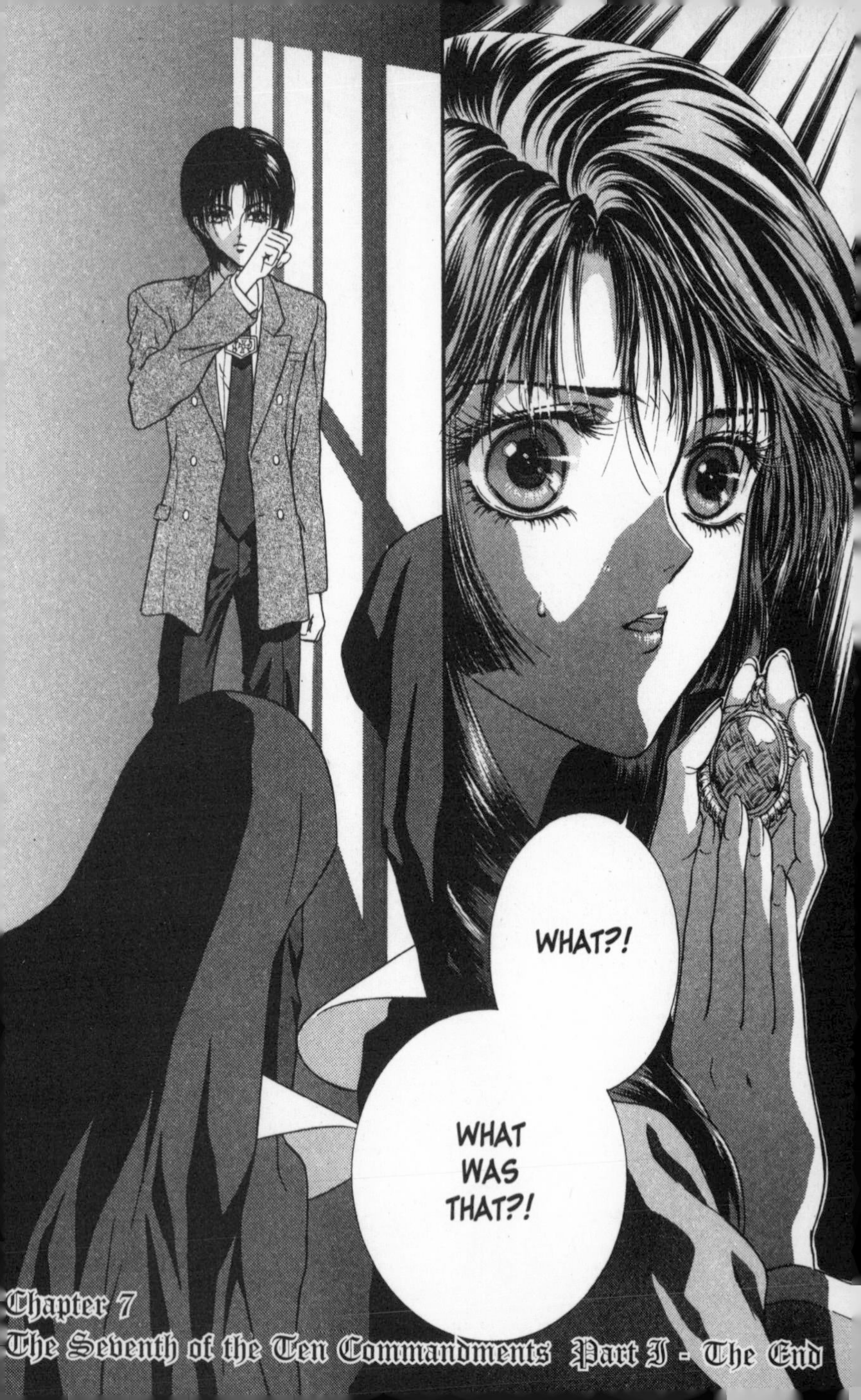
WHAT?!
WHAT WAS THAT?!
Chapter 7
The Seventh of the Ten Commandments Part I - The End

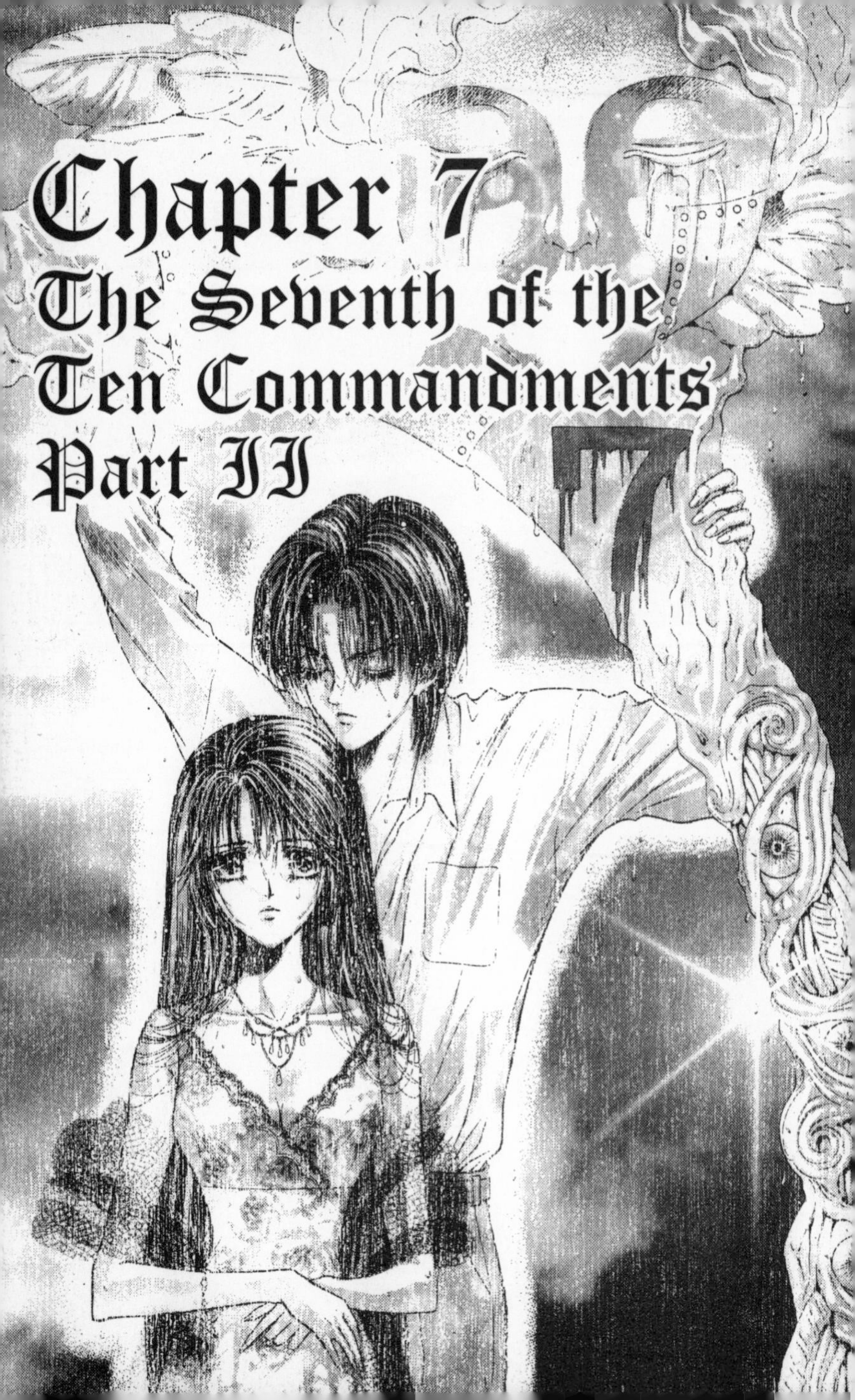
Chapter 7
The Seventh of the
Ten Commandments
Part II

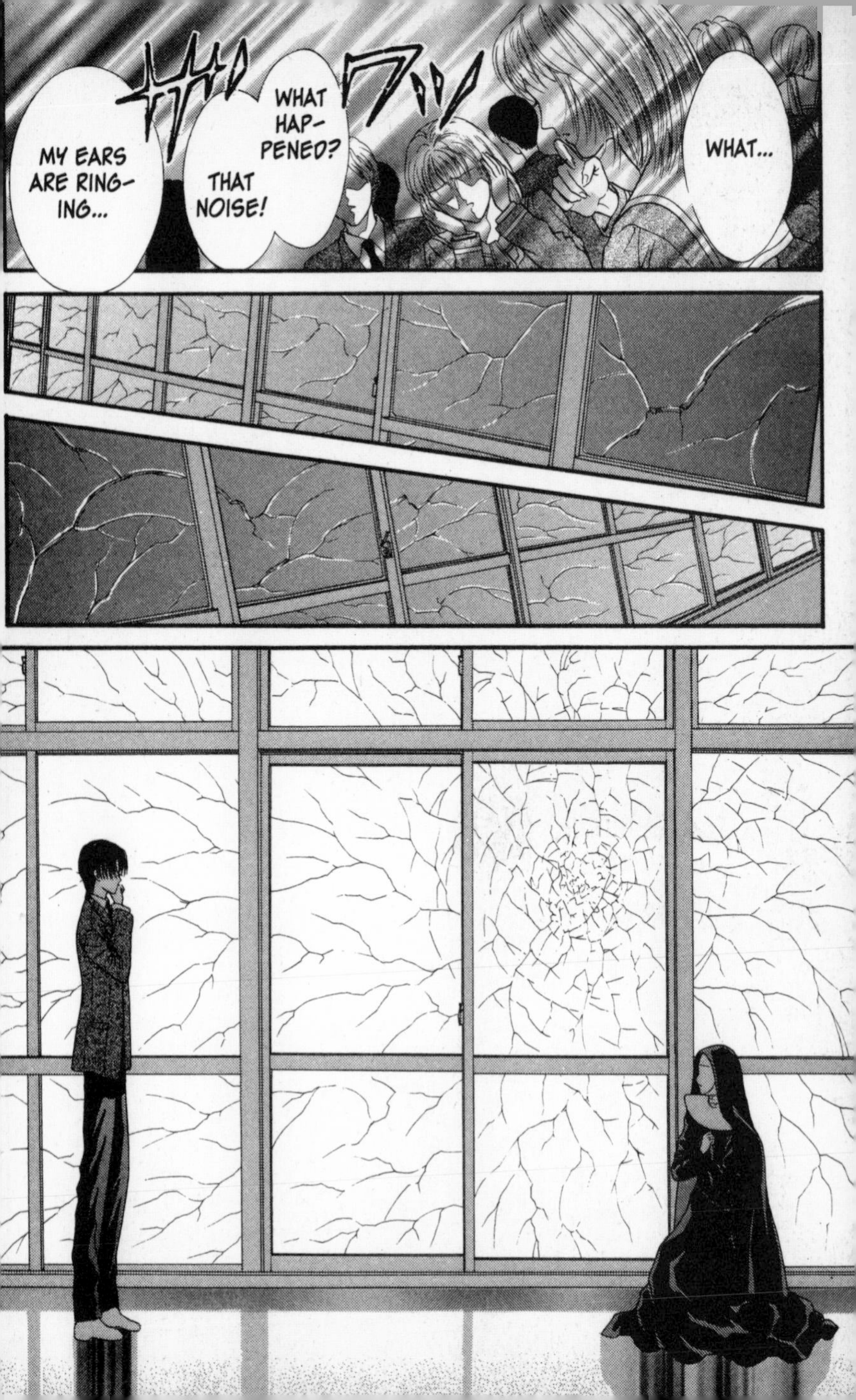
WHAT...
WHAT HAPPENED? THAT NOISE!
MY EARS ARE RINGING...

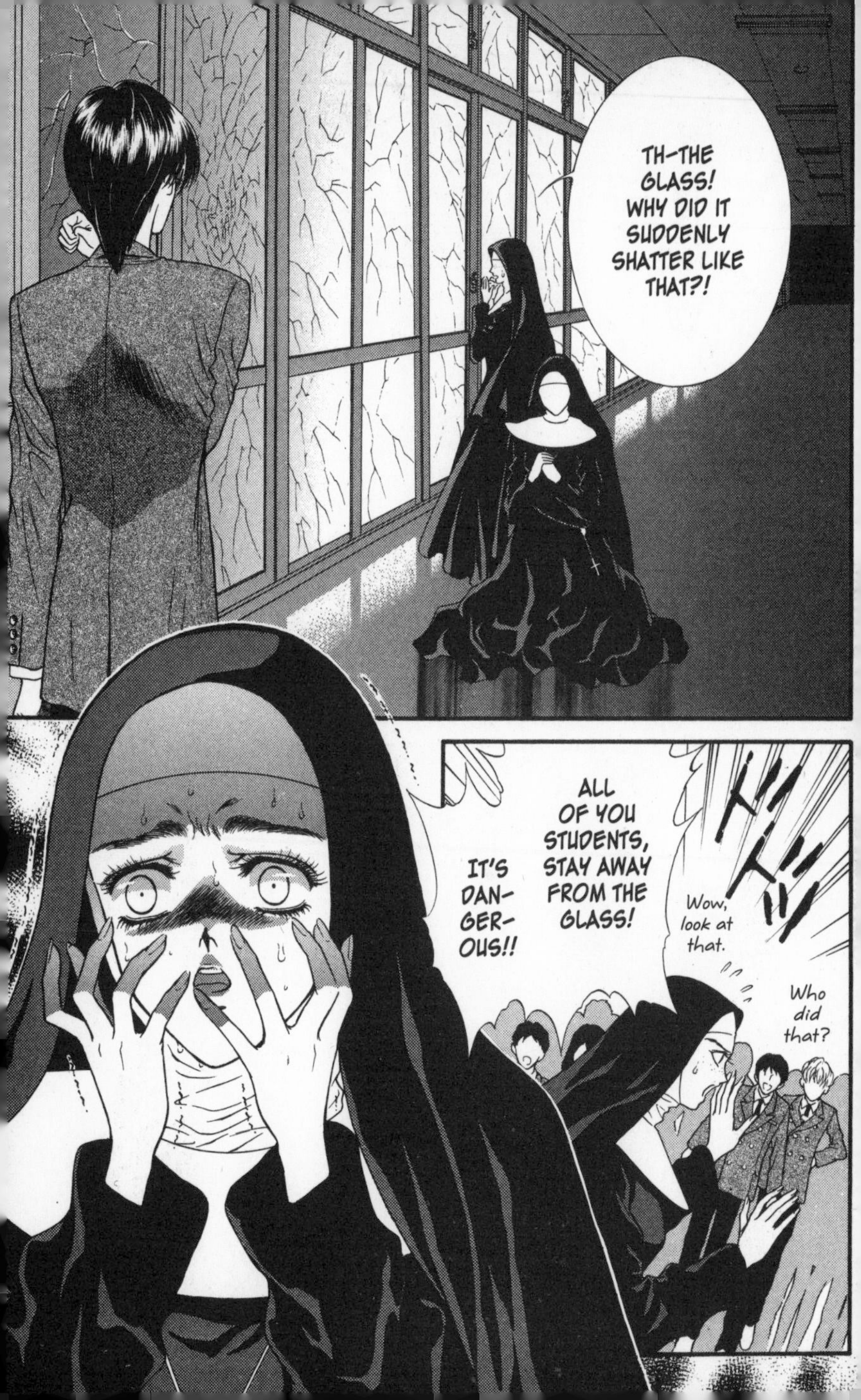
TH-THE GLASS! WHY DID IT SUDDENLY SHATTER LIKE THAT?!
Who did that?
Wow, look at that.
ALL OF YOU STUDENTS, STAY AWAY FROM THE GLASS!
IT'S DAN-GER-OUS!!

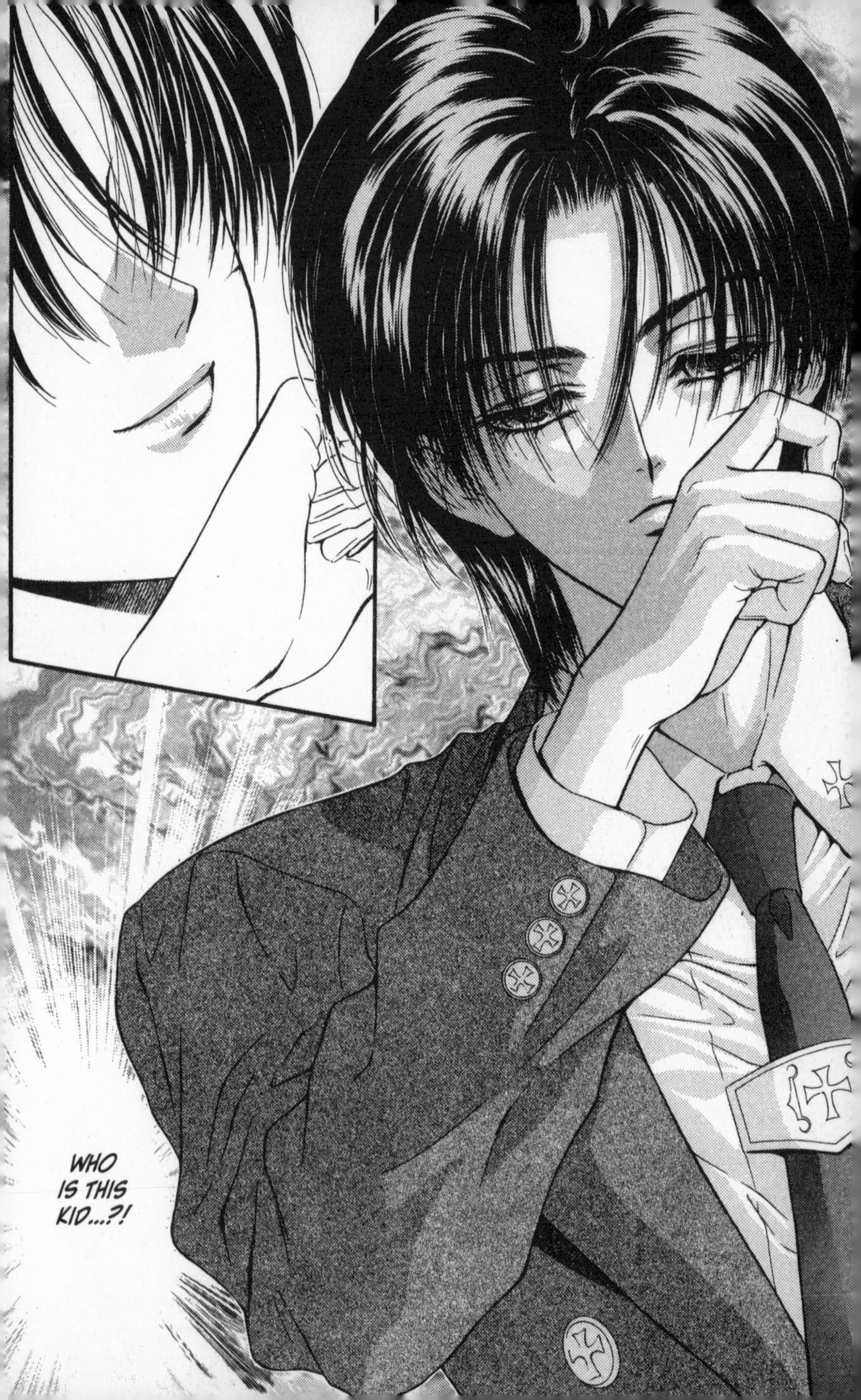
WHO IS THIS KID...?!

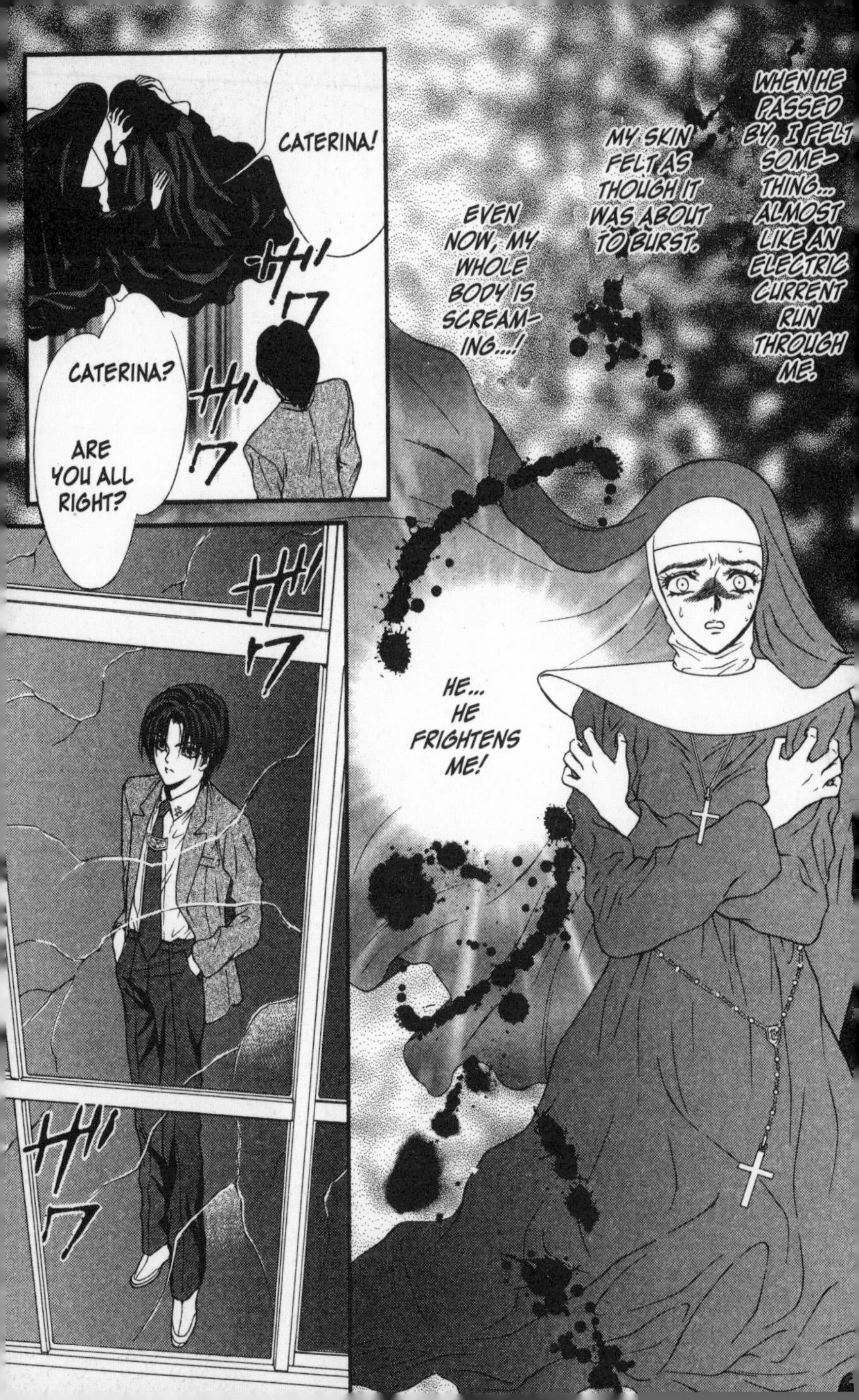
WHEN HE PASSED BY, I FELT SOMETHING... ALMOST LIKE AN ELECTRIC CURRENT RUN THROUGH ME.
MY SKIN FELT AS THOUGH IT WAS ABOUT TO BURST.
EVEN NOW, MY WHOLE BODY IS SCREAMING...!
HE... HE FRIGHTENS ME!
CATERINA!
CATERINA?
ARE YOU ALL RIGHT?

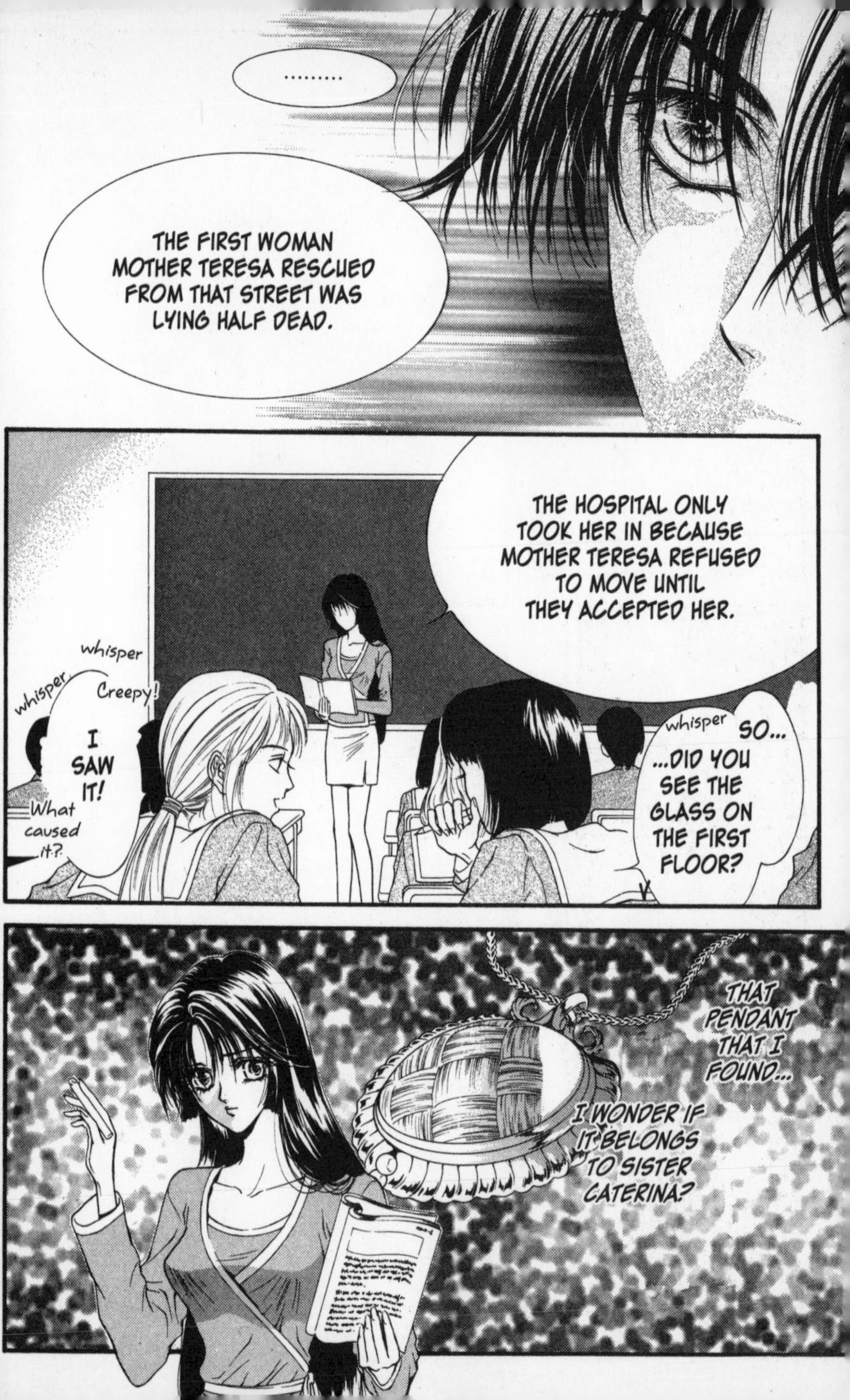
....
THE FIRST WOMAN MOTHER TERESA RESCUED FROM THAT STREET WAS LYING HALF DEAD.
THE HOSPITAL ONLY TOOK HER IN BECAUSE MOTHER TERESA REFUSED TO MOVE UNTIL THEY ACCEPTED HER.
whisper
SO...
...DID YOU SEE THE GLASS ON THE FIRST FLOOR?
whisper
Creepy!
whisper
I SAW IT!
What caused it?
THAT PENDANT THAT I FOUND...
I WONDER IF IT BELONGS TO SISTER CATERINA?

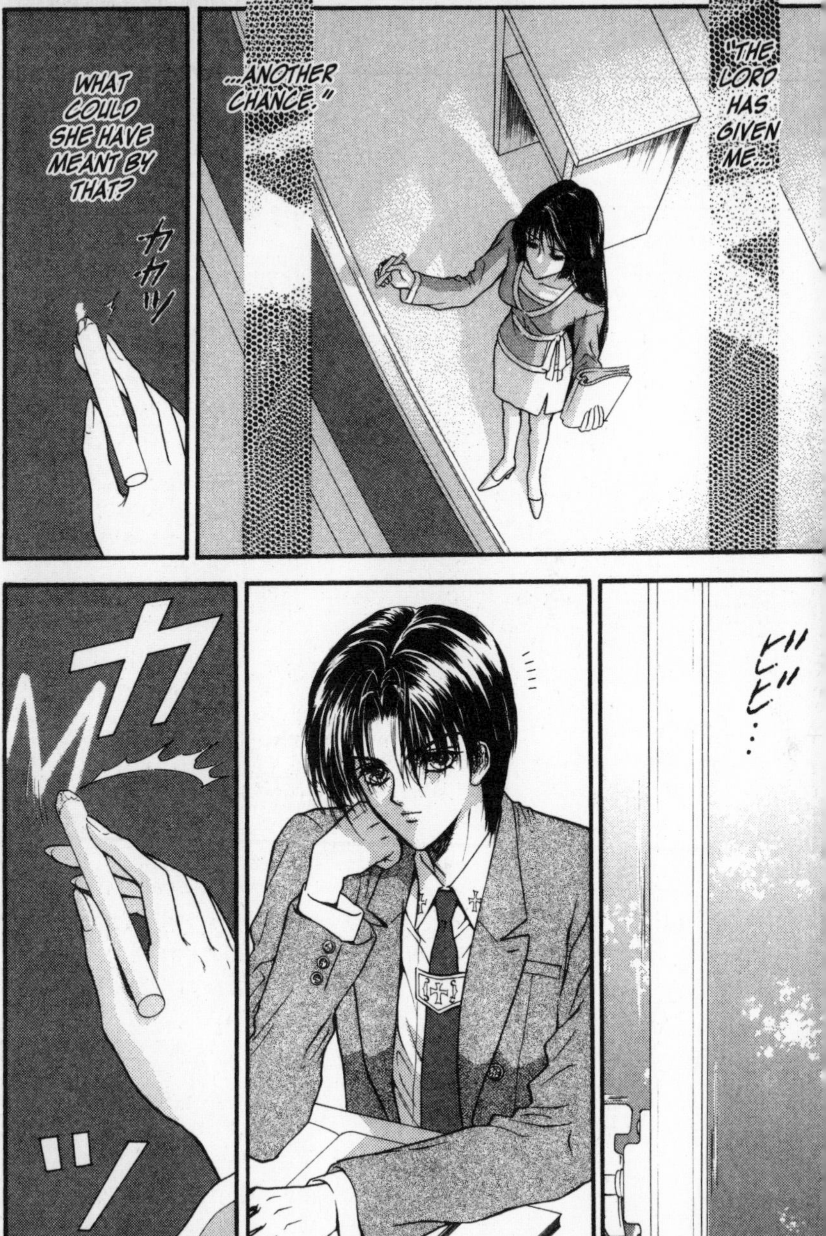

"THE LORD HAS GIVEN ME...
...ANOTHER CHANCE."
WHAT COULD SHE HAVE MEANT BY THAT?
カカッ
ビビビ…
カッ

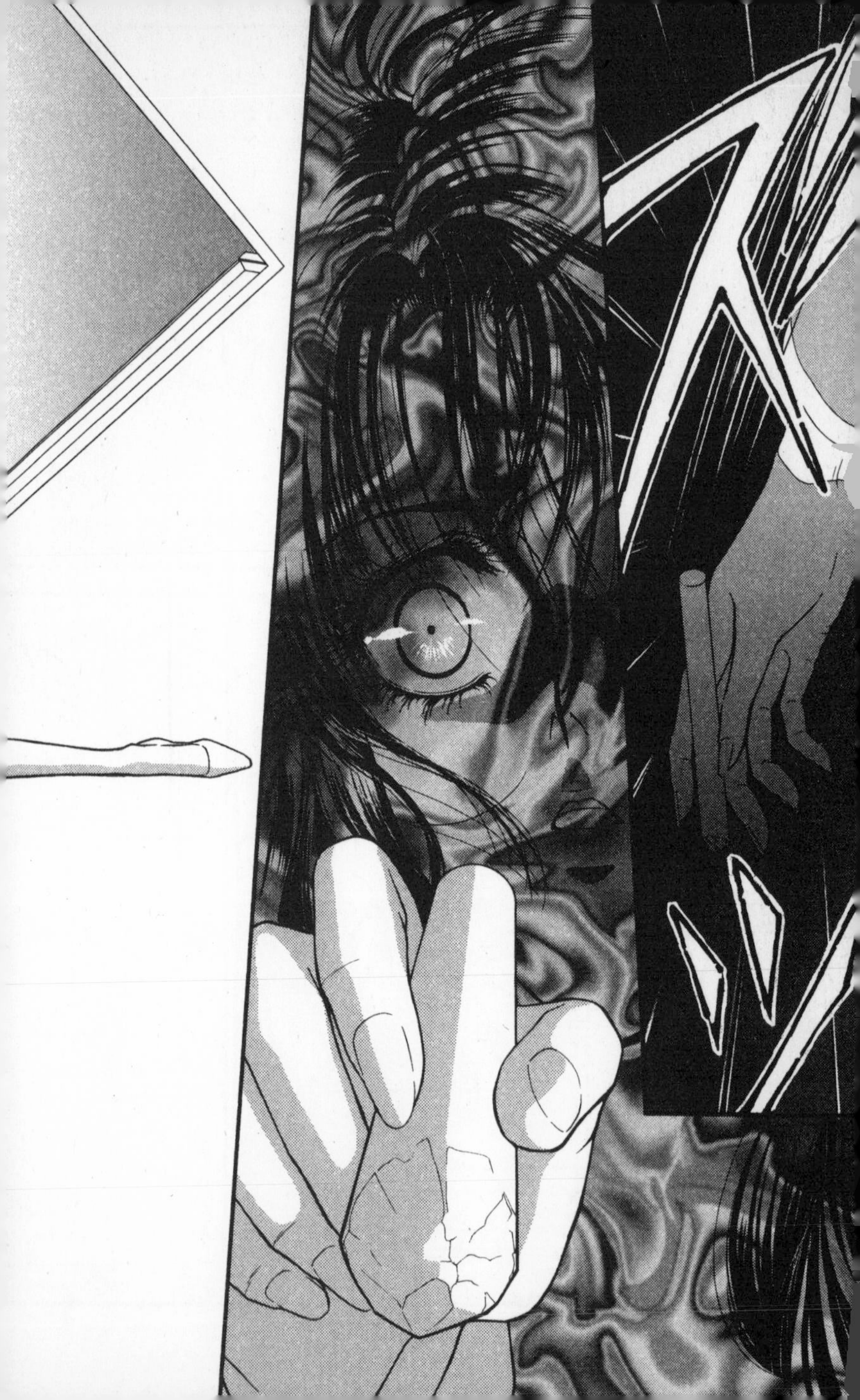

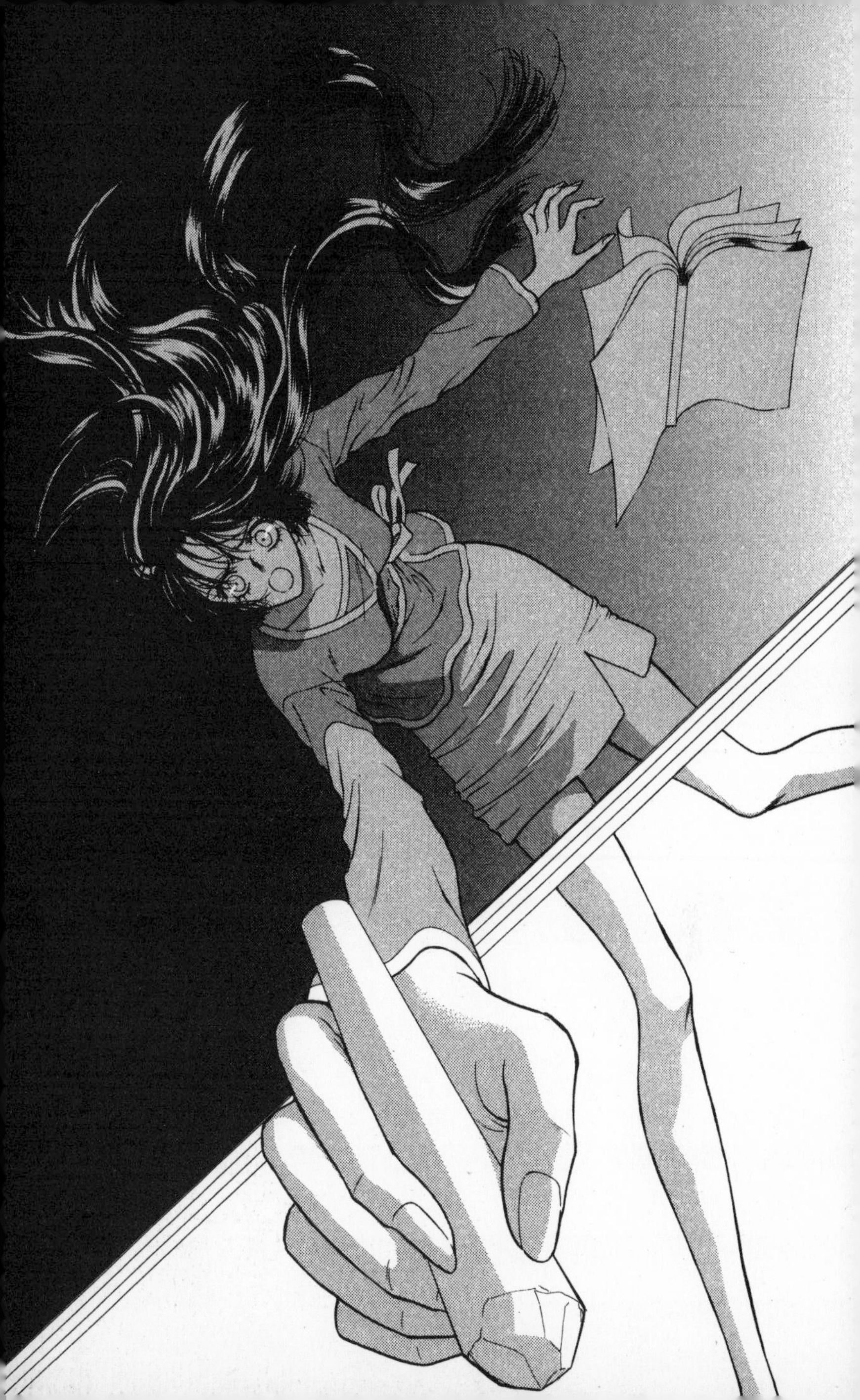

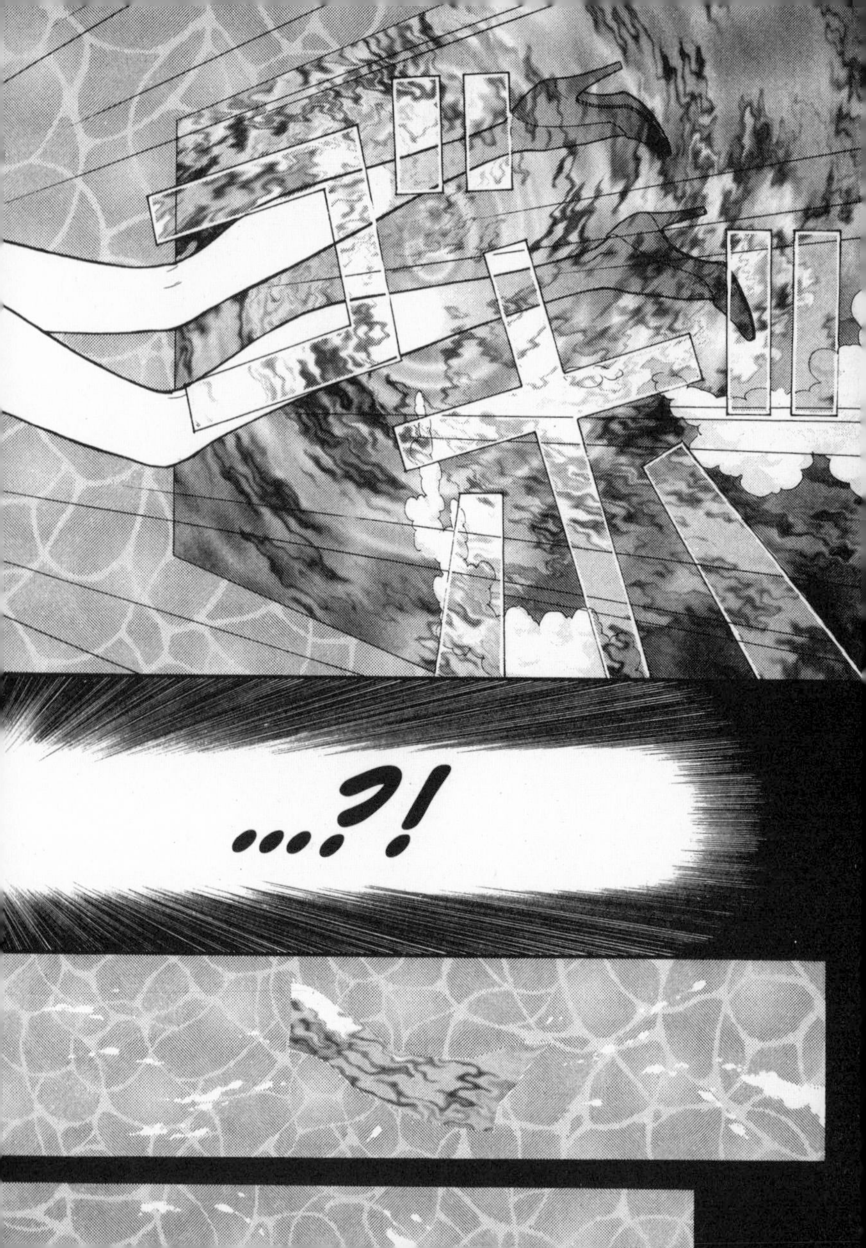
...?!

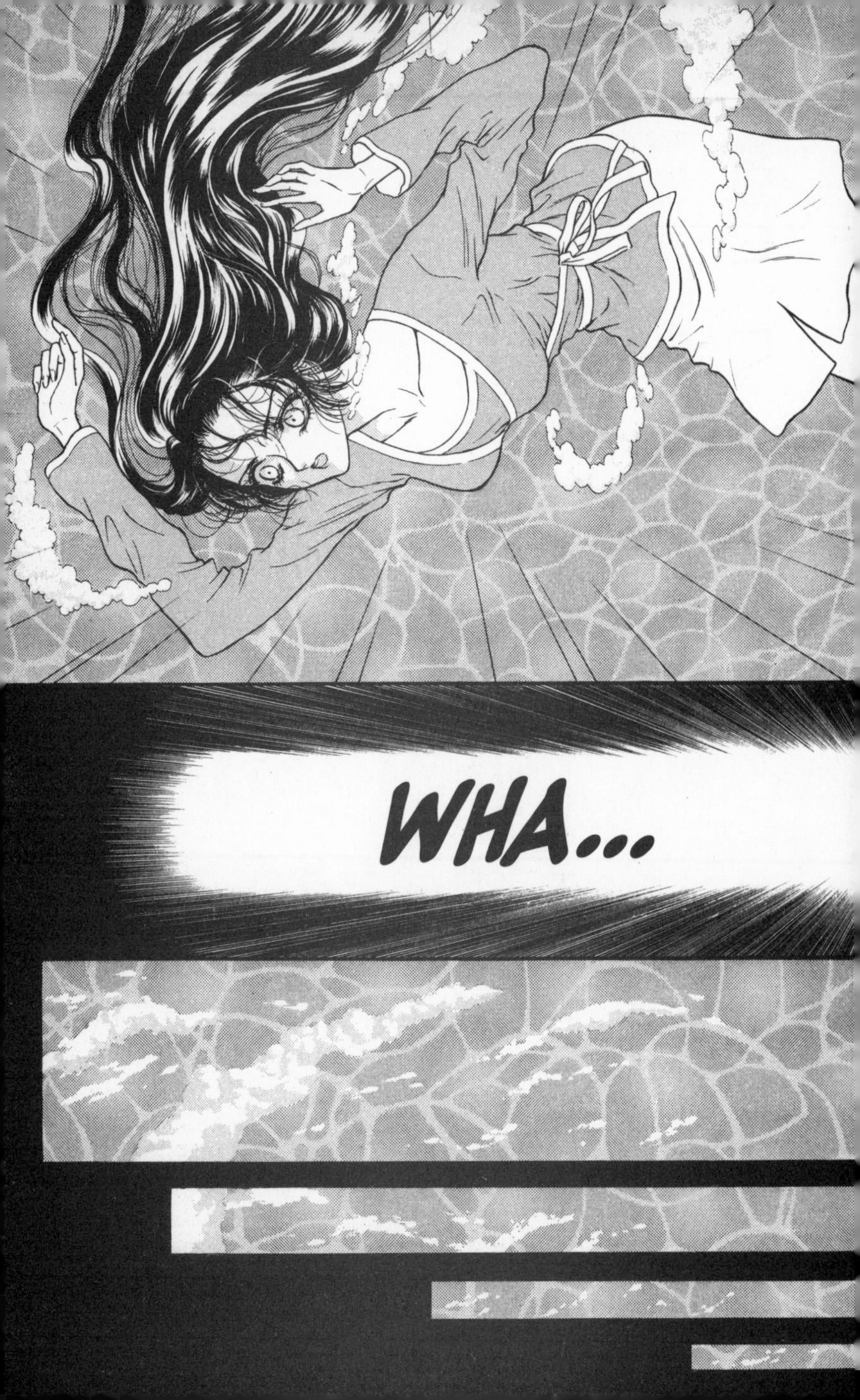
WHA...

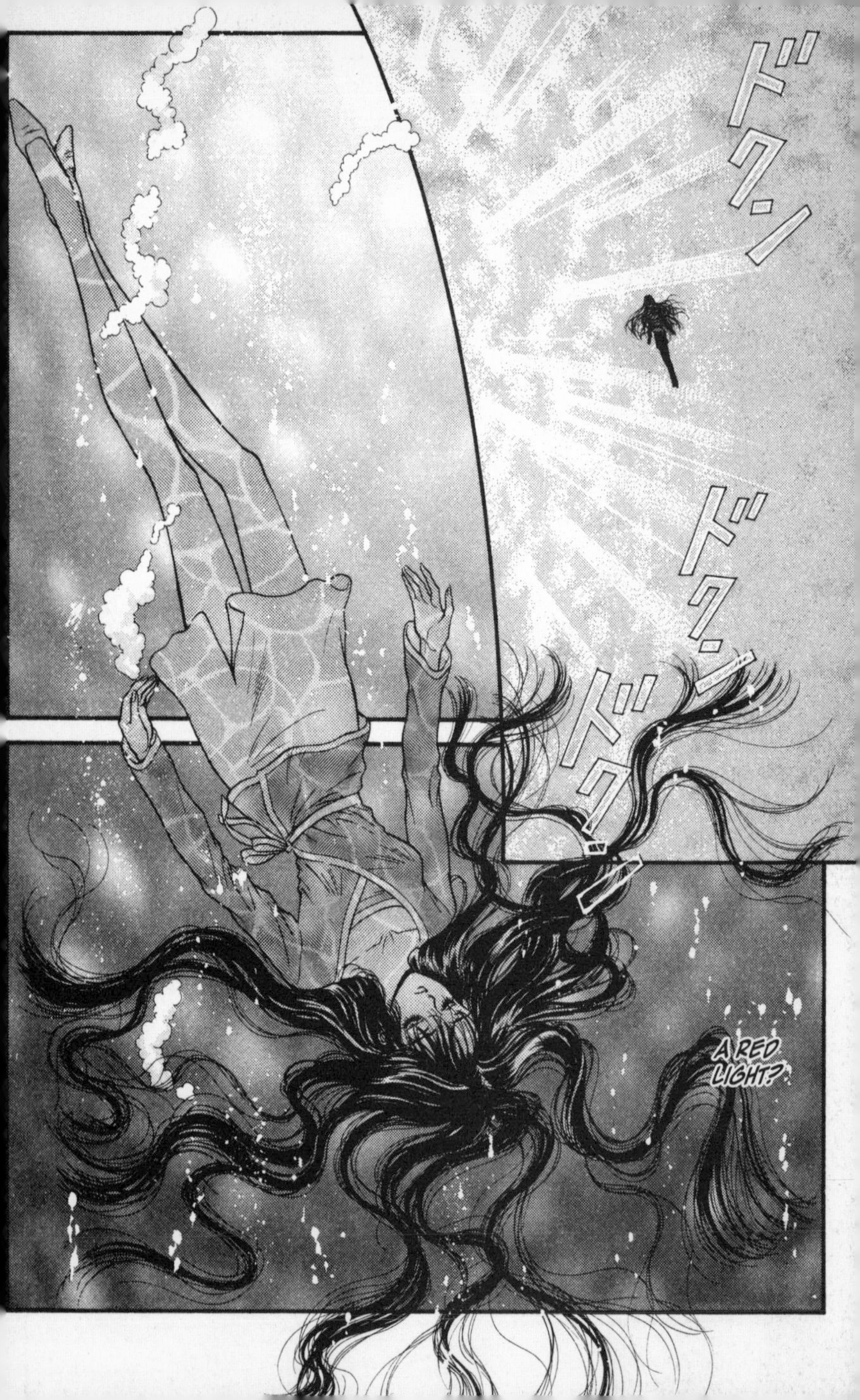
ドクン
ドクン
ドクン
A RED LIGHT?

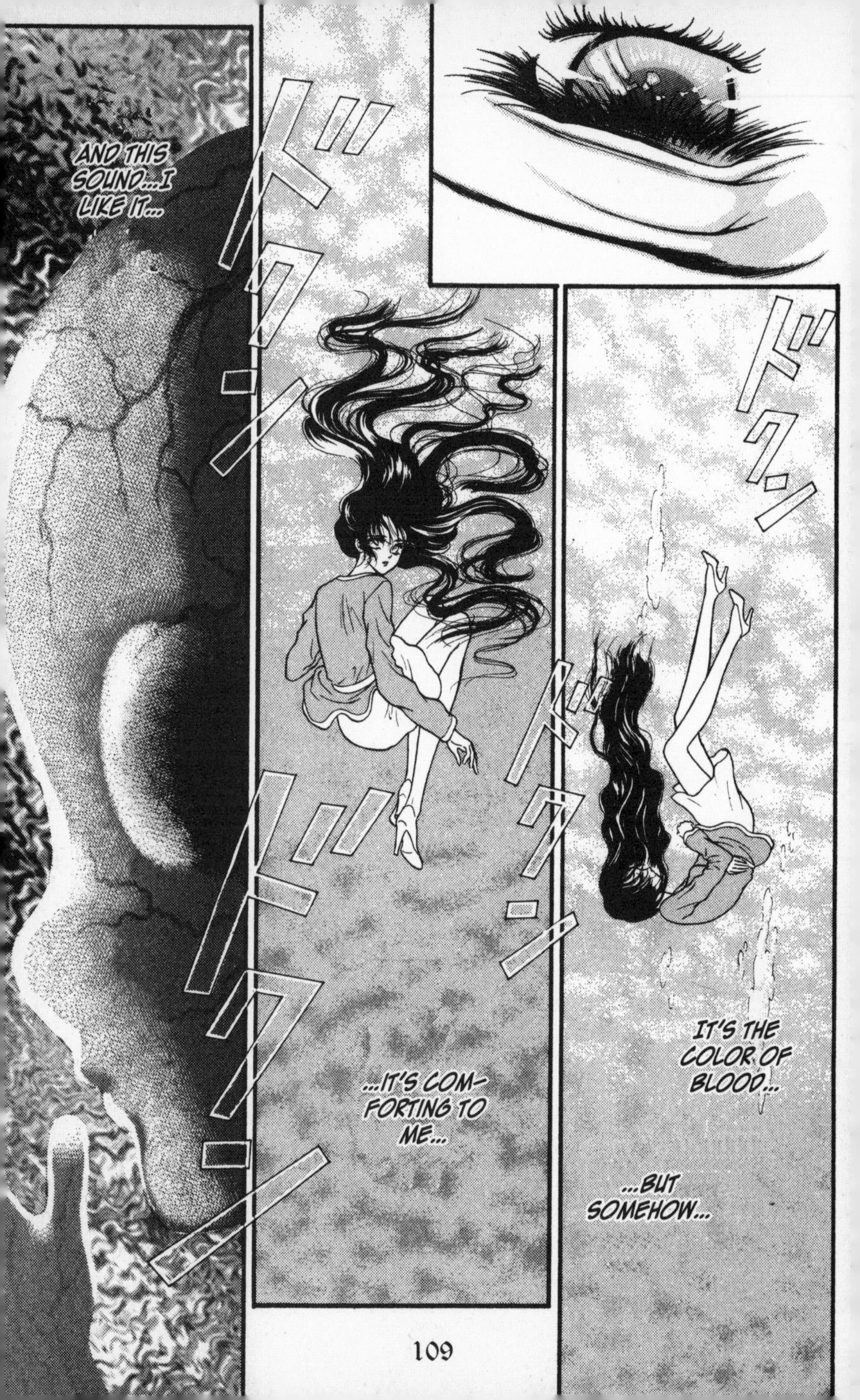
ドクン
IT'S THE COLOR OF BLOOD...
...BUT SOMEHOW...
ドクン
...IT'S COMFORTING TO ME...
ドクン
AND THIS SOUND...I LIKE IT...
ドクン

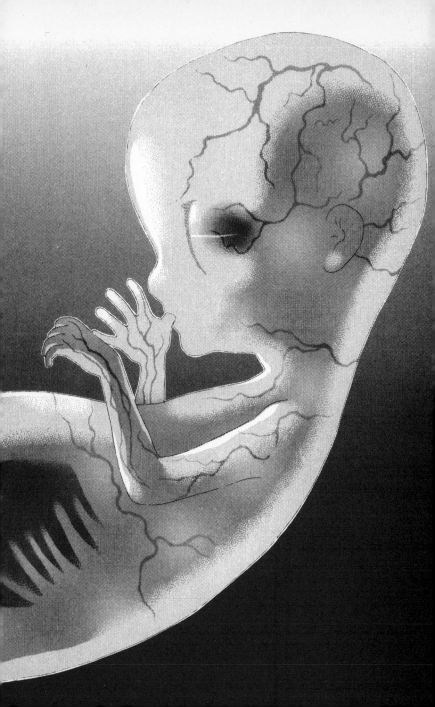

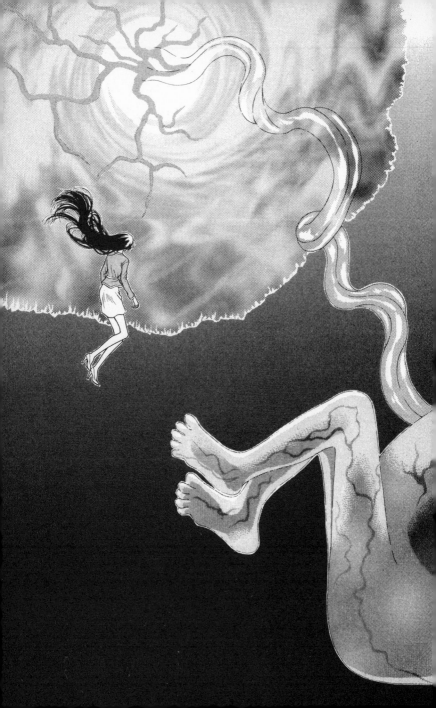

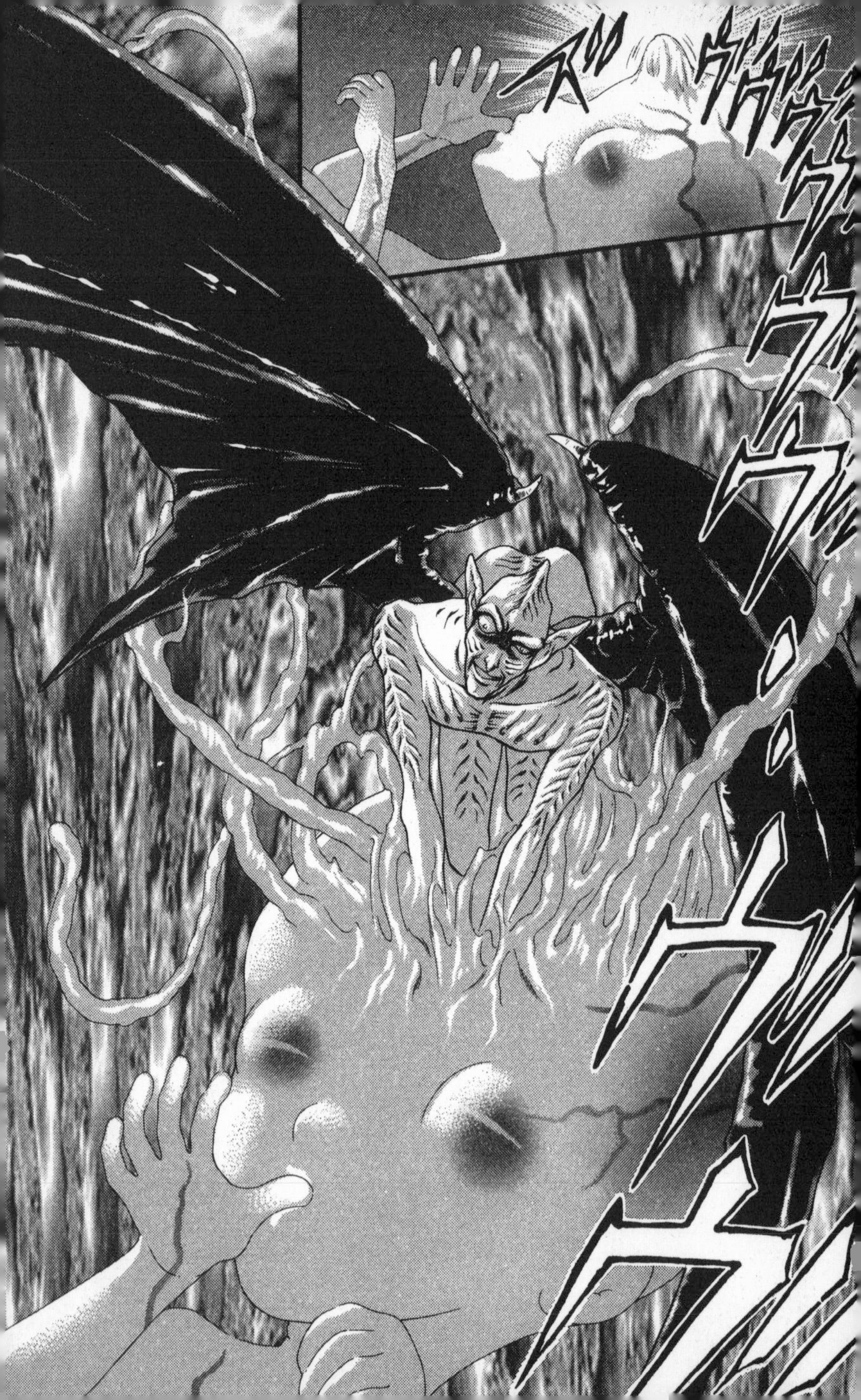

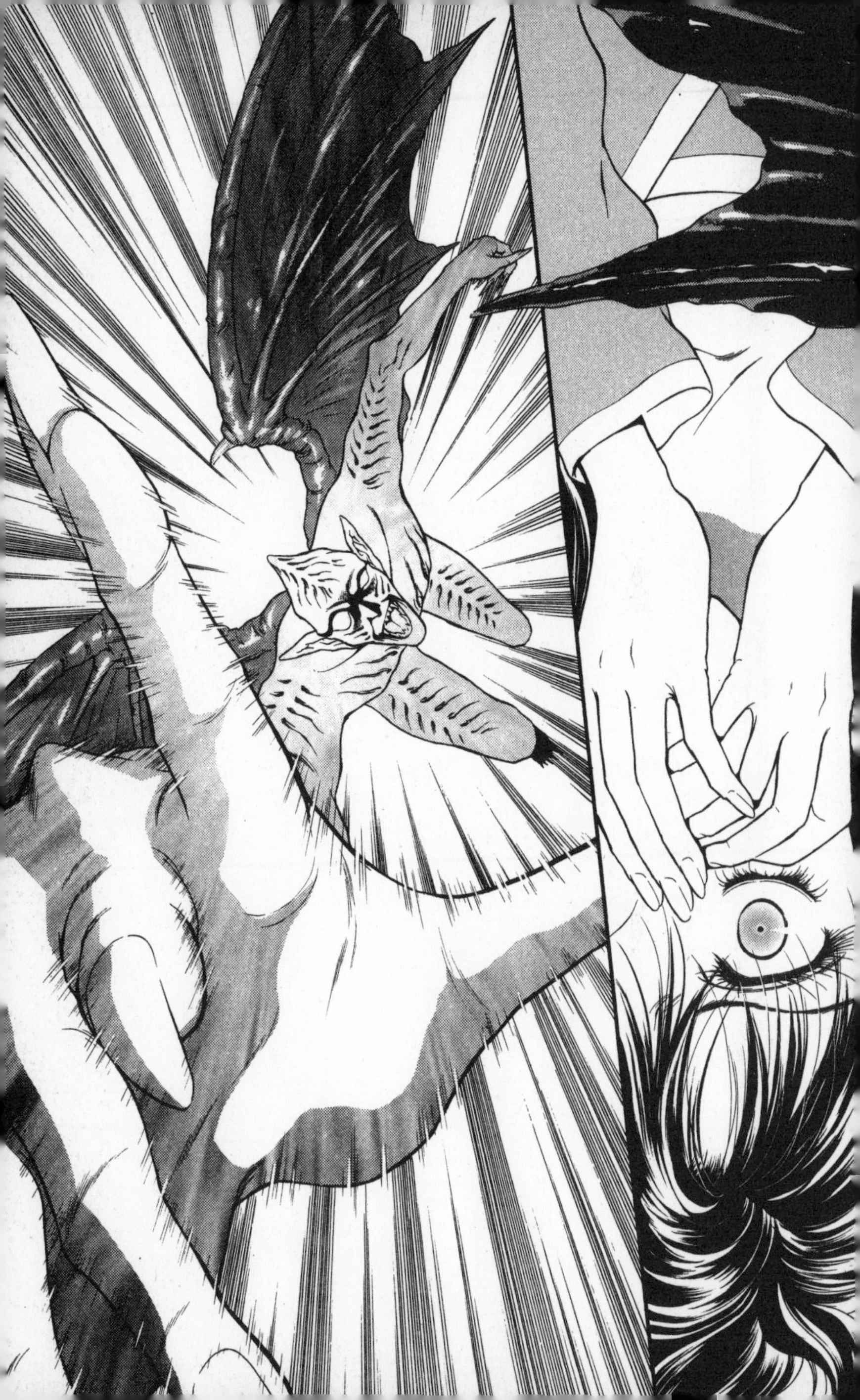

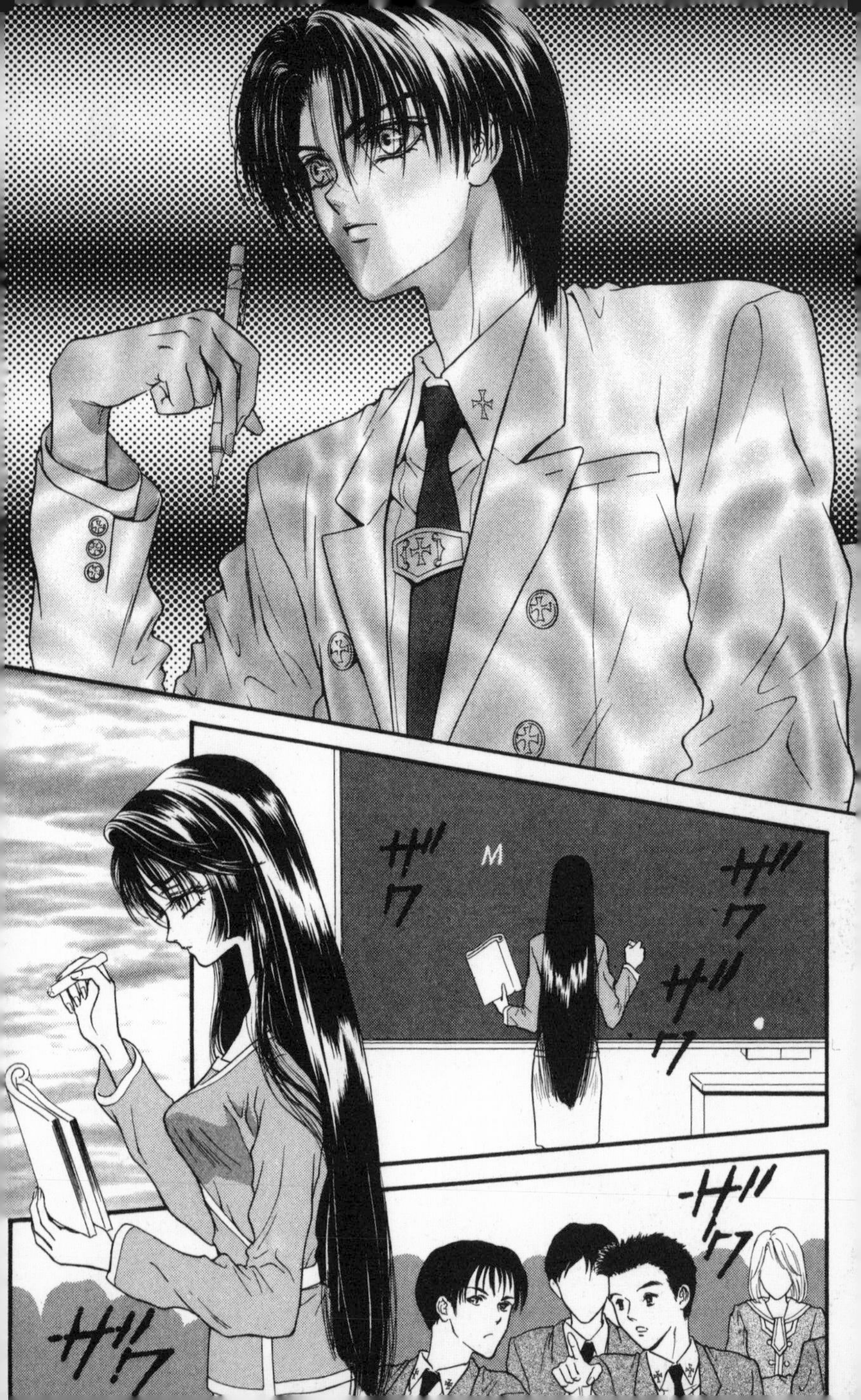
ザワ
ザワ
M
ザワ
ザワ
ザワ

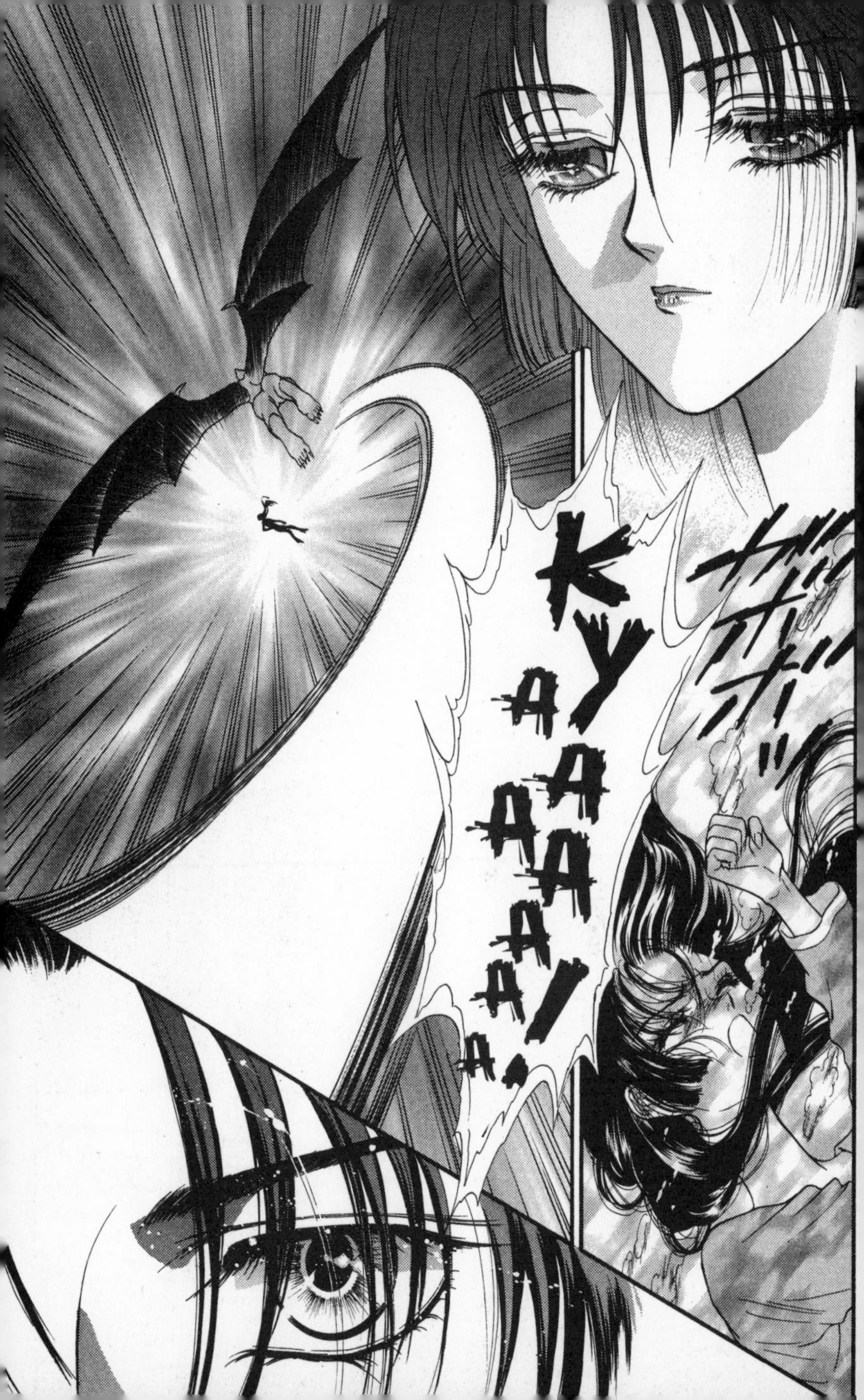
ガボォッ
KYAAAAAAA!

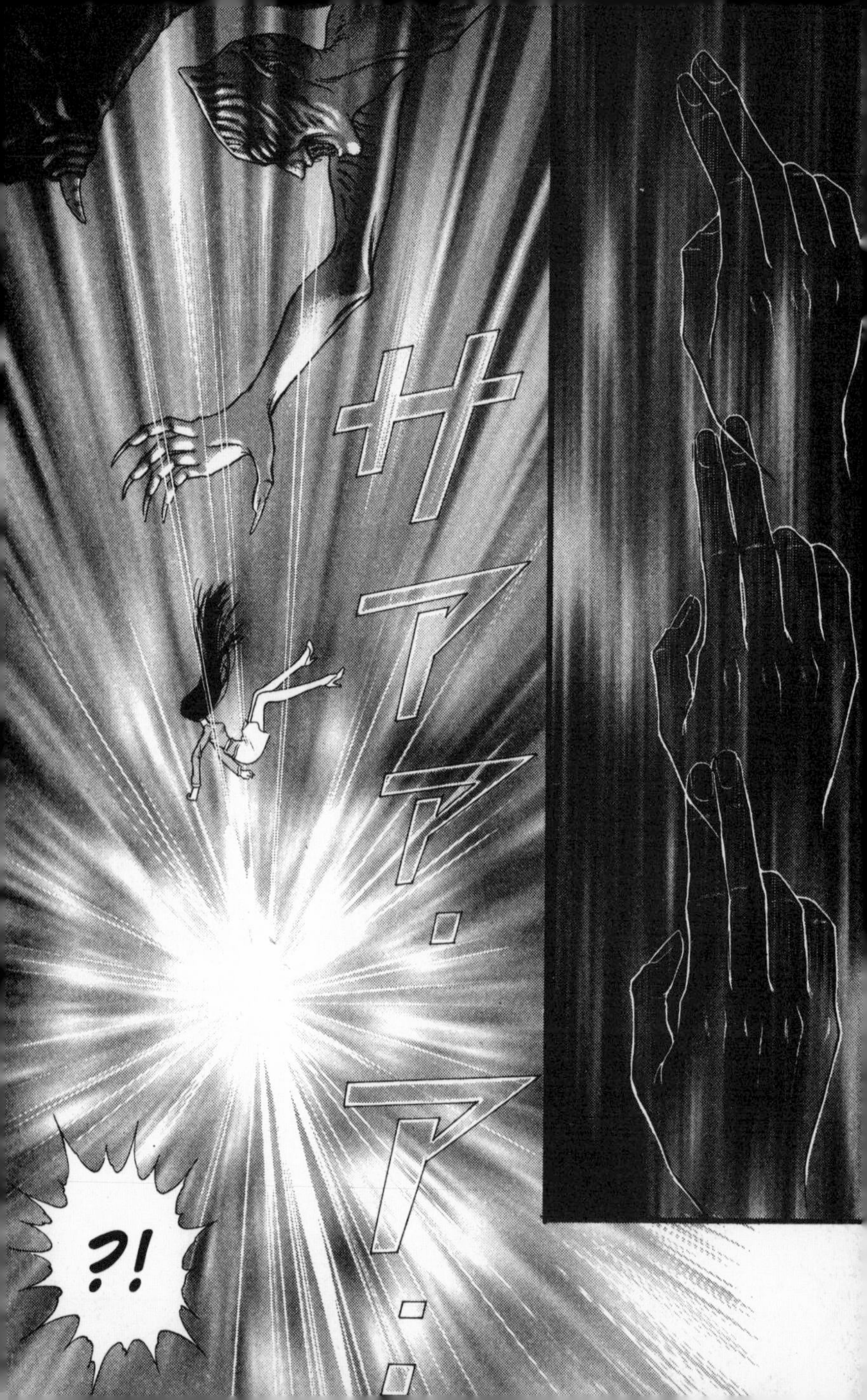
サアァ・ア・・
?!

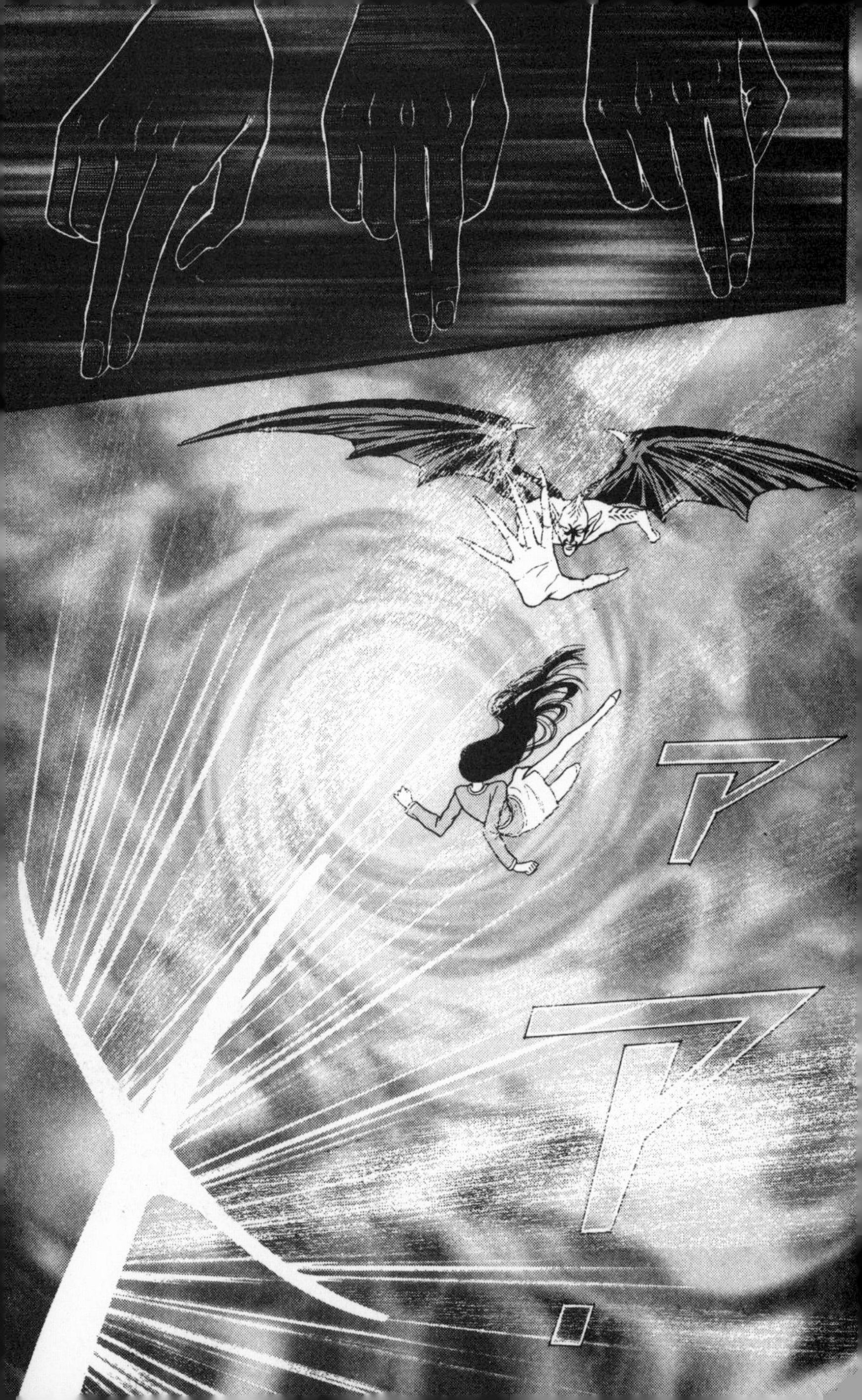
アア.

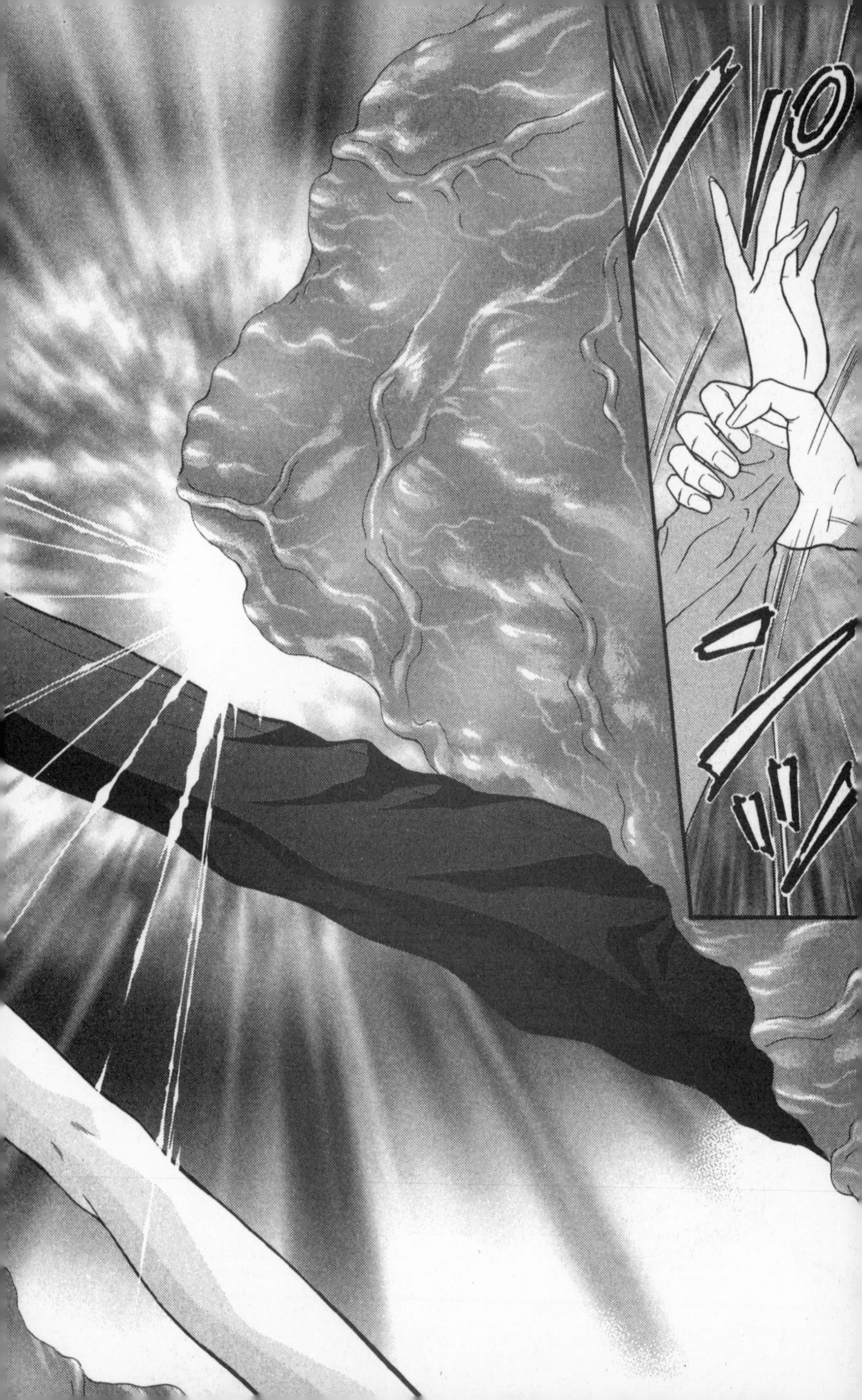

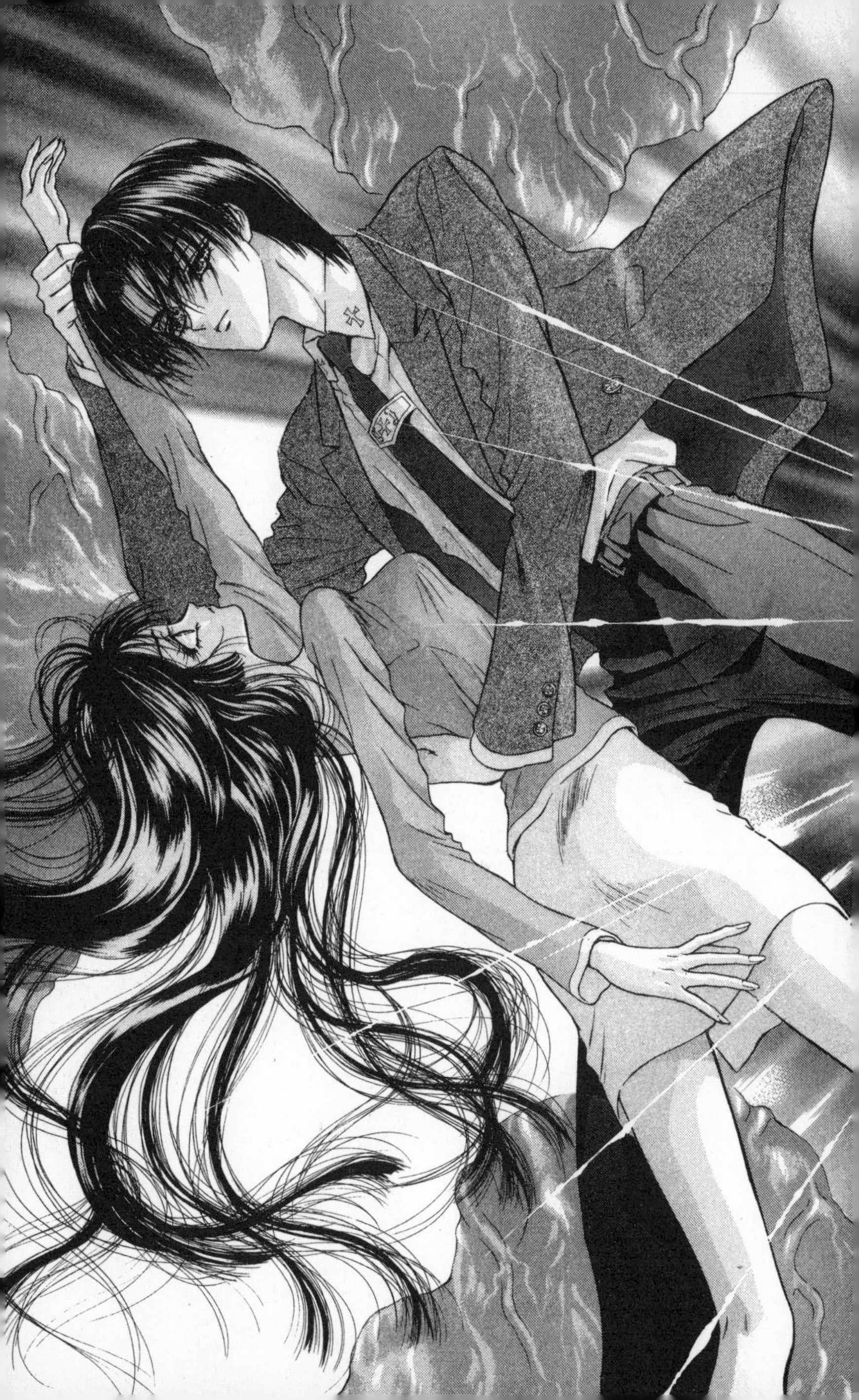

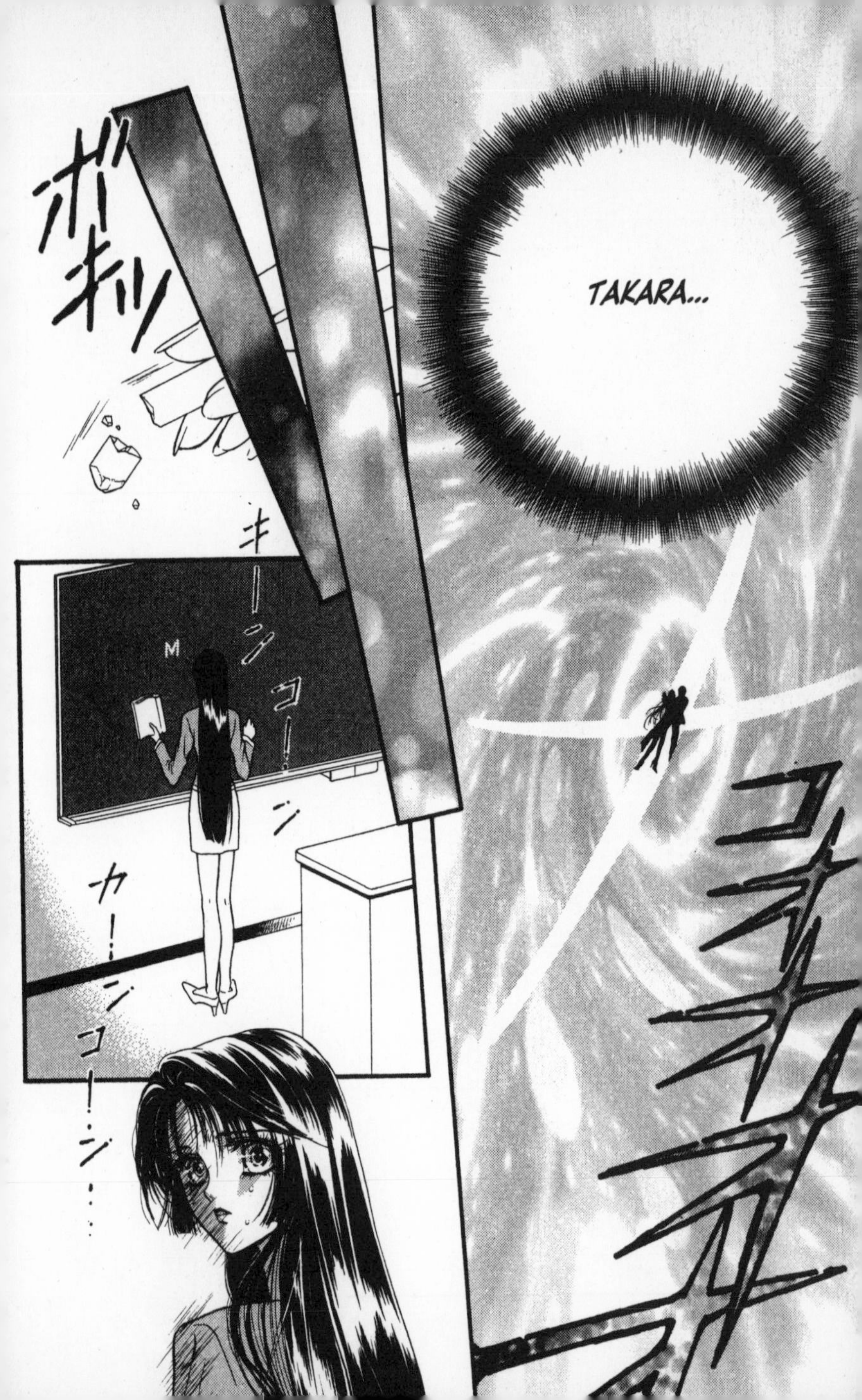
TAKARA...
ボキッ
キーンコーン
カーンコーン…

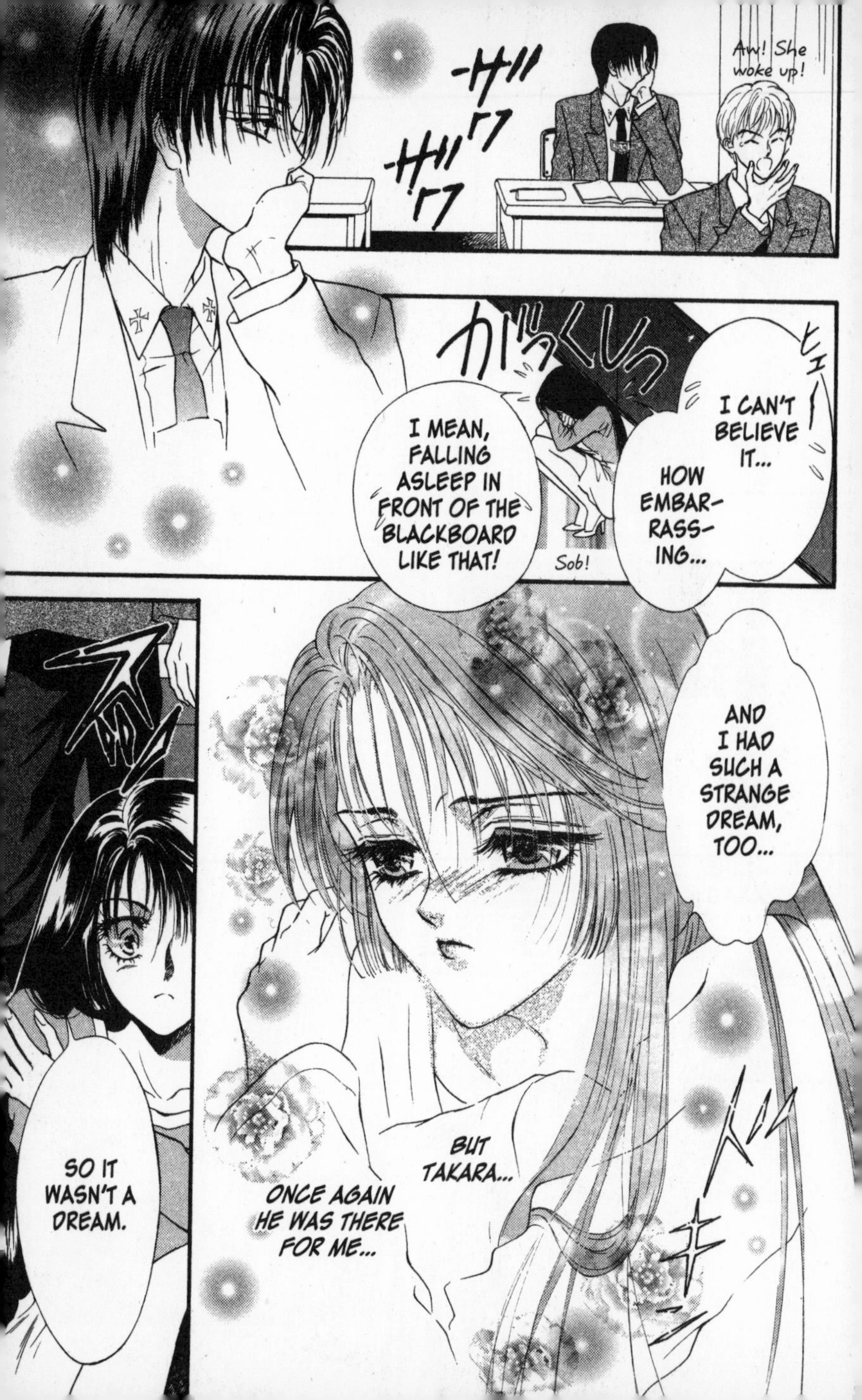
Aw! She woke up!
I CAN'T BELIEVE IT...
HOW EMBARRASSING...
I MEAN, FALLING ASLEEP IN FRONT OF THE BLACKBOARD LIKE THAT!
Sob!
AND I HAD SUCH A STRANGE DREAM, TOO...
BUT TAKARA...
ONCE AGAIN HE WAS THERE FOR ME...
SO IT WASN'T A DREAM.

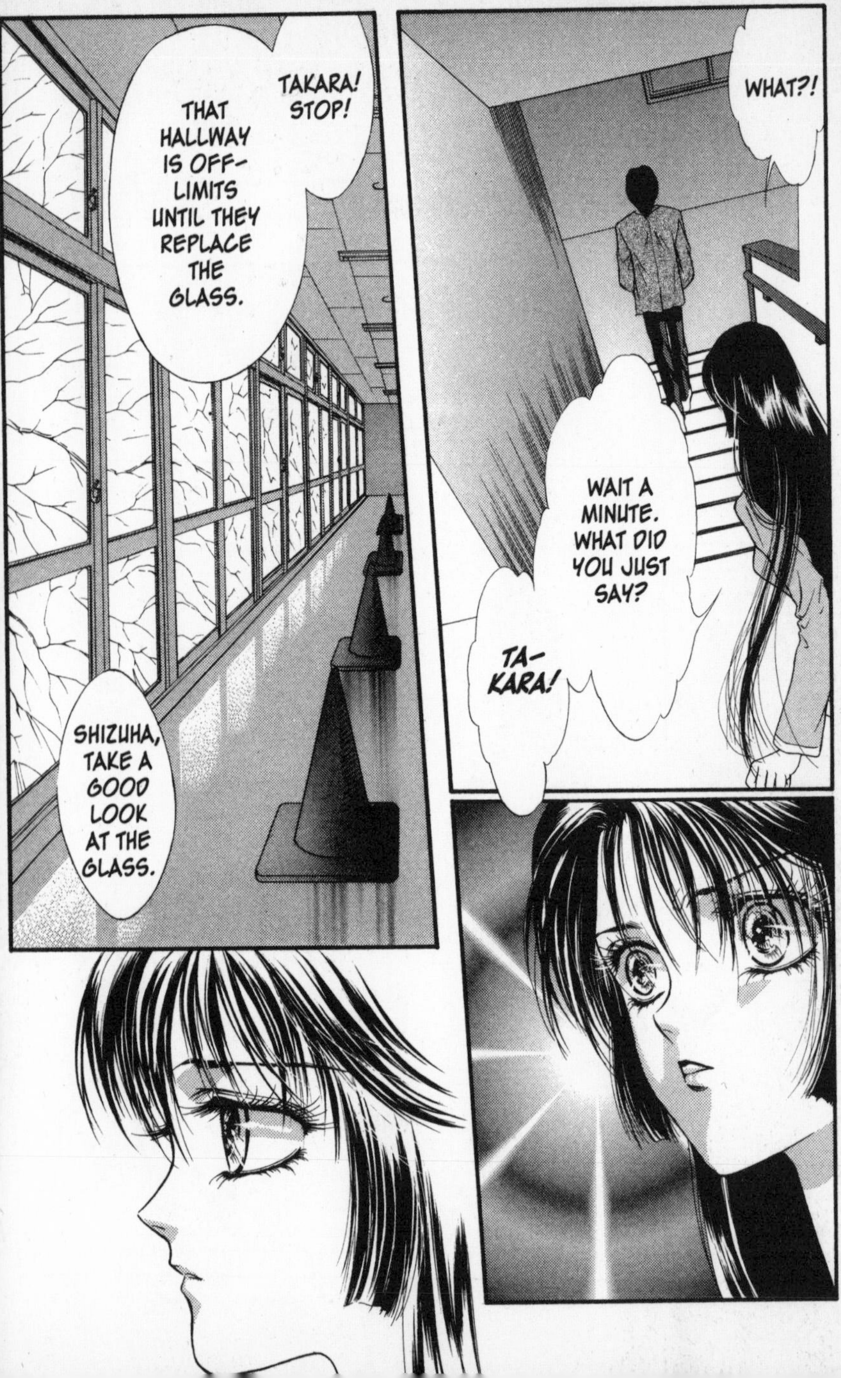
WHAT?!
WAIT A MINUTE. WHAT DID YOU JUST SAY?
TA-KARA!
TAKARA! STOP!
THAT HALLWAY IS OFF-LIMITS UNTIL THEY REPLACE THE GLASS.
SHIZUHA, TAKE A GOOD LOOK AT THE GLASS.

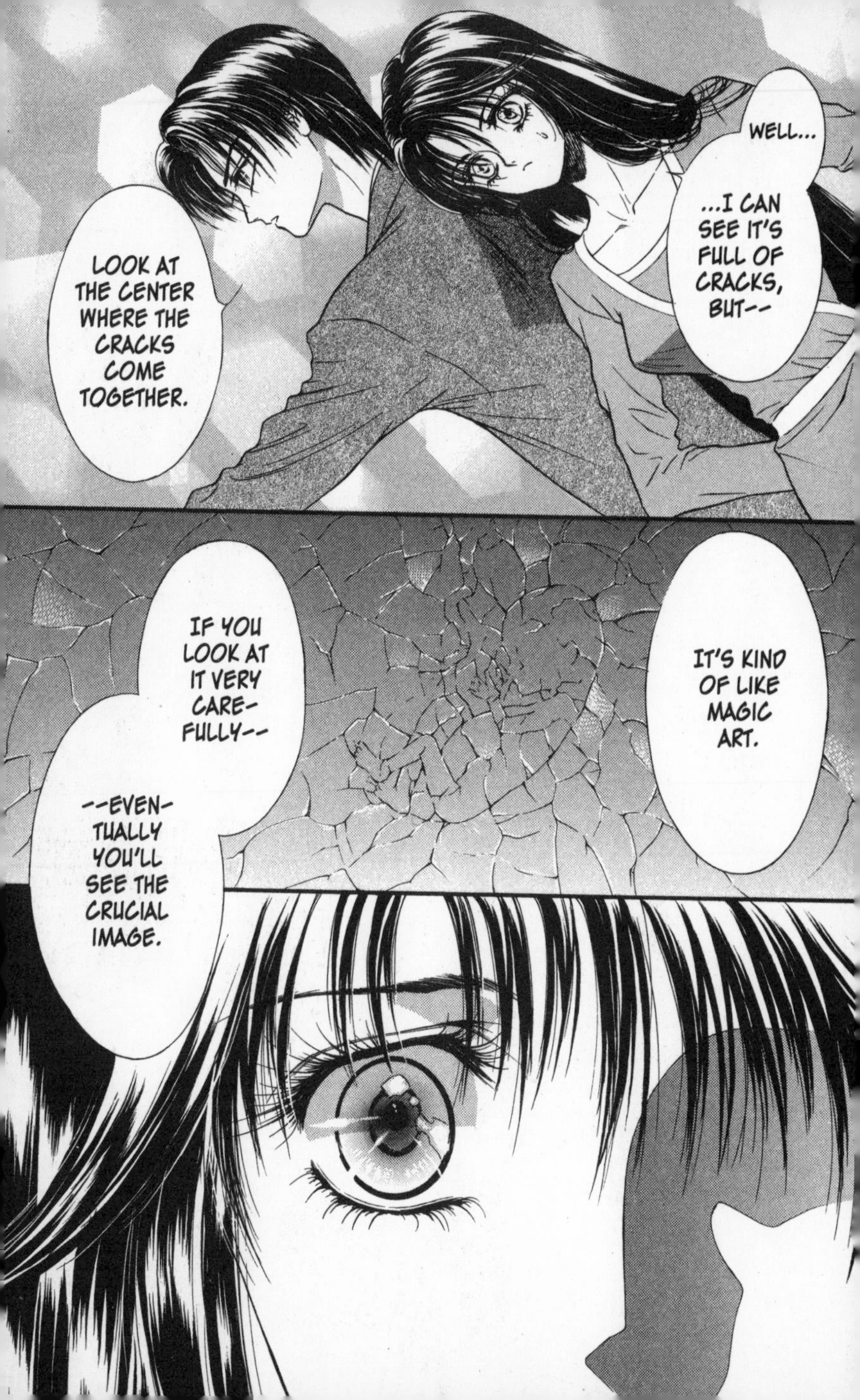
WELL...
...I CAN SEE IT'S FULL OF CRACKS, BUT--
LOOK AT THE CENTER WHERE THE CRACKS COME TOGETHER.
IT'S KIND OF LIKE MAGIC ART.
IF YOU LOOK AT IT VERY CARE-FULLY--
--EVEN-TUALLY YOU'LL SEE THE CRUCIAL IMAGE.

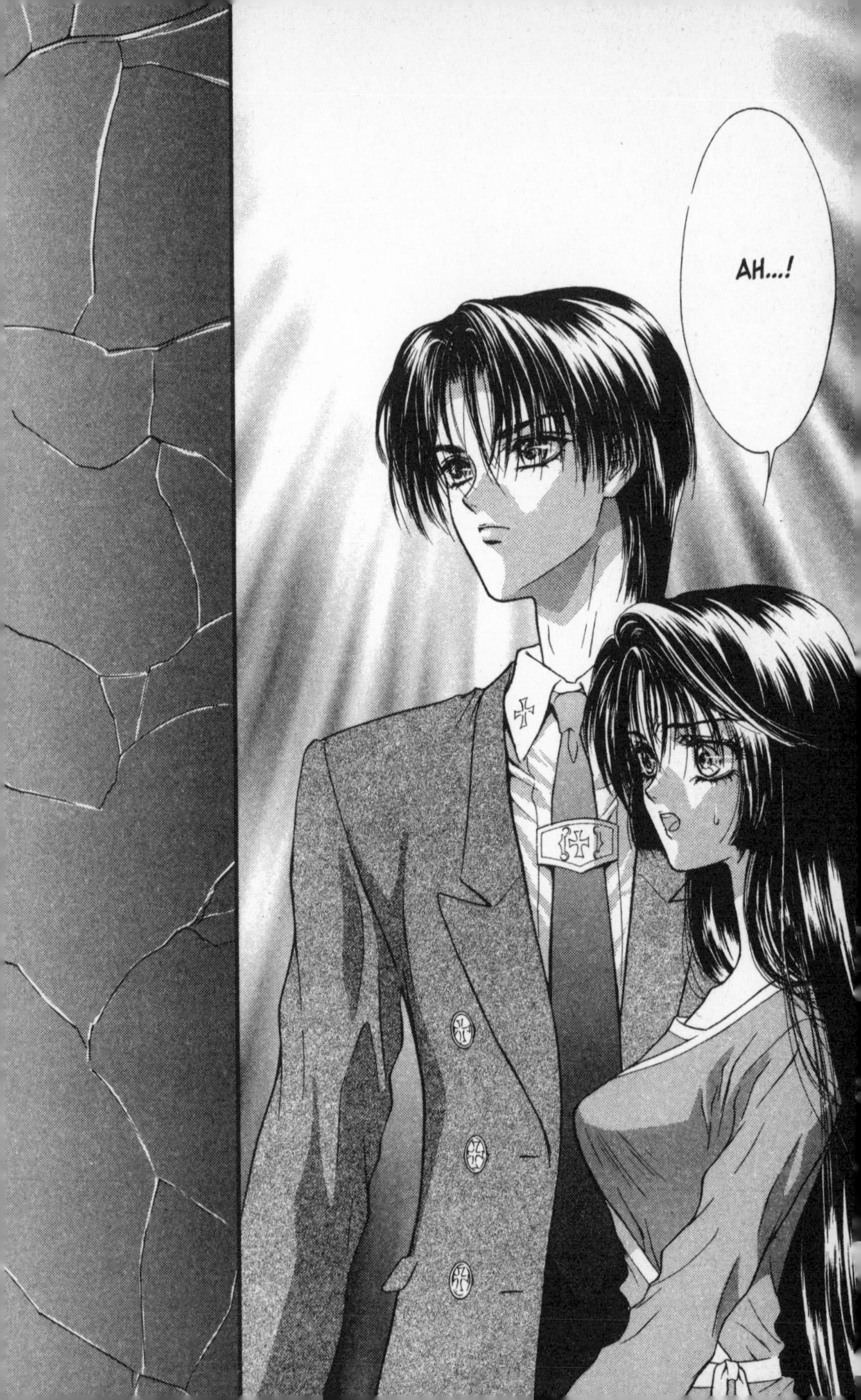
AH...!

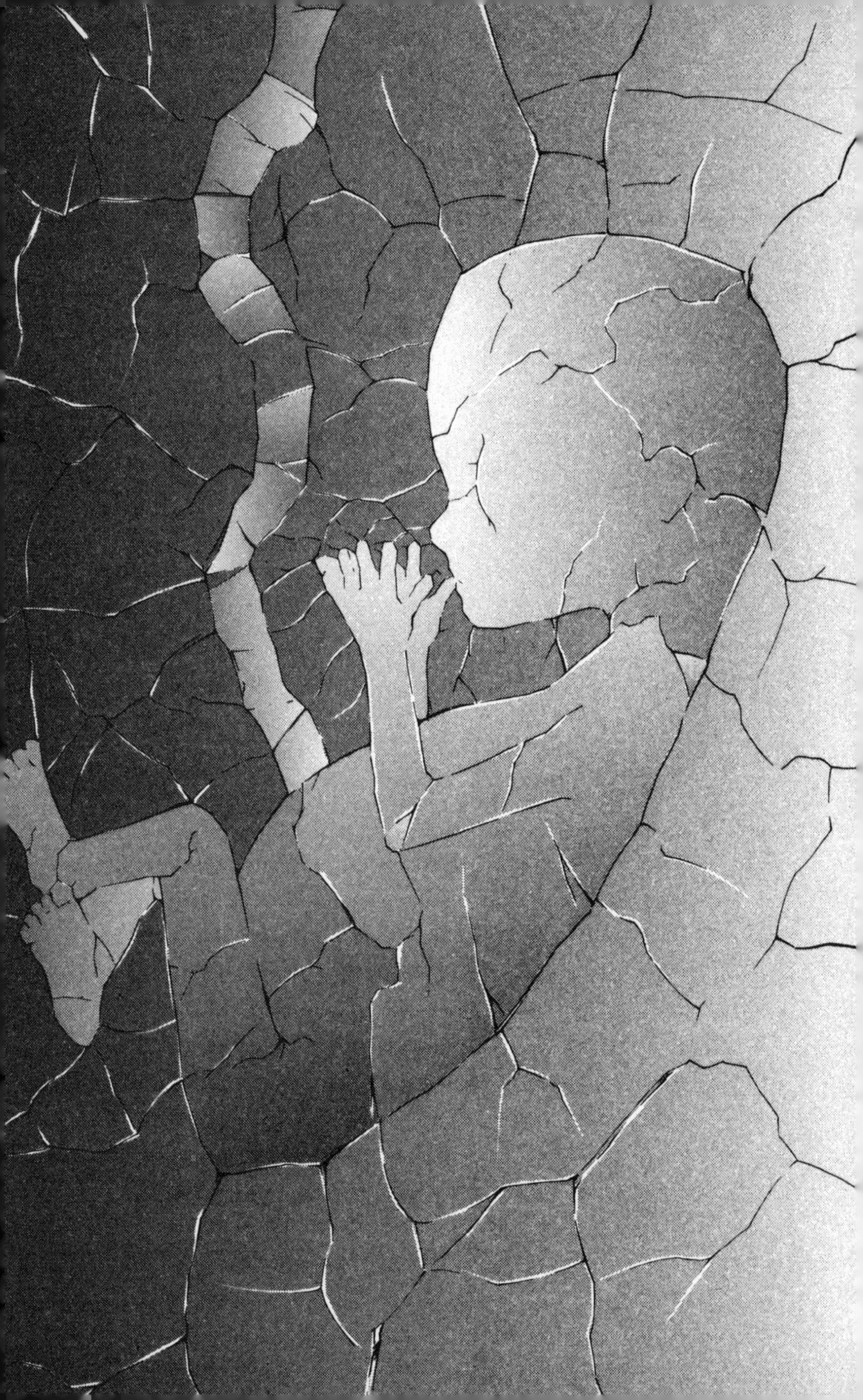

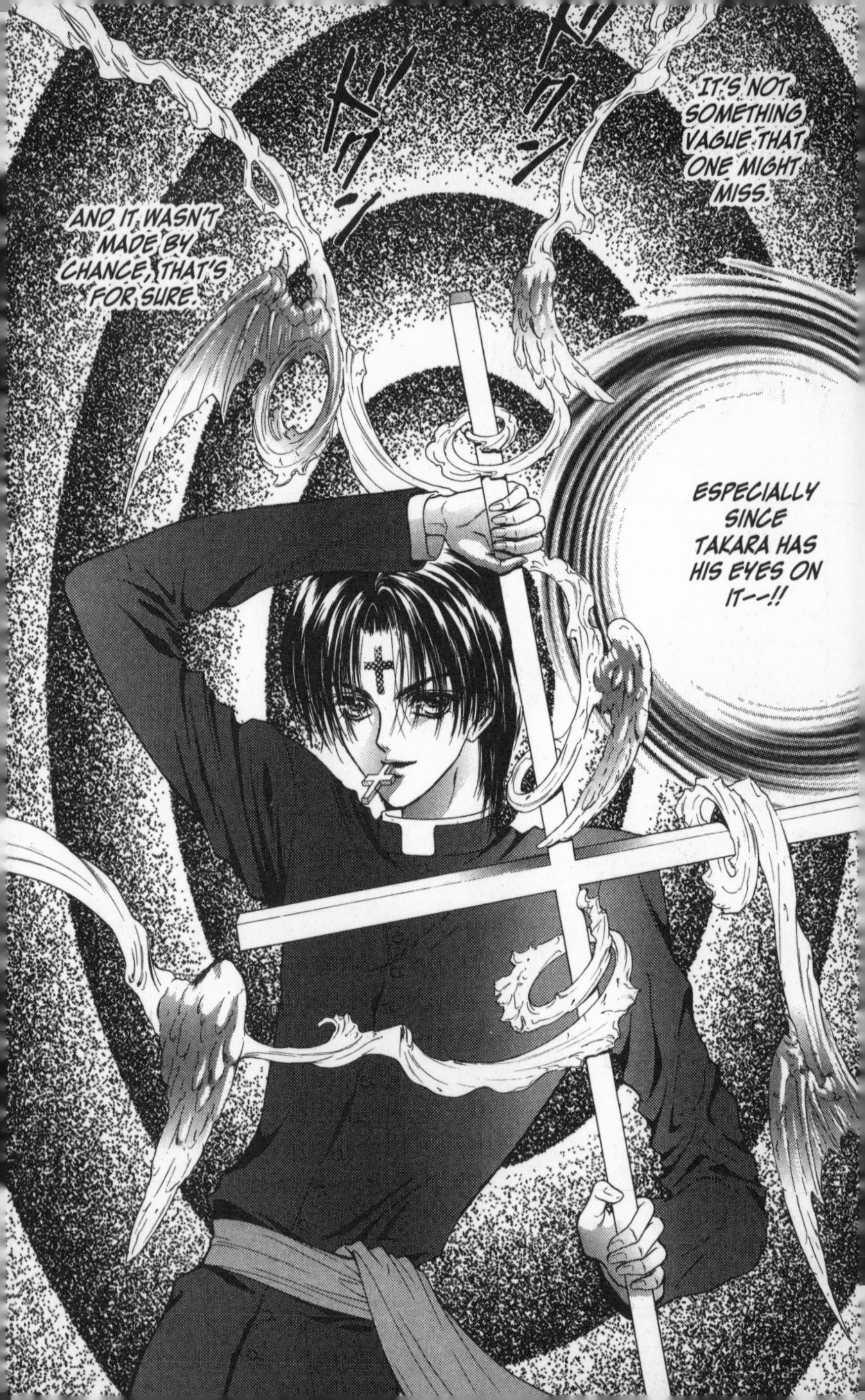
IT'S NOT SOMETHING VAGUE THAT ONE MIGHT MISS.
AND IT WASN'T MADE BY CHANCE, THAT'S FOR SURE.
ESPECIALLY SINCE TAKARA HAS HIS EYES ON IT--!!

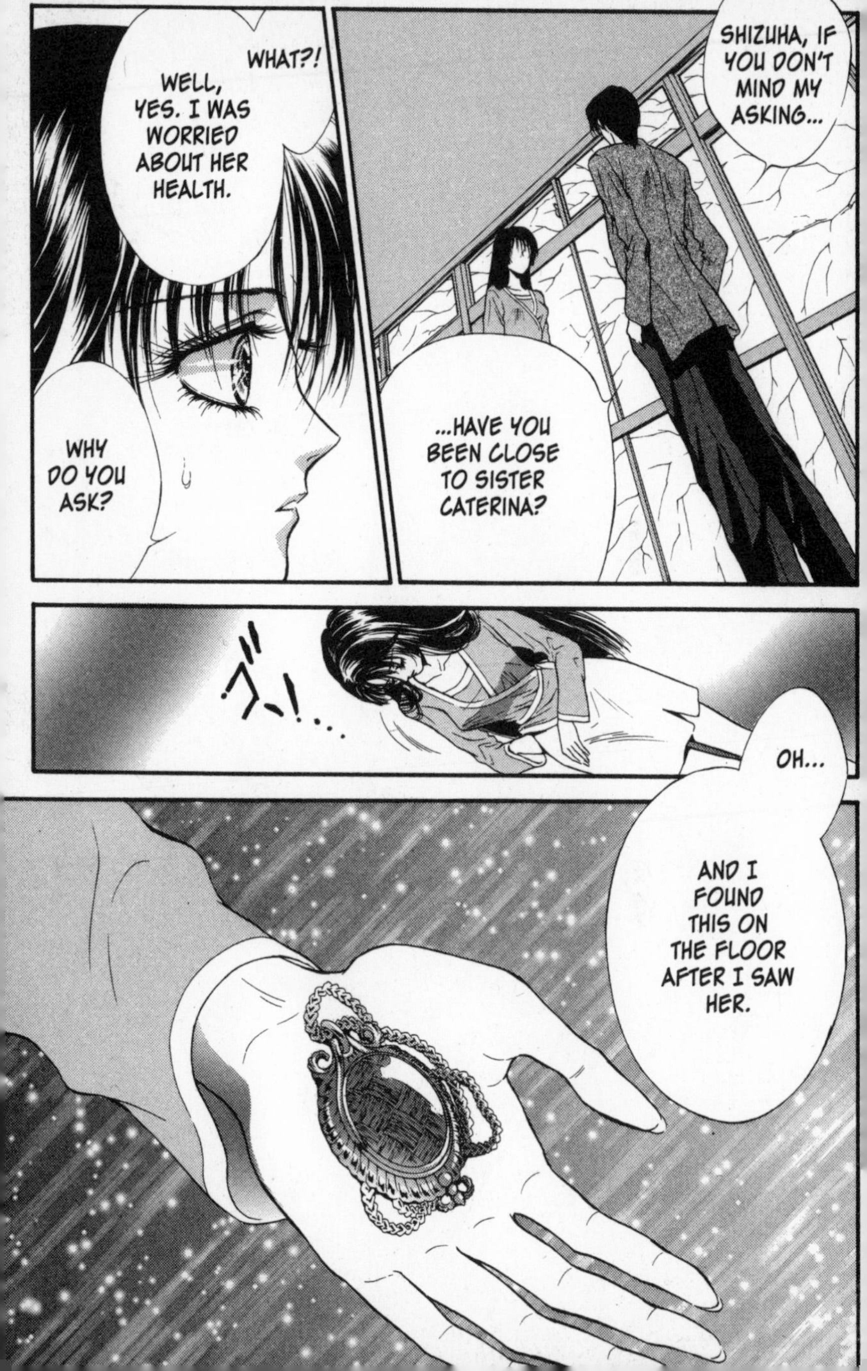
SHIZUHA, IF YOU DON'T MIND MY ASKING...
...HAVE YOU BEEN CLOSE TO SISTER CATERINA?
WHAT?!
WELL, YES. I WAS WORRIED ABOUT HER HEALTH.
WHY DO YOU ASK?
ズ!...
OH...
AND I FOUND THIS ON THE FLOOR AFTER I SAW HER.

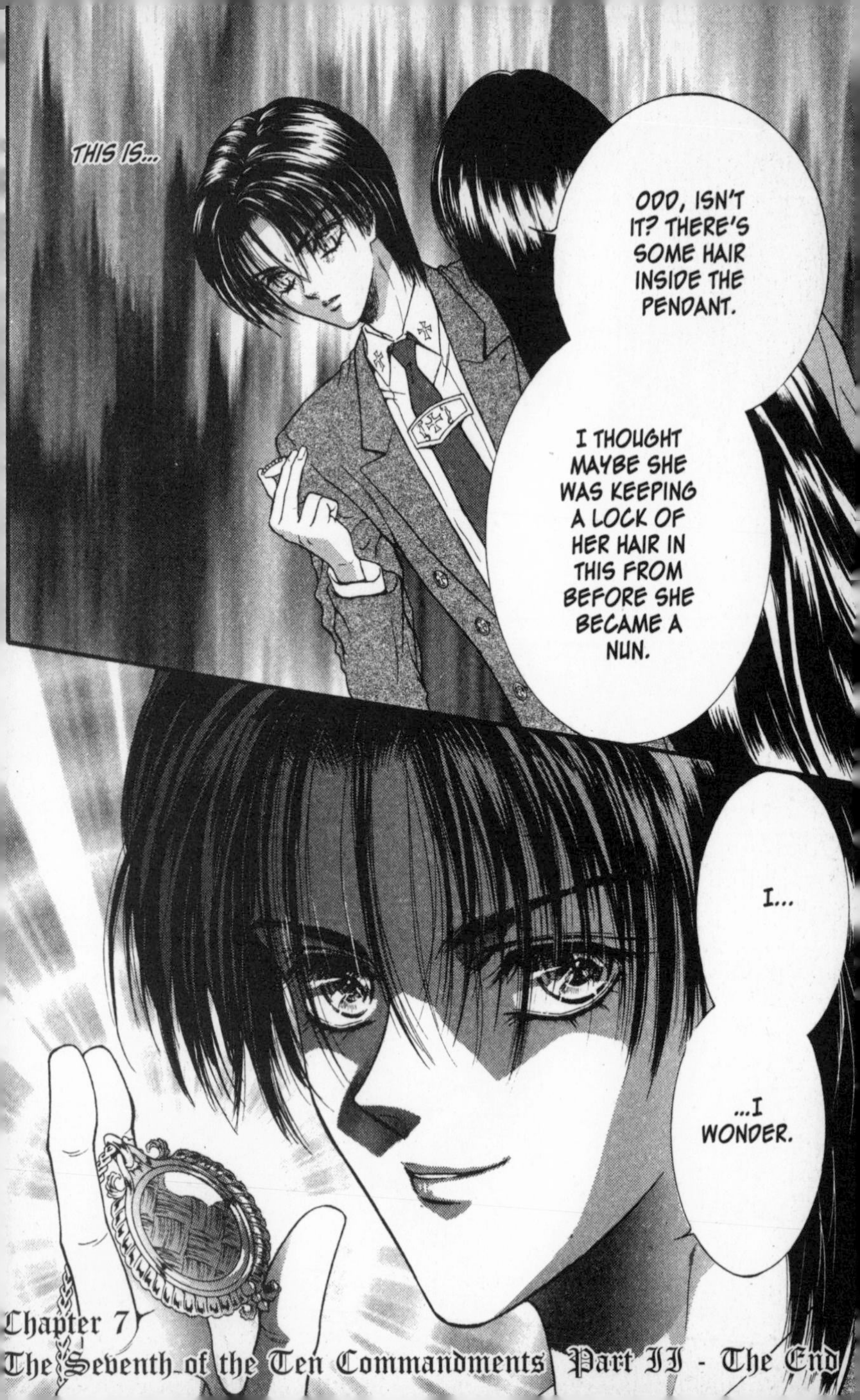
THIS IS...
ODD, ISN'T IT? THERE'S SOME HAIR INSIDE THE PENDANT.
I THOUGHT MAYBE SHE WAS KEEPING A LOCK OF HER HAIR IN THIS FROM BEFORE SHE BECAME A NUN.
I...
...I WONDER.
Chapter 7
The Seventh of the Ten Commandments Part II - The End

The Seventh of the Ten Commandments
Part III

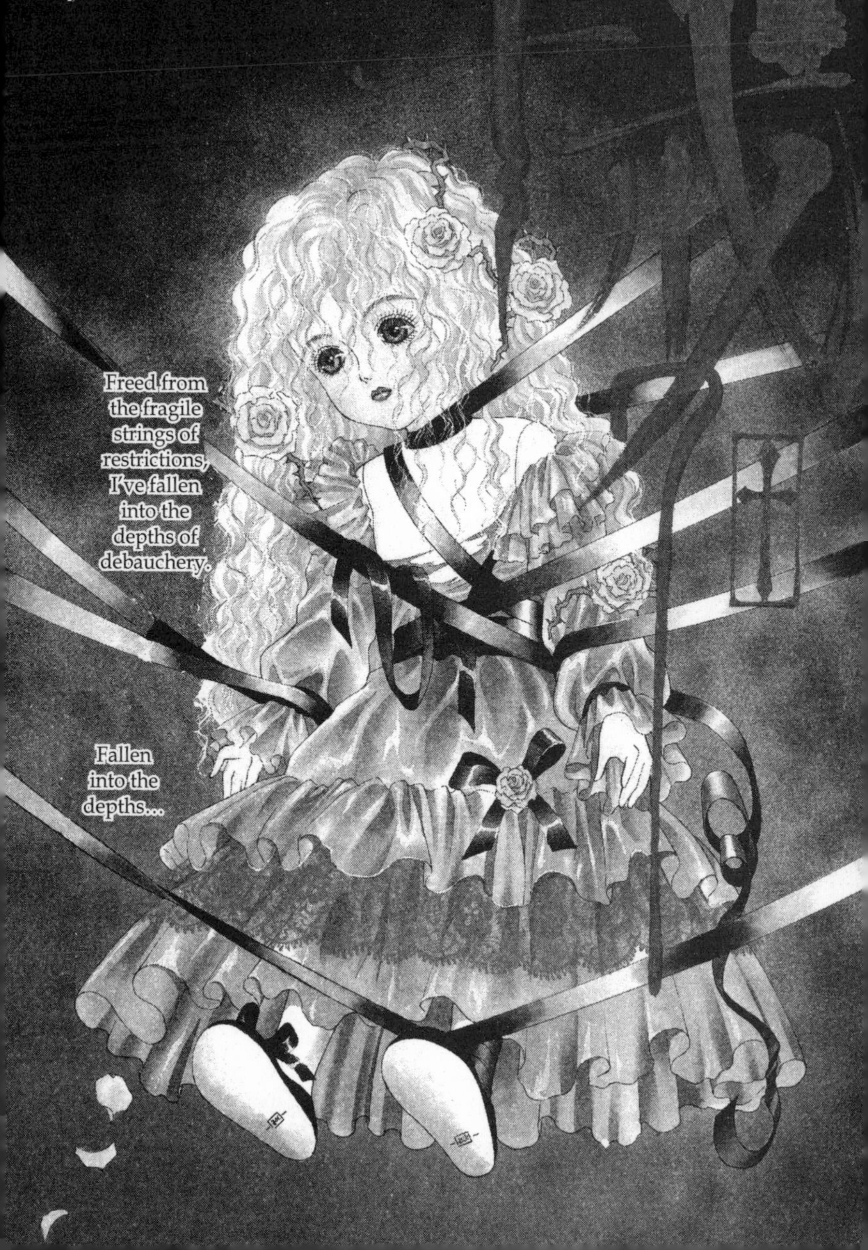
Freed from the fragile strings of restrictions, I've fallen into the depths of debauchery.
Fallen into the depths...

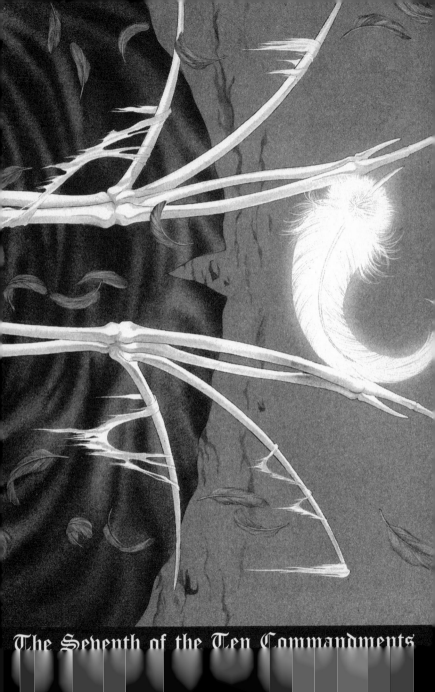

The Seventh of the Ten Commandments

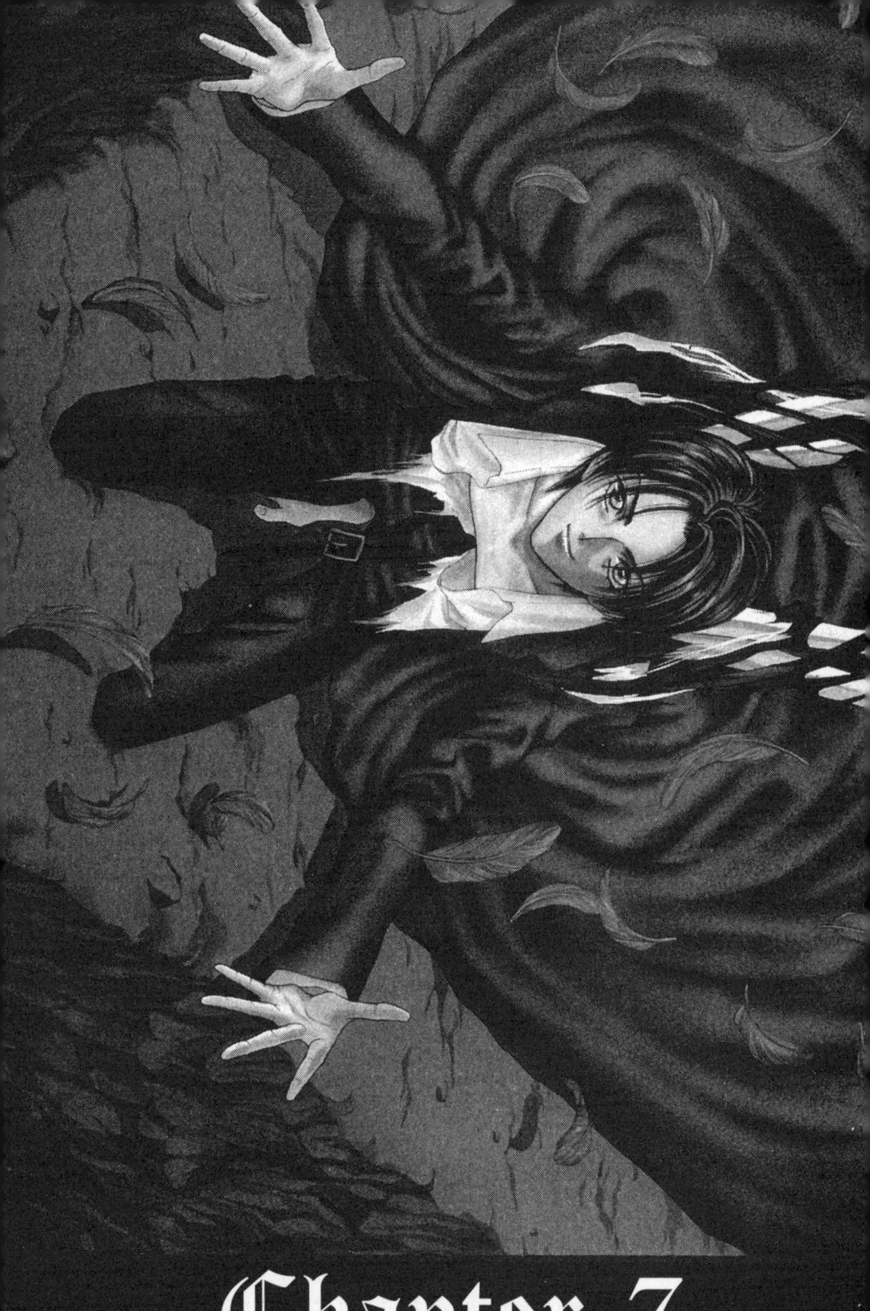

Chapter 7

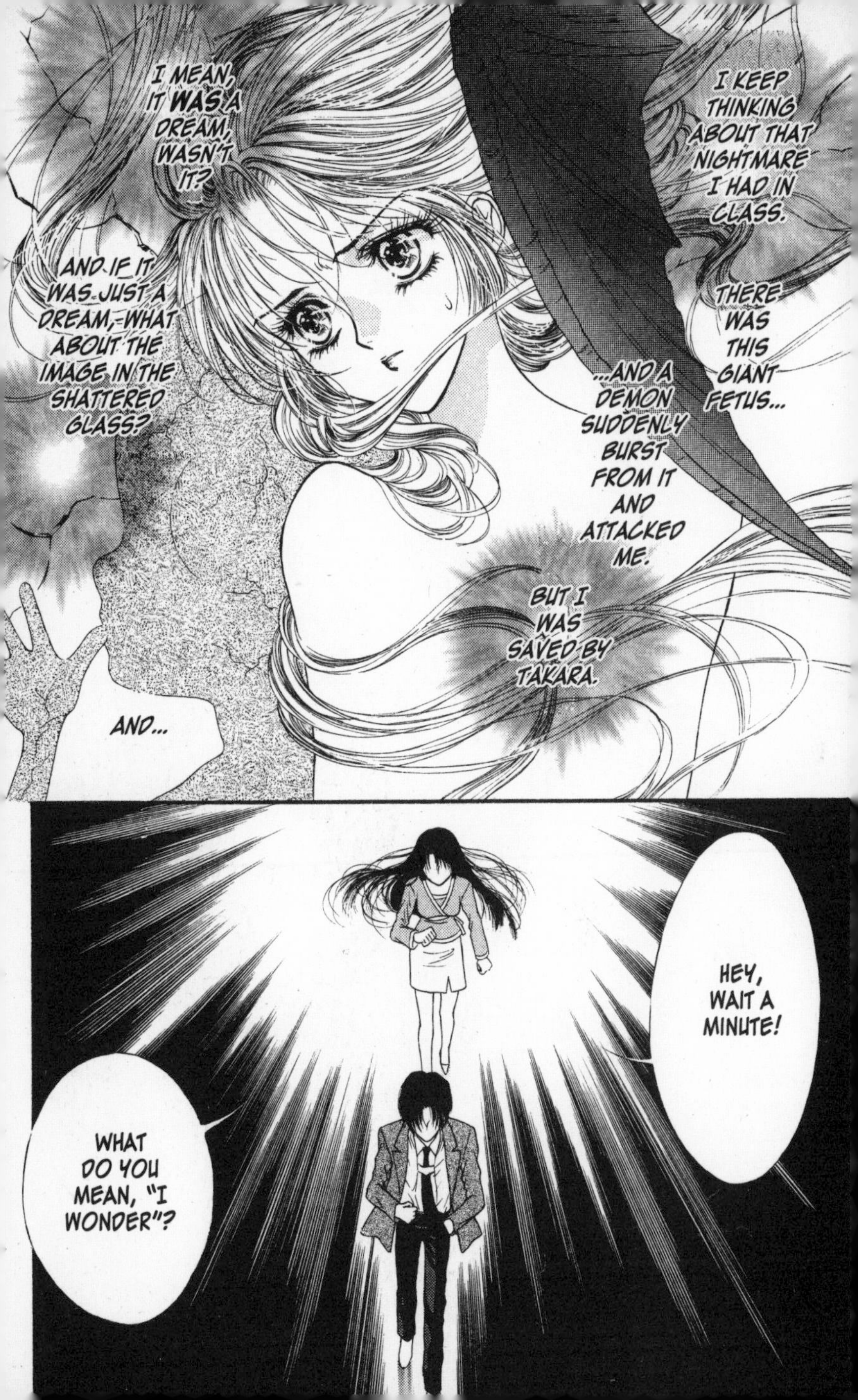
I KEEP THINKING ABOUT THAT NIGHTMARE I HAD IN CLASS.
THERE WAS THIS GIANT FETUS...
...AND A DEMON SUDDENLY BURST FROM IT AND ATTACKED ME.
BUT I WAS SAVED BY TAKARA.
I MEAN, IT **WAS** A DREAM, WASN'T IT?
AND IF IT WAS JUST A DREAM, WHAT ABOUT THE IMAGE IN THE SHATTERED GLASS?
AND...
HEY, WAIT A MINUTE!
WHAT DO YOU MEAN, "I WONDER"?

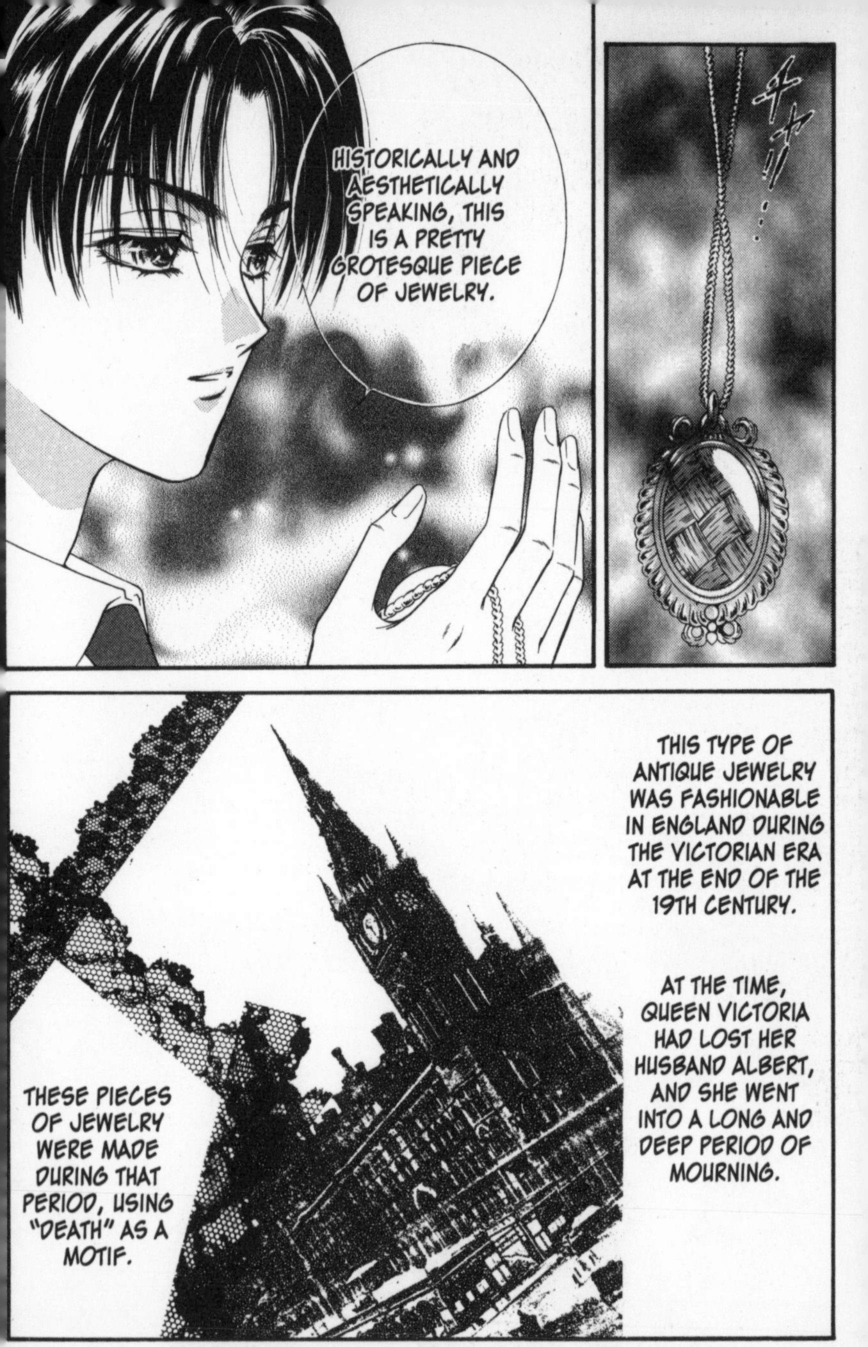
HISTORICALLY AND AESTHETICALLY SPEAKING, THIS IS A PRETTY GROTESQUE PIECE OF JEWELRY.
THIS TYPE OF ANTIQUE JEWELRY WAS FASHIONABLE IN ENGLAND DURING THE VICTORIAN ERA AT THE END OF THE 19TH CENTURY.
AT THE TIME, QUEEN VICTORIA HAD LOST HER HUSBAND ALBERT, AND SHE WENT INTO A LONG AND DEEP PERIOD OF MOURNING.
THESE PIECES OF JEWELRY WERE MADE DURING THAT PERIOD, USING "DEATH" AS A MOTIF.

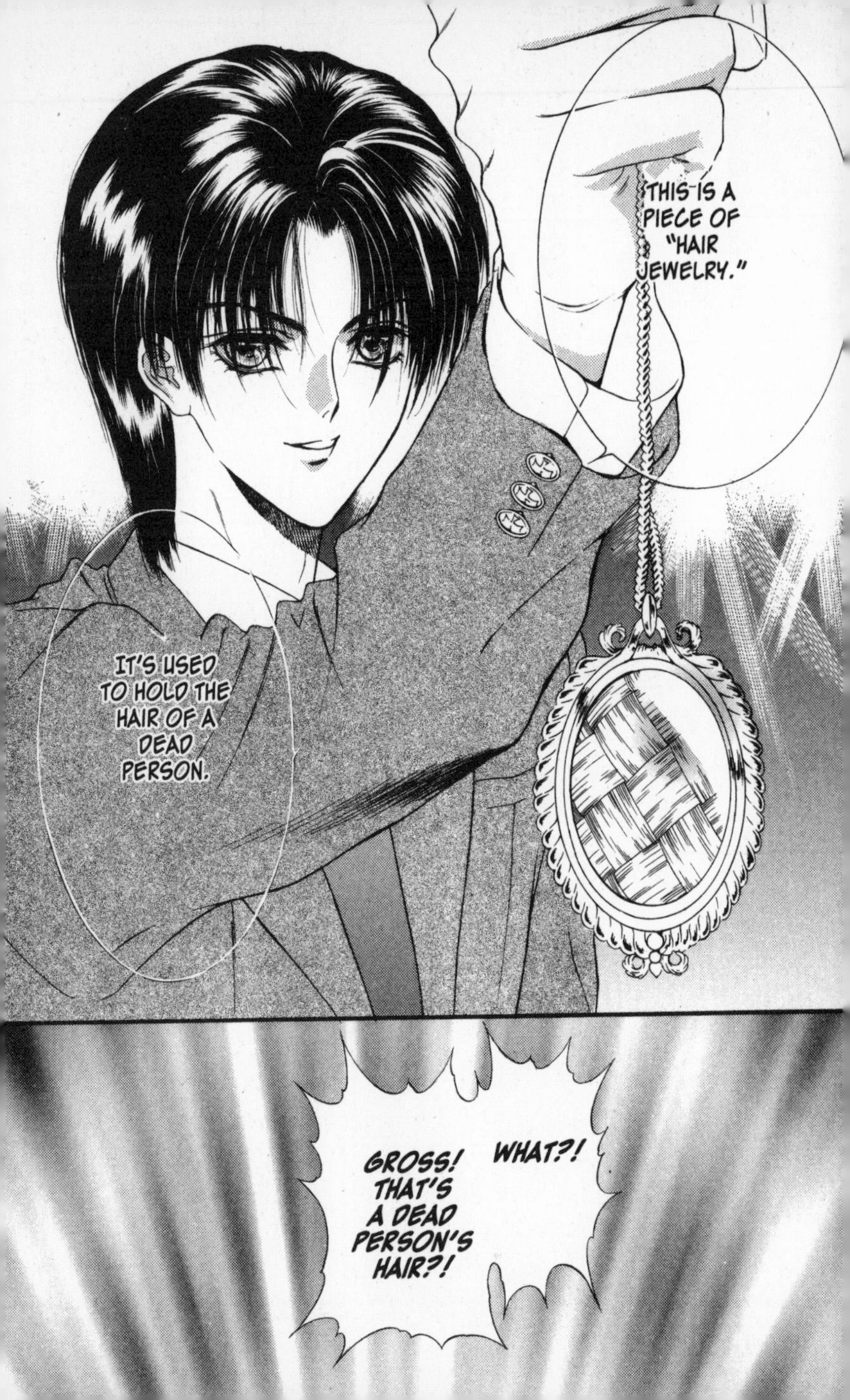
THIS IS A PIECE OF "HAIR JEWELRY."
IT'S USED TO HOLD THE HAIR OF A DEAD PERSON.
WHAT?!
GROSS! THAT'S A DEAD PERSON'S HAIR?!

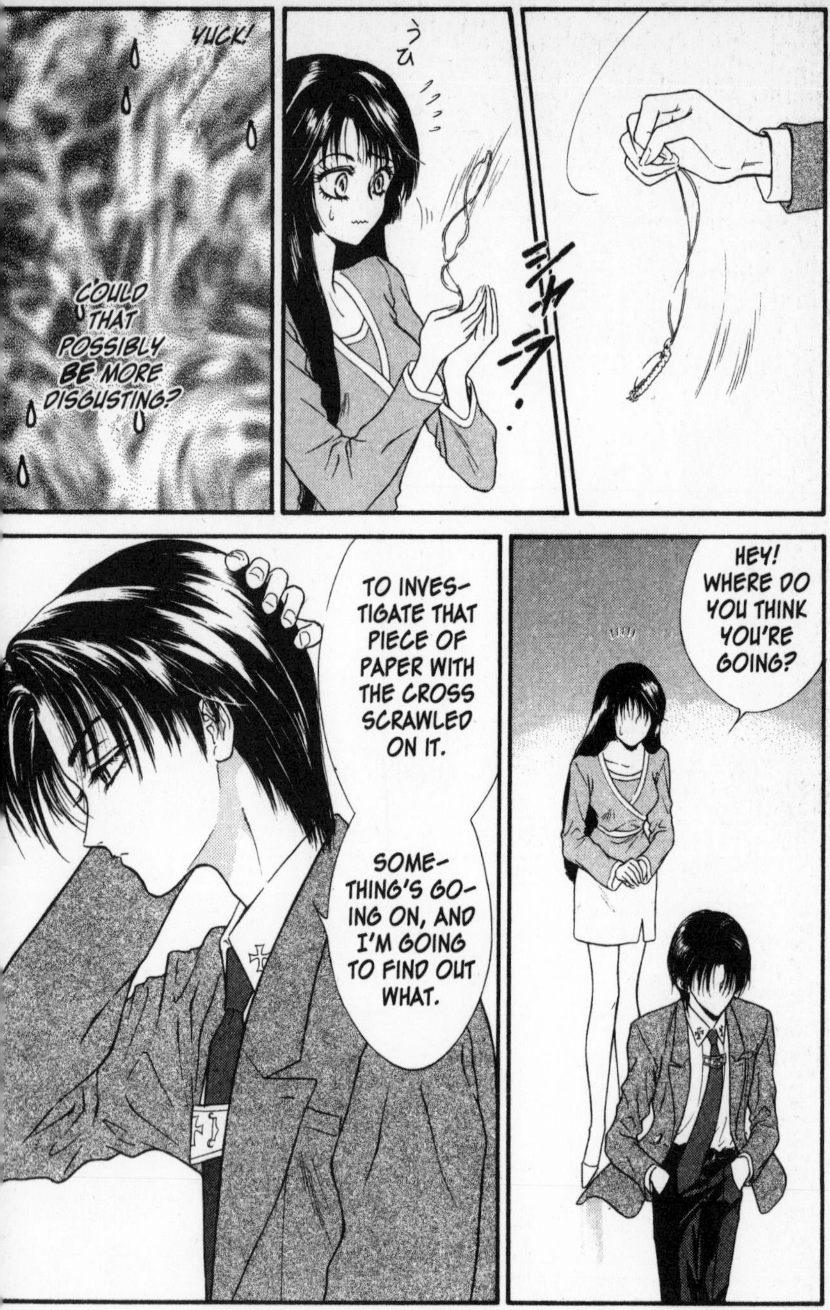
うひ
YUCK!
COULD THAT POSSIBLY BE MORE DISGUSTING?
HEY! WHERE DO YOU THINK YOU'RE GOING?
TO INVES-TIGATE THAT PIECE OF PAPER WITH THE CROSS SCRAWLED ON IT.
SOME-THING'S GO-ING ON, AND I'M GOING TO FIND OUT WHAT.

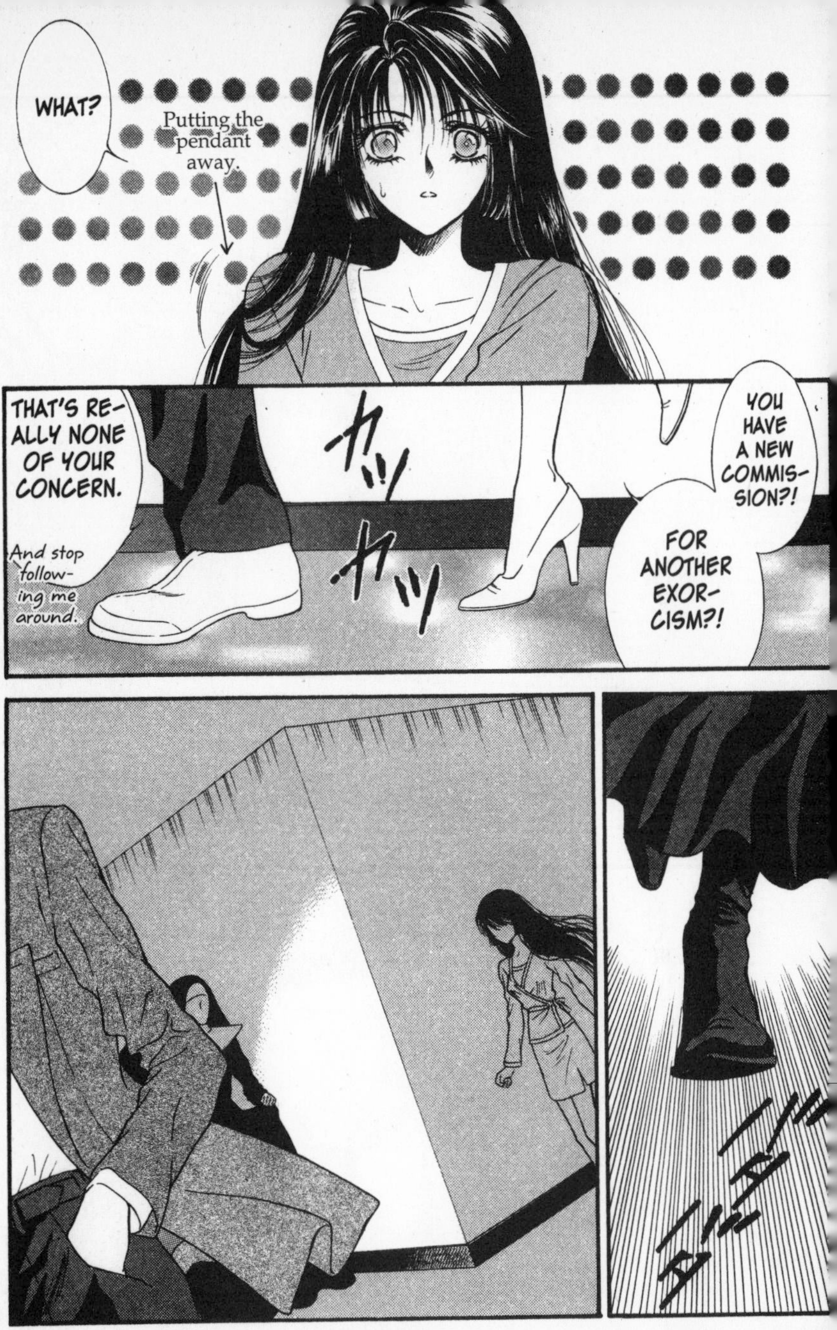
WHAT?
Putting the pendant away.
YOU HAVE A NEW COMMISSION?!
FOR ANOTHER EXORCISM?!
THAT'S REALLY NONE OF YOUR CONCERN.
And stop following me around.

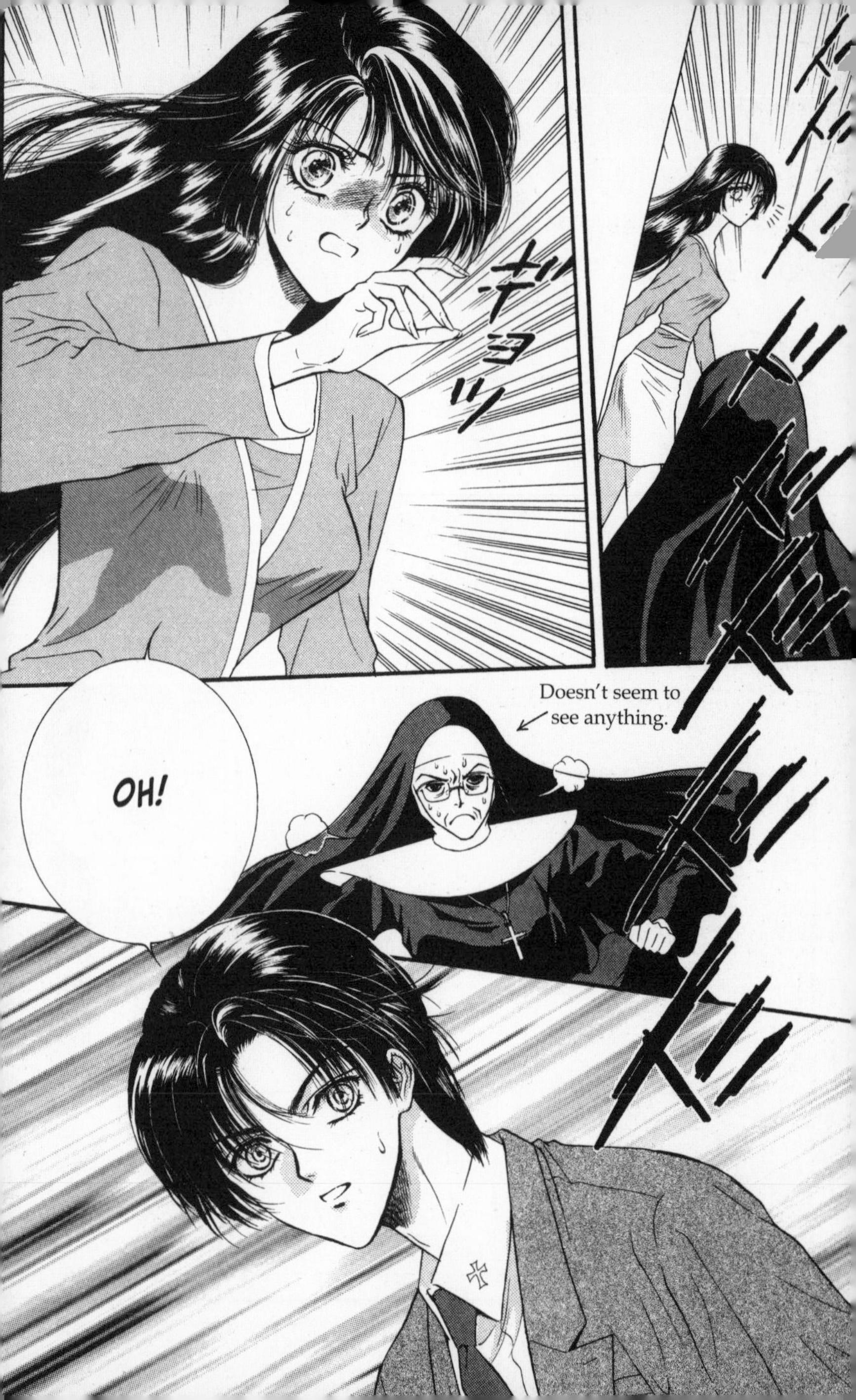
Doesn't seem to see anything.
OH!

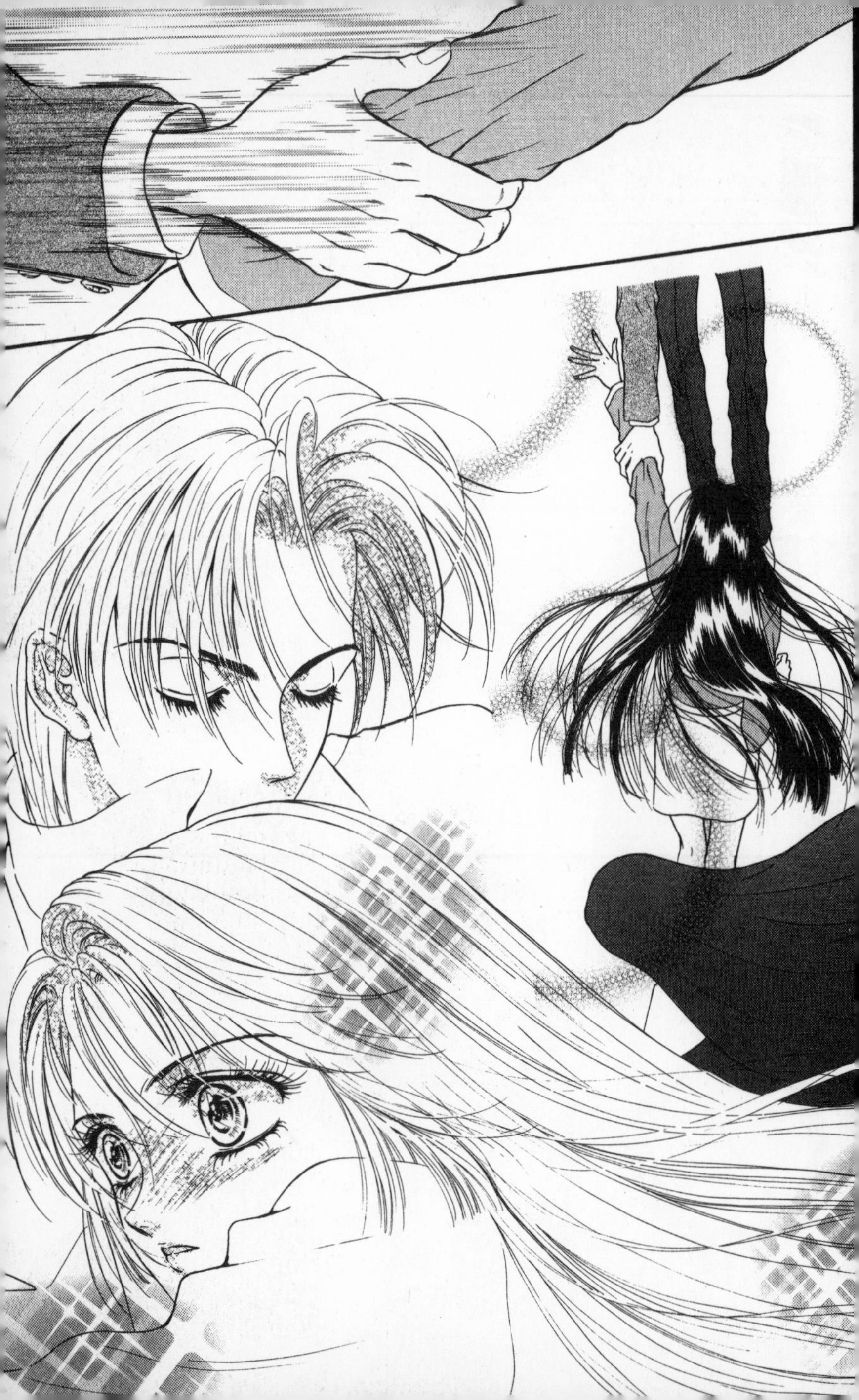

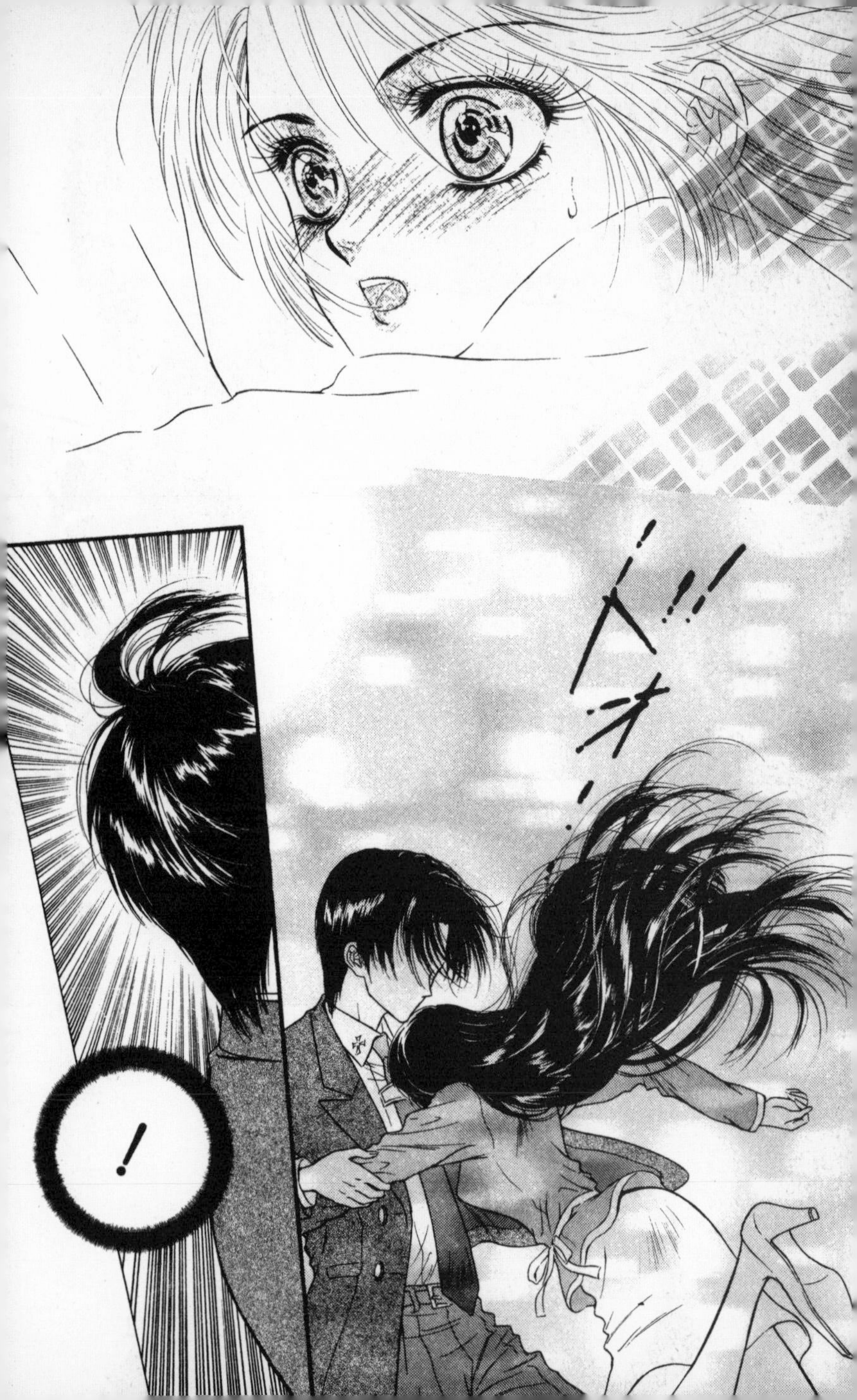
ドォ…
!

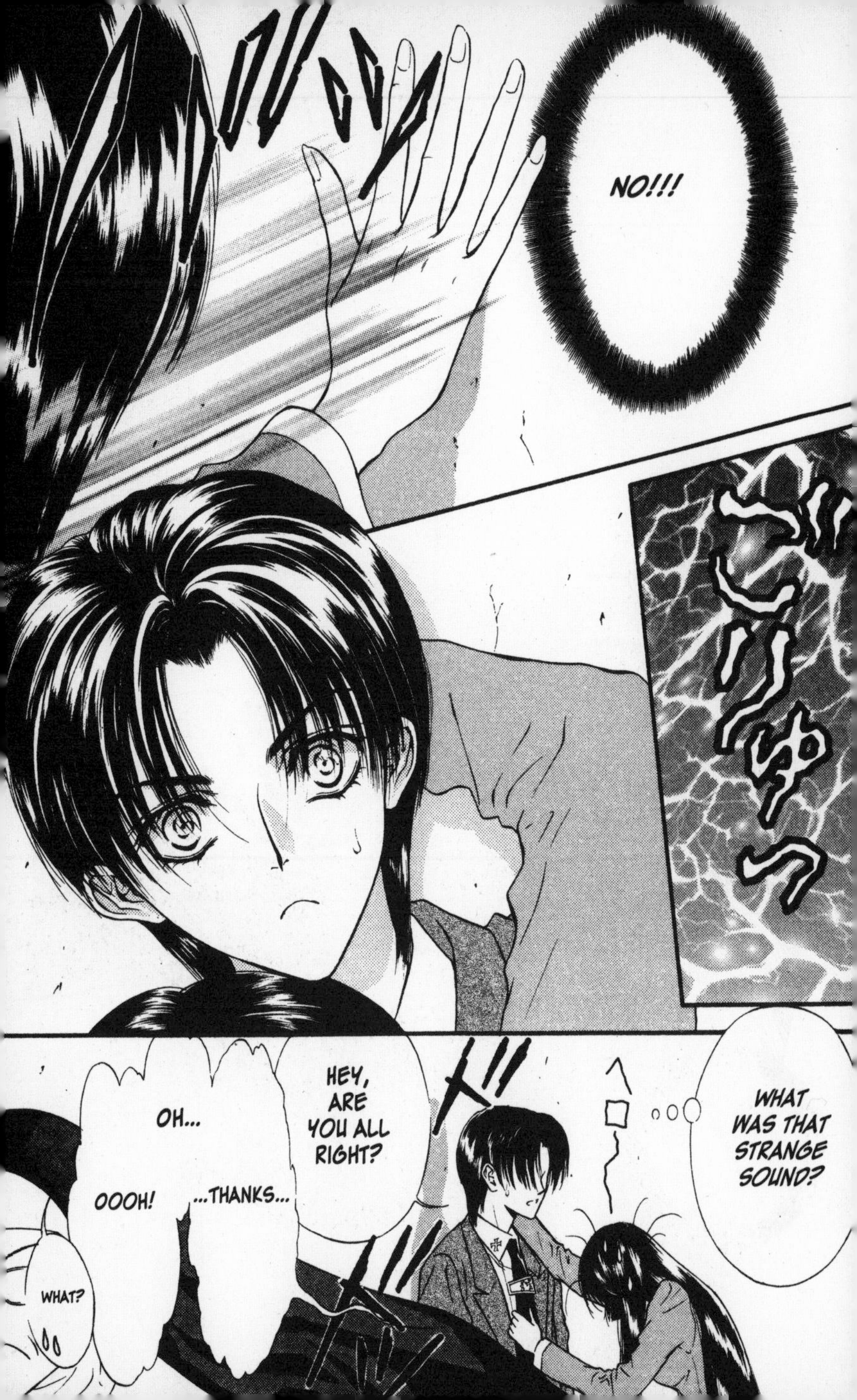
NO!!!
WHAT WAS THAT STRANGE SOUND?
HEY, ARE YOU ALL RIGHT?
OH...
...THANKS...
OOOH!
WHAT?

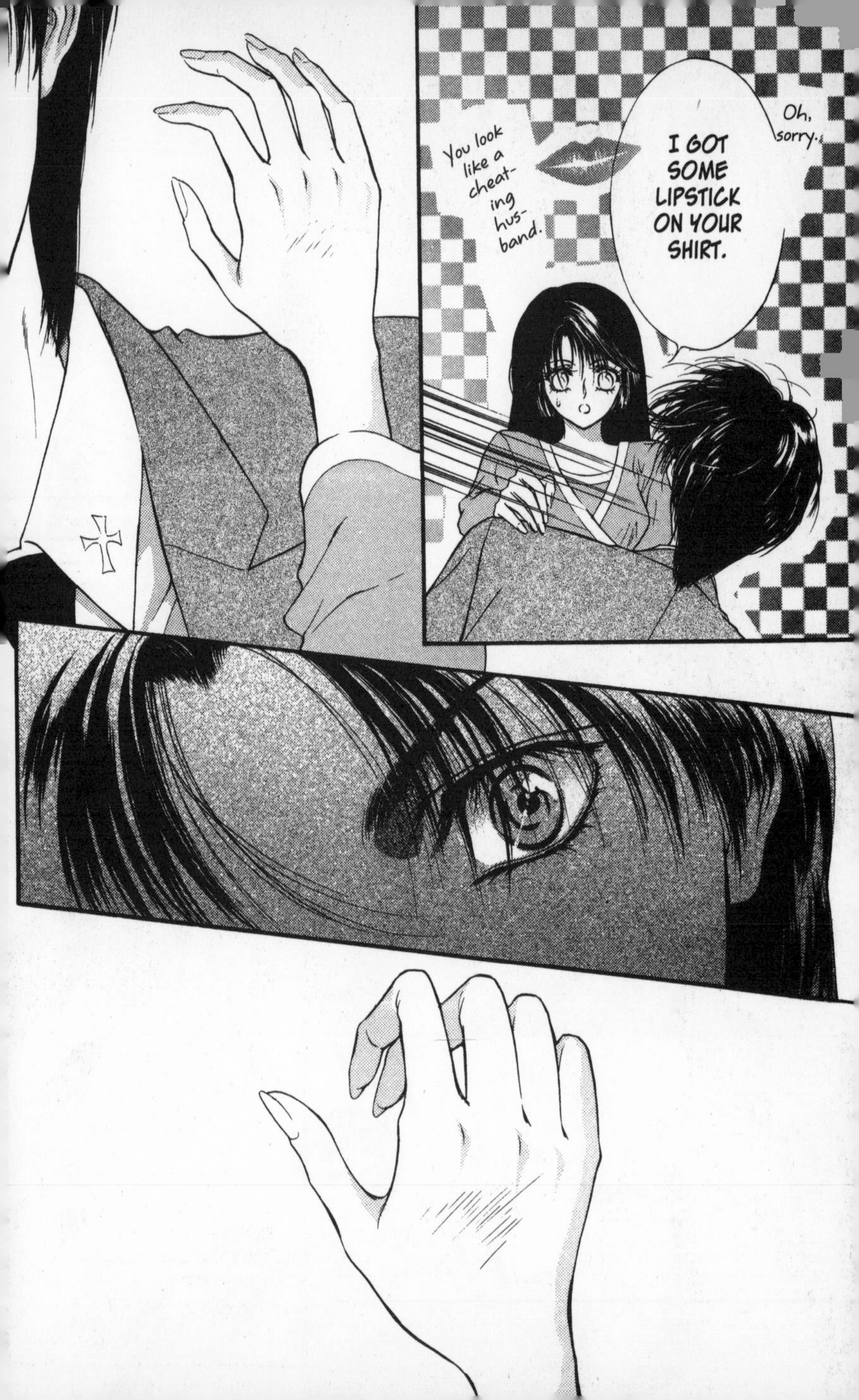
Oh, sorry.
I GOT SOME LIPSTICK ON YOUR SHIRT.
You look like a cheat-ing hus-band.

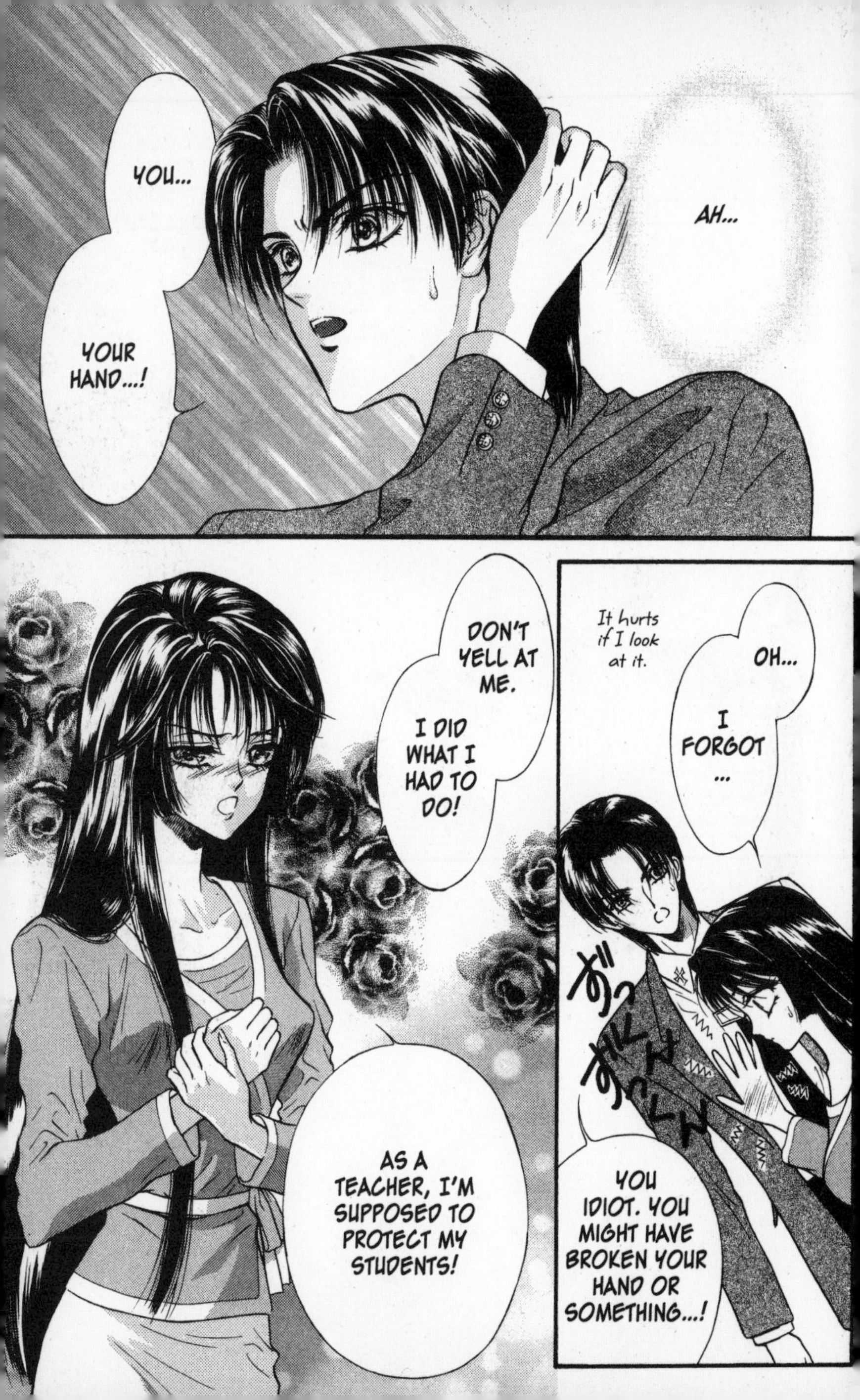
AH...
YOU...
YOUR HAND...!
It hurts if I look at it.
OH...
I FORGOT ...
YOU IDIOT. YOU MIGHT HAVE BROKEN YOUR HAND OR SOMETHING...!
DON'T YELL AT ME.
I DID WHAT I HAD TO DO!
AS A TEACHER, I'M SUPPOSED TO PROTECT MY STUDENTS!

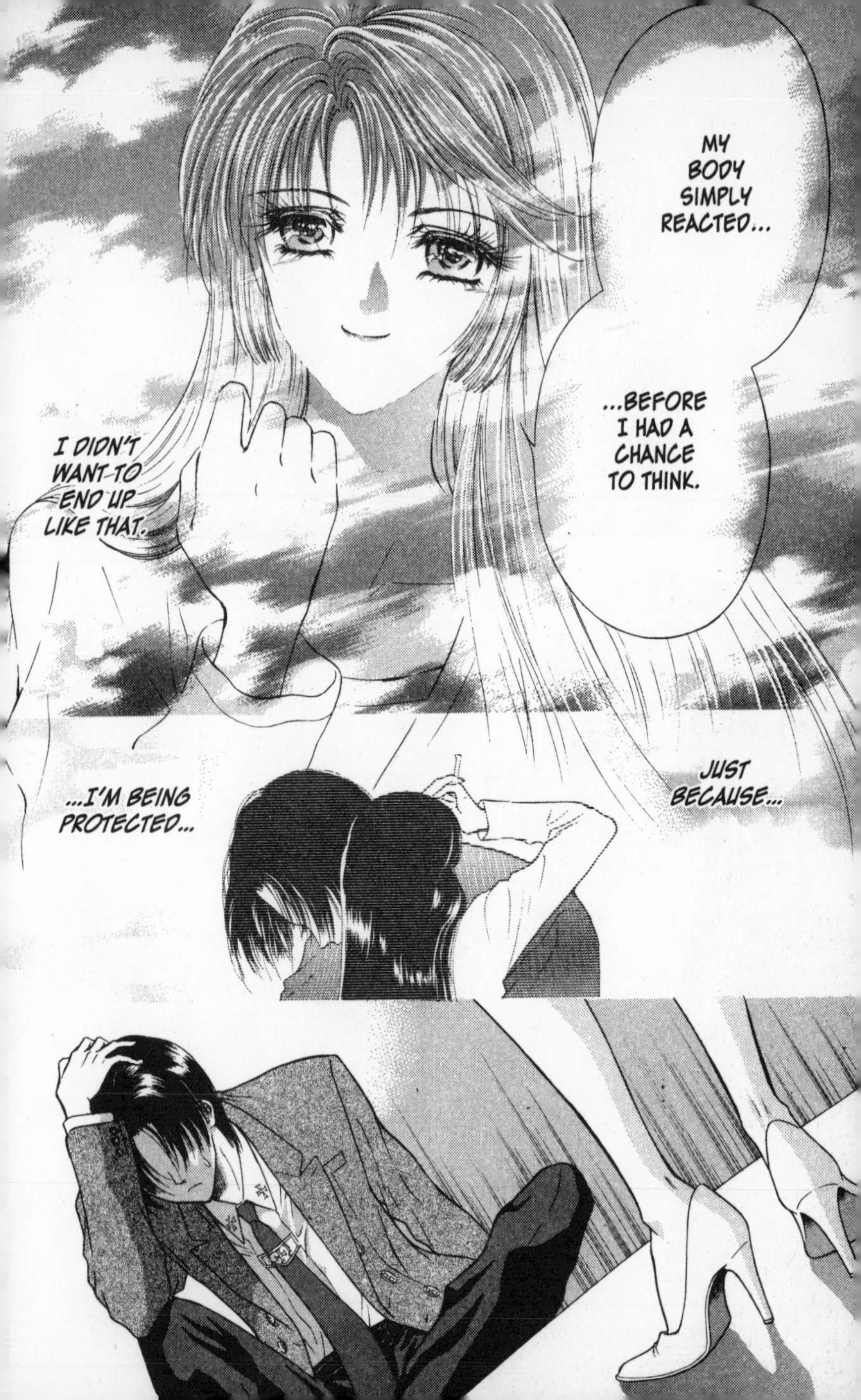
MY BODY SIMPLY REACTED...
...BEFORE I HAD A CHANCE TO THINK.
I DIDN'T WANT TO END UP LIKE THAT.
JUST BECAUSE...
...I'M BEING PROTECTED...

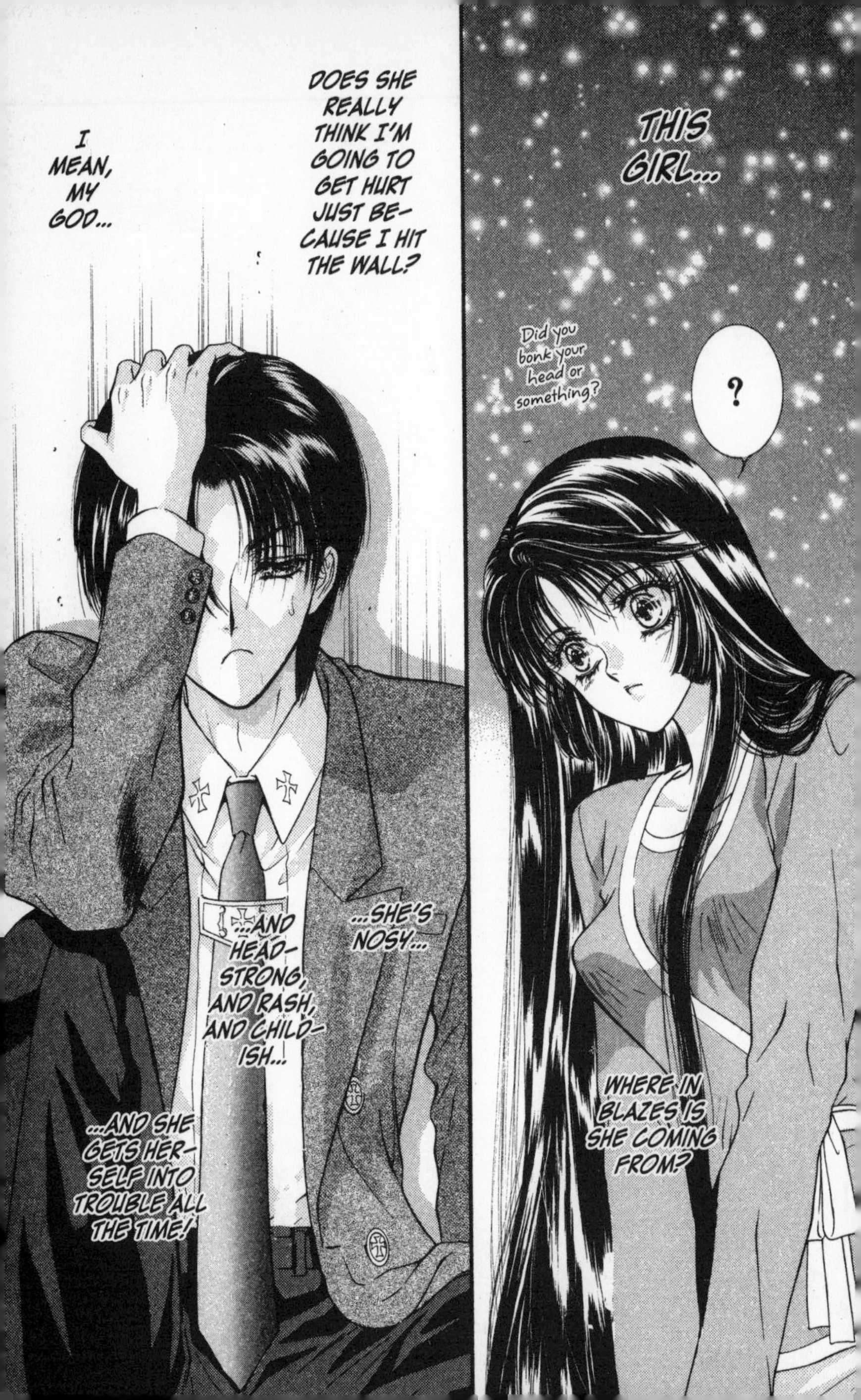
THIS GIRL...
?
Did you bonk your head or something?
WHERE IN BLAZES IS SHE COMING FROM?
DOES SHE REALLY THINK I'M GOING TO GET HURT JUST BECAUSE I HIT THE WALL?
I MEAN, MY GOD...
...SHE'S NOSY...
...AND HEADSTRONG, AND RASH, AND CHILDISH..!
...AND SHE GETS HERSELF INTO TROUBLE ALL THE TIME!

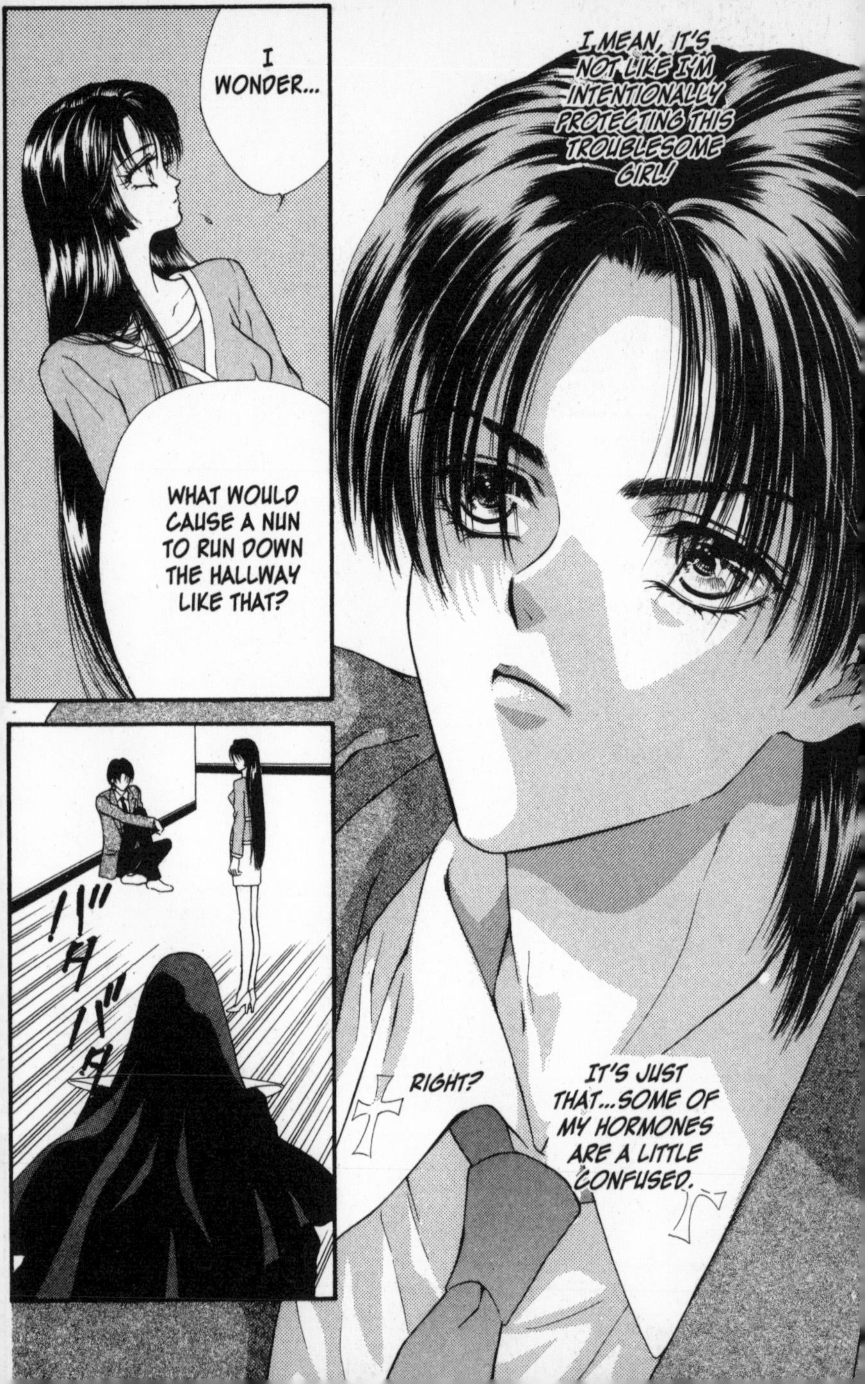
I MEAN, IT'S NOT LIKE I'M INTENTIONALLY PROTECTING THIS TROUBLESOME GIRL!
RIGHT?
IT'S JUST THAT...SOME OF MY HORMONES ARE A LITTLE CONFUSED.
I WONDER...
WHAT WOULD CAUSE A NUN TO RUN DOWN THE HALLWAY LIKE THAT?
バタバタ!

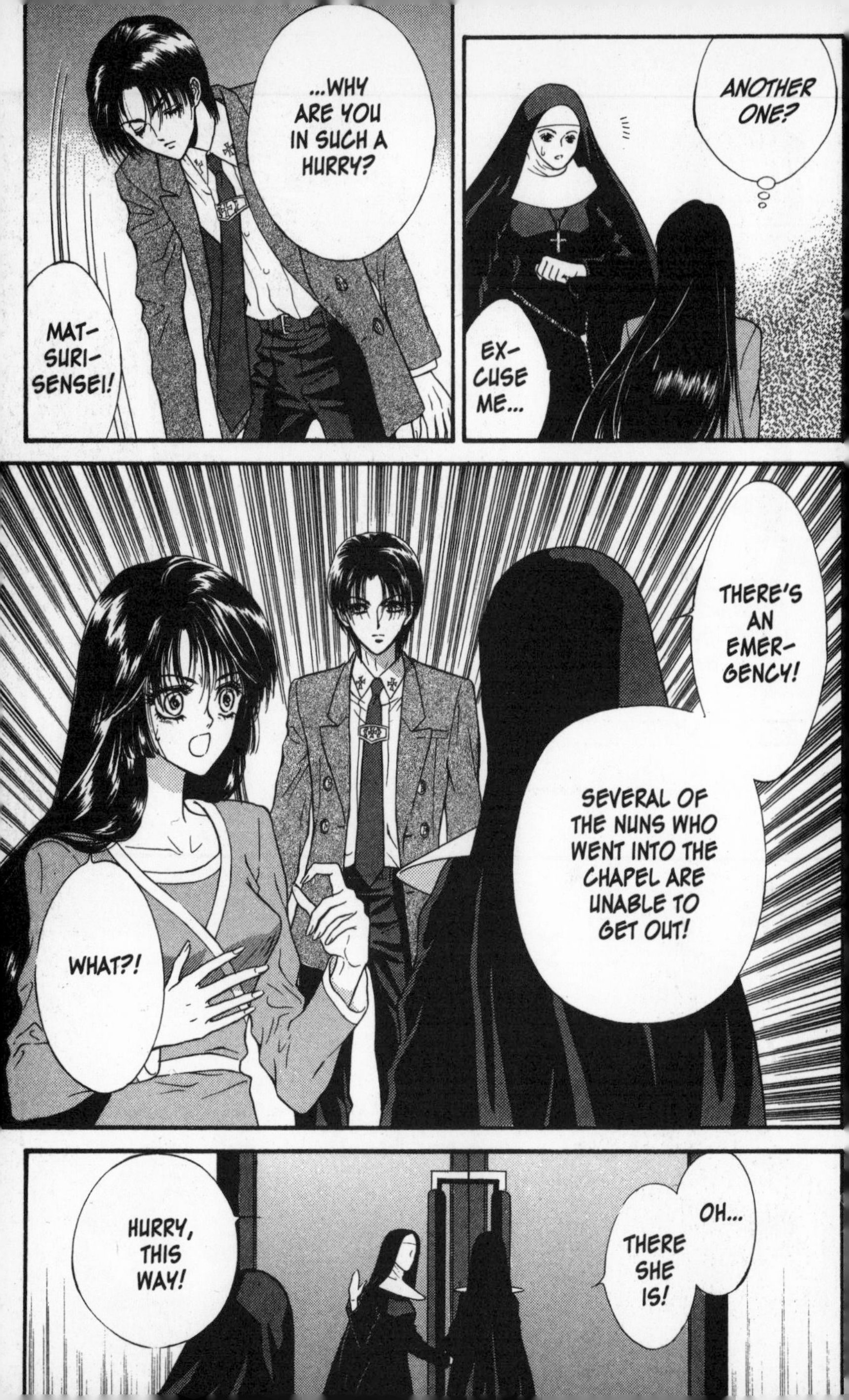
ANOTHER ONE?
EX-CUSE ME...
...WHY ARE YOU IN SUCH A HURRY?
MAT-SURI-SENSEI!
THERE'S AN EMER-GENCY!
SEVERAL OF THE NUNS WHO WENT INTO THE CHAPEL ARE UNABLE TO GET OUT!
WHAT?!
OH...
THERE SHE IS!
HURRY, THIS WAY!

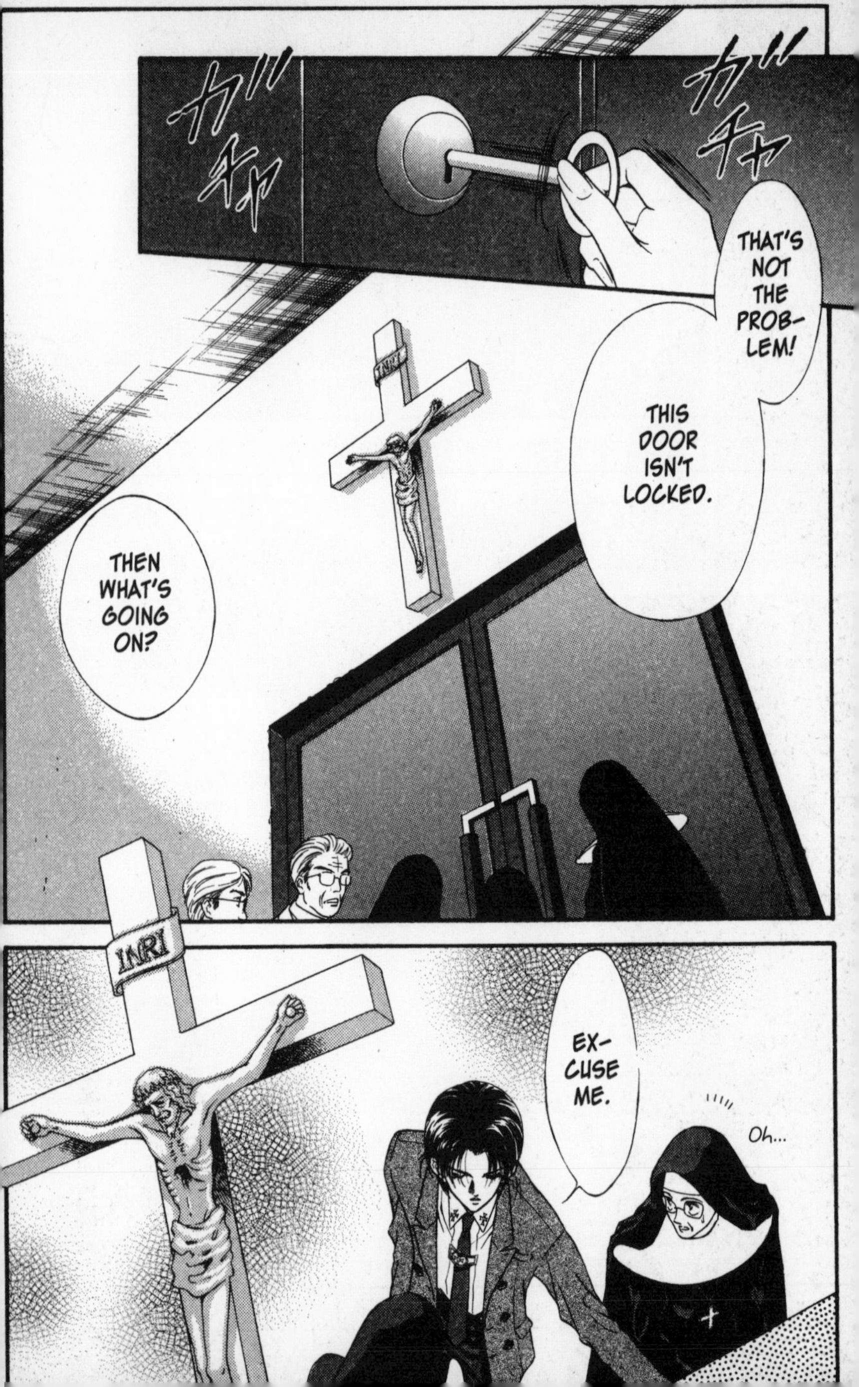
ガチャ
ガチャ
THAT'S NOT THE PROB-LEM!
THIS DOOR ISN'T LOCKED.
THEN WHAT'S GOING ON?
INRI
EX-CUSE ME.
Oh...

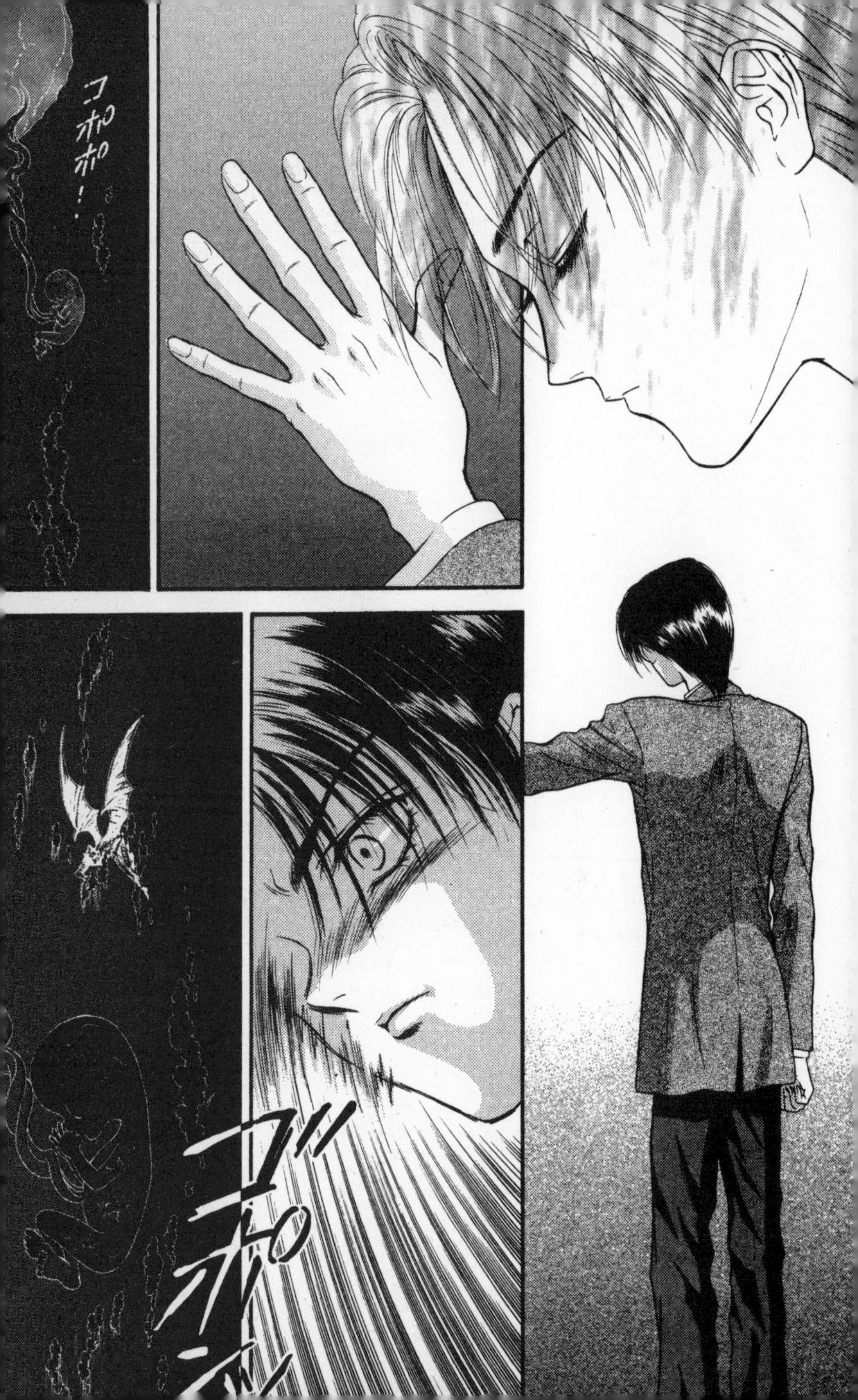
コポポ！！
ゴポ

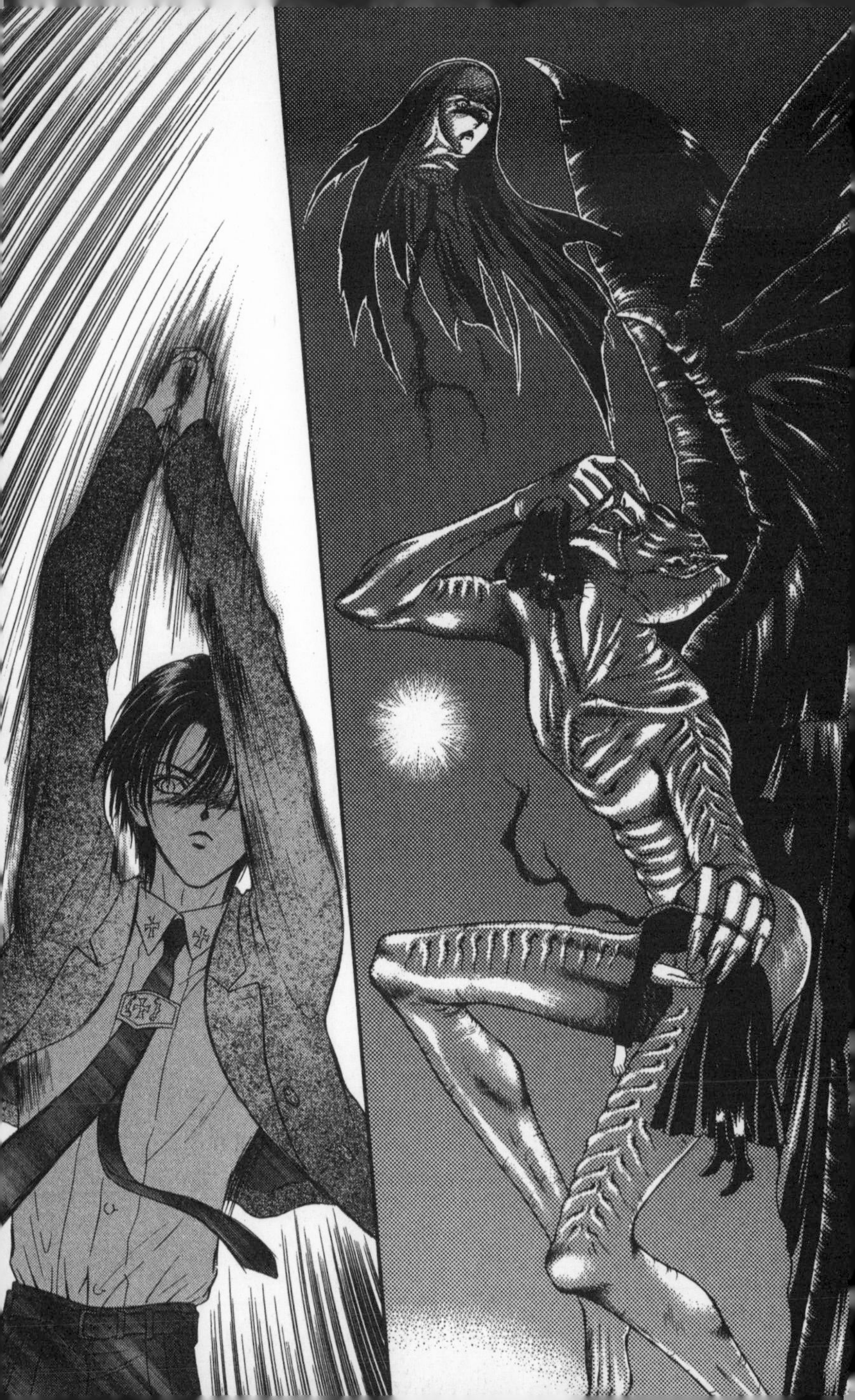

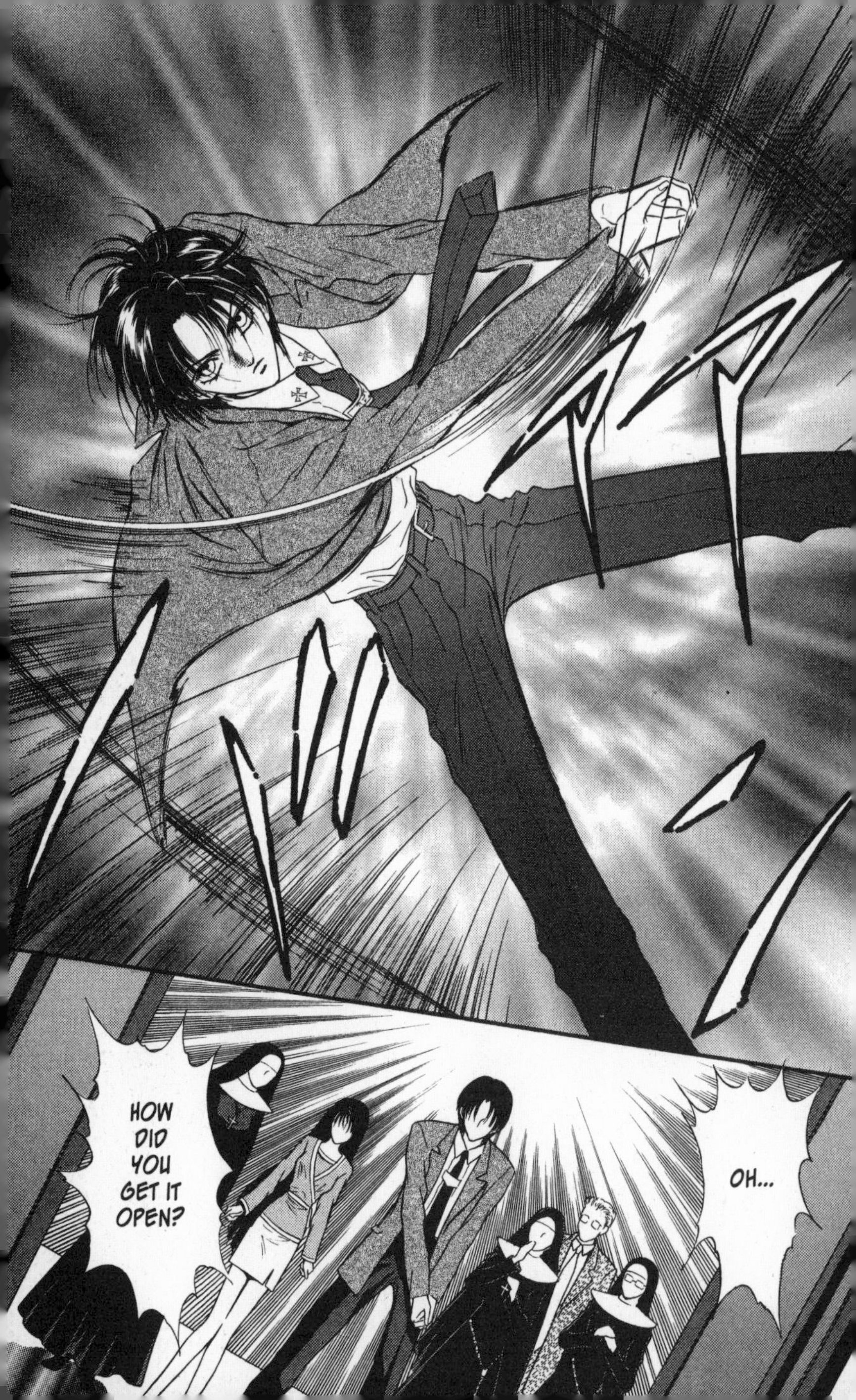
OH...
HOW DID YOU GET IT OPEN?

WE WERE TOO LATE.

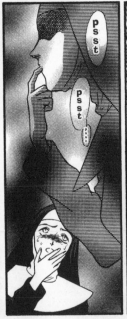

psst

psst

psst

ARE YOU ALL RIGHT?

ARE YOU...?

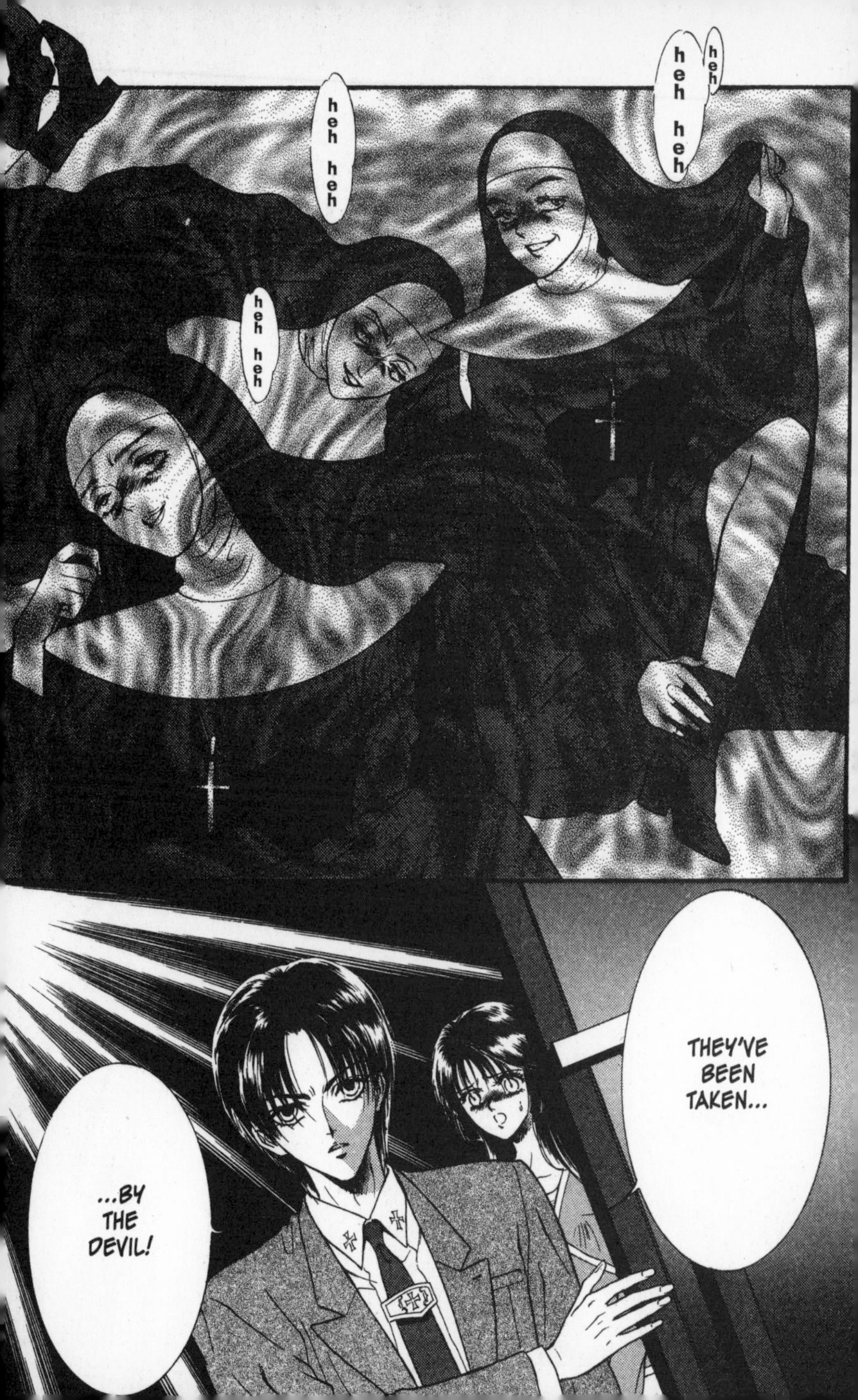
heh
heh heh heh
heh heh heh
heh heh
THEY'VE BEEN TAKEN...
...BY THE DEVIL!

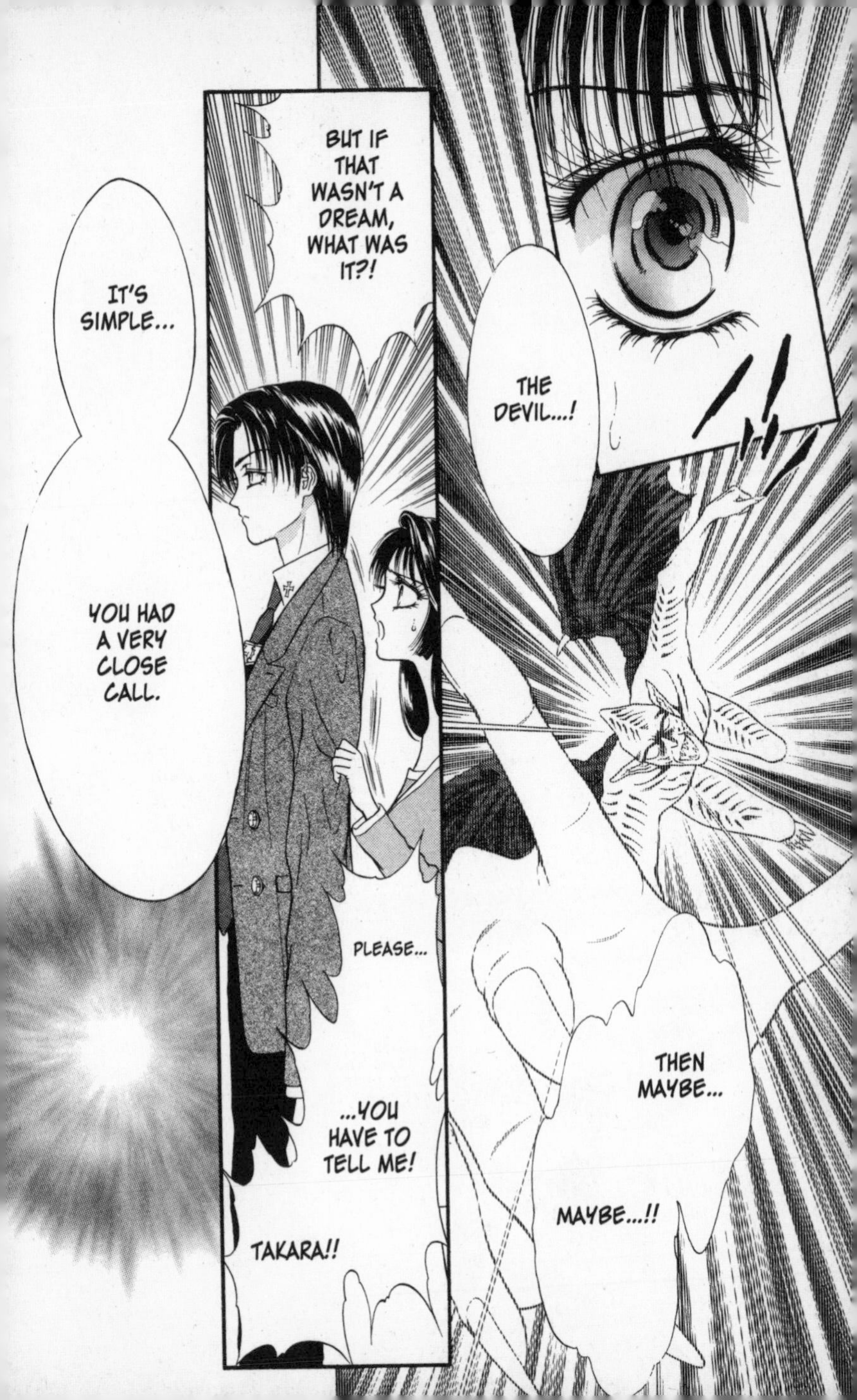
THE DEVIL...!
THEN MAYBE...
MAYBE...!!
BUT IF THAT WASN'T A DREAM, WHAT WAS IT?!
PLEASE...
...YOU HAVE TO TELL ME!
TAKARA!!
IT'S SIMPLE...
YOU HAD A VERY CLOSE CALL.

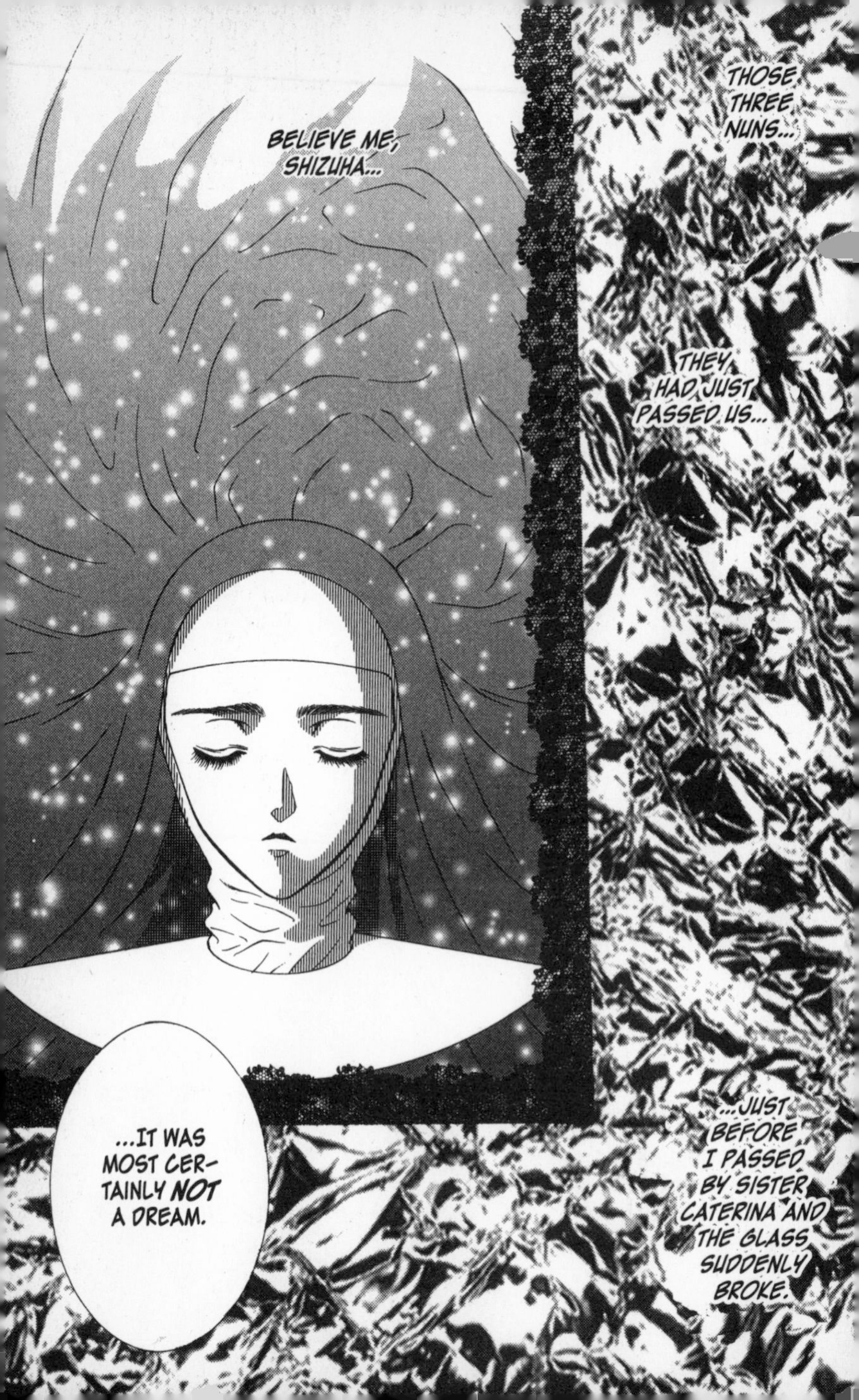
THOSE THREE NUNS...
THEY HAD JUST PASSED US...
...JUST BEFORE I PASSED BY SISTER CATERINA AND THE GLASS SUDDENLY BROKE.
BELIEVE ME, SHIZUHA...
...IT WAS MOST CER-TAINLY NOT A DREAM.

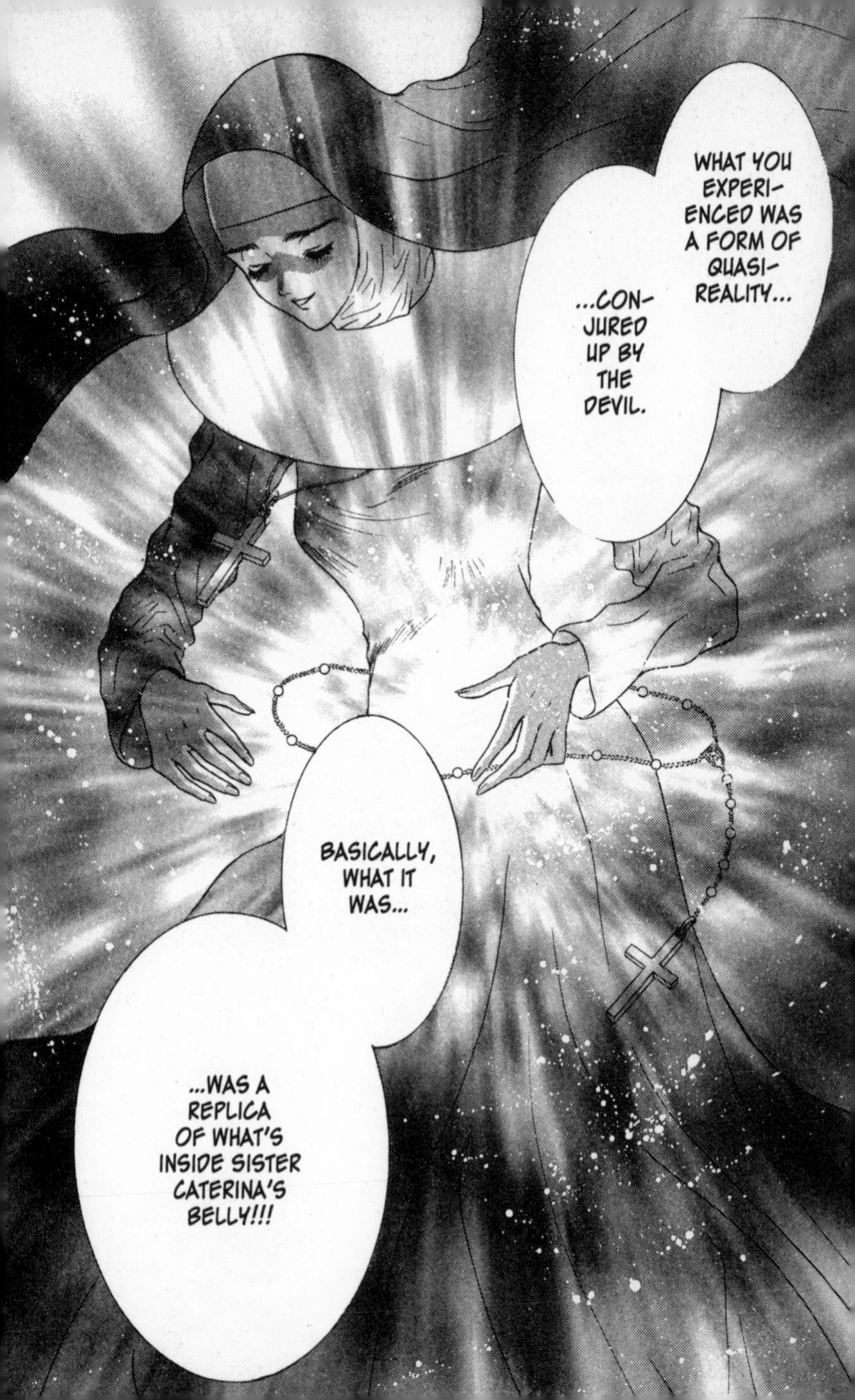
WHAT YOU EXPERI- ENCED WAS A FORM OF QUASI- REALITY...
...CON- JURED UP BY THE DEVIL.
BASICALLY, WHAT IT WAS...
...WAS A REPLICA OF WHAT'S INSIDE SISTER CATERINA'S BELLY!!!

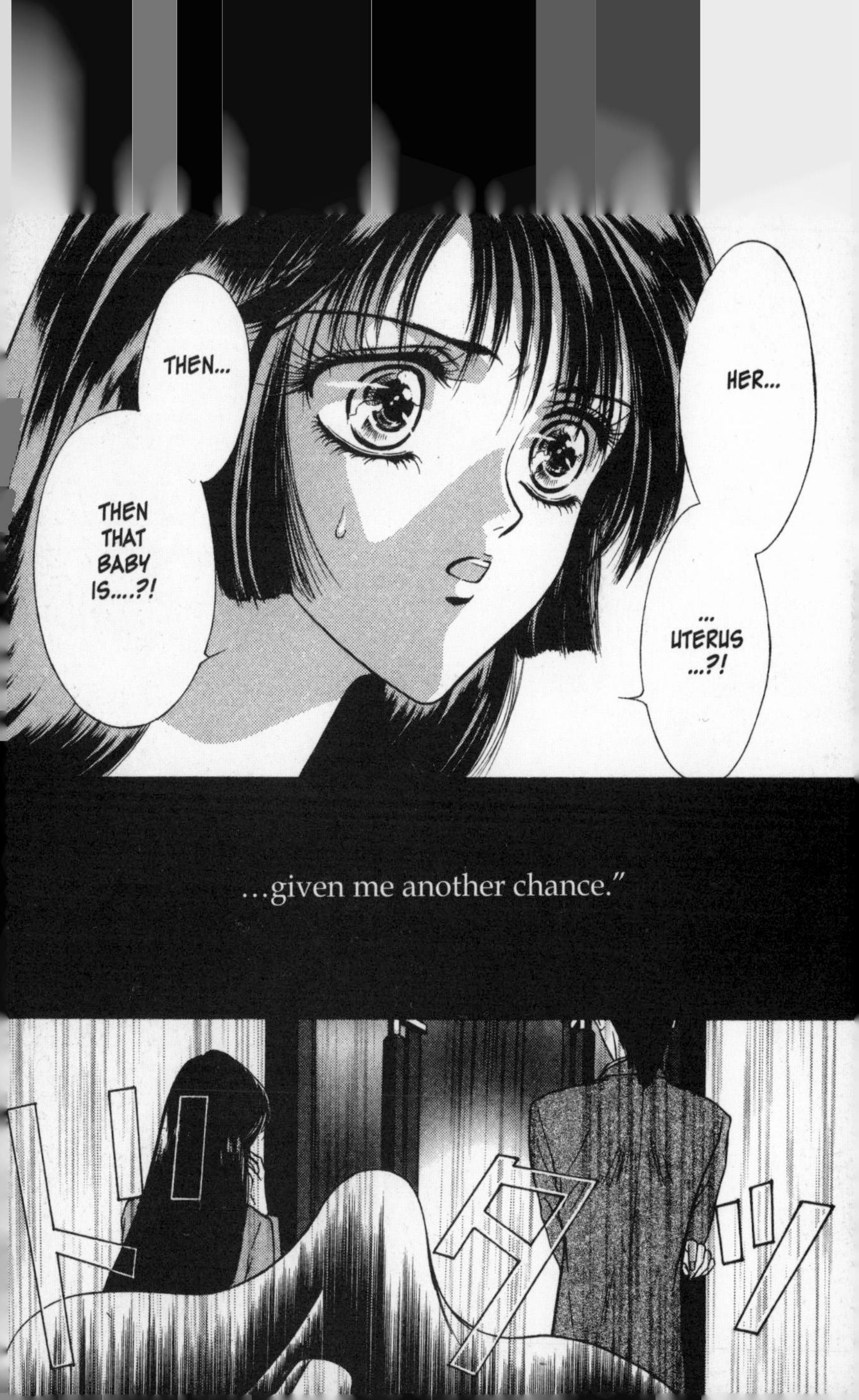
HER...
... UTERUS ...?!
THEN...
THEN THAT BABY IS....?!
...given me another chance."

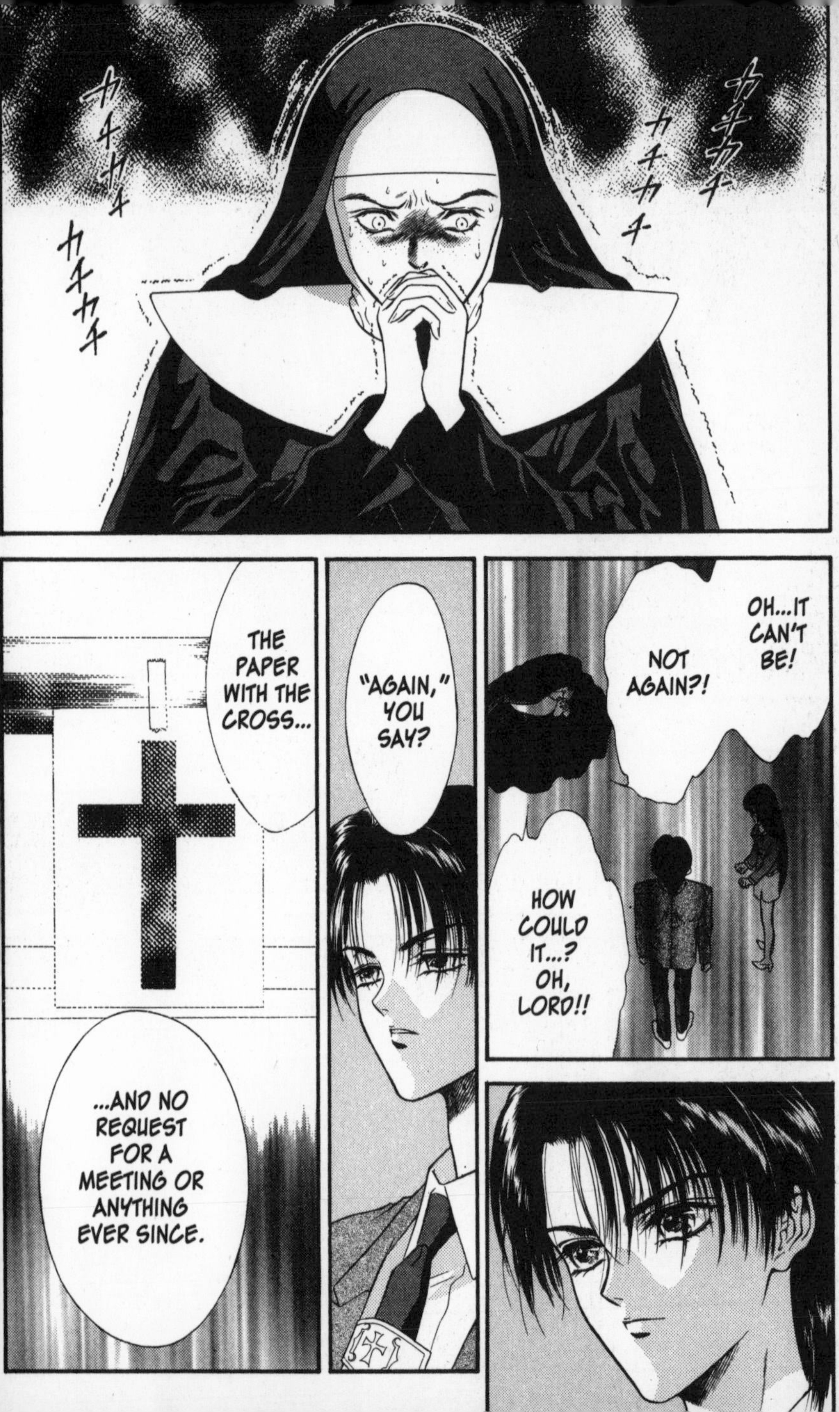
カチカチ
カチカチ
カチカチ
カチカチ
OH...IT CAN'T BE!
NOT AGAIN?!
HOW COULD IT...? OH, LORD!!
"AGAIN," YOU SAY?
THE PAPER WITH THE CROSS...
...AND NO REQUEST FOR A MEETING OR ANYTHING EVER SINCE.

THEN WAS IT YOU...?

THE ONE WITH THE STRANGE COMMIS- SION?

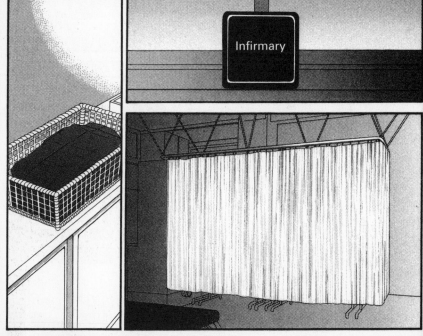

Infirmary

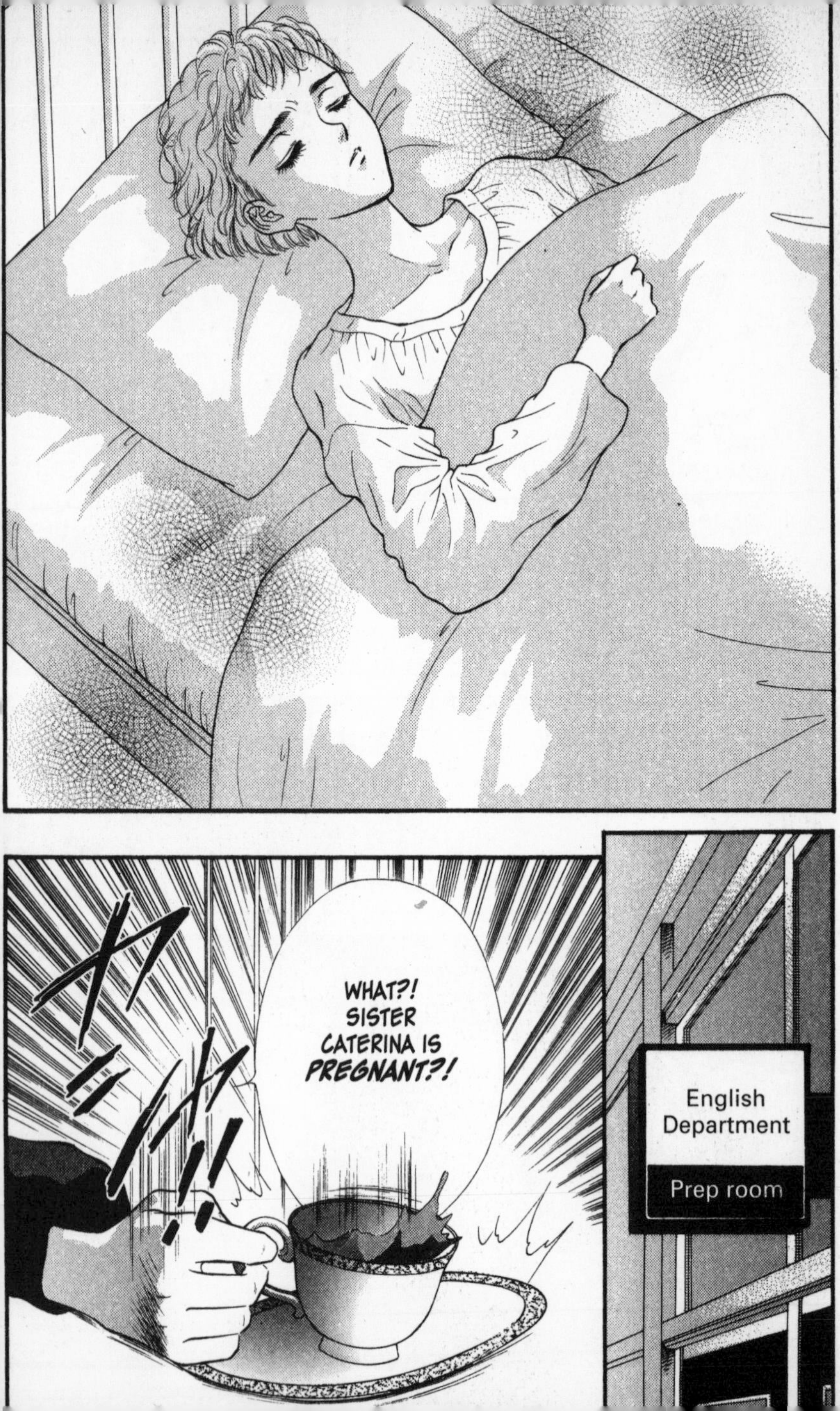
English Department
Prep room
WHAT?! SISTER CATERINA IS PREGNANT?!

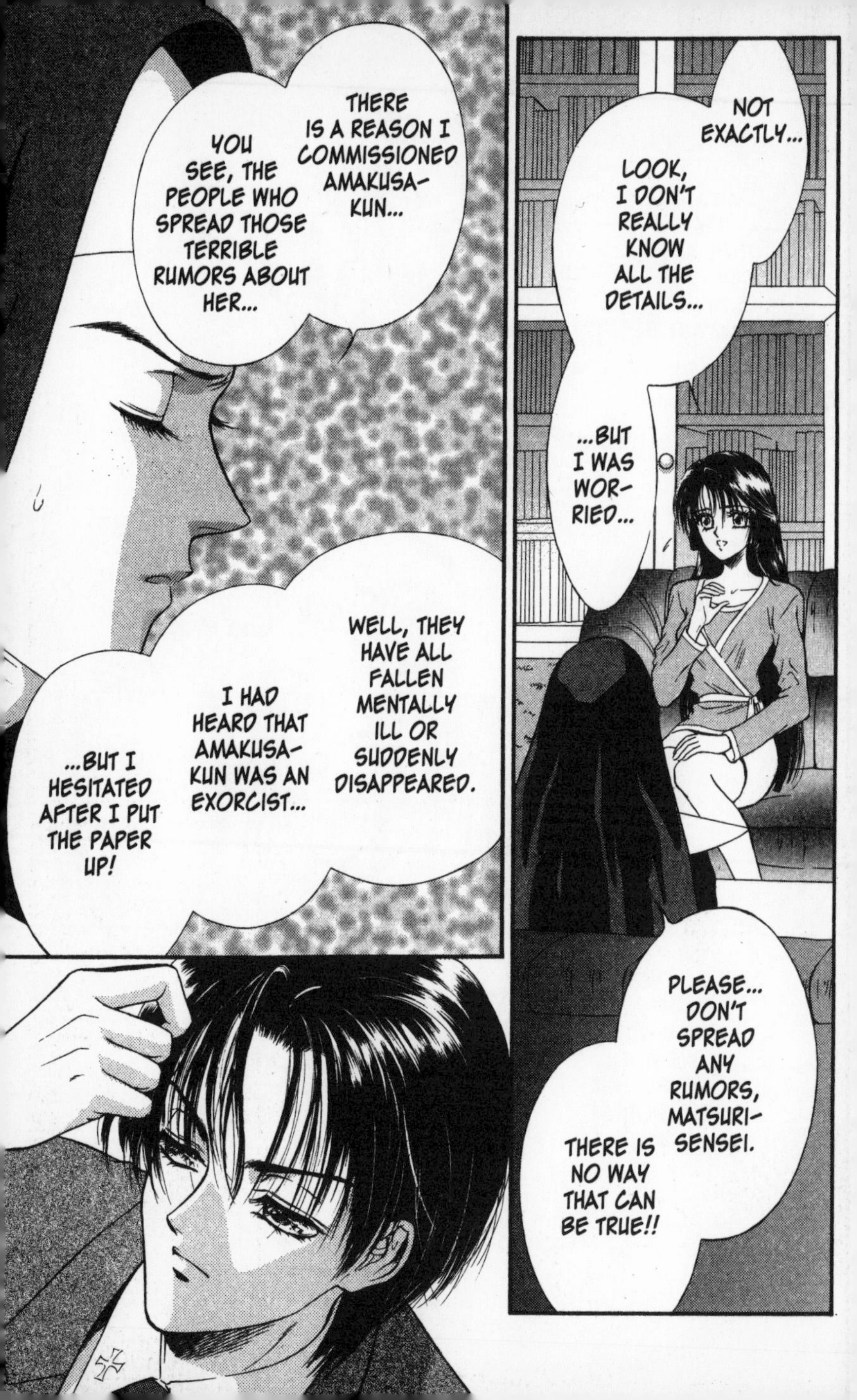
NOT EXACTLY...
LOOK, I DON'T REALLY KNOW ALL THE DETAILS...
...BUT I WAS WOR-RIED...
PLEASE... DON'T SPREAD ANY RUMORS, MATSURI-SENSEI.
THERE IS NO WAY THAT CAN BE TRUE!!
THERE IS A REASON I COMMISSIONED AMAKUSA-KUN...
YOU SEE, THE PEOPLE WHO SPREAD THOSE TERRIBLE RUMORS ABOUT HER...
WELL, THEY HAVE ALL FALLEN MENTALLY ILL OR SUDDENLY DISAPPEARED.
I HAD HEARD THAT AMAKUSA-KUN WAS AN EXORCIST...
...BUT I HESITATED AFTER I PUT THE PAPER UP!

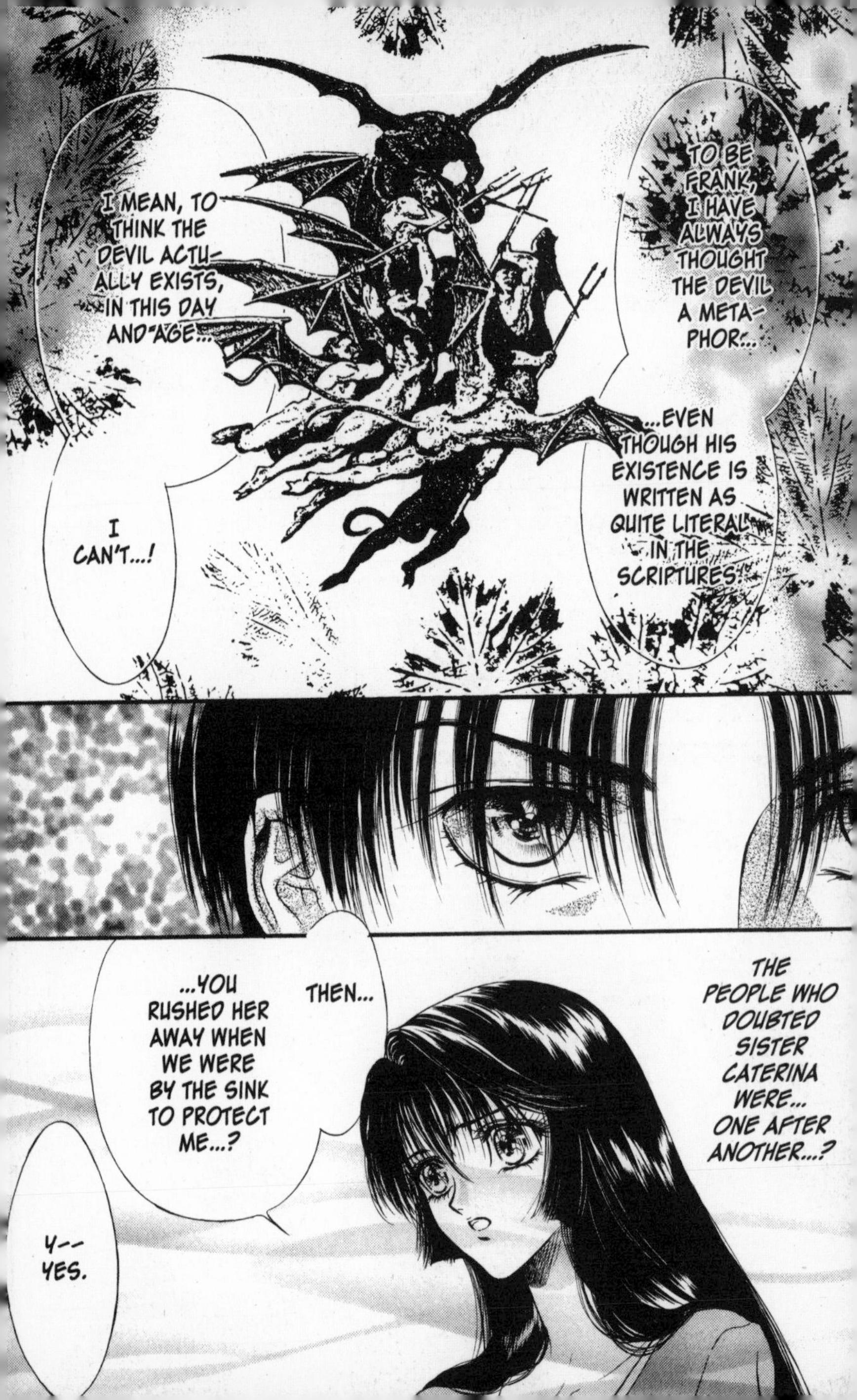
TO BE FRANK, I HAVE ALWAYS THOUGHT THE DEVIL A METAPHOR...
...EVEN THOUGH HIS EXISTENCE IS WRITTEN AS QUITE LITERAL IN THE SCRIPTURES.
I MEAN, TO THINK THE DEVIL ACTUALLY EXISTS, IN THIS DAY AND AGE...
I CAN'T...!
THE PEOPLE WHO DOUBTED SISTER CATERINA WERE... ONE AFTER ANOTHER...?
THEN...
...YOU RUSHED HER AWAY WHEN WE WERE BY THE SINK TO PROTECT ME...?
Y-- YES.

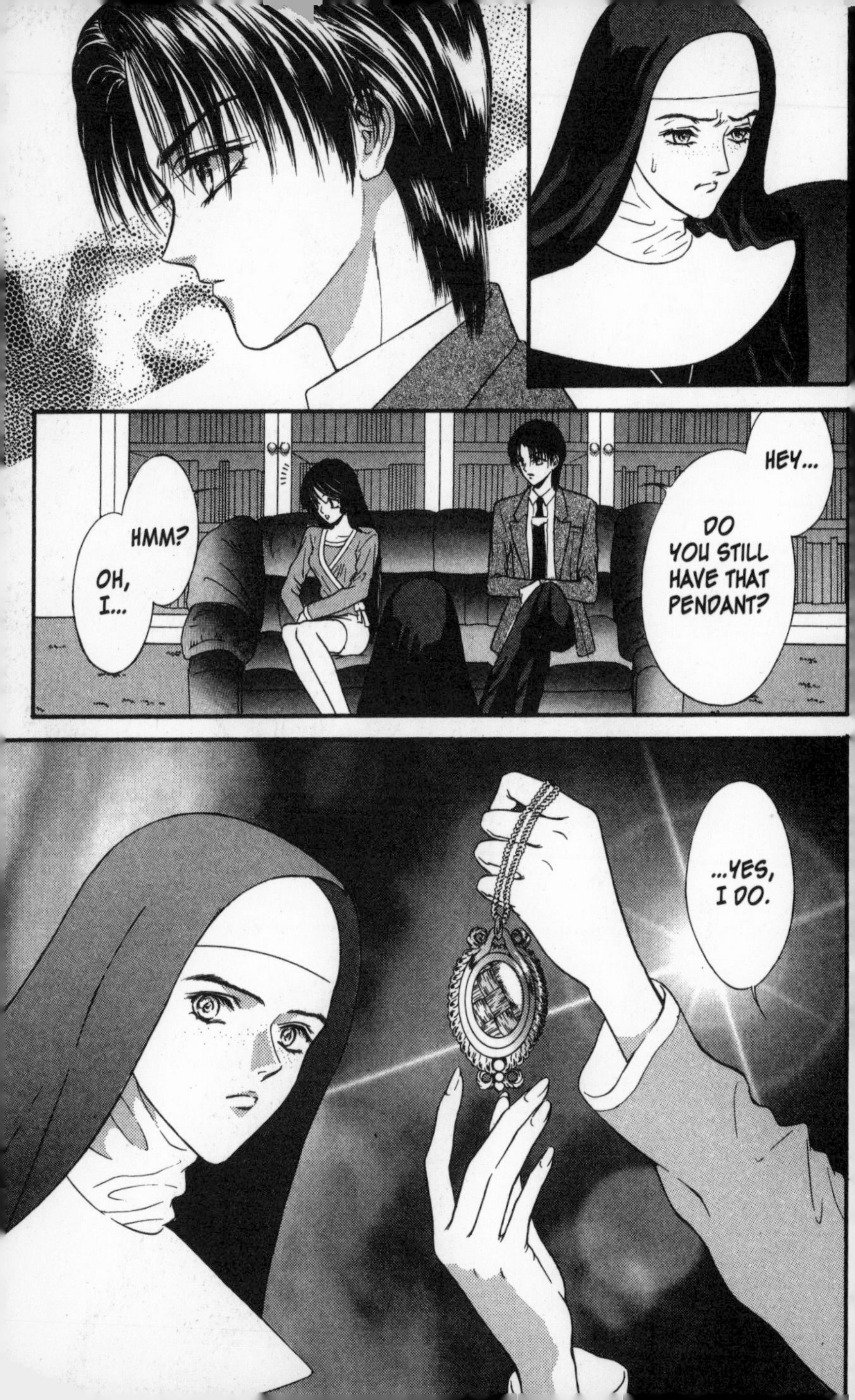
HEY...
DO YOU STILL HAVE THAT PENDANT?
HMM?
OH, I...
...YES, I DO.

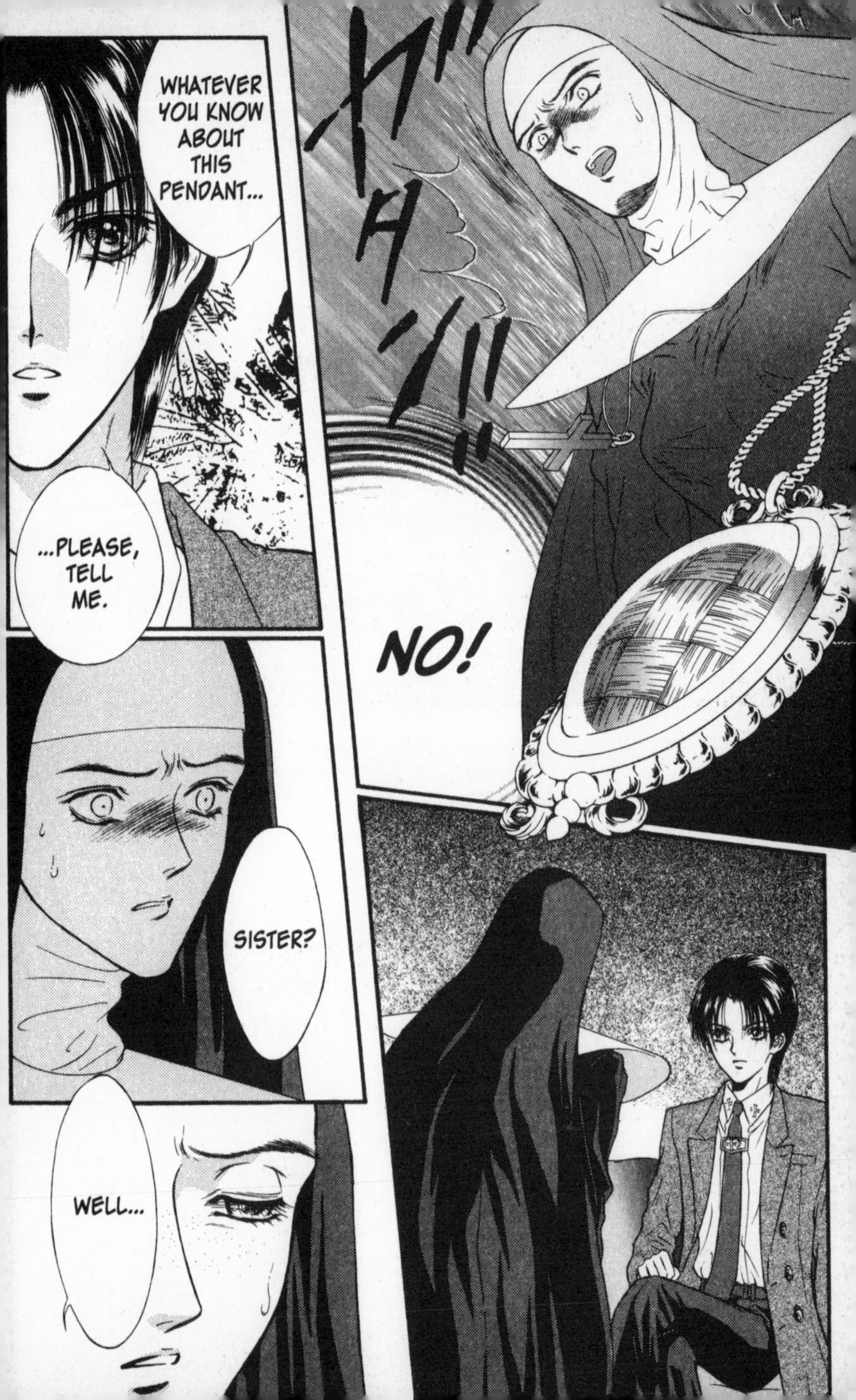

ガタン!!
NO!
WHATEVER YOU KNOW ABOUT THIS PENDANT...
...PLEASE, TELL ME.
SISTER?
WELL...

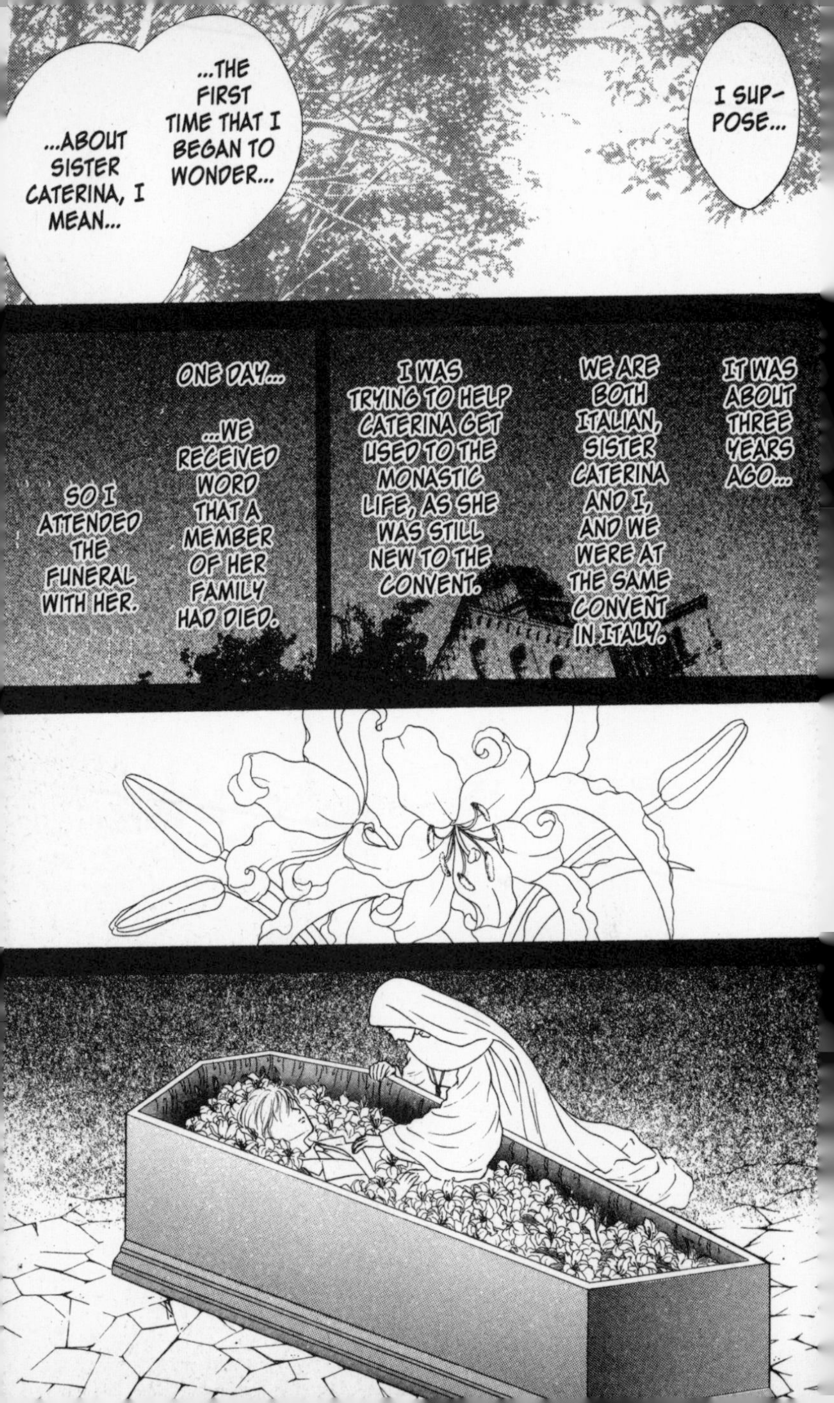
I SUP-POSE...
...THE FIRST TIME THAT I BEGAN TO WONDER...
...ABOUT SISTER CATERINA, I MEAN...
IT WAS ABOUT THREE YEARS AGO...
WE ARE BOTH ITALIAN, SISTER CATERINA AND I, AND WE WERE AT THE SAME CONVENT IN ITALY.
I WAS TRYING TO HELP CATERINA GET USED TO THE MONASTIC LIFE, AS SHE WAS STILL NEW TO THE CONVENT.
ONE DAY...
...WE RECEIVED WORD THAT A MEMBER OF HER FAMILY HAD DIED.
SO I ATTENDED THE FUNERAL WITH HER.

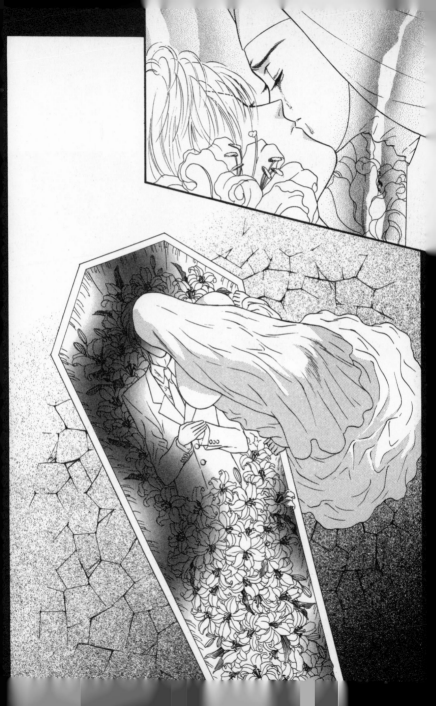

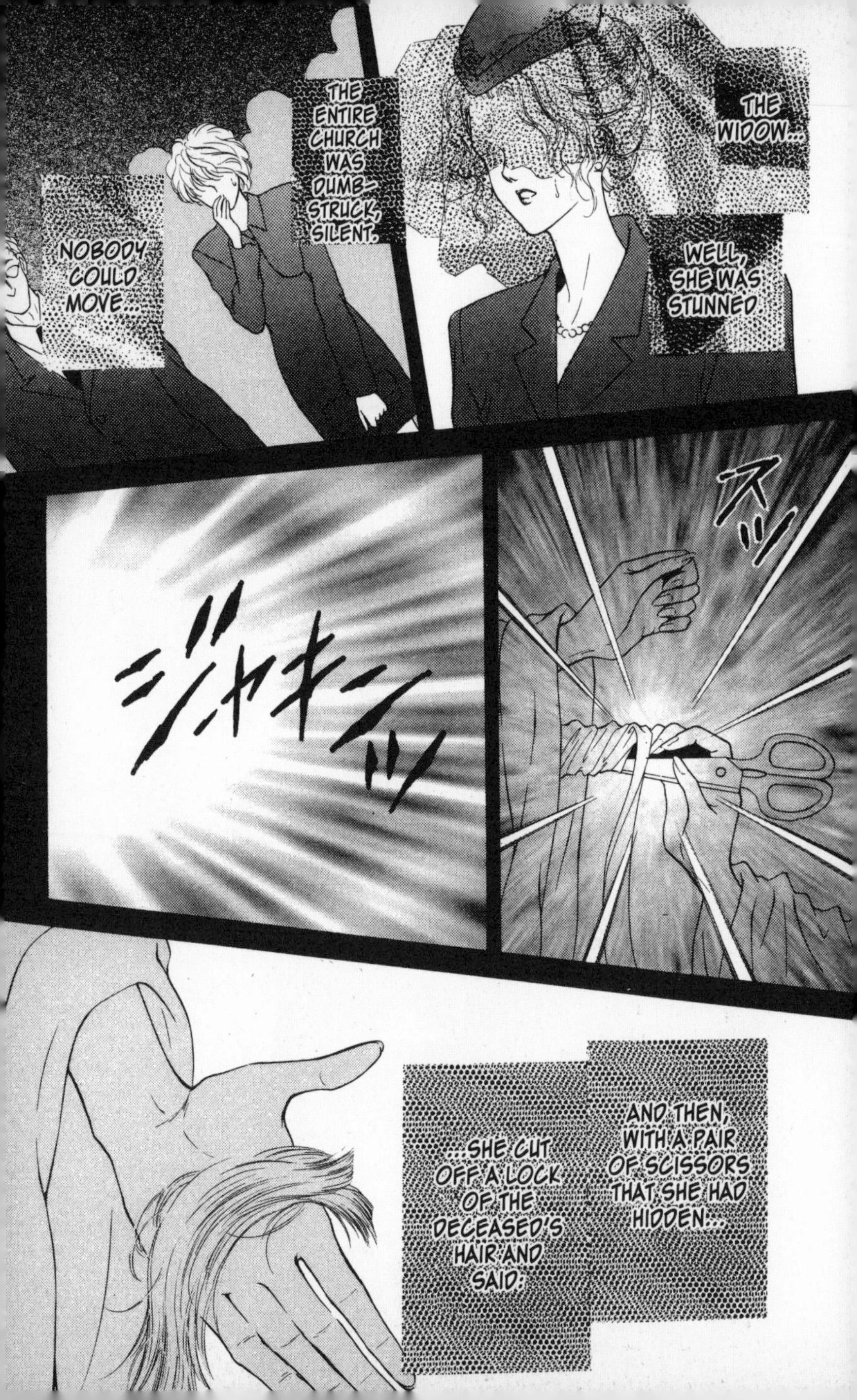
THE WIDOW...
WELL, SHE WAS STUNNED
THE ENTIRE CHURCH WAS DUMB-STRUCK, SILENT.
NOBODY COULD MOVE...
スッ
ジャキーンッ
AND THEN, WITH A PAIR OF SCISSORS THAT SHE HAD HIDDEN...
...SHE CUT OFF A LOCK OF THE DECEASED'S HAIR AND SAID:

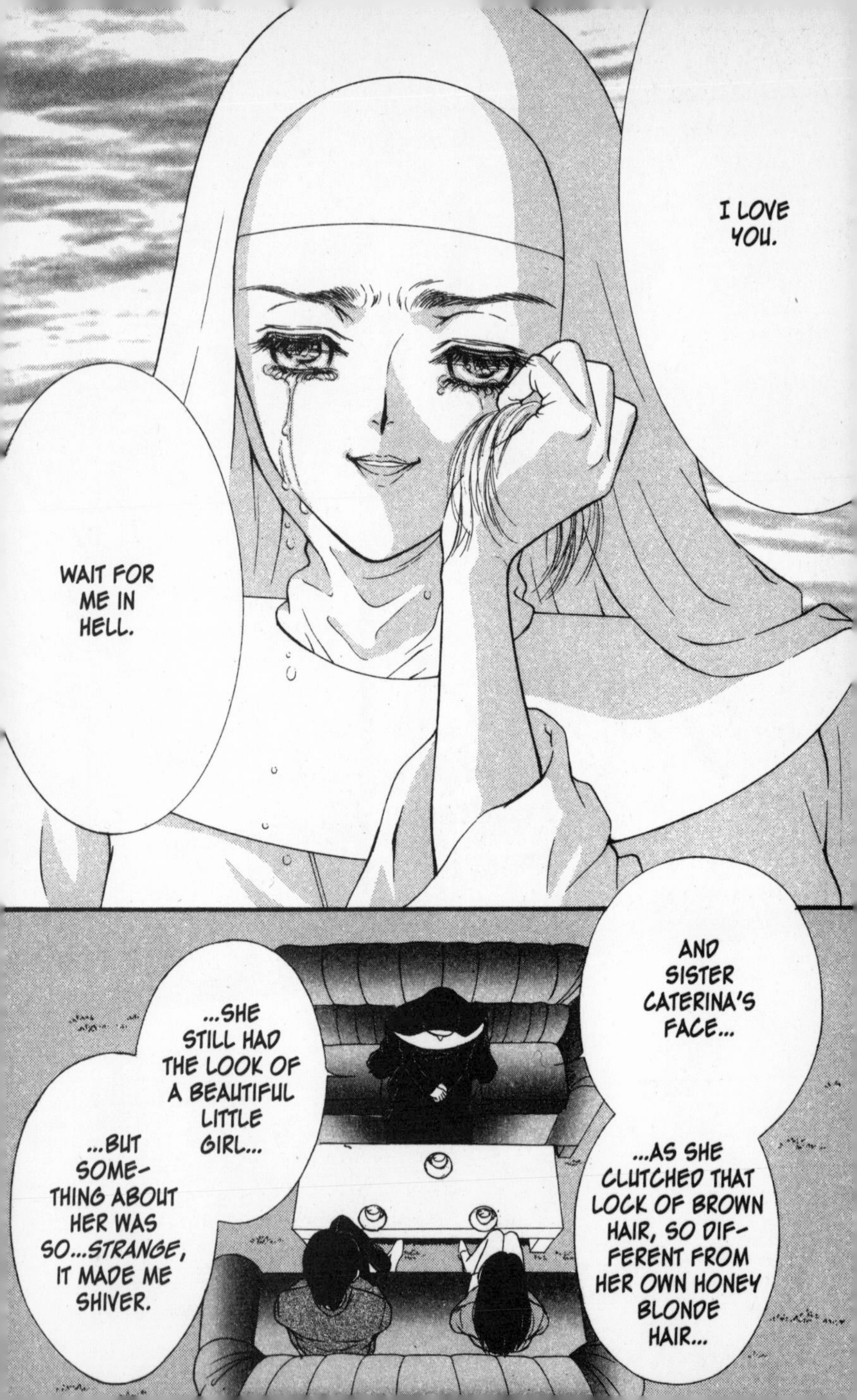
I LOVE YOU.
WAIT FOR ME IN HELL.
AND SISTER CATERINA'S FACE...
...AS SHE CLUTCHED THAT LOCK OF BROWN HAIR, SO DIF-FERENT FROM HER OWN HONEY BLONDE HAIR...
...SHE STILL HAD THE LOOK OF A BEAUTIFUL LITTLE GIRL...
...BUT SOME-THING ABOUT HER WAS SO...*STRANGE*, IT MADE ME SHIVER.

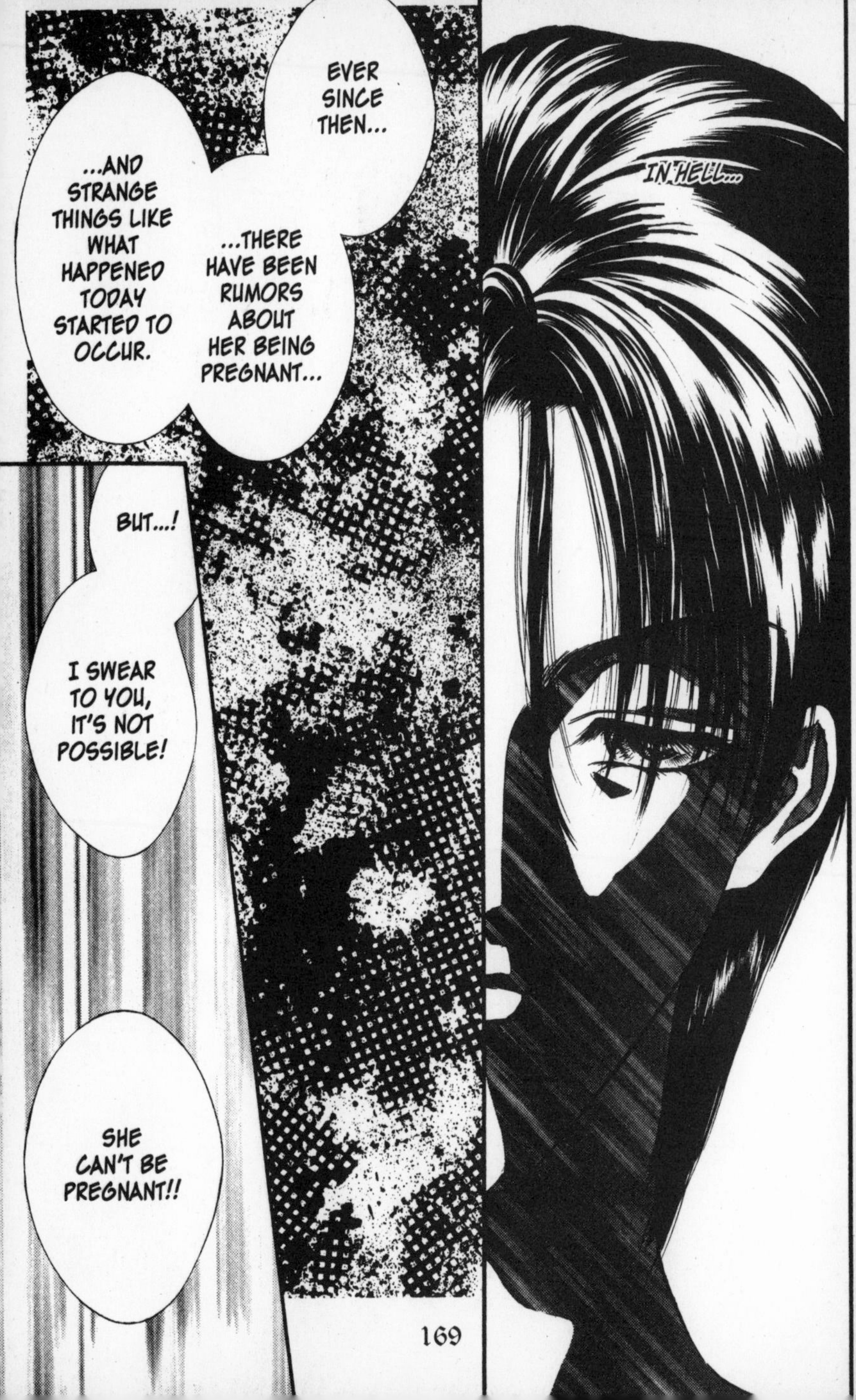
IN HELL...
EVER SINCE THEN...
...THERE HAVE BEEN RUMORS ABOUT HER BEING PREGNANT...
...AND STRANGE THINGS LIKE WHAT HAPPENED TODAY STARTED TO OCCUR.
BUT...!
I SWEAR TO YOU, IT'S NOT POSSIBLE!
SHE CAN'T BE PREGNANT!!

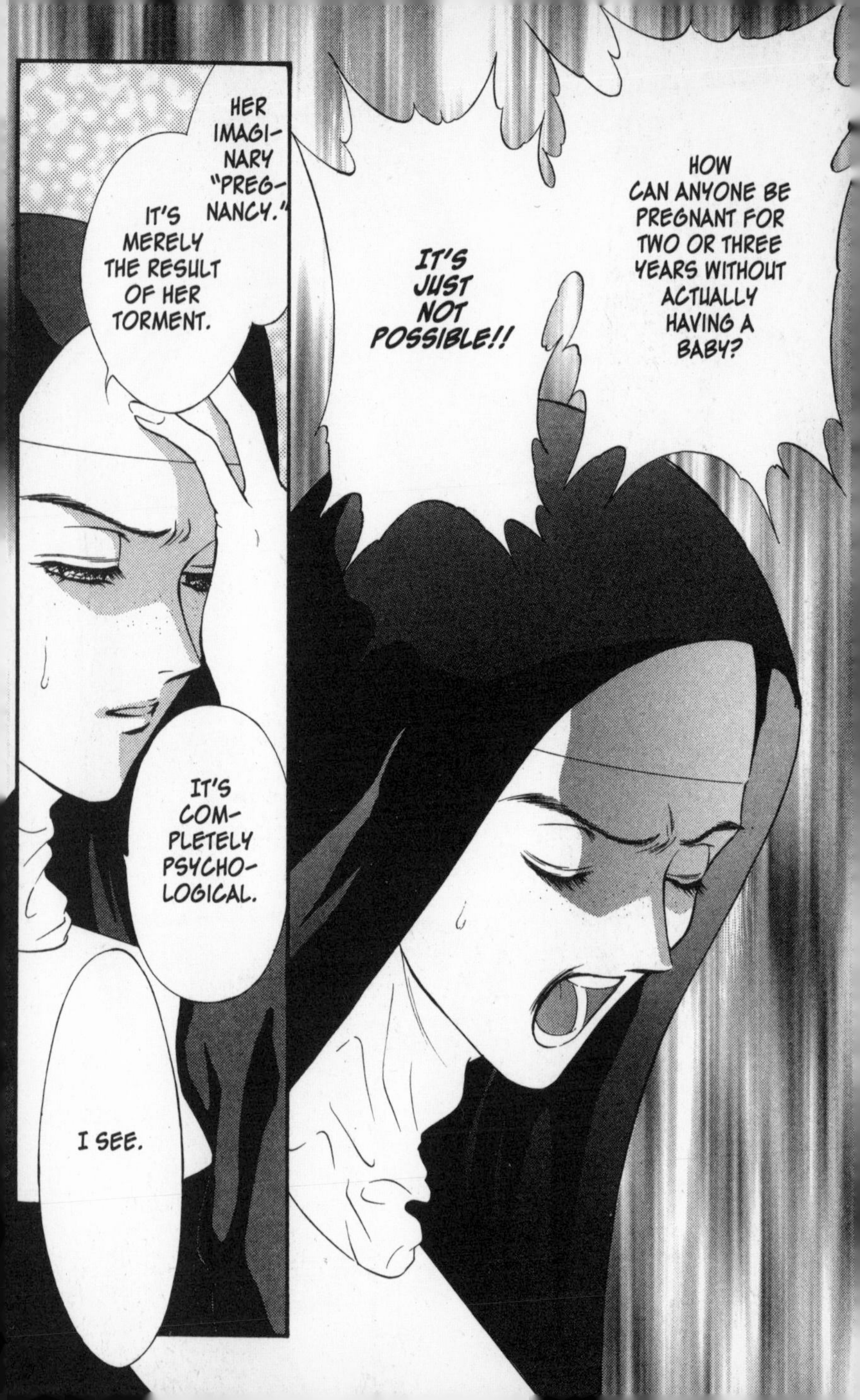
HOW CAN ANYONE BE PREGNANT FOR TWO OR THREE YEARS WITHOUT ACTUALLY HAVING A BABY?
IT'S JUST NOT POSSIBLE!!
HER IMAGINARY "PREGNANCY."
IT'S MERELY THE RESULT OF HER TORMENT.
IT'S COMPLETELY PSYCHOLOGICAL.
I SEE.

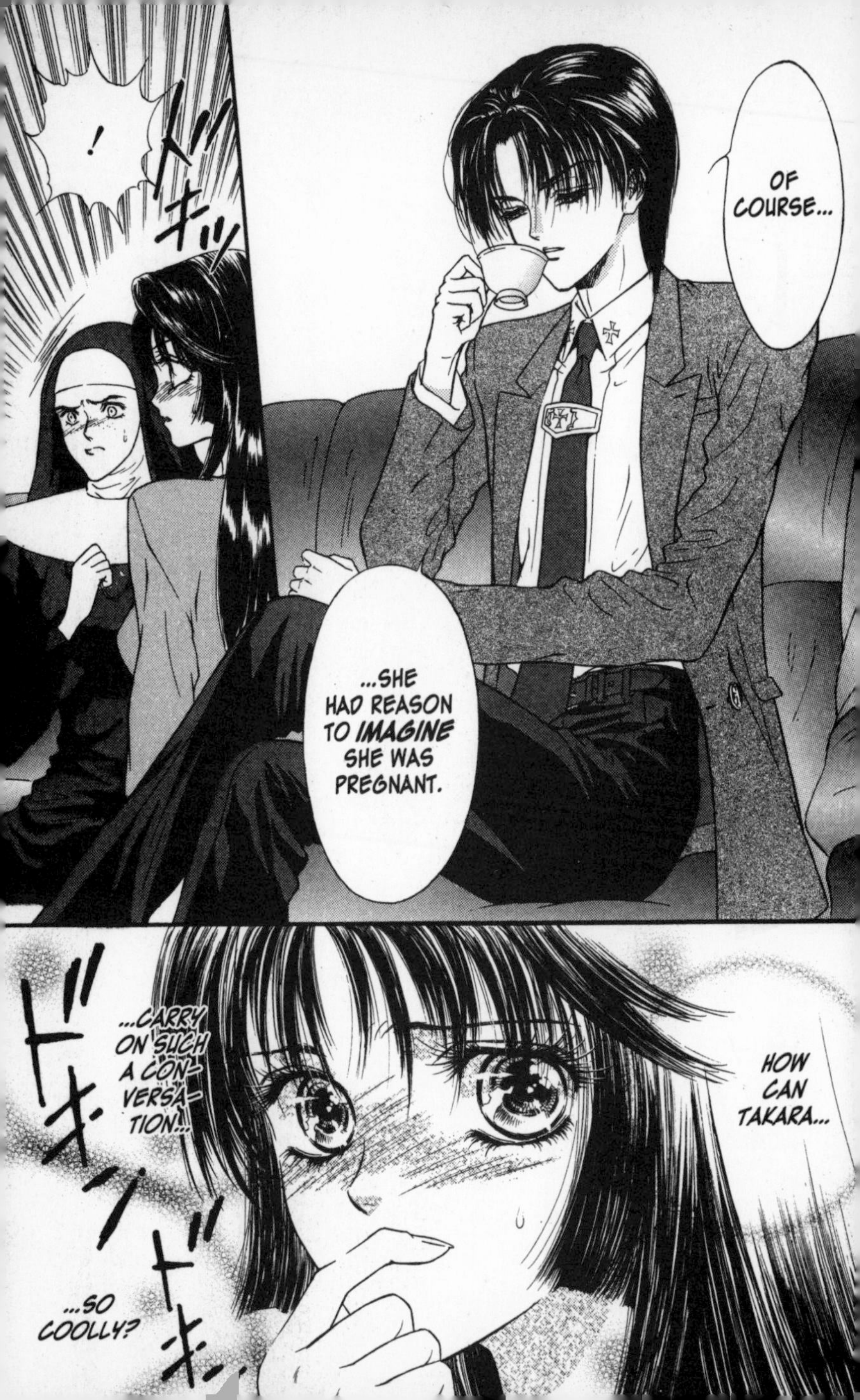
OF COURSE...
!
...SHE HAD REASON TO IMAGINE SHE WAS PREGNANT.
HOW CAN TAKARA...
...CARRY ON SUCH A CON-VERSA-TION...
...SO COOLLY?

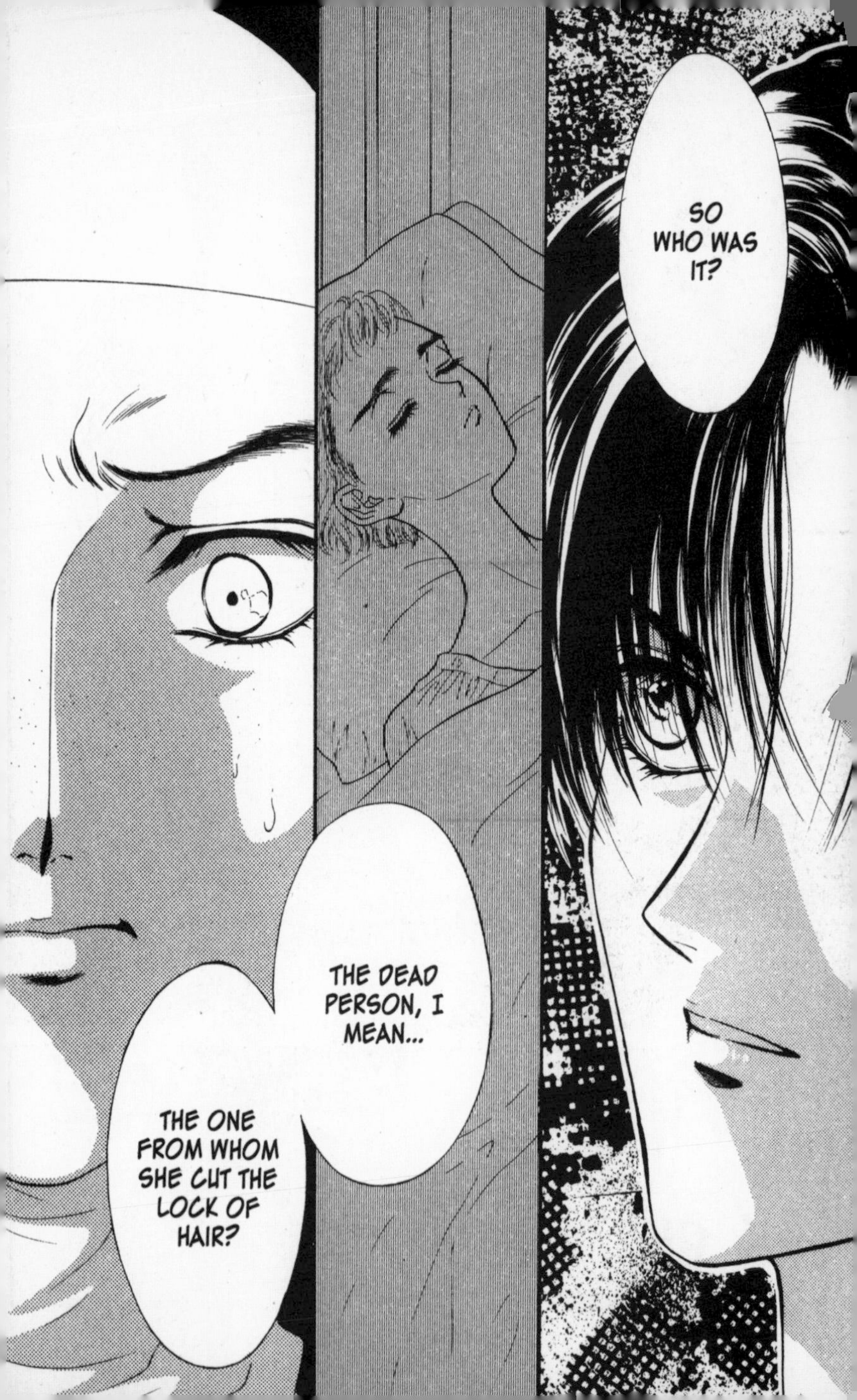
SO WHO WAS IT?
THE DEAD PERSON, I MEAN...
THE ONE FROM WHOM SHE CUT THE LOCK OF HAIR?

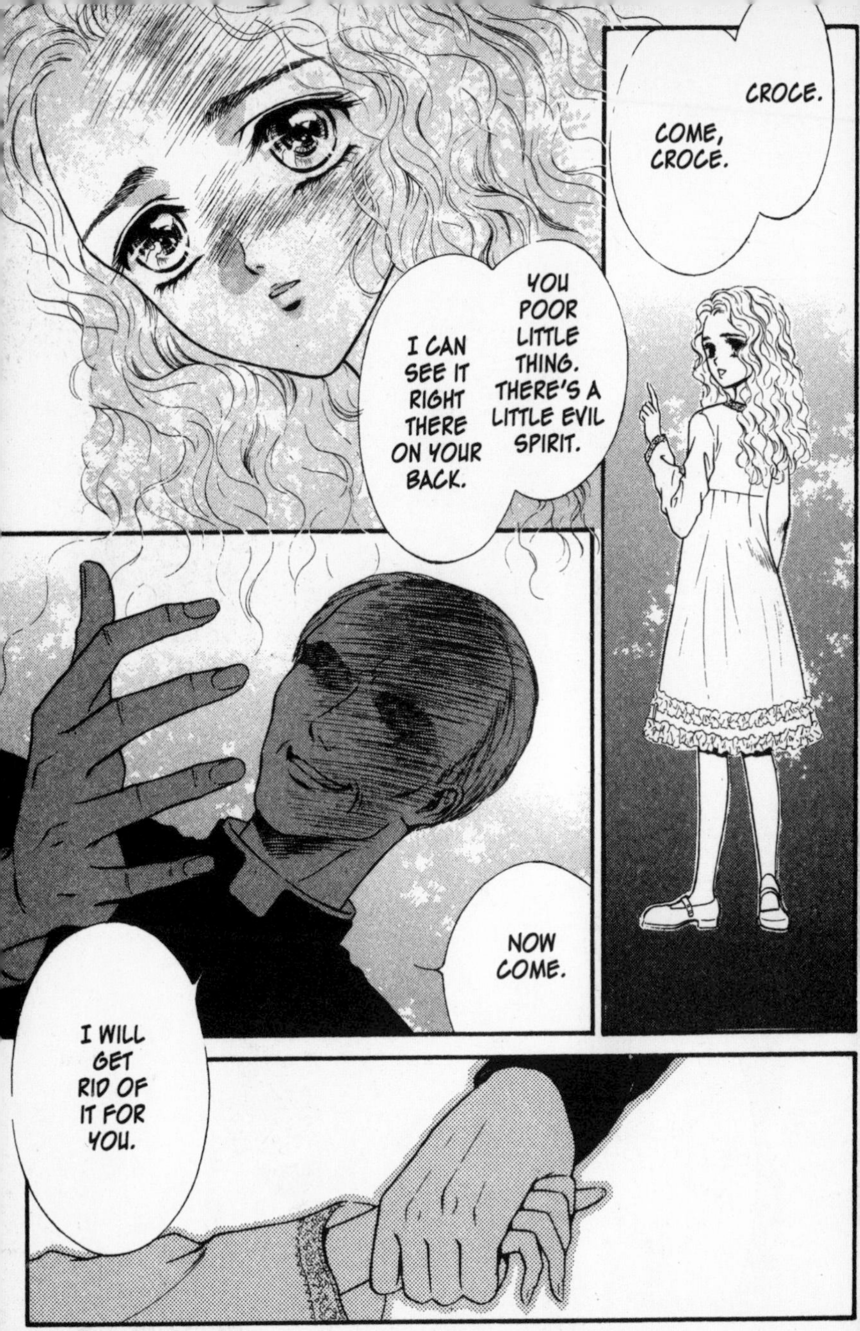
CROCE.
COME, CROCE.
YOU POOR LITTLE THING. THERE'S A LITTLE EVIL SPIRIT.
I CAN SEE IT RIGHT THERE ON YOUR BACK.
NOW COME.
I WILL GET RID OF IT FOR YOU.

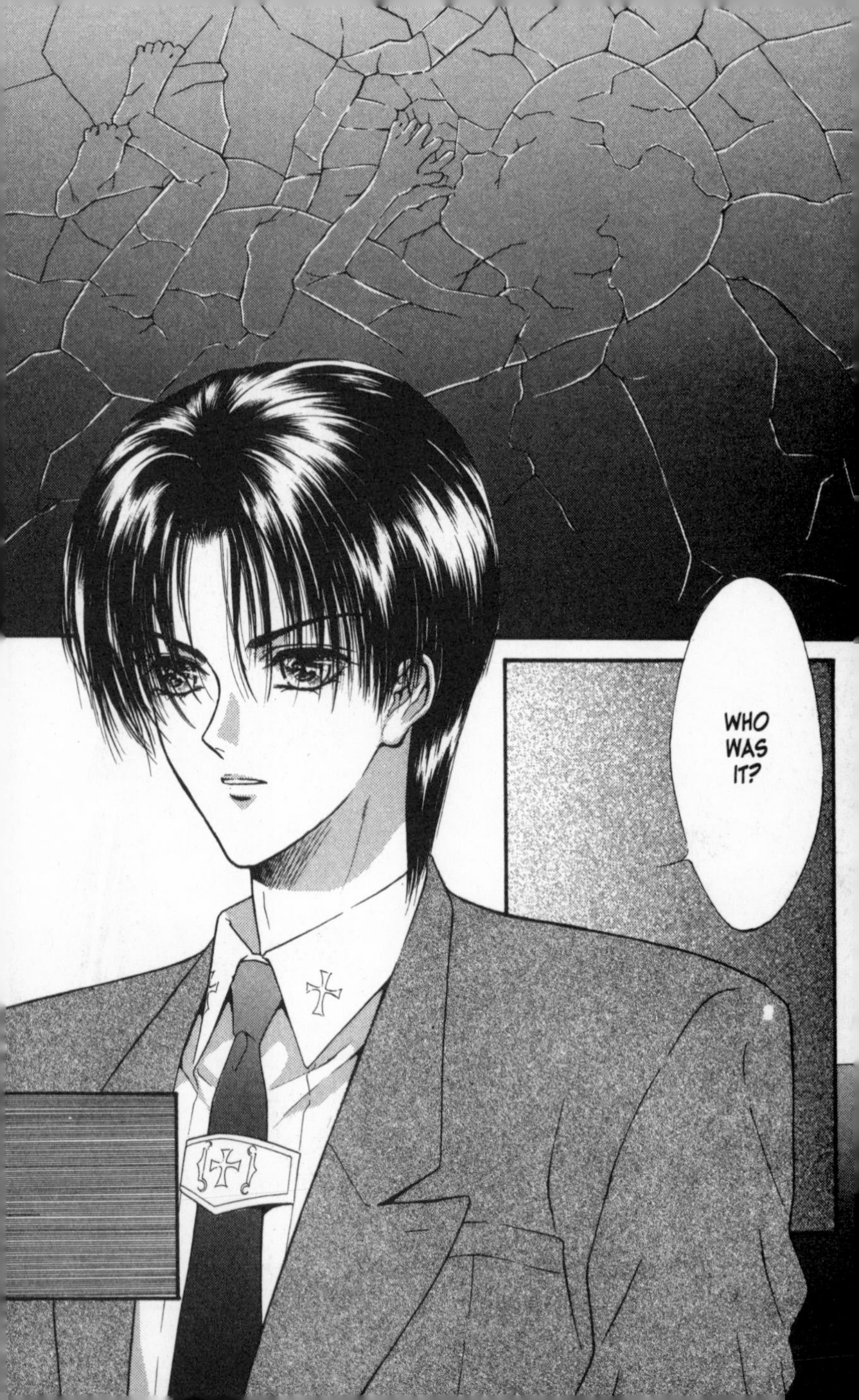
WHO WAS IT?

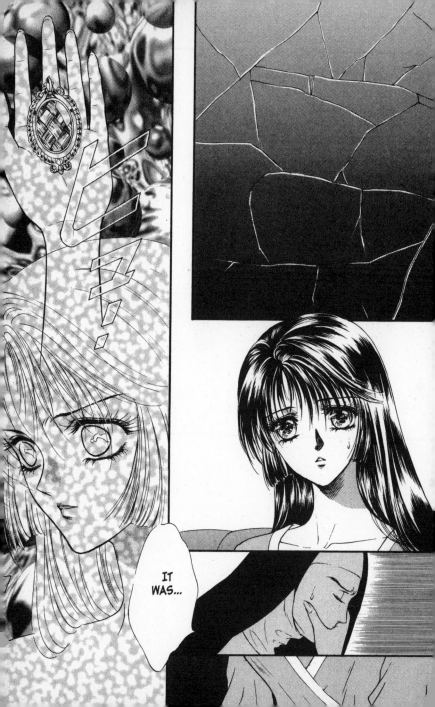

IT
WAS...

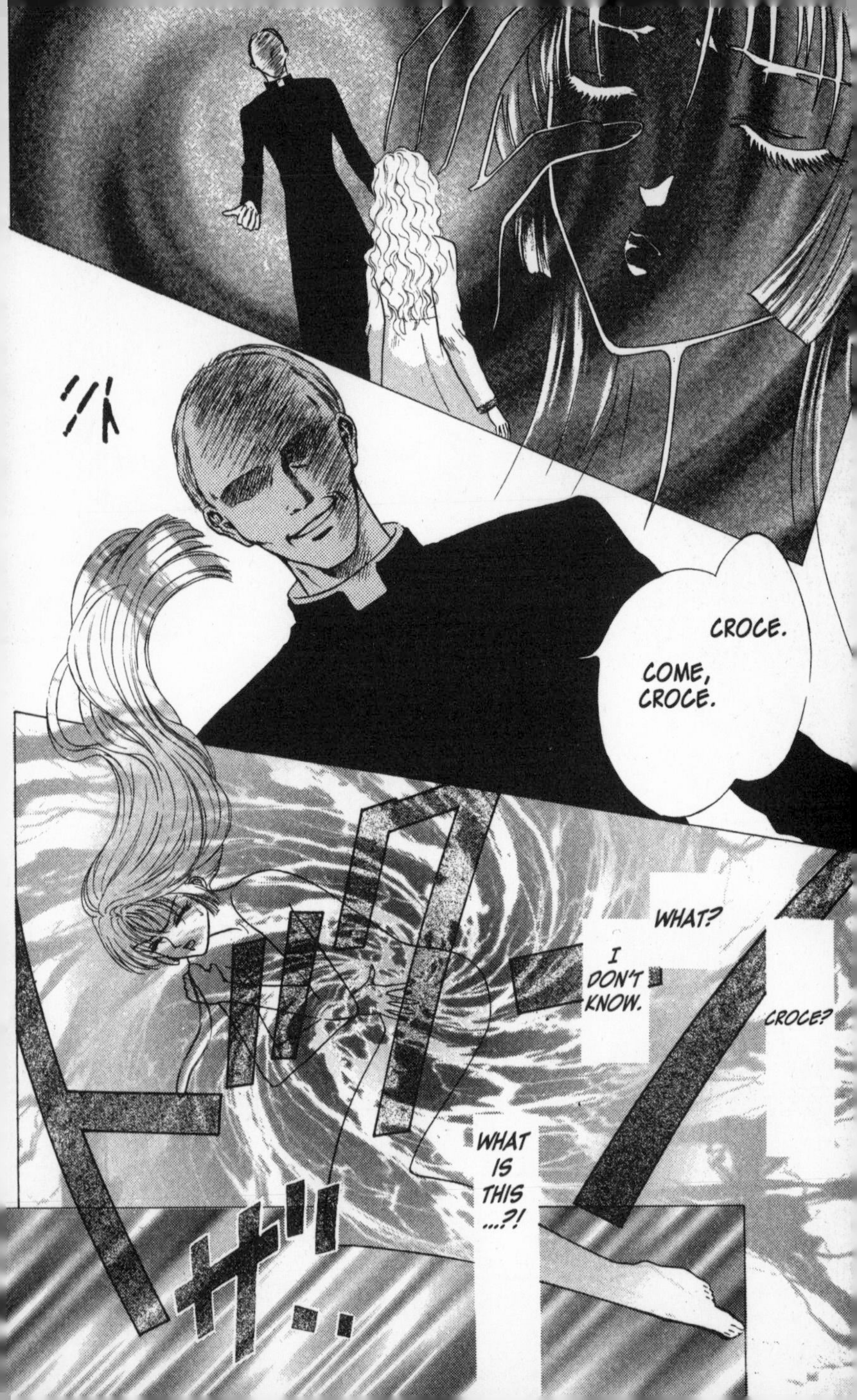

CROCE.
COME, CROCE.
WHAT?
I DON'T KNOW.
CROCE?
WHAT IS THIS ...?!

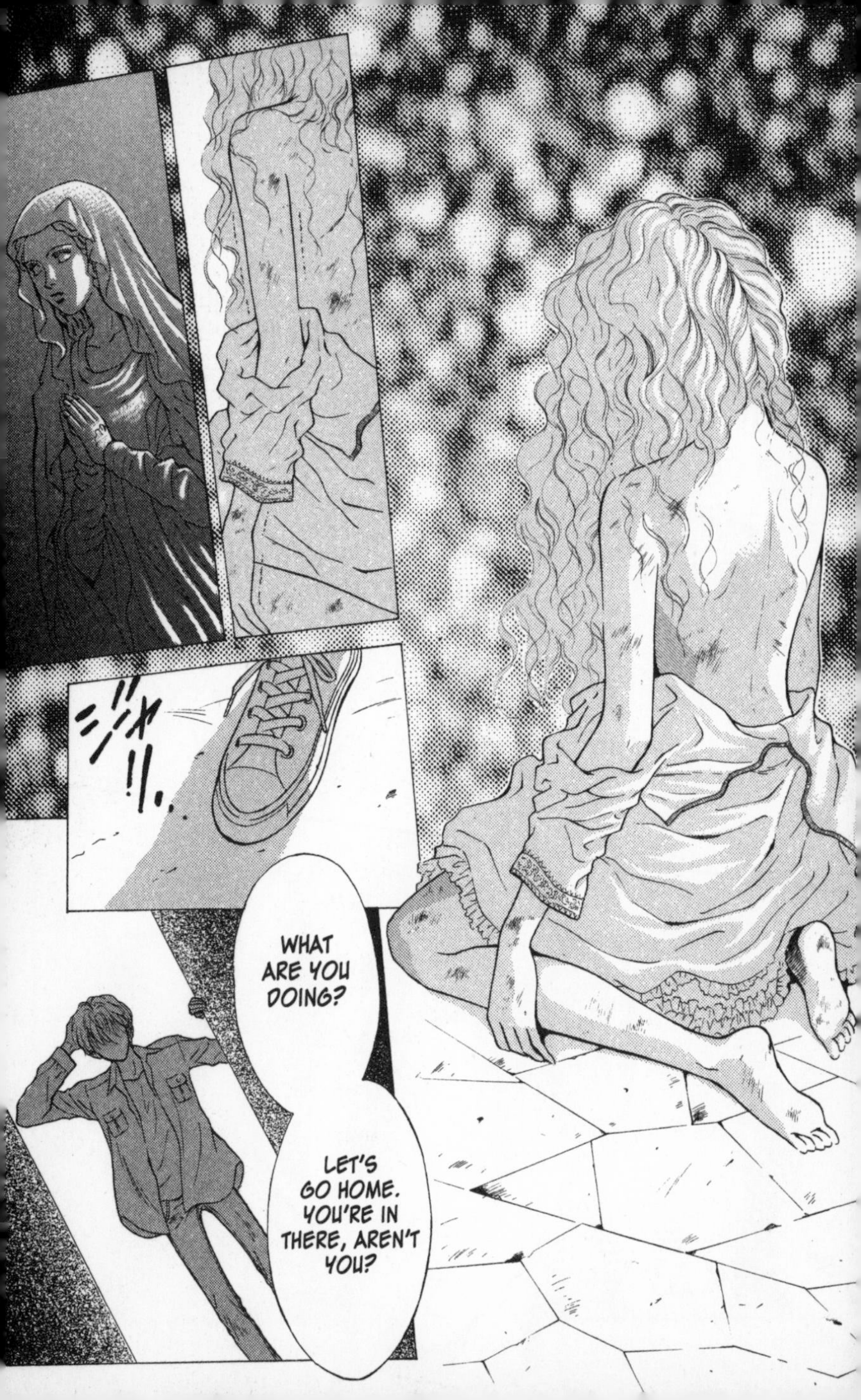
WHAT ARE YOU DOING?
LET'S GO HOME. YOU'RE IN THERE, AREN'T YOU?

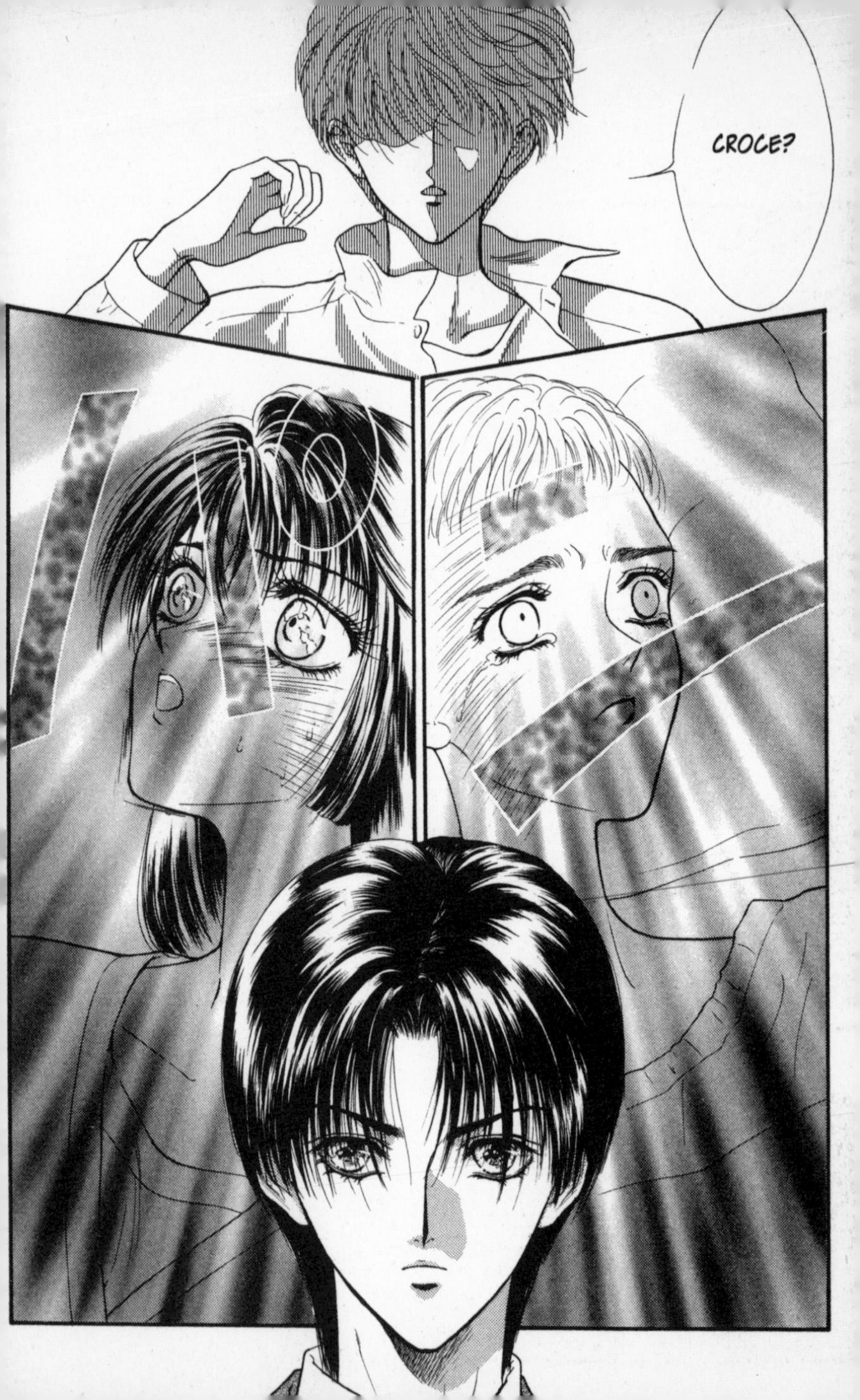
CROCE?

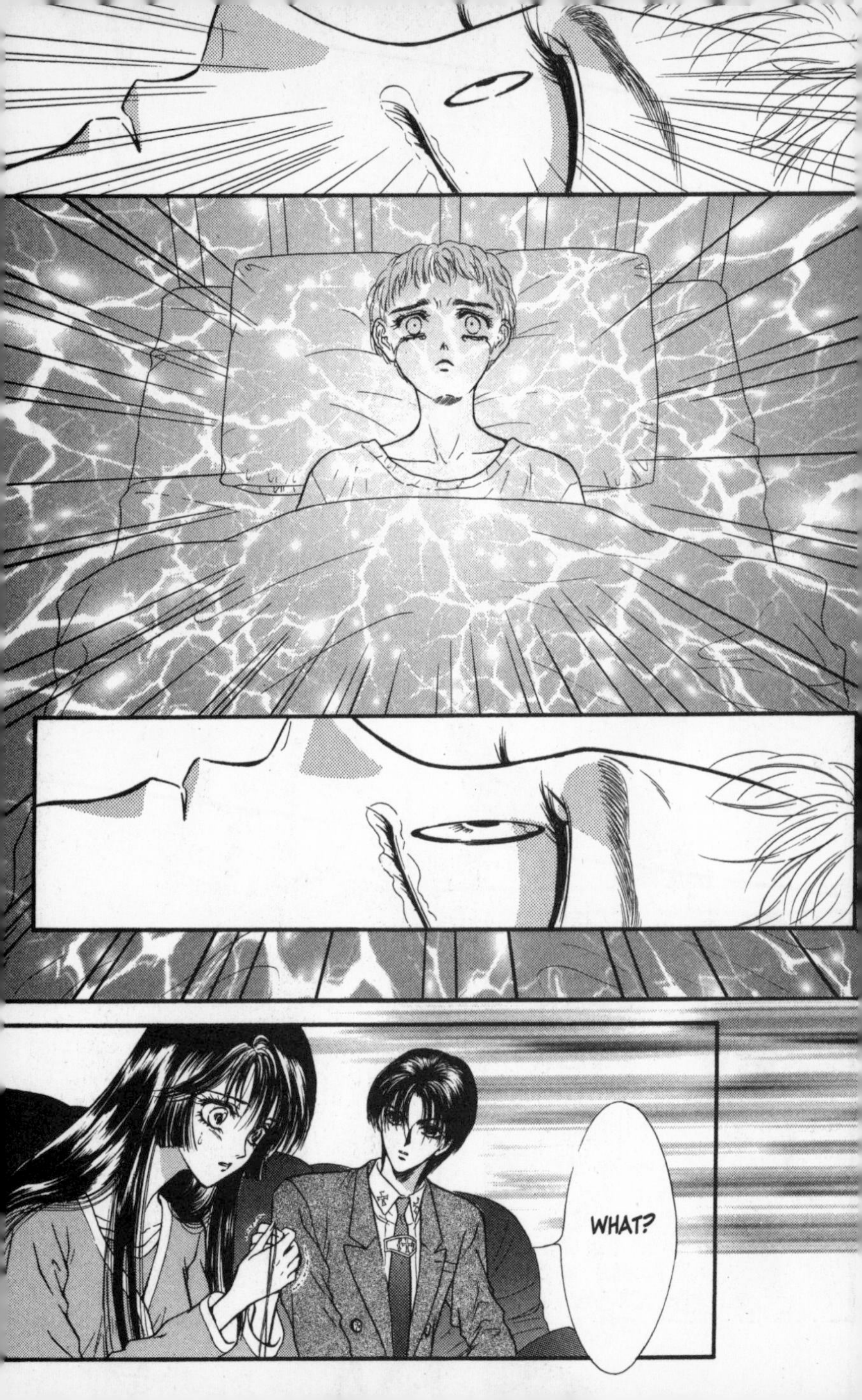
WHAT?

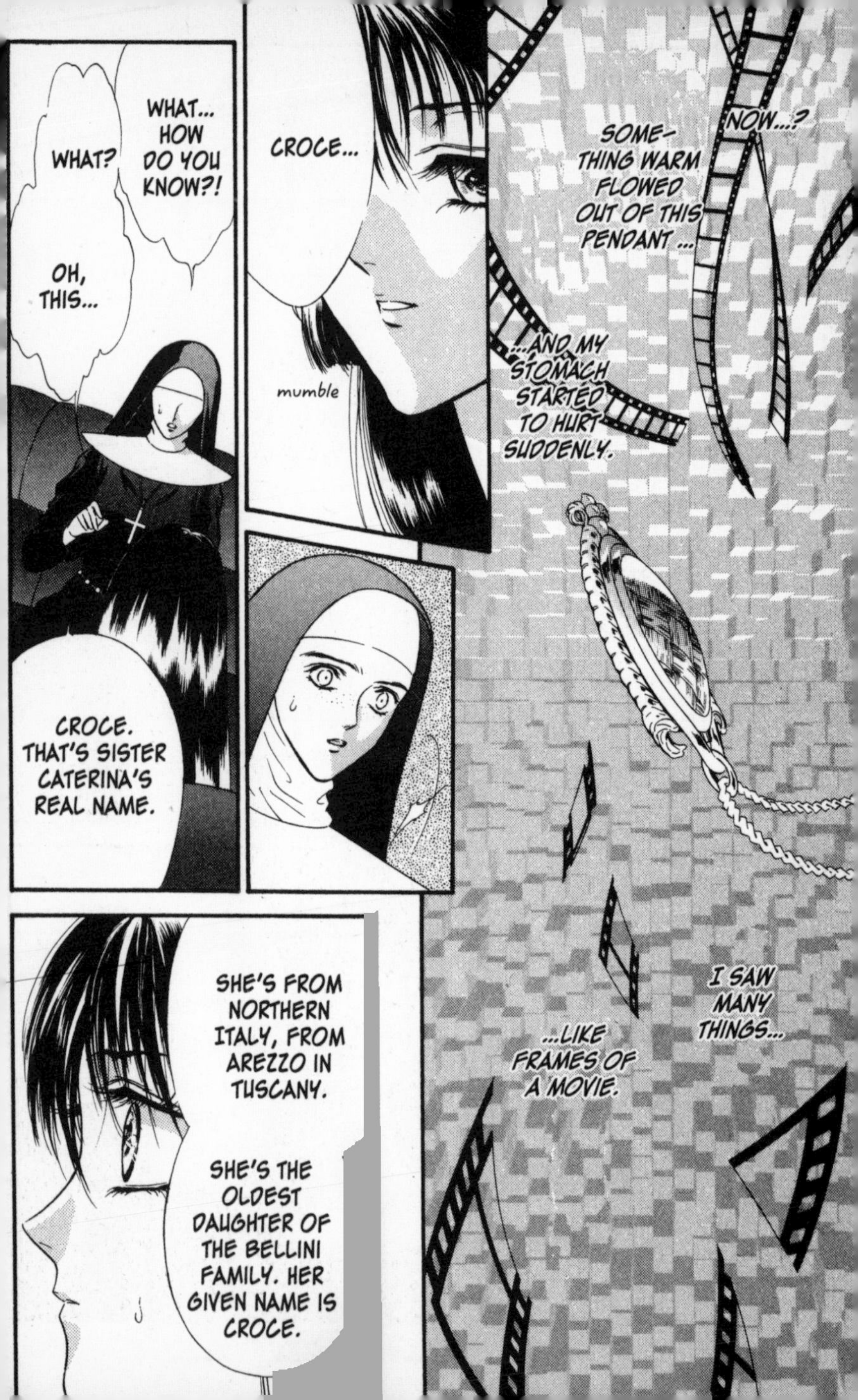
NOW...?
SOME-THING WARM FLOWED OUT OF THIS PENDANT ...
...AND MY STOMACH STARTED TO HURT SUDDENLY.
I SAW MANY THINGS...
...LIKE FRAMES OF A MOVIE.
CROCE...
mumble
WHAT... HOW DO YOU KNOW?!
WHAT?
OH, THIS...
CROCE. THAT'S SISTER CATERINA'S REAL NAME.
SHE'S FROM NORTHERN ITALY, FROM AREZZO IN TUSCANY.
SHE'S THE OLDEST DAUGHTER OF THE BELLINI FAMILY. HER GIVEN NAME IS CROCE.

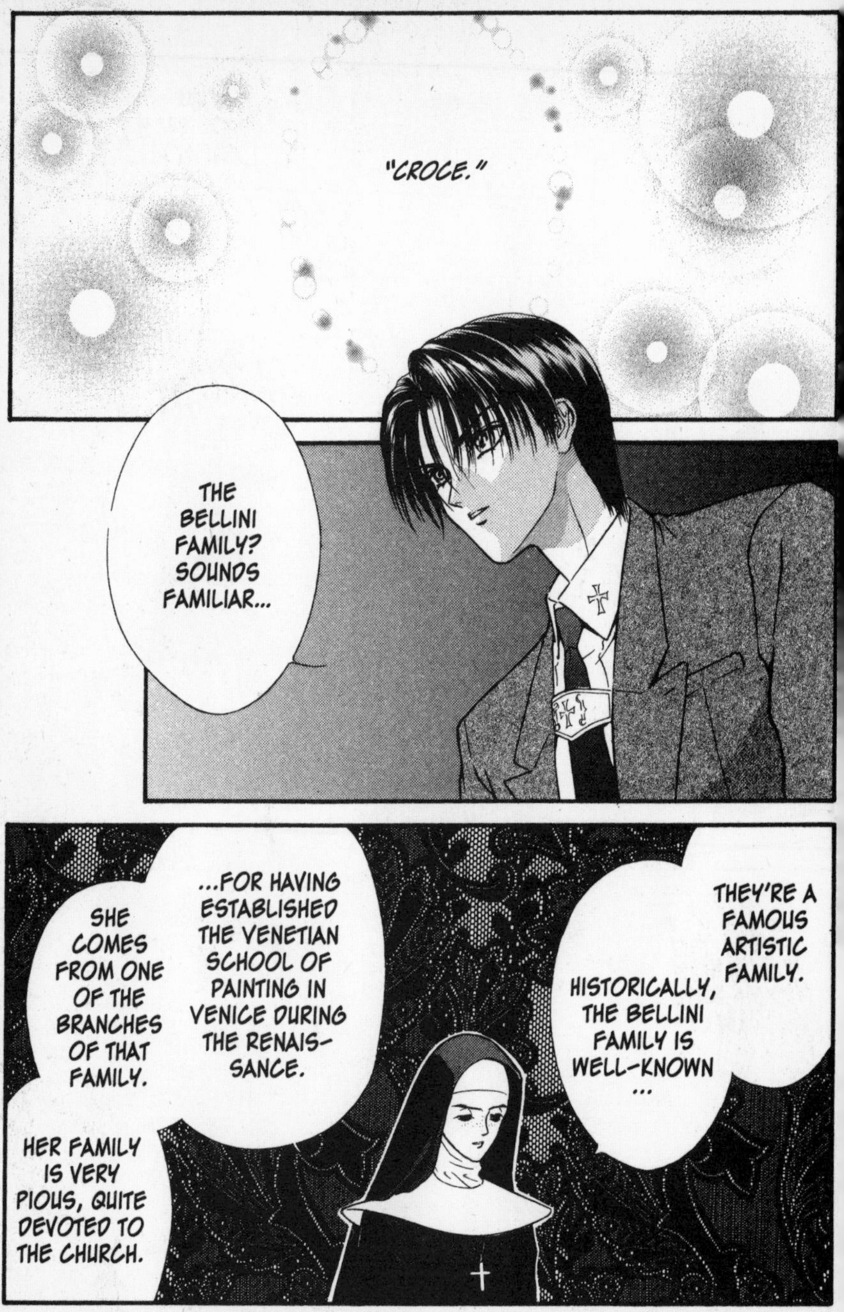
"CROCE."
THE BELLINI FAMILY? SOUNDS FAMILIAR...
THEY'RE A FAMOUS ARTISTIC FAMILY.
HISTORICALLY, THE BELLINI FAMILY IS WELL-KNOWN ...
...FOR HAVING ESTABLISHED THE VENETIAN SCHOOL OF PAINTING IN VENICE DURING THE RENAIS-SANCE.
SHE COMES FROM ONE OF THE BRANCHES OF THAT FAMILY.
HER FAMILY IS VERY PIOUS, QUITE DEVOTED TO THE CHURCH.

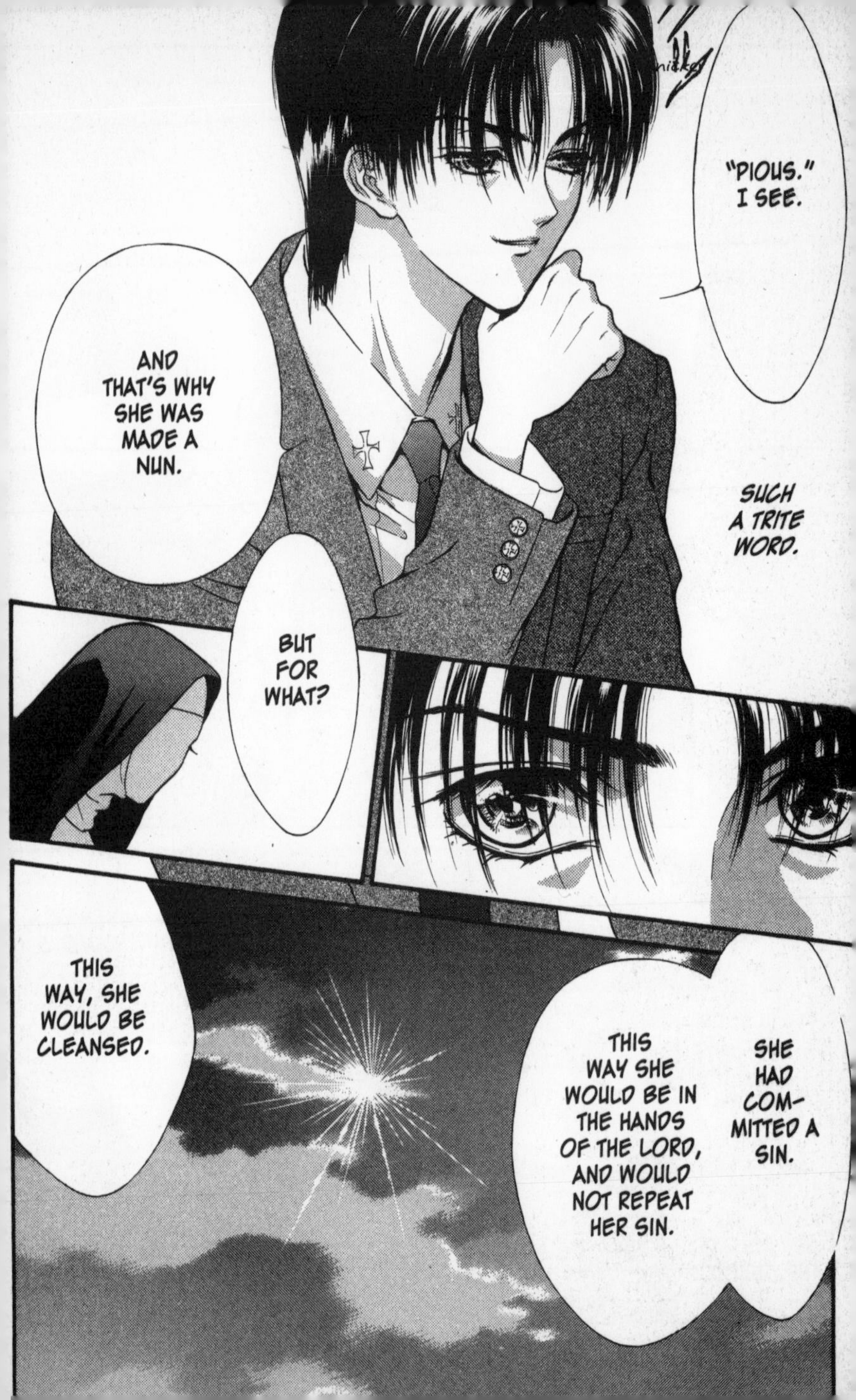
snicker
"PIOUS." I SEE.
SUCH A TRITE WORD.
AND THAT'S WHY SHE WAS MADE A NUN.
BUT FOR WHAT?
SHE HAD COM-MITTED A SIN.
THIS WAY SHE WOULD BE IN THE HANDS OF THE LORD, AND WOULD NOT REPEAT HER SIN.
THIS WAY, SHE WOULD BE CLEANSED.

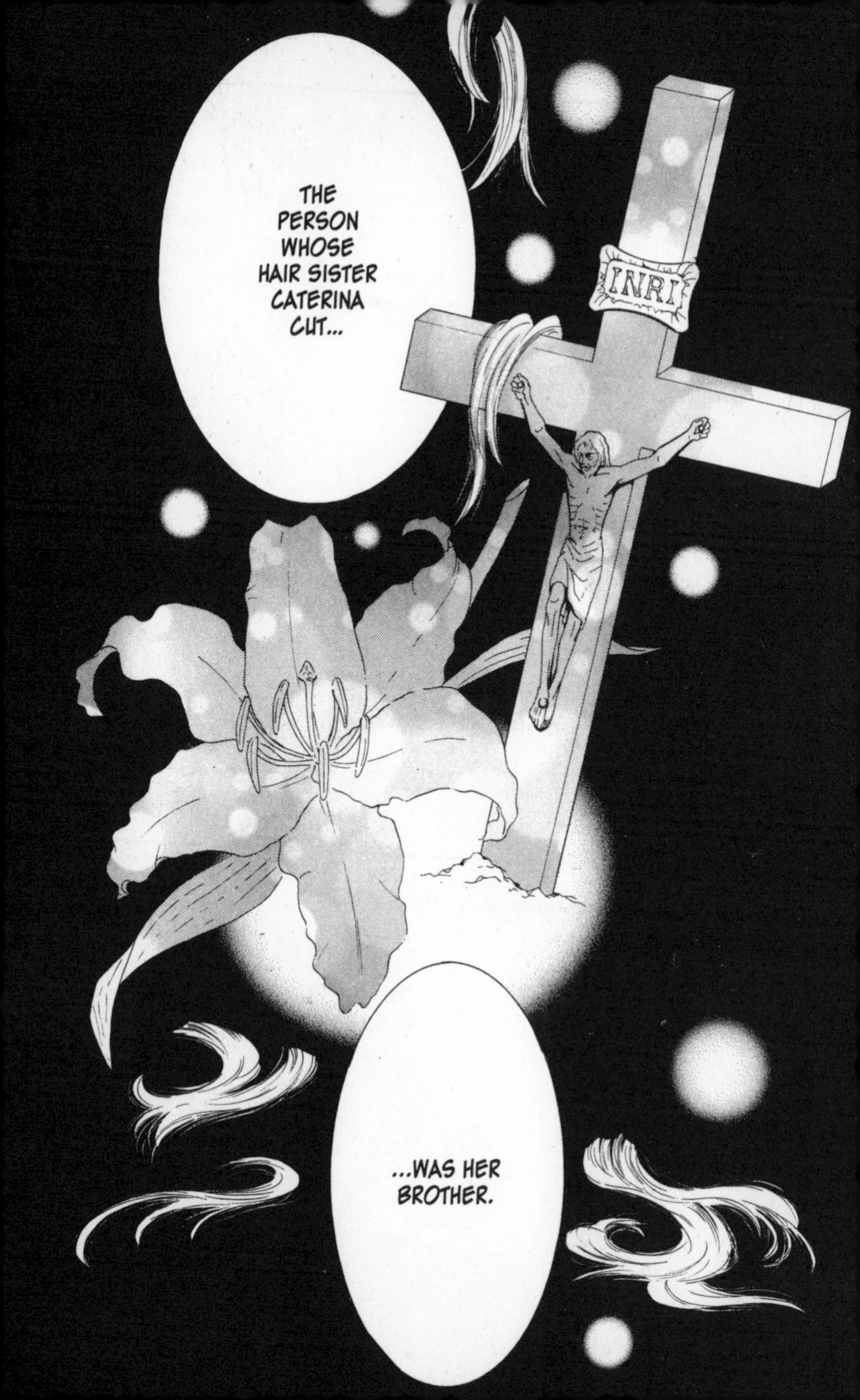
THE PERSON WHOSE HAIR SISTER CATERINA CUT...
INRI
...WAS HER BROTHER.

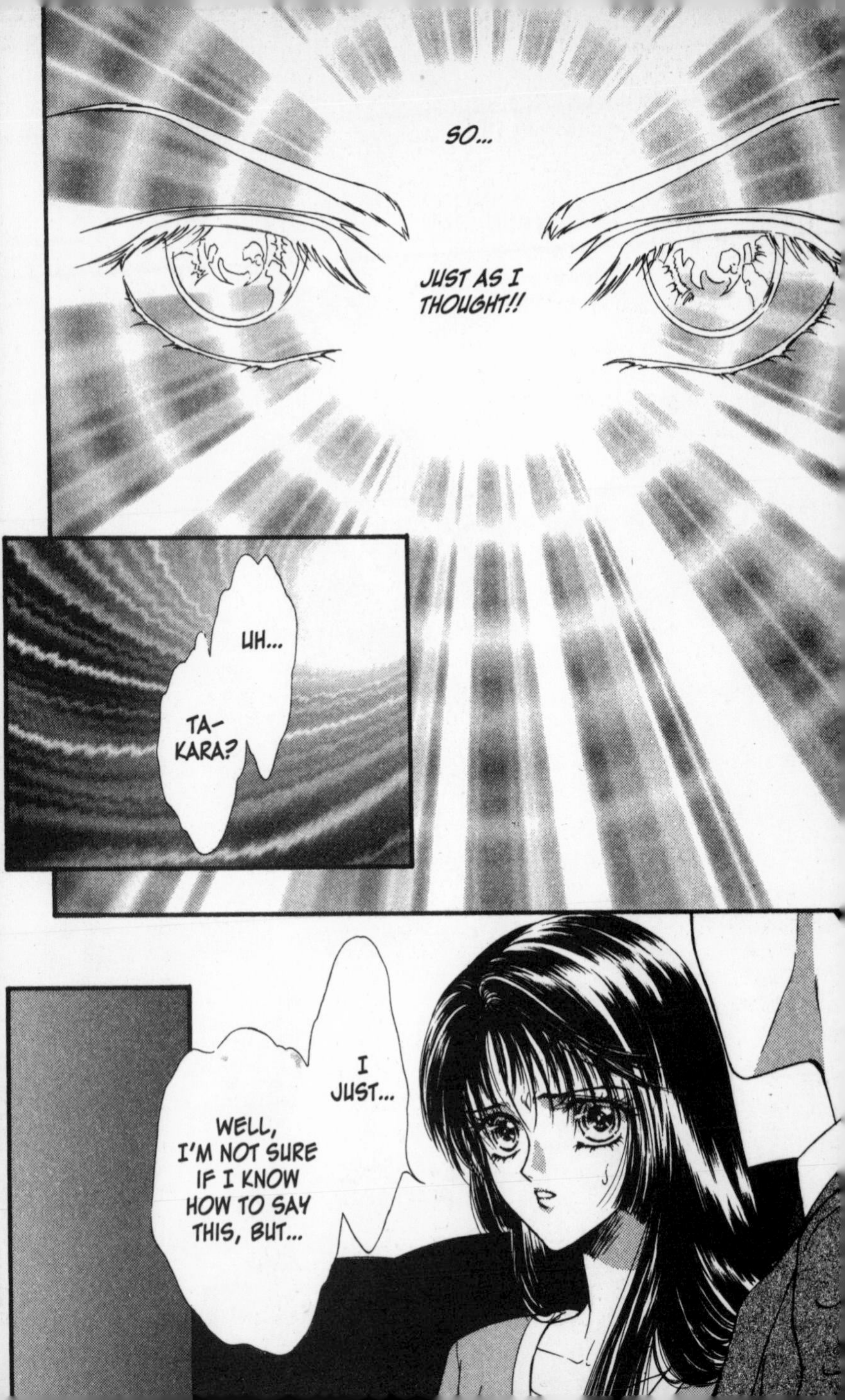
SO...
JUST AS I THOUGHT!!
UH...
TA-KARA?
I JUST...
WELL, I'M NOT SURE IF I KNOW HOW TO SAY THIS, BUT...

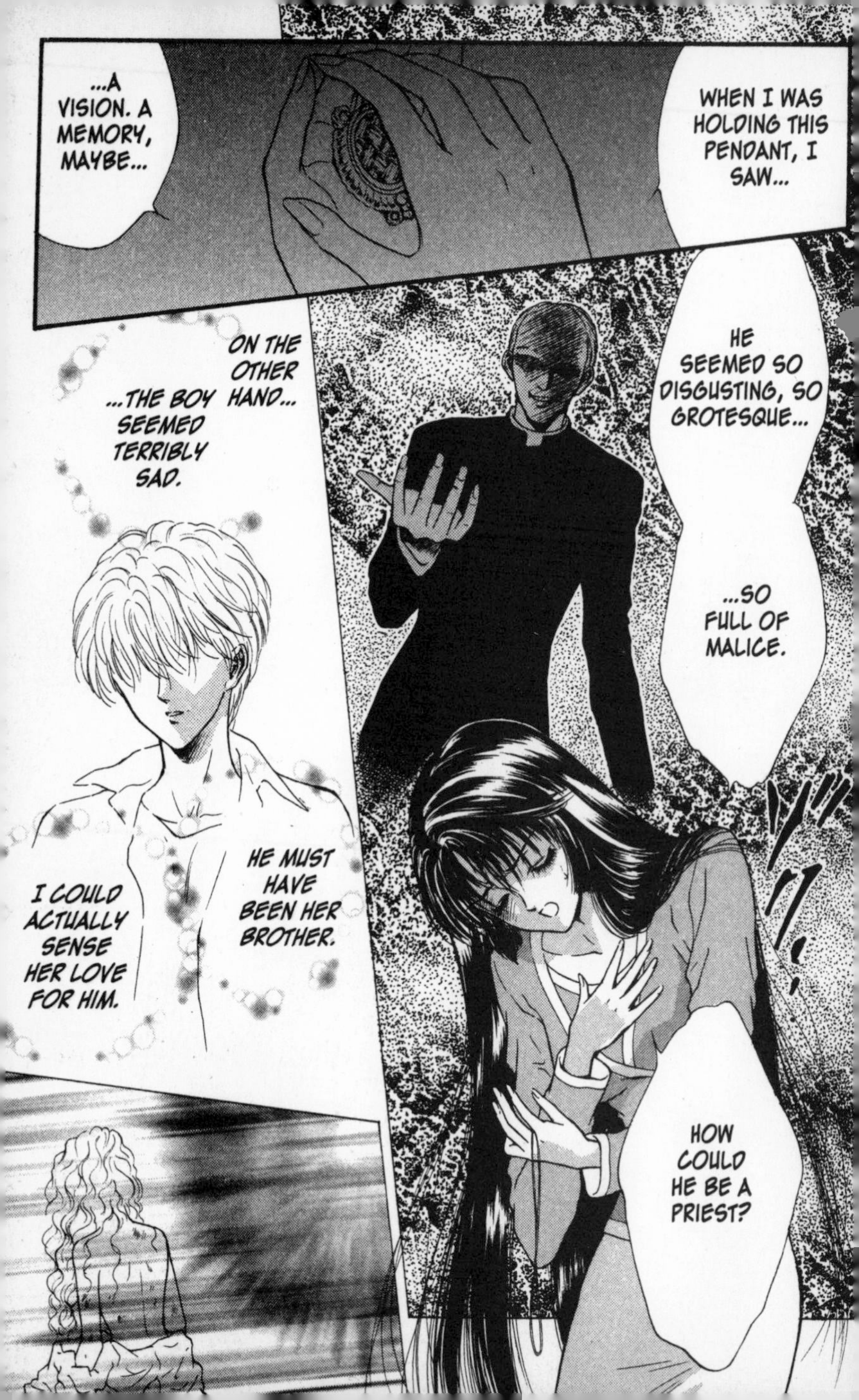
WHEN I WAS HOLDING THIS PENDANT, I SAW...
...A VISION. A MEMORY, MAYBE...
HE SEEMED SO DISGUSTING, SO GROTESQUE...
...SO FULL OF MALICE.
HOW COULD HE BE A PRIEST?
ON THE OTHER HAND...
...THE BOY SEEMED TERRIBLY SAD.
HE MUST HAVE BEEN HER BROTHER.
I COULD ACTUALLY SENSE HER LOVE FOR HIM.

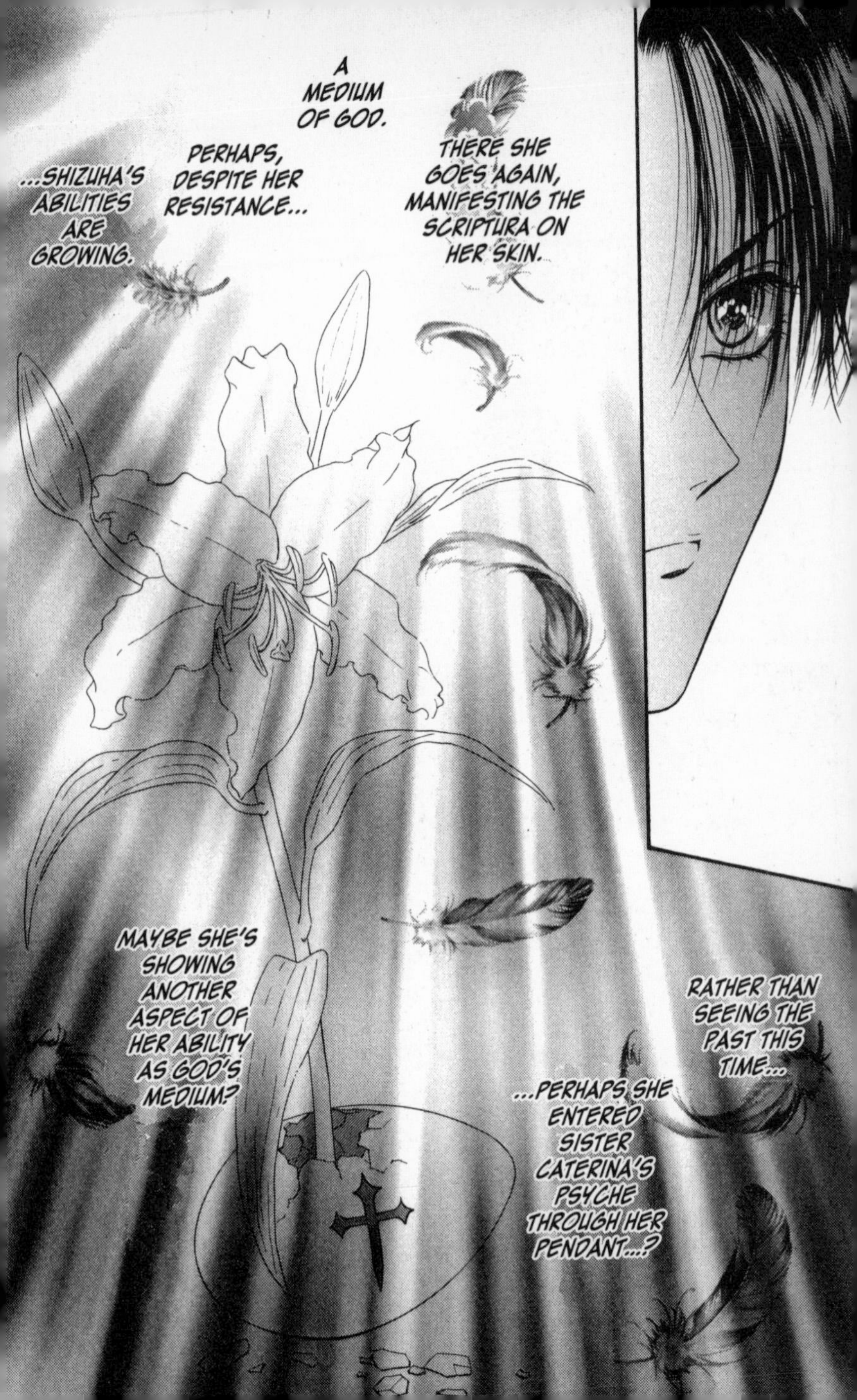

THERE SHE GOES AGAIN, MANIFESTING THE SCRIPTURA ON HER SKIN.
A MEDIUM OF GOD.
PERHAPS, DESPITE HER RESISTANCE...
...SHIZUHA'S ABILITIES ARE GROWING.
RATHER THAN SEEING THE PAST THIS TIME...
...PERHAPS SHE ENTERED SISTER CATERINA'S PSYCHE THROUGH HER PENDANT...?
MAYBE SHE'S SHOWING ANOTHER ASPECT OF HER ABILITY AS GOD'S MEDIUM?

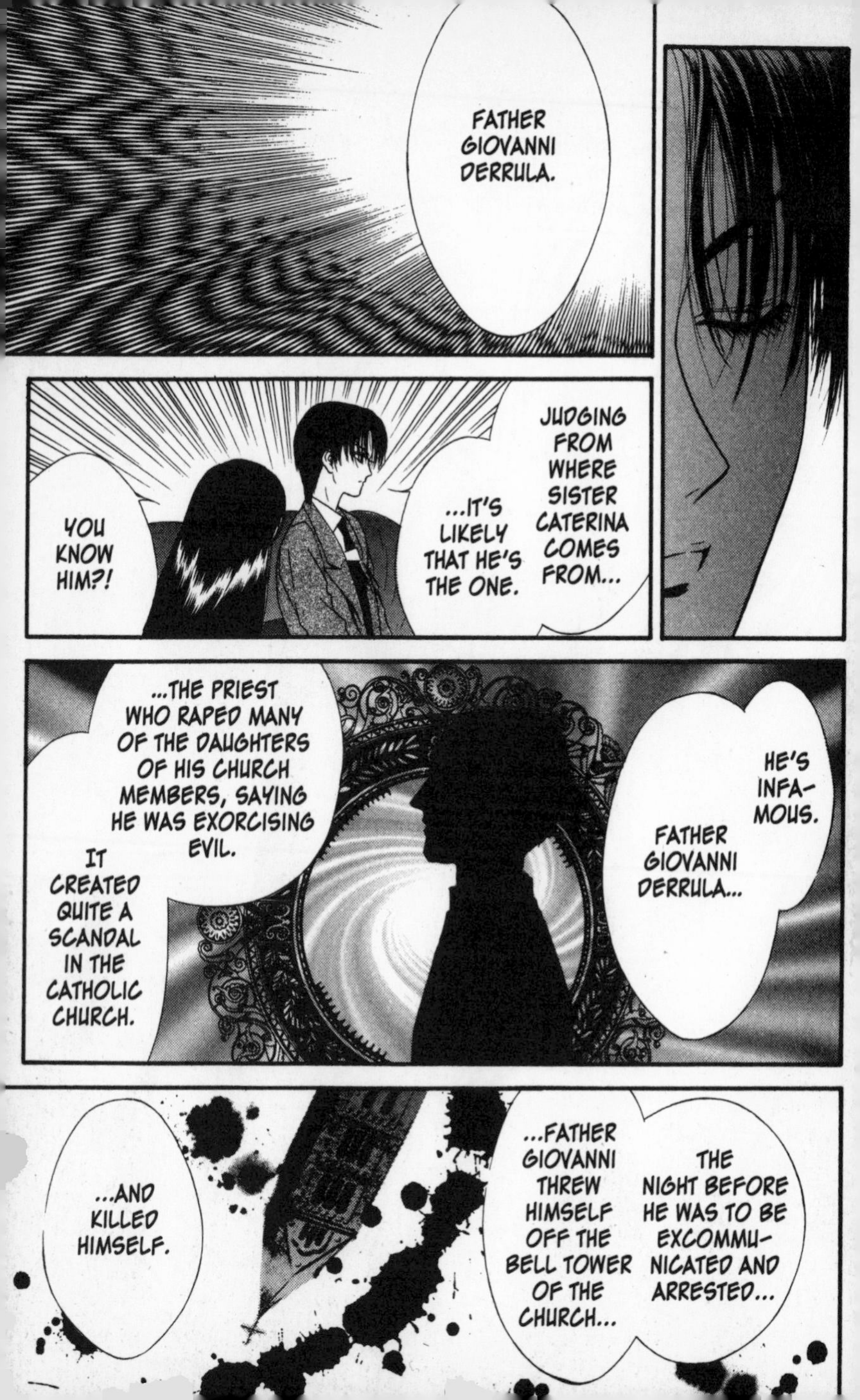
FATHER GIOVANNI DERRULA.
JUDGING FROM WHERE SISTER CATERINA COMES FROM...
...IT'S LIKELY THAT HE'S THE ONE.
YOU KNOW HIM?!
HE'S INFA-MOUS.
FATHER GIOVANNI DERRULA...
...THE PRIEST WHO RAPED MANY OF THE DAUGHTERS OF HIS CHURCH MEMBERS, SAYING HE WAS EXORCISING EVIL.
IT CREATED QUITE A SCANDAL IN THE CATHOLIC CHURCH.
THE NIGHT BEFORE HE WAS TO BE EXCOMMU-NICATED AND ARRESTED...
...FATHER GIOVANNI THREW HIMSELF OFF THE BELL TOWER OF THE CHURCH...
...AND KILLED HIMSELF.

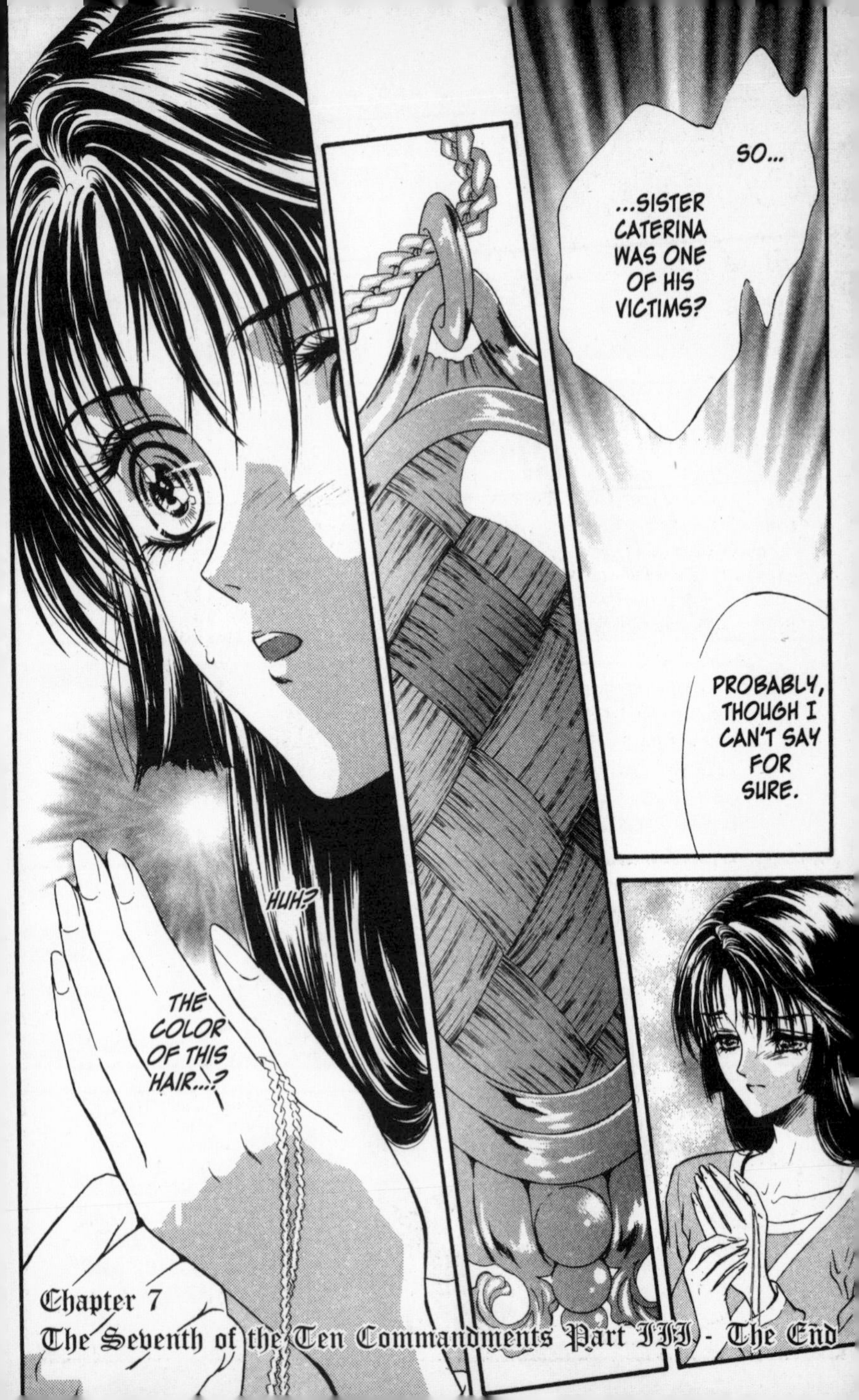
SO...
...SISTER CATERINA WAS ONE OF HIS VICTIMS?
PROBABLY, THOUGH I CAN'T SAY FOR SURE.
HUH?
THE COLOR OF THIS HAIR...?
Chapter 7
The Seventh of the Ten Commandments Part III - The End

Okay, People, It's Afterword Time.

Area where the author is inexperienced.

According to friends, there was someone at a Comic Market who was dressed up as Takara. I was astonished, but happy. Are monastic robes easy to make? (It seems like you'd need a lot of fabric.) The hair should be made smooth and flowing with a straight perm, and colored dark brown with green high-lights. Wear blue-gray contact lenses, and you've got it!!

You ought to try it now!!

たる

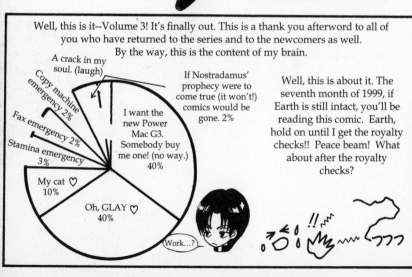

Well, this is it--Volume 3! It's finally out. This is a thank you afterword to all of you who have returned to the series and to the newcomers as well.
By the way, this is the content of my brain.

A crack in my soul. (laugh)
If Nostradamus' prophecy were to come true (it won't!) comics would be gone. 2%
Copy machine emergency 2%
Fax emergency 2%
Stamina emergency 3%
I want the new Power Mac G3. Somebody buy me one! (no way.) 40%
My cat ♡ 10%
Oh, GLAY ♡ 40%

Well, this is about it. The seventh month of 1999, if Earth is still intact, you'll be reading this comic. Earth, hold on until I get the royalty checks!! Peace beam! What about after the royalty checks?

Work...?

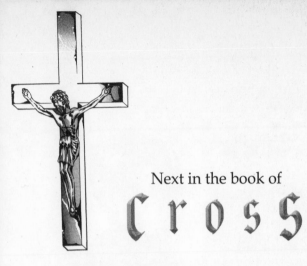

Next in the book of

Cross

The mystery of Sister Caterina continues.
When Takara discovers the abhorrent secret of her
past and the truth behind her current "pregnancy,"
he decides to perform an exorcism. Meanwhile,
Shizuha's empathic abilities come to the fore, as
she too suffers Caterina's pain. And when a
confrontation with a student reveals yet another
case of possession, Takara imbues Shizuha with the
power of the Cross so that she may aid him in the
battle against evil. All the while, it is becoming
increasingly difficult for these two to contain their
feelings for one another.

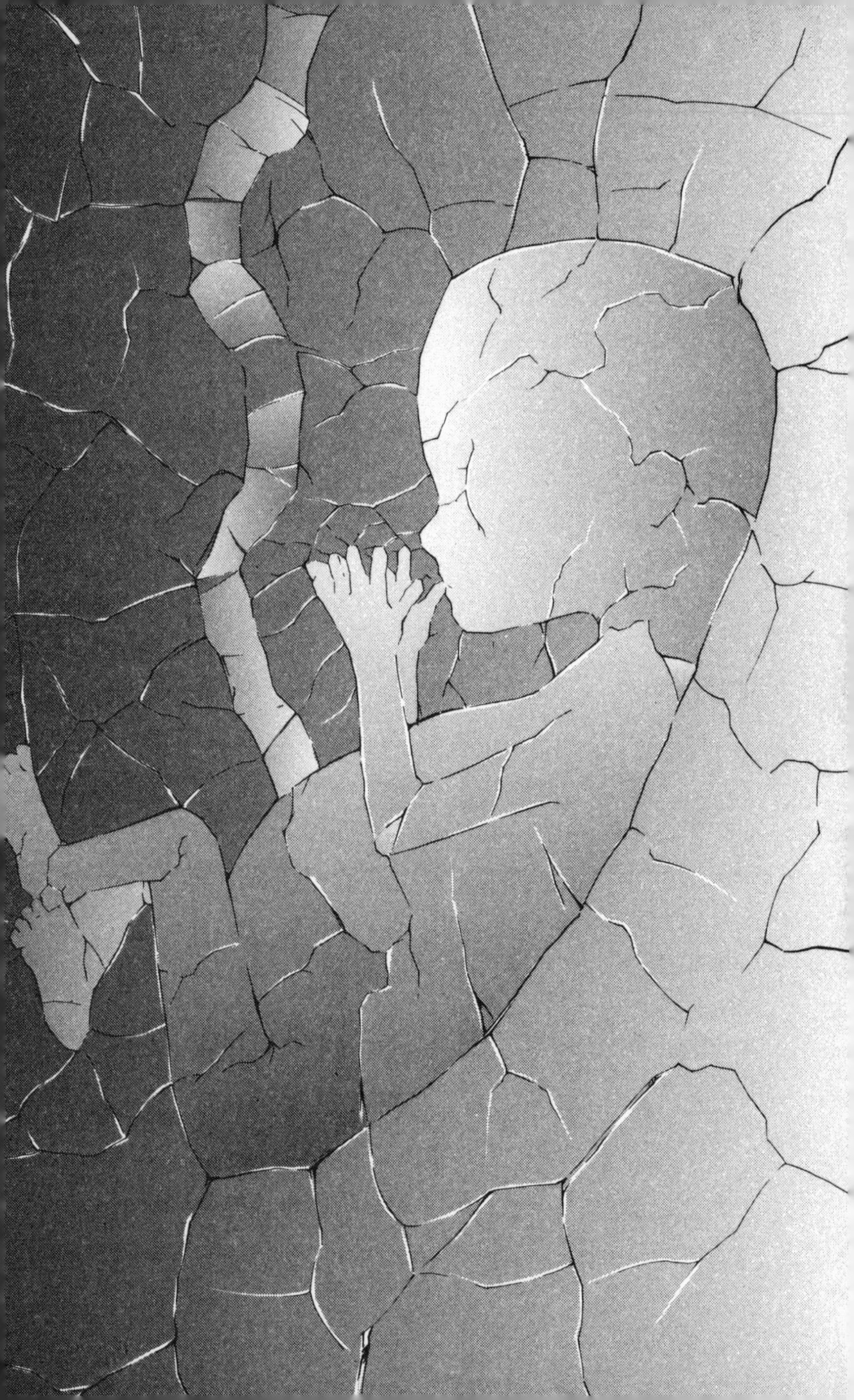

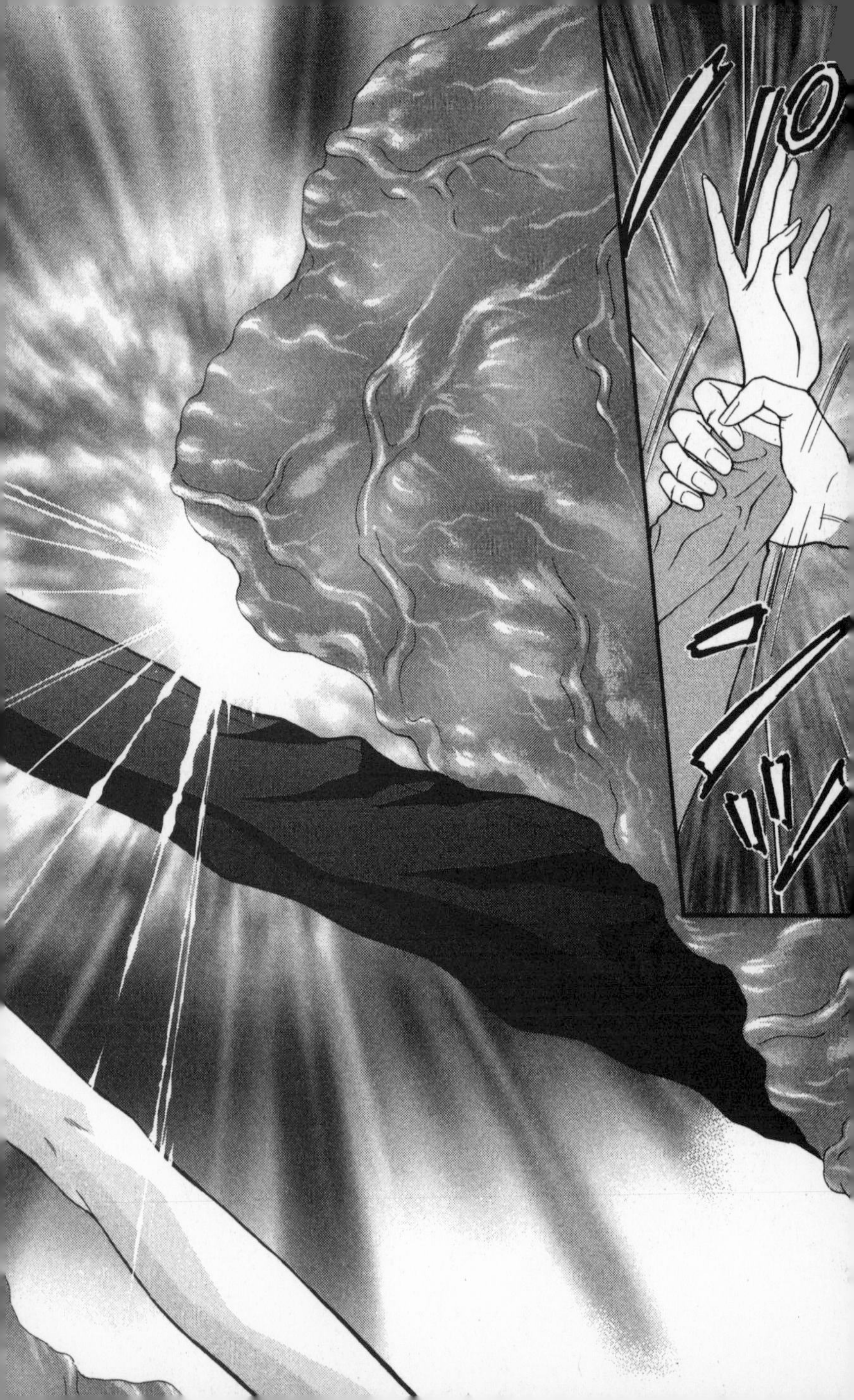

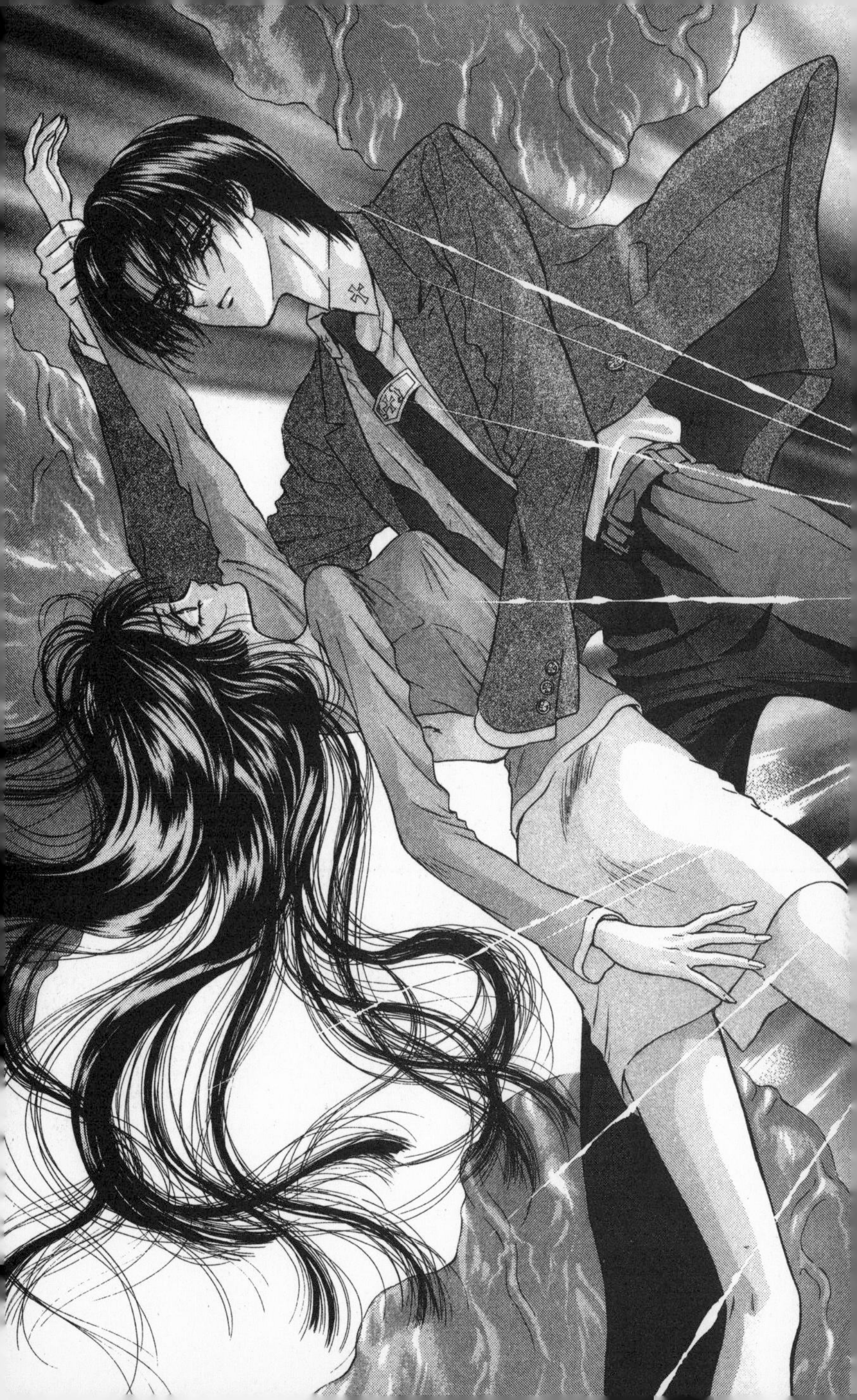

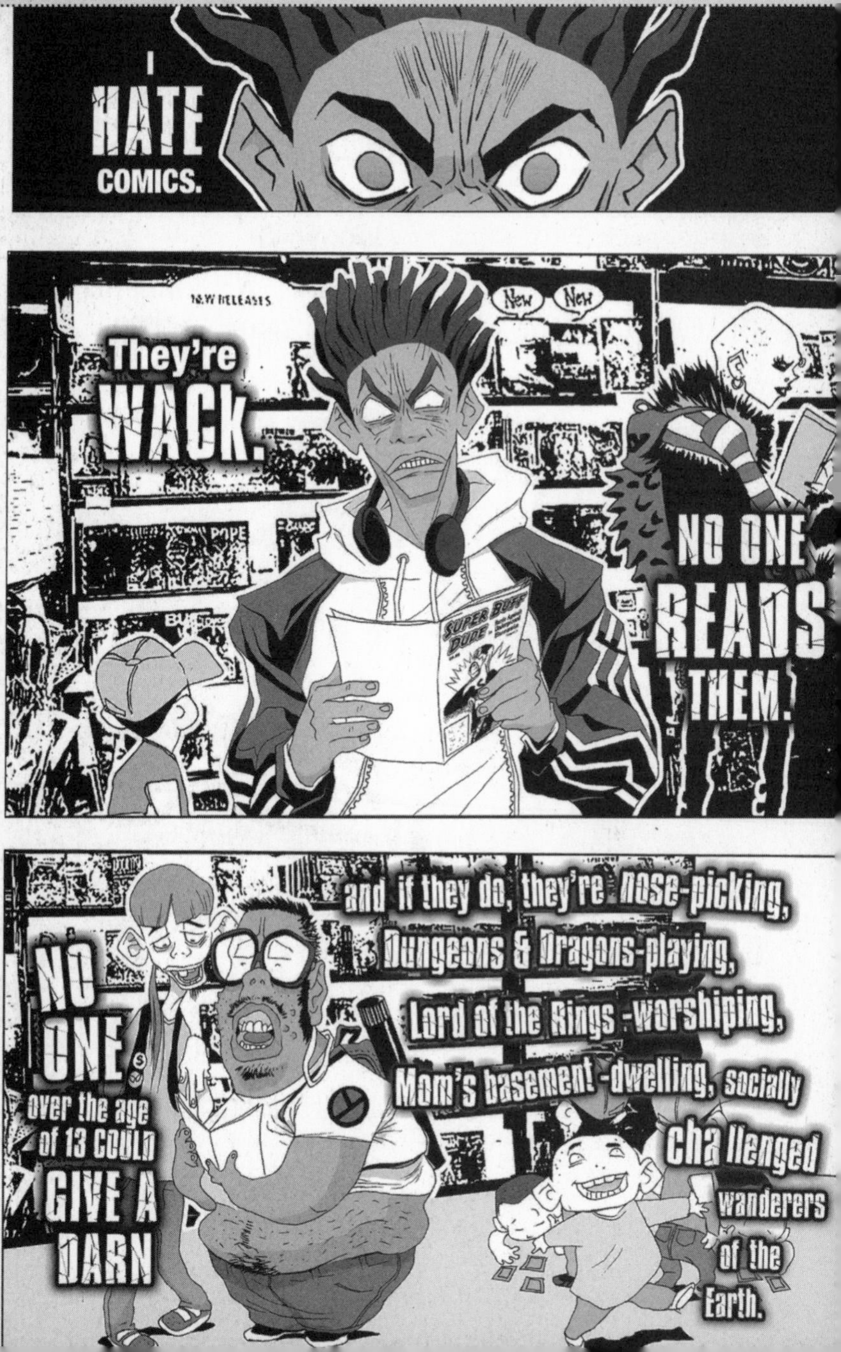
I HATE COMICS.
They're WACK.
NO ONE READS THEM.
New
New
SUPER BUFF DUDE
NO ONE over the age of 13 COULD GIVE A DARN
and if they do, they're nose-picking, Dungeons & Dragons-playing, Lord of the Rings -worshiping, Mom's basement -dwelling, socially challenged wanderers of the Earth.

SPOTLIGHT TOKYOPOP MANGA SUPPLEMENT

BLAZIN' BARRELS

Sting may look harmless and naïve, but he's really an excellent fighter and a wannabe bounty hunter in the futuristic Wild West. When he comes across a notice that advertises a reward for the criminal outfit named Gold Romany, he decides that capturing the all-girl gang of bad guys is his ticket to fame and fortune!

MIN-SEO PARK HAS CREATED ONE WILD TUMBLEWEED TALE FILLED WITH ADVENTURE GALORE AND PLENTY OF SHOTGUN ACTION!

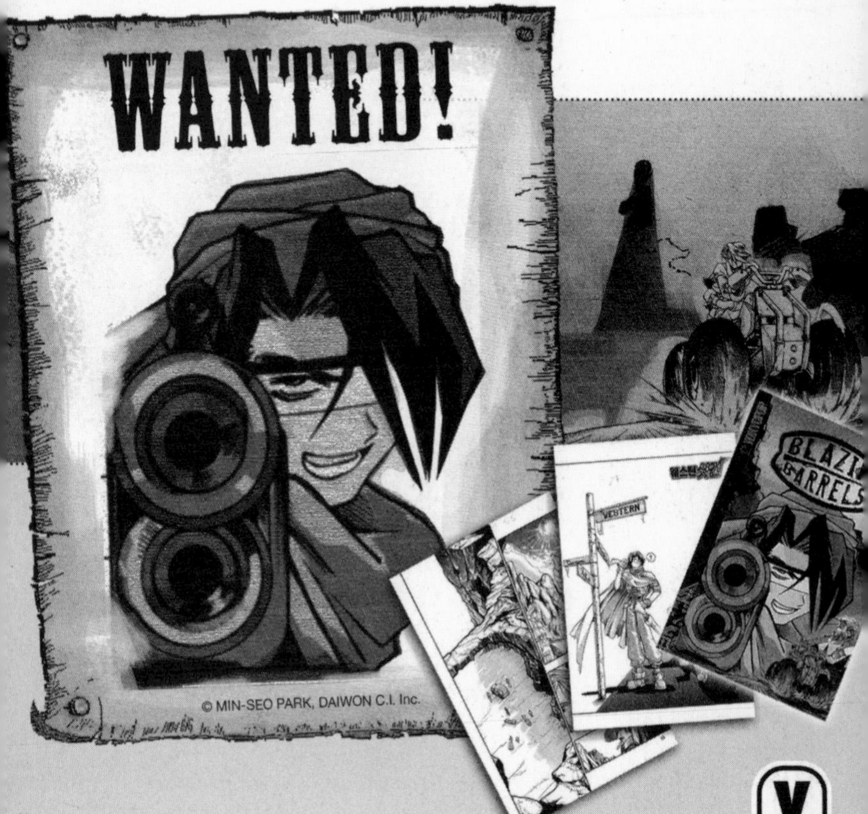

WANTED!
WESTERN
BLAZIN' BARRELS

FOR MORE INFORMATION VISIT: WWW.TOKYOPOP.COM

Y YOUTH AGE 10+

TOKYOPOP SHOP

WWW.TOKYOPOP.COM/SHOP

HOT NEWS!
Check out the
TOKYOPOP SHOP!
The world's best
collection of manga in
English is now available
online in one place!

RG VEDA

VISITOR

Van Von Hunter and other hot titles are available at the store that never closes!

VAN VON HUNTER

- • LOOK FOR SPECIAL OFFERS
- • PRE-ORDER UPCOMING RELEASES!
- • COMPLETE YOUR COLLECTIONS

EDITORS' PICKS ~ TOKYOPOP MANGA SUPPLEMENT

BY MASAKAZU YAMAGUCHI

ARM OF KANNON

Good and evil race to find the mysterious Arm of Kannon—an ancient Buddhist relic that has the power to bring about the end of humanity. The relic has been locked in a sacred temple for thousands of years. However, it is released and its demonic form soon takes over the will of a young boy, Mao, who must now flee from the evil forces that hunt the arm for control of its awesome power. This sexually charged action/horror story, traversing a vast landscape of demons, swordsmen, magicians, street gangs and government super-soldiers, will make the hairs on the back of your neck stand on edge.

~Rob Valois, Editor

BY YURIKO NISHIYAMA

DRAGON VOICE

I have to admit that Yuriko Nishiyama's *Dragon Voice* was not at all what I was expecting. As more a fan of action/ adventure stories like *Samurai Deeper Kyo*, the singing and dancing hijinks of a Japanese boy-band seemed hardly like my cup of tea. But upon proofreading Volume 3 for fellow editor Lillian Diaz-Przybyl, I found *Dragon Voice* to be one of my favorites! Rin and his fellow Beatmen dazzle their way past all obstacles—rival boy-band Privee, theme-park prima donnas, or TV production pitfalls—and do it with style! This book is one of the most fun reads I've had in a long time!

~Aaron Suhr, Sr. Editor

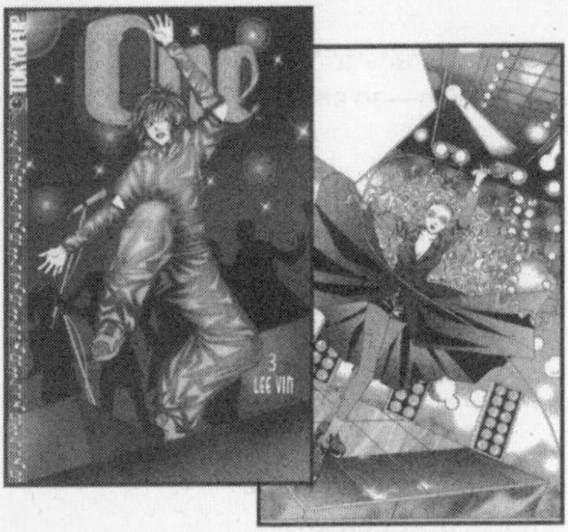
One
TOKYOPOP
3
LEE VIN

BY LEE VIN

ONE

Like American Idol? Then you'll love *One,* an energetic manga that gives you a sneak peek into the pop music industry. Lee Vin, who also created *Crazy Love Story,* is an amazingly accomplished artist! The story centers on the boy band One, a powerhouse of good looks, hot moves, and raw talent. It also features Jenny You, a Britney-Avril hybrid who's shooting straight for the top. But fame always comes at a price—and their path to stardom is full of speed bumps and roadblocks. But no matter what happens, they keep on rockin'—and so does this manga!

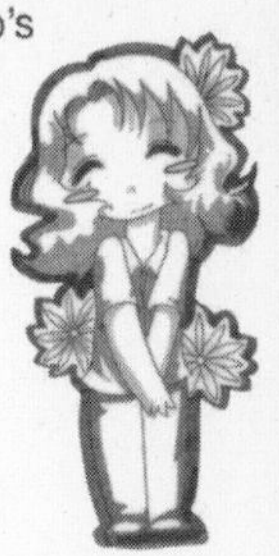

~Julie Taylor, Sr. Editor

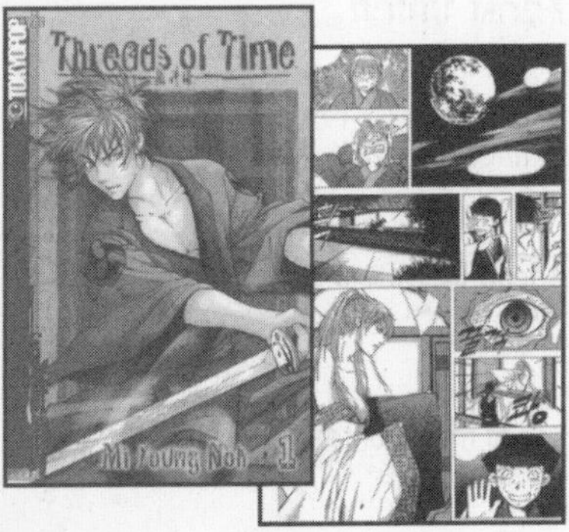
Threads of Time
TOKYOPOP
Mi Young Noh 1

BY MI-YOUNG NOH

THREADS OF TIME

The best thing about *Threads of Time* is its richly dramatic depiction of Korea's struggle to push back the Mongol Hordes in the 13th century. The plot focuses on a 20th century boy who ends up back in time. However, this science fiction conceit retreats to the background of this thrilling adventure in war-torn ancient Korea. Imagine a Korean general riding into battle with a battery of twelve men against two hundred Mongol warriors! Imagine back-stabbing politicians murdered in the clear of night. Imagine an entire village raped and slaughtered by Mongol hounds only to be avenged by a boy who just failed his high school science test.

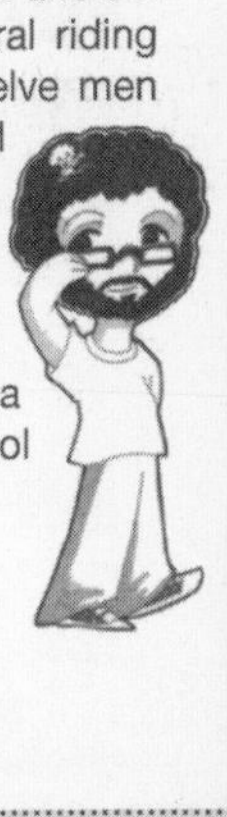

~Luis Reyes, Editor

STOP!

This is the back of the book.
You wouldn't want to spoil a great ending!

This book is printed "manga-style," in the authentic Japanese right-to-left format. Since none of the artwork has been flipped or altered, readers get to experience the story just as the creator intended. You've been asking for it, so TOKYOPOP® delivered: authentic, hot-off-the-press, and far more fun!

DIRECTIONS

If this is your first time reading manga-style, here's a quick guide to help you understand how it works.

It's easy... just start in the top right panel and follow the numbers. Have fun, and look for more 100% authentic manga from TOKYOPOP®!